Time, History, and Literature

Time, History, and Literature

Selected Essays of Erich Auerbach

Edited and with an introduction by James I. Porter

Translated by Jane O. Newman

PRINCETON UNIVERSITY PRESS

Princeton & Oxford

Copyright © 2014 by Princeton University Press
Published by Princeton University Press, 41 William Street, Princeton, New Jersey 08540
In the United Kingdom: Princeton University Press, 6 Oxford Street,
Woodstock, Oxfordshire OX20 1TW

press.princeton.edu

JACKET ART: Paolo Uccello (1397–1475), *The Great Flood*, S. Maria Novella, Florence, Italy.
Photo: George Tatge for Alinari, 1998. Courtesy of Alinari / Art Resource, NY

LIBRARY OF CONGRESS CATALOGING-IN-PUBLICATION DATA
Auerbach, Erich, 1892–1957.
Time, history, and literature : selected essays of Erich Auerbach / edited and with an
introduction by James I. Porter ; translated by Jane O. Newman.
pages cm
Includes bibliographical references and index.
ISBN 978-0-691-13711-7 (acid-free paper) 1. Literature—History and criticism—Theory,
etc. 2. Critics—Germany. 3. Criticism—Germany. 4. Literary historians—Germany. I.
Porter, James I., 1954– editor of compilation. II. Newman, Jane O., translator. III. Title.
PN504.A94 2014
809–dc23   2013013528

British Library Cataloging-in-Publication Data is available

The translation of this work was supported by a grant from the Goethe-Institut, which is
funded by the German Ministry of Foreign Affairs.

This book has been composed in Minion and Ideal Sans

Printed on acid-free paper ∞

Printed in the United States of America

1 3 5 7 9 10 8 6 4 2

CONTENTS

ACKNOWLEDGMENTS

James I. Porter

This collection arose out of a discrepancy that struck me as I grew increasingly interested in the writings and career of the Romance philologist Erich Auerbach. Despite his recognition as one of the great literary critics of the twentieth century, a large portion of his essays were going uncited, and apparently also unread—with palpable consequences for the way Auerbach's image has been shaped since the translation of *Mimesis* in 1953, his best read work in the anglophone world, but by no means his only work.

Auerbach's output was considerable, and it took numerous forms, including essays, many of which have been unavailable in English until now. I am extremely grateful to Princeton University Press for responding without hesitation to my proposal to put together a new edition of Auerbach's most significant essays. First and foremost, I wish to thank Hanne Winarsky, who gave this project its initial momentum. I am further grateful to Brigitta van Rheinberg, Alison MacKeen, Larissa Klein, and Kathleen Cioffi, all of whom made my communications with the Press as pleasurable and efficient an experience as one could hope for. Jane Newman brought Auerbach's prose to life in English. Without her dedication (and patience with my various editorial intrusions) this collection would not have seen the light of day. Thanks also go to Eva Jaunzems for her expert copyediting. Kevin Batton built the index. The project has benefited from a number of helping hands besides, some of whom are listed in the acknowledgments to my introduction below, and others in my other published essays on Auerbach. Among the greatest of my debts are those I owe to Martin Vialon, whose contributions to this volume are too many to name, and not easily repaid.

Note: All translations from the German are by Jane O. Newman, with the exception of Chapter 9 ("On the Anniversary Celebration of Dante"), which was translated by James I. Porter.

INTRODUCTION

James I. Porter

What we are we have become in the course of our history, and it is only
in history that we can remain what we are, and develop.

—Auerbach, "The Philology of World Literature"

Frequently credited with having shaped the modern study of comparative
literature, and famous above all for his daring study, *Mimesis: The Representation of Reality in Western Literature* (German original 1946; English translation 1953), Erich Auerbach has been the beneficiary of a surge of attention
from literary and cultural critics in the humanities over the past two decades,
above all in Germany and in the United States.[1] It is therefore an opportune
moment to produce a new selection of his essays, many of which have never
been available in English, and so continue to go unappreciated even by those
who are most concerned to reassess Auerbach's life and circumstances.

Quite apart from their obvious evidentiary value (they span the full length
of his career), the essays in this collection have an indisputable immediate
value. All of them are gems. None is very long or forbiddingly learned, apart
from two ("*Figura,*" here Chapter 7, and "*Passio* as Passion," here Chapter
14). And taken as an ensemble, they permit us to observe Auerbach responding to a variety of occasions in a wide range of venues, from a feuilleton
piece commemorating the six-hundredth anniversary of Dante's death in
1921 to his inaugural postdoctoral lecture at Marburg (July 1929) to a talk
recorded after the War (March 1948) at the Pennsylvania State College (now
Pennsylvania State University) to the obligatory run of articles produced for
academic journals and edited volumes—though Auerbach always wears his

---

[1] Four major edited collections chart this trend: Seth Lerer, ed., *Literary History and the Challenge of Philology: The Legacy of Erich Auerbach* (Stanford: Stanford University Press, 1996); Walter Busch and Gerhart Pickerodt, eds. (with the assistance of Markus Bauer), *Wahrnehmen Lesen
Deuten: Erich Auerbachs Lektüre der Moderne* (Klostermann: Frankfurt am Main, 1998); Aamir R.
Mufti, ed., *Critical Secularism*. Special issue of *boundary 2: an international journal of literature and
culture* 31.2 (2004); and Karlheinz Barck and Martin Treml, eds., *Erich Auerbach: Geschichte und
Aktualität eines europäischen Philologen* (Berlin: Kulterverlag Kadmos, 2007). The bibliography is
extensive and growing. For a selection, see the readings listed in the bibliographical overview at
the end of this book.

learning lightly and is never dry or pedantic: he tends to use footnotes, the weapon of choice for German scholars, in a sparing fashion, and even quotations from originals are kept to a minimum. On the other hand, what Auerbach forgoes in academic niceties he makes up for in radical impulses: he is constantly challenging his colleagues in Romance philology and in nearby fields to press their disciplines towards ever broader and more searching limits. Finally, underlying all of his writings is a deep intellectual coherence that is as admirable as it is rare. Auerbach has the potential to inspire readers even today. Students in the humanities would do well to emulate his example.

Auerbach's Life and Afterlife

Erich Auerbach (1892–1957) was caught in the crosshairs of history. A German-Jewish intellectual who fought for his country in the First World War and was decorated with an Iron Cross (2nd class), Auerbach was removed from his teaching post in Marburg and effectively forced into exile by the Nazis in 1935 in the wake of the racially discriminatory Nuremberg Laws of that same year. The laws, which banned Jews from public employment on the basis of bloodlines while imposing a host of further stigmas and restrictions, effectively annuled the rather fragile immunity Auerbach had enjoyed since 1933. At that time, an earlier law was passed that spared Jewish and some non-Jewish but politically suspect veterans from being removed from their posts in the civil service (others were less fortunate—for example, Auerbach's colleague, Leo Spitzer [1887–1960]).[2] Unsafe in Germany, he sat out the Second World War in Istanbul and later emigrated to the States in 1947 to live out the last decade of his life as an *éminence grise* in the American academy—first at the Pennsylvania State College, then briefly at the Institute for Advanced Studies in Princeton (1949–50), and finally at Yale where he held a professorship and then a chair in Romance philology until his death. Some half a century on, Erich Auerbach is now being reexamined and celebrated, whether as a founder of comparative literature, an example of the exilic intellectual, or as a prophet of global literary studies.

Despite all this attention, the Auerbach who has been received to date and made into a canonical figure that looms larger than life remains a somewhat filtered version of himself. The Auerbach who is most familiar today is defined by a certain time period: he is the scholar who fled Germany and who wrote under duress in impoverished conditions (most memorably, but

---

[2] That Auerbach's situation was anything but safe in 1933 and earlier is clear from the retrospective account of his former student and assistant, Werner Krauss ("Marburg unter dem Naziregime, *Sinn und Form* 35.5 [1983] 941–45; here 942), and from Auerbach's letter to Ludwig Binswanger from October 28, 1932 (n. 54 below).

least significantly, without a research library) and then later reflected on this tumultuous era, the Auerbach of "Figura" (1938), *Mimesis* (1946), and "The Philology of World Literature" (1952). Celebrated are the literary comparatist who can deftly juxtapose the Bible, Homer, and James Joyce's *Ulysses* in a sentence, the ecumenical and global thinker, and the lonely exilic victim—a romantic image, to be sure. Rarely is Auerbach viewed as a Romance philologist who went about making his mark in the university system of Weimar Germany, a system that produced a long line of distinguished critics like himself (among them, Karl Vossler [1872–1949] and Werner Krauss [1900–76]). Neither is he viewed as the supreme Dantist of his generation (and Auerbach's 1929 book on Dante is arguably his finest single achievement), as a student of the Christian Church and its intricate theological and philosophical debates (accessible to him in both Latin and the vernaculars), or as an expert on courtly life and culture from the Middle Ages to the Renaissance, and into the early modern era, subjects that occupied him in the years before he was forced into exile and that continued to preoccupy him down to his final, posthumous publication.

The tacit assumption behind the popular and dominant image of Auerbach is that just as his world changed on October 16, 1935 when he received word of his official termination at the University of Marburg, so did his view of the world. Therefore, his earlier writings are of little relevance to the later writings, or at any rate they must be of lesser moment, given the historical circumstances that interrupted his *curriculum vitae* and caused him to flee German soil. But this is merely to beg the question, for *Mimesis*, after all, is the fruit of a lifetime of learning: what is to be made of the man and his work before his expulsion to Istanbul at the mature age of forty-three? Are there no deeper continuities running through his thought? And did the world really take a turn for the worse only starting in 1935?

The earliest years of Auerbach's life may be quickly sketched. Born in Berlin to an upper-middle-class family of assimilated Jews, Auerbach studied law and received a doctoral degree in jurisprudence from Heidelberg in 1913. After serving in the army during the war (and a subsequent wounding and convalescence), he changed fields to Romance philology, earning his doctorate in 1921 from Greifswald. Unable to land a teaching post and while researching his postdoctoral thesis on Dante under Leo Spitzer from Marburg, he found temporary employment at the Prussian State Library in Berlin from 1923 to 1929 as a field librarian in law. Upon the publication of his thesis, and with the backing of Spitzer and Vossler (at Munich), the two main powerhouses in his field, he assumed a professorship at the University of Marburg in Romance philology, which he held from October 1930 until he was forced out by the Nazis in October 1935. It is at this point that the life of the Auerbach who is revered among scholars and aspiring students of literature alike begins.

A closer look at his writings from before 1935—both his books and his essays, nine of which are reproduced in this volume (nearly half the sum total)—will rapidly dispel any notion of a radical break, as will a deeper grasp of Auerbach's thought before and after this date. What stands out clearly at all points in his development are three distinguishing features: first, his complex relationship to the Judaeo-Christian tradition; next, his underlying philosophy of time and history, which he owes largely to Vico but also to Hegel; and lastly, his unique theory of ethics and responsible action, which emerges as a deeply committed stance toward human history and human reality, but also as an original and provocative view about the rise of modern, post-Christian subjectivity and individuality. Together, these form the bedrock of Auerbach's more familiar theory of literary mimesis, without which that theory cannot be truly fathomed.

Behind everything lies an additional, subtly determinative factor, which becomes evident once it is named: the fact that for the greater part of his career Auerbach was a Jew writing in an increasingly hostile environment, one that would eventually be dominated by the National Socialists under Hitler. While all of these threads run through Auerbach's writings from start to finish, some are more pronounced in certain parts of his corpus than in others. The essays presented here have been selected with the aim of foregrounding each of these elements of Auerbach's profile as a thinker and a writer in all their complexity, in order to contribute not only to a broader and more informed reception of his work but also to a more engaged reading of his intellectual "project"—if the phrase may be permitted, as it surely must be. For one of the most admirable hallmarks of Auerbach's writings is the profound consistency that quietly informs them. Behind them all one can sense a searching mind and a vision that are bent on comprehending a seemingly endless variety of historical phenomena, personalities, and forms within a single framework, one that continually circles back to a series of carefully chosen and richly productive questions, almost as if this program for inquiry had been planned years in advance of its final execution.

By training a Romance philologist and by inclination a literary comparatist, in reality Auerbach transcended both labels. This is only to be expected of a thinker who continues to exert so powerful a fascination over both general readers and professional scholars a half-century after his death. Auerbach's signature insights are not primarily stylistic in the way that his nearest contemporaries tended to read texts, for example Ernst Robert Curtius (1886–1956) or Leo Spitzer, both of whom viewed style as a window onto transcendent and transhistorical aesthetic forms (be these impersonal classical *topoi* or tokens of a romanticized expressionism) and whose positions, viewed from today, resemble a kind of New Criticism *avant la lettre*. His interests lay elsewhere. Provisionally, we can say that he sought to derive something like a history of mentalities under the guise of Romance philology. And he carried out this project with a formidable degree of philosophical rigor and sophistication that is partially concealed by his elegant literary sensibilities and his astonishing depth of cultural knowledge.

Taking literature as his starting point (often under the rubric of a concrete *Ansatzpunkt*, be this a phrase, an isolated feature of style, or a self-contained logical sequence), Auerbach restlessly sought to establish nothing less than an intellectual—or better yet, spiritual (he often calls it "inner")—history of the Western European mind as it lunged into contemporary modernity. As we read in the foreword to his *Four Studies in the History of French Thought and Culture*,[3] literary forms were for Auerbach a gateway to forms of thought, feeling, and expression. Such was the premise already of his 1921 dissertation on the early Renaissance novella in Italy and France (on which more below). And while it would take more than a brief introduction to unfold Auerbach's insights in the way they deserve, it will be possible to name and explicate some of them briefly, in the hope that readers will then recognize these themes as they appear, like so many musical motifs, at different moments and in different configurations in the essays that follow.

Key Concepts

A number of key words in Auerbach's vocabulary stand out as utterly characteristic of his thought: *life, feeling, sensuousness, concreteness, history, (tragic) realism, historical perspectivism* and *relativism, unconscious (habits), historical consciousness, earthly (matters), (horizontal) secularization, de-Christianization, (vertical) ethics, autonomy,* and *(lay) public.* What these terms begin to suggest are the outlines of a series of developments in the West as it passed from the classical era into late antiquity, the Middle Ages, the Renaissance, early modernity, the nineteenth century, and finally into Auerbach's present. And while Auerbach marks each of these eras with symbolically charged canonical literary figures (Homer, sundry classical authors from Plato to Tacitus, St. Paul, Augustine and other early Christian writers, Dante, Montaigne, Pascal, Racine, Vico, Rousseau, Stendhal, Balzac, Proust, and Virginia Woolf), his narrative charts much more than a progression in literary history. What he is capturing is the evolution of Western historical consciousness as it moves out of a universe filled with myths into one that is saturated with history, while the intervening ground is colored by the spiritual beckonings of Judaism and then Christianity. In a word, Auerbach's writings effectively chart and then explore the difficult discovery of the sensuous, the earthly, and the human and social worlds.

More schematically, the passage Auerbach traces is from an era in which human meaning is sought out in some transcendental sphere above to an era in which it is discovered and consciously made here on earth. Auerbach

---

[3] *Vier Untersuchungen zur Geschichte der französischen Bildung* (Bern: A. Francke, 1951) 8.

applauds this conquest of historical awareness as a process that allows individuals and societies to realize the nature of their ever-changing and ever-adapting humanity, even as he acknowledges the enormous risks and the terrifying lack of guarantees that such a venture entails, and even as he at times appears—but *only* appears—to lament the passing of the more stable moral frameworks of religion.[4] In point of fact, in the passage from religion to secularism one kind of uncertainty is traded for another. As he writes in his book on Dante, in an intensely beautiful passage that gives a taste of that work and of Auerbach's writings at their best, what Dante describes in the *Divine Comedy* is not the promise of eternal salvation, but rather

> the narrow cleft of *earthly human history*, the span of *man's life on earth*, in which the great and dramatic decision [of a person's destiny] must fall. The cleft is truly open, the span of life is short, uncertain, and decisive for all eternity; it is the magnificent and terrible gift of potential freedom which creates the urgent, restless, *no less human than Christian-European* atmosphere of the irretrievable, fleeting moment that must be made the most of.[5]

If uncertainties continue to linger even during the secular era on this view of history, that is because the process of self-realization in time is for Auerbach ongoing, and the work of historical awareness is never complete. Human possibilities are no less compellingly intense in later periods than in the Christian poem of Dante. It is the experience of these possibilities, not their realization *per se*, that Auerbach seeks to capture with his rubric, which he did not coin but merely made his own, "tragic realism."

Earthly Philology

Auerbach's perspective on history is avowedly indebted to Giambattista Vico, the great Neapolitan thinker of the early eighteenth century who may well have inaugurated modern historicism. Auerbach certainly believed this to be the case. In fact, it is in his essays on Vico that we find some of Auerbach's

---

[4] An example is *Das französische Publikum des 17. Jahrhunderts* (Munich: Max Hueber Verlag, 1933) 52–53, where classical French tragedy is said to supplant Christianity through a radical process of "de-Christianization" by heralding a "new ideal world of value," one that celebrates the autonomy of human passions and the "triumph" of the newly discovered "moral person." Tellingly, what Auerbach laments here is less the passing of religion than the reduction of historicity and worldliness to "a bare minimum." In return, a new moral world comes to light with values of its own, one that eventually will take root again in this world. Differently, Jane O. Newman, "Force and Justice: Auerbach's Pascal," in *Political Theology and Early Modernity*, Julia Reinhard Lupton and Graham Hammill, eds. (Chicago: University of Chicago Press, 2012) 159–80.

[5] *Dante: Poet of the Secular World*, Ralph Manheim, trans. (Chicago: University of Chicago Press, 1961; German original 1929) 132; trans. adapted, emphasis added.

own philosophy of history set forth at its clearest, for instance in "Vico and Herder" (1932; here Chapter 2).[6] The text of a lecture, the essay has added point, as it showcases the literary critic instructing his fellow humanists in what he takes to be their actual activity and mission: "The majority of you, as students of the humanities, are pursuing history, be this the study of change in political and economic spheres or the history of language, writing, or art."

This formulation must have come as quite a shock to the members of the German-Italian Research Institute assembled in Cologne in 1931 and headed at the time by Leo Spitzer. Auerbach's choice of theme was admittedly some- what brazen. Spitzer's deep reservations about historical method were, and are, well known. Auerbach, moreover, was just a year into his first teaching post at Marburg, and Spitzer had left almost as soon as Auerbach arrived (a turn of events that would repeat itself in 1936 in Istanbul, when Spitzer, having helped appoint Auerbach as his own successor, left for Johns Hop- kins before Auerbach could even arrive). Was Auerbach being deliberately provocative?[7] And anyway, how could history possibly provide a foundation for the humanities, and specifically for literary study?

Undaunted, Auerbach goes on to outline the role of the modern researcher in relation to the mission he has just proclaimed: because history is not a for- tuitous sequence of events, historians in the fullest sense of the word must seek to unravel the logic inherent in those events; and doing so is premised on the belief, which must not only be premised but also deeply cherished, that "the wealth of events in human life which unfold in earthly time con- stitutes a totality, a coherent development or meaningful whole, in which each individual event is embedded in a variety of ways and through which it can be interpreted." The language is taken almost verbatim from Auerbach's dissertation, *On the Technique of the Early Renaissance Novella in Italy and France*, which further emphasizes the "infinite" character of these events in all their "wealth" and the "sensuousness of life."[8] Alas, a perfect grasp of any such totality is forbidden, and so one is thrown back upon some less than perfect means of intuiting the logic of events—call this feeling, intuition, or speculation. The inquirer proceeds by such means; she interprets, but "often

[6]See also "Vico's Contribution to Literary Criticism" (here Chapter 1), a brief and accessible statement, and its expansion in Auerbach's introduction to *Literary Language and Its Public in Late Latin Antiquity and in the Middle Ages*, Ralph Manheim, trans. (New York: Pantheon, 1965; rpt. Princeton University Press, 1993; German original 1958) 6–24.

[7]Their tensions were publically visible. See Hans Ulrich Gumbrecht, *Vom Leben und Sterben der großen Romanisten: Karl Vossler, Ernst Robert Curtius, Leo Spitzer, Erich Auerbach, Werner Krauss* (Munich: Hanser, 2002) 164.

[8]*Zur Technik der Frührenaissancenovelle in Italien und Frankreich* (Heidelberg: C. Winter, 1921) 38. Similarly, *Dante* (n. 5 above) 144: "wealth of experiences" (trans. adapted); and *Literary Lan- guage and Its Public* (n. 6 above) 21, on the historical method which compels us "to set forth our consciousness of ourselves here and now, in all its wealth and limitations."

unconsciously"; and when she does, she is driven as much by "practical and ethical needs" as by scholarly ones.

Philology is the name that Auerbach, following Vico, gives to all such interpretive activity.[9] It was in redirecting the thrust of his field that Auerbach's originality lay, not in his characterization of historical inquiry *per se*, which if anything was a fairly well developed (if not universally accepted) view in much of the German academy at the time, in the wake of Hegel, Dilthey, Croce, and Troeltsch, though not in Romance philology. On the contrary, Auerbach's mentors and peers—Karl Vossler, Victor Klemperer, Ernst Robert Curtius, Leo Spitzer, and Eugen Lerch—sought to understand the meaning of culture through language and literature, often treating these latter as self-standing aesthetic phenomena that were best grasped through immediate intuition—an enterprise that tended to sunder art from reality, and both from history.[10] Where they pressed philology in the direction of stylistics and aesthetics in reaction to the dry positivism of nineteenth-century Romance philology, Auerbach at times appeared to be conducting something more akin to historical sociology, which rendered his nomenclature all the more idiosyncratic.

What he has in mind with "philology" is an endeavor that goes well beyond the conventional meaning of the term, which had roughly the same

[9] See Auerbach's "Vorrede" [Preface] to Giambattista Vico, *Die neue Wissenschaft über die gemeinschaftliche Natur der Völker*. Abridged and translated with an introduction by Erich Auerbach (Berlin: de Gruyter, 1924) 9–39; here 29: "Vico understands by *philology* everything that we label as the human sciences today: all of history in the narrower sense: sociology, national economy, history of religion, language, law, and art; and he demands that these empirical sciences should become one with philosophy." He is paraphrasing Vico, *Scienza Nuova* 1744, "Spiegazione della dipintura" and "Degli elementi" X (Vico, *Opere*, 3rd ed. [A. Battistini, ed. Milan: Arnaldo Mondadori, 2001] 1: 419, 498. See further, "Giambattista Vico and the Idea of Philology" (here Chapter 3) and "Vico's Contribution to Literary Criticism" (here Chapter 1).

[10] Compare Vossler, *Sprache als Schöpfung und Entwicklung: Eine theoretische Untersuchung mit praktischen Beispielen* (Heidelberg: C. Winter, 1905): "*Pure intuition is art*" (emphasis in original). Hence, "the elaborations of art cannot be measured against reality" (15). Nothing could be more alien to Auerbach than a view like this. Leaning on Bergson, the younger Curtius arrived at parallel views (*Die literarischen Wegbereiter des neuen Frankreich* [Potsdam: G. Kiepenheuer, 1920] 31–38). Curtius eventually abandoned his infatuation with Bergsonian vitalism, only to retreat into another form of ahistoricism. See his *Deutscher Geist in Gefahr* (Stuttgart: Deutsche Verlags-Anstalt, 1932) 13, 33; further, Karlheinz Barck, "'Flucht in die Tradition': Erfahrungshintergründe Erich Auerbachs zwischen Exil und Emigration," in Aleida Assmann and Anselm Haverkamp, eds., *Stimme, Figur: Kritik und Restitution in der Literaturwissenschaft* (Stuttgart and Weimar: J. B. Metzler, 1994) 47–60; here 58–60; Gumbrecht, *Vom Leben und Sterben der großen Romanisten* (n. 7 above) 9–71. Curtius clung to his stance to the bitter end. See Robert Fitzgerald, *Enlarging the Change: The Princeton Seminars in Literary Criticism, 1949–1951* (Boston: Northeastern University Press, 1985) 22, summarizing the rather heated exchange of views at Auerbach's 1949 Gauss lectures at Princeton ("Curtius replied flatly that words make shapes of beauty, not states of consciousness but artistic states"); ibid. 36–37 (a sample). Auerbach's reply was characteristically indirect and deeply felt (ibid. 26, repeated in "Baudelaire's *Fleurs du Mal* und das Erhabene" [1951], in Erich Auerbach, *Gesammelte Aufsätze zur romanischen Philologie* [Bern and Munich: A. Francke, 1967] 290).

set of connotations in the 1930s as it does today—namely, the love of words and literature manifested through the study of texts, their language, meaning, transmission, classification, translation, and so on. Not that Auerbach was uninterested in philology in the narrow sense, or that he was unequipped to handle its steepest challenges. "*Figura*," his classic essay on the meaning of a single term and its vicissitudes from classical antiquity to Dante, shows Auerbach coming as close as he ever does to putting on display, in a magisterial fashion, all the skills of a German philologist, while ranging over a millennium and a half of recondite grammatical, literary, rhetorical, and theological learning. But, in the end, not even "*Figura*" can be shelved alongside philological scholarship, because it too is an exercise in deep intellectual history, not lexicography. There is something faintly paradoxical, or else subtly polemical, about the essay, tracking as it does the relentlessly linear history of a phenomenon that, Auerbach claims, insists on locating events in concrete historical time from within a tradition whose *telos* and ultimate meaning ought to lie outside time altogether: Christianity. But more on this in a moment. We must first return to Auerbach's understanding of history, which he owed in no small part to his encounters with Vico, Herder, and Hegel.

History for Auerbach is a rich concept. In the essay on Vico and Herder we begin to understand why. The first element that stands out in his definition of history is the word "earthly"—*irdisch* in German, which can also mean "secular" or "(this-)worldly." History is plainly—even militantly—a secular concept in Auerbach's mind. But it is this because it designates the full scope of human and humane activity: it maps out life in all its vital richness. Further, history is made up of specific, individual elements (events in life), not abstract universals, and these are multiply related to one another and to the whole that meaningfully contains them. Discerning their meaning is an essential, if not *the* essential, human activity for Auerbach. It involves what he calls a "horizontal reading of history's unfolding," because history works itself out across time in a linear, developmental fashion, in contrast to a "vertical" assignment of meaning from above. To read along the former axis of meaning is to grasp history as a process that is immanent to the world. To read "vertically" is to grasp history as providential, transcendent, and divinely ordained. "Earthly" carries this mark of difference wherever it occurs in Auerbach's writings, as it does with astonishing frequency—which is not to say that earthly history is altogether devoid of vertical meaning. At its richest, human history reveals vertical significance, not of the sort that descends from above, but the kind of meaning that resides in the very depths of the (worldly) surfaces of life, which is to say human history as it is "re-evok[ed] . . . from the depth of our own consciousness" ("Vico and Aesthetic Historism," here Chapter 4; cf. *Mimesis*, 43–44, 444, 552).

All of these notions combined—history as secular, vital, and concrete, as human and humane—are the singular object of Auerbach's philology, which is what makes it in the end an earthly, this-worldly philology, a true philology of world history.[11] In "The Philology of World Literature" (1952, here Chapter 20), Auerbach goes so far as to count himself among "the philologists of the world," virtually coining a new label for his discipline: *Weltphilologie. Weltphilologie* is not, in fact, a new coinage, because the term had enjoyed a limited circulation since the late eighteenth century as a marker of progressive and radical thought. Whether or not Auerbach knew these precedents, he was nevertheless pressing ahead in the same spirit of conceptual and practical reform. In this light, contemporary extrapolations of "world philology" in the direction of "global literature" are probably over-readings of Auerbach's more limited intentions. By "world" Auerbach understands either "this world" of the here and now or else the world of the European West, much along the lines of the theologian and philosopher of history Ernst Troeltsch (1865–1923), with whom Auerbach studied while he was at Heidelberg and Berlin and whom he acknowledges for having awakened his interest in Vico ("Vorrede" 39).[12]

"Earthly" occurs as a virtual leitmotif in Auerbach's writings. The word features conspicuously in the title of the first book he published after his 1921 dissertation, *Dante als Dichter der irdischen Welt* (1929), which appeared under the English title of *Dante: Poet of the Secular World* (1961). The rendering is unfortunate, as it gets the accent wrong. Of concern to Auerbach in this study is not the world as a secular entity, but the earthly character of the world in its experiential particularity, vividness, and proximity to life. The word "earthly" continues to resonate in all of Auerbach's writings, down to his posthumously published *Literary Language and Its Public in Late Latin Antiquity and in the Middle Ages* (German edition 1958; English translation 1965), for instance on the penultimate page, where Auerbach describes "the strange moral dialectic of Christianity," which is his way of glossing "the *scandal* of [Christianity's] corruption" from the previous page:

> God's realm is not of this world; *but how can the living remain aloof from the earthly realm?* And are they justified in doing so, seeing that Christ himself entered into earthly affairs? Their duty as Christians is not to remain stoically aloof from earthly concerns but to submit to suffering. And

[11] Cf. *Literary Language and Its Public* (n. 6 above) 16: "The systematic context of all human history . . . is Vico's subject, which, in line with Vico's own terminology, we may equally well call philology or philosophy." Such study "is concerned with only one thing—mankind."

[12] Troeltsch actually *equates* Europeanism with world history: "For us there is only a world history of Europe" (*Der Historismus und seine Probleme* 1: *Das logische Problem der Geschichtsphilosophie* [Tübingen: J.C.B. Mohr (Paul Siebeck), 1922] 708). Elsewhere, too, Troeltsch sounds uncannily like Auerbach (or rather, vice versa). See his pages on "Europeanism," ibid. 703–30, esp. 704–5. And see the translation of Auerbach's 1941–42 lecture, "Realism in Europe in the Nineteenth Century," reproduced in Kader Konuk, *East West Mimesis: Auerbach in Turkey* (Stanford: Stanford University Press, 2010) 182.

how can one tolerate the fact that the Church itself, the Pope, the bishops, and the monasteries sink into the depths of earthly corruption, with the result that souls are led astray and fall victim to eternal damnation?[13] Is this to be endured? And if not, how can it be averted if not by energetic counteractivity in the earthly world, *where on the other hand the activity of the living can never be anything but biased in favor of earthly existence*? (337; trans. adapted; emphasis added)

Auerbach's analysis is rather astonishing. Is it the work of a philologist? Surely it is not the work of a Romance philologist, though perhaps it is that of an earthly, worldly philologist. Here, he is taking as his object a dilemma—indeed, a "paradox" (338)—that lies at the heart of the Christian faith and practice, and diagnosing this as a form of spiritual and psychological "anxiety," which he goes on, a page later, to describe as the "eschatological disquiet of the Christian." Auerbach then proceeds to make two further remarkable points: first, this anxiety is as fundamental to the Christian faith as is its belief in salvation itself; and second, this same anxiety has been an essential catalyst of moral, political, and philosophical change in the *secular* world in the West. As Auerbach sees things, Christianity posited an ineradicable paradox for mankind—namely, the problem of reconciling an eternal ideal with earthly temporality, and above all the riddle of God's Incarnation, which is to say his engagement with history (Christ's own historicity). Moreover, Christ's messianic project crucially *failed*. In Auerbach's words, Christianity was "a movement which by its very nature could not remain fully spiritual" and was "never fully actualized . . . in the world"—"all that was a lamentable failure" (*Dante* 12, 13).[14] And yet, it was by means of this very paradox that Christianity helped to propel the world forward into time and history, by serving as a (gradually) vanishing mediator and "creating the conditions for its own suppression and withering away."[15]

While there is much to ponder in this judgment from Auerbach's posthumous work, of equal note is its longevity in his thought. The same theme happens to structure one of his most compelling essays, "On Rousseau's Place

---

[13] Most spectacularly as displayed in Dante's *Inferno*. See also "The Three Traits of Dante's Poetry" (here Chapter 15).

[14] See also *Mimesis: The Representation of Reality in Western Literature*, W.R. Trask, trans. (Princeton, NJ: Princeton University Press, 1953; rpt. 2003) 76: "Such attempts *were bound to founder*. . . ." Further, Martin Treml, "Auerbachs imaginäre jüdische Orte," in Barck and Treml, eds., *Erich Auerbach* (n. 1 above) 244.

[15] For this last concept, see Fredric Jameson, "The Vanishing Mediator, or, Max Weber as Storyteller," in *The Ideologies of Theory: Essays, 1971–1986* 2 (Minneapolis: University of Minnesota Press, 1988) 3–34; and Étienne Balibar, "Europe as Vanishing Mediator," *Constellations* 10.3 (2003) 312–38; quotation 334. The classic example of this concept is Protestantism as analyzed by Max Weber, whose work of 1904/5 (rev. ed. 1920) was very likely familiar to Auerbach, at the very least *via* Troeltsch.

in History" (1932, here Chapter 19). A mere five pages long in the original, the essay is a brilliant cameo of this great Enlightenment thinker standing athwart the threshold of modernity, bewildered by competing allegiances, caught in a double bind between faith and reason. In a nutshell, Rousseau "was constitutionally Christian, a Christian *in potentia*"; but by the same token, "he was unable to actualize this potential Christianity." The consequences of this dilemma are devastating for Rousseau. Auerbach describes him as a clinical disaster: he presents neurological symptoms, and a morbid insecurity in the face of life. He felt unwell, irresolute, tortured, and estranged from a world that appeared to him fundamentally wrong and corrupted—in short, he was not a pretty sight. We might call him a post-Christian neurotic. Rousseau's pessimism toward the world and its disappointments was, Auerbach says, as much a natural consequence of his loss of faith in Christianity itself (his "crisis of Christianity") as it was of his lingering attachment to the Christian schema of values and attitudes despite his adoption of Enlightenment principles. It was not so much that the world had lost value as it was that religion could no longer redeem the world. Formally and "dispositionally" speaking, Rousseau remained a Christian (this was apparent in the very *habitus* by which he grasped the world and his place in it), but not confessionally speaking, and in no other respect either. Caught between conflicting stances, Rousseau vacillated uncomfortably in between, with no refuge in sight.

As plausible as all this may sound as a psychological portrait of a complex figure on the cusp of our own modernity (even though Auerbach insists that his account is historically and not clinically motivated), the truly interesting point is that Rousseau's condition betrays something symptomatic about Christians generally, and not only in their "critical epochs," such as the one through which Rousseau exemplarily lived: namely, that "*uncertainty*"—or "*insecurity*"—"*in the earthly world is a Christian motif.*" This last observation is found elsewhere in Auerbach's writings, for instance in his 1941 essay "On Pascal's Political Theory" (Chapter 17, this volume).[16] There, Auerbach exposes in Pascal's ultra-Christian thinking the germs of an un-Christian and even anti-Christian logic—a logic that, in the essay on Rousseau, he had described as a form of Christian ambivalence and which he also found em-

---

[16] The essay has a complex publication history. It first appeared in 1946 in a Turkish journal, *Felsefe Arkivi* [Archives of Philosophy], under the title, "Der Triumph des Bösen: Versuch über Pascals polische [sic] Theorie" [The Triumph of Evil: An Essay on Pascal's Political Theory], though the essay was completed in 1941, as Auerbach indicates on the last page of the article. A revised and expanded version appeared as a chapter of *Vier Untersuchungen zur Geschichte der französischen Bildung* (1951), under the title, "Über Pascals politische Theorie" [On Pascal's Political Theory] (rpt. Gesammelte Aufsätze, 1967). In the same year, an English version, presumably produced by Auerbach himself, was published in the *Hudson Review* ("The Triumph of Evil in Pascal"). Chapter 17 below is based on the 1967 version. But because the core of all four versions goes back to 1941, this is the reference date being adopted in the present volume.

bedded in Dante's peculiar form of realism (to be discussed momentarily). The irony of the essay from 1941 is that Pascal, the devout and grimly ascetic believer, paves the way for the atheistic Enlightenment and its "polemic against Christianity," a polemic that ironically originated from *within* Christianity itself. One need look no further, Auerbach reasons, than to the precarious logic of Christian self-hatred (of which asceticism is but a species), to the Christian duty to submit to worldly suffering, or to "God's sacrifice of Himself"—literally, his "submission"—"to earthly reality," which in turn is the source of all subsequent religious pathos and "tragic realism" ("all of European tragic realism depends on this"[17]), in order to find an explanation for this kind of "de-Christianization" from within. "De-Christianization" is another rubric-like theme that runs through Auerbach's writings from start to finish as one of their more insistent, if subterranean, motifs.

Dante's *Summa Vitae Humanae*

Finally, in order to tie together some of the major strands of thinking that weave in and out of Auerbach's writings over the course of his career, it will be necessary to go back to his 1929 masterpiece on Dante. There we see how the shrewd diagnosis of Christianity's dilemmas found in Auerbach's 1932 essay on Rousseau had already taken form in his mind three years earlier—indeed, it actually lay at the center of his view of Dante's great work. In *Dante as Poet of the Earthly World*,[18] we read how Christianity is in fact founded upon the same lack of quiet that tormented Rousseau—indeed, how "Christ himself lived in continuous conflict" about his own calling, thereby creating the prototype of Christian ambivalence (14). All such ambivalence goes beyond the awkward balancing act of a subject who is caught with one foot in this world and another in the Beyond, because it marks an antinomy that is rooted within the Christian faith itself and is part of its defining DNA (Auerbach will later call this its inner "antagonism"). Consequently, in his work on Dante, Auerbach offers nothing less than a reassessment of Christianity in its psychological and phenomenological core, which he locates in sheer paradox and tension, starting with its "historical kernel," which consists of a man, Christ, who embodies godhood, and the terrible clash between these

---

[17] *Introduction aux études de philologie romane* (Frankfurt am Main: V. Klostermann, 1949) 57; see "Romanticism and Realism" (here Chapter 12).

[18] This is also how Auerbach renders the title in the English version of his *curriculum vitae* that he submitted to the Emergency Committee in Aid of Displaced Foreign Scholars in February 1941 when he petitioned, unsuccessfully, for asylum (a process he had initiated starting at least in September 1935, and then reactivated virtually every year thereafter until May/June 1943). I am grateful to Martin Vialon for making these documents available to me in advance of his own publication of this extraordinary find.

two poles (11; trans. adapted; see also 178: "that entirely Christian tension and intensity, which was Dante's gift to posterity"; trans. adapted).

Auerbach is keen to compare this phenomenon to its classical precedents, and just as in *Mimesis* it is the biblical tradition that stands out as superior in richness, complexity, and compelling power:

> The historical core of Christianity . . . offers a more radical paradox, a wider range of contradiction, than anything known to the ancient world, either in its history or in its mythical tradition. . . . This entire episode [sc., of God's Incarnation and Passion] was to provoke the greatest of all transformations in the inner and outward history of our civilized world. (*Dante* 11)

Nor is this all. One might have imagined that Christianity entailed a disparagement of this earth and a pining for the Beyond, but Auerbach introduces an unexpected wrinkle: it was the classical traditions of wisdom (Auerbach names Epicureanism and Stoicism) that had detached themselves from the here and now, while Christianity by contrast *intensified* the sensibility for, and attachment to, earthly existence, a fact that its core "myth" both advertises and embodies symptomatically (12–13). That is, Christianity intensified the potential for a subjective embrace of human reality, which (as we saw) can only occur through the convergence of three factors: history, lived experience in the present, and a (tragic, i.e., fleeting) sense of meaning and depth, which is to say, of potentials that exceed the surfaces of life.

This reversal of the accustomed roles of the pagan and Christian worlds is highly provocative, to say the least. Attachment to this world in Christianity, however, comes not in the form of an unequivocal embracing of the mundane (a yearning for the Hereafter remains potent), but in the form of an utter submission to earthly destiny—an acceptance of one's mortal lot, of one's humility and humanity, of historical time, and (not least) of the historicity of Christ—"of the appearance of Christ as a *concrete* event, as a central fact of *world history*" (16; trans. adapted; emphasis added). Hence the significance, which Auerbach repeatedly underscores, of Christ's Incarnation and his Passion, as opposed to his Resurrection and Ascension. Auerbach is not drawing a fine theological distinction. On the contrary, he is making a critical and historical point, very much in line with the writings of his teacher Troeltsch, who sought to bracket, through historical analysis, the *mysterium* of Christ.[19] Like Auerbach, Troeltsch viewed the story of Christ as a "decisive"

---

[19] See esp. Ernst Troeltsch, *Die Absolutheit des Christentums und die Religionsgeschichte*, 2nd rev. ed. (Tübingen: Mohr, 1912). Troeltsch's influence on Auerbach's view of history is well recognized. See, most recently, Graf's introduction to Ernst Troeltsch, *Der Historismus und seine Probleme*, 1: *Das logische Problem der Geschichtsphilosophie*, Friedrich Wilhelm Graf and Matthias Schlossberger, eds. (Berlin: W. De Gruyter, 2008) 1–157. But in the areas of theology and religion the impact of Troeltsch's critical historicism on Auerbach has been neglected. Troeltsch's views are

step forward in the historical awareness of mankind; unlike Troeltsch, Auerbach adds the crucial twist of existential agony. Approaching the foundational fact of Christianity in this way, as residing in Christ's Incarnation and Passion ("the true heart of the Christian doctrine," *Mimesis* 72) and not in his Ascension to a Beyond, allows Auerbach to treat Christian faith as an encounter with a "story" or "narrative," but above all as a "history" (*Geschichte*), which is to say as an event in time, and an emotionally fraught one at that, because it was rooted in deeply unsettling paradox. Christianity thus shows itself to be the incarnation less of Spirit than of conflicting aspirations.[20]

Dante's achievement was to capture this unsettled frame of mind through the compelling mimetic character that he gave to his souls: though they are mere wraiths, nominally dead and transported to another world, they talk, have consciousness, memories, passions, and seem to us (and even to themselves) very much as if they were still alive in the here and now. In fact, "the souls of Dante's otherworld are not dead men," Auerbach insists, almost counterintuitively, though he is merely rephrasing the logic of Dante's poem: "No, . . . they are the truly living," more real than dead, more *earthly* and *concrete* than they seem spirited away into a Beyond (134). This is the triumph of Dante's "naturalism" (146),[21] which is more than a triumph of mimetic realism in the narrow literary sense: it wrests from the afterlife the vitality of living creatures conditioned by time and presents them in all their "contingent and particular" glory (150; trans. adapted). Auerbach dubs them for this reason *Zeitmenschen* (creatures of time), a term used in German philosophy and theology from the middle of the eighteenth century onward to distinguish the temporal aspect of humanity from its eternal and spiritual quality, but which in Auerbach's hands takes on a somewhat stronger meaning: for he is insisting, along with Dante, that temporal beings are to be found in the

---

laid out in a number of his writings, above all in *Die Bedeutung der Geschichtlichkeit Jesu für den Glauben* [The Significance of the Historicity of Jesus for the Chistian Faith] (Tübingen: J.C.B. Mohr, 1911); *Der Historismus und seine Probleme* (n. 12 above) 14–16; *Glaubenslehre: Nach Heidelberger Vorlesungen aus den Jahren 1911 und 1912* (Munich: Duncker & Humblot, 1925); and in *Die Absolutheit des Christentums*. That the paradoxes of Incarnation were in the air at the time is shown by Lothar Helbing's *Der dritte Humanismus* (Berlin: Verlag Die Runde, 1932) 42.

[20] Auerbach repeats part of his argument from *Dante* in his later essay on Baudelaire ([n. 10 above] 285), noting the relevance of Christ's Incarnation and Passion to "every Christian interpretation of *life*" (emphasis added). See further *Literary Language and Its Public* (n. 6 above) 40–47, 52, 315–16. Cf. also Auerbach's telling letter to Croce about Vico, dating from March 1936: "On the other hand, even those who are Christians among today's scholars will no longer claim that Genesis is an exact and scientific description of physical creation. . . . And I believe that a philosopher who was more liberal in his interpretation of faith [such as Vico] would not be compelled to regard the birth of Christ as a fact of material [viz., "embodied"] transcendence" (Ottavio Besomi, ed., *Il carteggio Croce-Auerbach* [Bellinzona: Archivio Storico Ticinese, 1977] 29).

[21] See Max Dvořák's *Idealismus und Naturalismus in der gotischen Skulptur und Malerei* (Berlin: R. Oldenbourg, 1918), which is referred to by Auerbach for this very concept (*Dante* [n. 5 above] 20).

eternal afterlife, and that this temporality captures an essential aspect of their being ("man requires a temporal process, history or destiny, in order to fulfill himself," 85). Though superficially in line with Thomist psychology, Auerbach's reading in fact points elsewhere.[22]

Dante, Auerbach believes, made two significant innovations over his predecessors, and these were linked: he "discovered" the individual *living* person, and he achieved a novel "vision of reality."

> With the discovery of individual destiny, modern mimesis discovered the person. It lifted him out of the two-dimensional irreality of a remoteness that was only constructed or imagined and placed him in *the realm of history, which is his true home*. . . . The immanent realism and historicism that are found in the eschatology of the *Divine Comedy* flowed back into actual history and filled it with the lifeblood of authentic truth. . . . Radiating out from here, history as such—the life of the human being as this is given and in its earthly character—underwent a vitalization and acquired a new value. Even the *Divine Comedy* barely manages to subdue the wild spirits of life within the framework of its eschatology, and one senses how quickly and forcefully these spirits will soon prise themselves loose from their constraints. With Petrarch and Boccaccio the historical realm becomes a fully earthly and autonomous entity, and from there the fecundating stream of sensuous and historical evidence [*Evidenz*: a principle of empirical discernibility and proof] spills forth over Europe—to all appearances utterly removed from its eschatological origins, and yet secretly connected to these by the bonds that hold man fast to his concrete and historical destiny. (217; my translation; emphasis added; Engl. trans. 178)

Dante's poem documents a turning point in history that was all the harder to track because it was history itself that was coming to life. Against all odds, Auerbach's counterintuitive interpretation is unflinching and radical: "Thus, even though the *Divine Comedy* describes the state of souls after death, *its subject, in the last analysis, remains earthly life in all its complexity*; everything that happens below or in the heavens above relates to *human drama here on earth*" (132; trans. adapted; emphasis added). Auerbach's subsequent readings of Dante, whether in "The Discovery of Dante by Romanticism"

---

[22] For the Thomist theory of self-realization in the afterlife, see Étienne Gilson, *Le thomisme: Introduction au système de Saint Thomas D'Aquin*, revised and expanded ed. (Paris: J. Vrin, 1922; 1st ed. 1920) esp. 138–151 and 208–12. Acknowledging this influence, Auerbach also notes the poet's various licenses and divergences from Catholic orthodoxy (e.g., *Dante* [n. 5 above]) 71–73, 81, 87, 116; cf. 27–28). See further Helmut Kuhn, "Literaturgeschichte als Geschichtsphilosophie," *Philosophische Rundschau* 11.3–4 (1964) 222–248, esp. 248 (quoted n. 43 below), which in this and several other respects remains unsurpassed as a study of Auerbach's thought—with one stunning exception (see n. 24 below).

(1929, here Chapter 11), "Dante and Vergil" (1931, here Chapter 10), *Mimesis* (1946), "The Three Traits of Dante's Poetry" (1948, here Chapter 15), or "Typological Symbolism in Medieval Literature" (1952, here Chapter 8), are all embellishments on this single interpretive premise, which is adumbrated already in "On the Anniversary Celebration of Dante" (1921, here Chapter 9).

In reading the poem in this way, Auerbach could not have taken a line more unlike his mentor's had he wished to do so. In his several works on Dante, Vossler held that the poet was an unwavering dogmatic, steeped in Thomist theology and psychology, whose poem could nevertheless be finally understood only as a work of art: it bore no relation to reality—not even a figural one—because Dante had so stylized his poem's contents with his imagination as to cut them off entirely from all "earthly existence," and virtually from all other forms of cultural expression as well.[23] The *Divine Comedy* for Vossler was not a document of the historical world of the *trecento*, but merely an instance of one man's religious belief transposed into an idiosyncratic aesthetic form.

By contrast, Dante's vision was for Auerbach an agent of profound cultural change. The logic of his poetry led not to an embrace of transcendence but to "something new," an unprecedented sense of historical immediacy and a rich capacity for grasping human experience in its most vital if vulnerable aspects. As a result, Dante was realizing a potential within the Christian theological worldview that led to the dissolution of that worldview altogether. In Dante, "the indestructibility of the whole historical and individual man turns *against* [the divine] order . . . and obscures it. The image of man eclipses the image of God. Dante's work realized the Christian-figural essence of man, and destroyed it in the very process of realizing it" (*Mimesis* 202; trans. adapted).[24] The general picture of secularization starting in the latter half of the twelfth century and eventuating in "the autonomous value of earthly things" was widely accepted at the time.[25] Auerbach complicates this narrative through a series of dark and riveting readings, in the present case by locating the secular turn, *nolens volens*, within the impeccably devout mind of Dante—a

[23] Karl Vossler, *Die philosophischen Grundlagen zum "süssen neuen Stil" des Guido Guinicelli, Guido Cavalcanti und Dante Alighieri* (Heidelberg: C. Winter's Universitätsbuchhandlung, 1904); *Dante als religiöser Dichter* (Bern: Seldwyla, 1921) esp. 9–10; *Die göttliche Komödie*, 2nd rev. ed., 2 vols. (Heidelberg: C. Winter, 1925) esp. 1:124–26 and 2:625.

[24] Kuhn ("Literaturgeschichte als Geschichtsphilosophie" [n. 22 above] 242) misses the boat here: "How can consummation be destructive?" But to ask this is to misapprehend the fundamental logic that governs cultural and historical change according to Auerbach, both here and everywhere else (cf. "Rousseau": "in historical occurrences, culminating moments and the first signs of crisis coincide"; "The Philology of World Literature": if the number of languages in the world were to be reduced to a few or even to one, as they appear to be headed, "the idea of world literature would simultaneously be realized and destroyed").

[25] See Dvořák's art-historical work, *Idealismus und Naturalismus* (n. 21 above; the quotation is from p. 91); Troeltsch, *Der Historismus und seine Probleme* (n. 12 above).

rather heretical stance.[26] As it happens, the kernel of this idea was already in place in Auerbach's dissertation of 1921: "The passionate contemplation of earthly life [which emerges with the early Renaissance novella in Italy and France] derives from him" (*Zur Technik* 3)—that is, from Dante, who after all was for Auerbach a poet not of the other world, but of the *earthly* world.

Vico, History, and the Ethics of the Real

Dante was without a doubt Auerbach's most adored literary author long before he learned to identify with him as a fellow political exile (see "On the Anniversary Celebration of Dante" and "Three Traits"). The kindred sympathy that he felt with the poet was very likely based on a deeper form of exilic experience that Auerbach knew in his own person and that he leaves all but unstated.[27] And yet, as original, powerful, and convincing as Auerbach's reading of Dante may be, in some ways he is merely retracing Hegel's own reading of the *Divine Comedy* (he names this debt explicitly in "The Discovery of Dante by the Romantics" and in *Mimesis*), and in other respects he is freely transposing a Hegelian template onto the great medieval poet. Also palpable in Auerbach's revisioning of Dante is the philosophical imagination of Vico, to whom Auerbach owed his sense of the particular, the concrete, and the contingent. Vico's critical empiricism and realism, possibly filtered through Auerbach's reading of Croce,[28] serve as a healthy antidote to Hegelian speculativeness and universalism for Auerbach. On the other hand, both Hegel and Vico believed in history as a providential force. Not so Auerbach, whose overarching vision of history knows no redemptive safeguards and no supervising providential instance.[29] On the contrary, history for Auerbach is riddled with uncertainties, and historical awareness means nothing less than

[26] Vossler certainly thought so, and criticized Auerbach on these very grounds in his mixed review of the book (*Deutsche Literaturzeitung* 50.2 [1929] 69–72). Vossler's verdict was only to be expected. Auerbach had anticipated it himself (letter to Vossler, 9 January 1929, in *Und wirst erfahren wie das Brot der Fremde so salzig schmeckt: Erich Auerbachs Briefe an Karl Vossler 1926–1948*, Vialon, ed. [Warmbronn: Ulrich Keicher, 2007] 6).

[27] See Vialon, ed., *Und wirst erfahren wie das Brot der Fremde so salzig schmeckt* (n. 26 above) 30–38, and the end of this introduction.

[28] And possibly also filtered through Troeltsch's brilliant analysis of Croce in the light of both Vico and Hegel in *Der Historismus und seine Probleme* (n. 12 above) 617–32.

[29] Vico, he claims, was the last person on earth who succeeded in achieving such a vision of faith ("Giambattista Vico," in *Der neue Merkur* 6 (1922) 249–52; here 249. He later qualifies this view, calling Vico's system "godless" ("Vorrede" [n. 9 above] 35). And in a 1935 letter to Croce he goes further still, doubting that Vico's work is redemptive at all, and concluding that it cannot be considered Christian at its core—while referring back to his "Vorrede" of 1924 for supporting arguments (Besomi, *Il carteggio Croce-Auerbach* [n. 20 above] 29). The same premise is articulated in the 1932 essay, "Montaigne the Writer" (here Chapter 16): "[T]here is practically no trace of hope or salvation in the *Essays*," which is why he finds them "un-Christian."

the acceptance of this difficult fact over time, and the wisdom that comes with it.

The largest historical pattern that Auerbach's writings chart is carefully designed to exemplify this vision. History for Auerbach is marked by two major ruptures, each constituting moments when vertical, transcendental meaning is shattered in the course of the horizontal, forward propulsion of history, while history is etched in turn with the scars of these traumatic unfoldings, and so acquires a depth of its own. First there is the devaluation (*Entwertung*) of Judaism through Christianity, then there is the de-Christianization (*Entchristung*) of Christianity (from both within and without). Occupying the two extremes are pagan antiquity, which is essentially depthless (despite some exceptions, Sophoclean tragedy above all), and post-Enlightenment modernity, the fate of which has yet to be determined. Auerbach has more than a historian's investment in documenting what today would be called this "historical turn," by which the religious insecurity witnessed above is overcome and the sensuous, earthly, and secular world is ushered in. It is the this-worldly elements of reality, its human, earthly side, that constitute the source of every value that matters to Auerbach in the end, be it historical or ethical or, as is most often the case, both of these combined. "The realm of history," after all, is mankind's "true home."

In Auerbach's dynamic scheme, history entails sure gains and certain losses. Thus, Christianity absorbed the Jewish tradition of reinterpretation, "now applied with incomparably greater boldness" to the Jewish Scriptures themselves, with a consequential "devaluation" of the Jewish religion (*Mimesis* 48; cf. 15–16). This is the famous origin of figural revision. Christianity could not, however, have succeeded without the lessons it learned from Judaism's capacity first to conceive and interpret the world historically (based on its notion of universal, "world-historical" events) and then to organize this history into a single coherent transcendental order (ibid. 17). In doing so, Christianity inherited not merely a religious sensibility, but an ineluctable *antagonism*: "the antagonism between sensory appearance and meaning, an antagonism which permeates the early, and indeed the whole, Christian view of reality" (ibid. 49). Christianity rose and fell on the rock of this antagonism, which troubled the very heart of its figural recuperation of history, of Judaism, and of earthly life itself, while this last ingredient remained both a reservoir of dynamic energy and an indigestible element:

> The figural interpretation of history emerged unqualifiedly victorious. *Yet it was no fully adequate substitute for the lost comprehension of rational, continuous, earthly connections between things,* and it could not be applied to any random occurrence, although of course there was no dearth of attempts to submit everything that happened to an interpretation directly from above. Such attempts *were bound to founder* on the

multiplicity of events and the unfathomableness of the divine councils. *And so vast regions of events remained without any principle by which they might be classified and comprehended*—especially after the fall of the Roman Empire. . . . It was a very long time before the germs contained in Christian thought (the mixture of styles, a deep insight into the processes of becoming), sustained by the sensuality of peoples who were not yet exhausted,[30] could take root in all their vigor. (*Mimesis* 75–76; trans. adapted; emphasis added)

In Auerbach's eyes, gaps existed in the Christian theory of the world, which were in fact more than mere gaps because they represented systematic flaws in that theory, being symptoms of its manifold inheritances but also of its innermost inconsistency, which not even invoking the divine mystery could paper over, and which eventually would lead to the collapse of Christianity as a dominant worldview altogether. When it finally arrived, the new world of secular, historicized reality proved to be infinitely "richer, deeper, *and more dangerous* than pagan antiquity's culture of the person, *for it inherited from the Christian religion* out of which it sprang and which it finally overcame *a sense of disquiet and a drive towards excessiveness*" (*Dante* 215; my translation; emphasis added; Engl. trans. 176).

This is a striking diagnosis. Christianity may be a source of psychological disquiet, but can it actually be labeled a source of excessive tendencies? For Auerbach this is most unambiguously the case. Christianity dwells in a permanent state of crisis and insecurity, as we saw, and now we can add that it does so *out of a fundamental lack*. Its restless impulse—its being driven not simply by a need for more, but by a need for "too much," for excess (*das Zuviel*), as illustrated by a promised Beyond, Last Judgment, and final salvation—is *compensatory* (in relation to a felt deficiency), but also forever inadequate given the structural role of this impulse within the larger edifice of Christian metaphysics. Once again, history is seen to be the transmission of gains and losses, but also of transformative effects. Only now it becomes apparent that secular modernity inherits one more feature from Christianity—a dangerous set of impulses.

---

[30] "Exhausted," which is to say, by the process of Christianization, which in turn drew upon their as yet untapped reservoirs of sensuality. None of this is apparent from the rendering by Trask ("reinforced by the sensuality of new peoples"), though Auerbach's formulation is admittedly rather compressed and somewhat brutal (*unterstützt von der Sinnlichkeit noch unzermürbter Völker*). Contrast the Jewish interpretive dynamic described earlier: "Doctrine and the search for enlightenment are inextricably connected with the sensuous aspect of the narrative (*mit der Sinnlichkeit der Erzählung*)," which Christianity threatened to banish altogether (ibid. 15; trans. adapted). The same idea appears in *Dante* (n. 5 above) 13: the "innermost sensory ground" of world views held by various peoples and races, to which "the apparatus of Christian dogma could be adapted more easily," etc.

Caught between competing cultural forces, mankind also appears to be caught between competing instincts—for instance, between the powerful pull of sensuality, immediacy, and lived experience on the one hand, and the need for deeper significance on the other. Can these ever be reconciled? The question leads to another: whether historical experience and deeper meaning can ever take on an immediately sensuous form, and thus become a transformative experience in its own right. As it happens, the satisfying union of these two needs represents the ideal trajectory of the human condition in Auerbach's view of it. Each of the moments that he singles out for description in his writings either approaches or briefly touches or else falls tragically short of this correlation between self and reality, what he sometimes describes as the revealed coincidence of man with his or her "fate" (the course of life one has led or will be seen to have led, insofar as this is dialectically informative of one's character; see, for example, "On the Anniversary Celebration of Dante"), but what he also recognized can take the form of profound *self*-consistency (the unwavering commitment to one's character in the face of circumstances; see *Dante*, ch. 1 and *passim*, and the theme of *sibi constare*, which is announced there and which appears throughout his writings). In those rare moments when this coincidence of self and reality is either intimated or made concrete, be this in the Old Testament or in the Passion of Christ or in such writers as Dante, Proust, or Virginia Woolf, the result is what Auerbach calls "tragic realism."

"Tragic realism" is Auerbach's way of naming the troubling juncture between the surfaces of life and language, which one can both know and feel, and the plunging vertical aspect of some other dimension altogether, which one can only sense. It is at such moments that mimesis is achieved—the representation of the essential unity of a character with its fate in all their blinding reality and luminous "evidence," as revealed in a singular act of the self.[31] Anticipating Foucault by half a century, Auerbach calls such moments "problematizations" of the ordinary—though what he is designating is in fact the substratum of reality that underlies all ordinary experience (e.g., *Dante* 13; *Mimesis* 18–19, 22, 27, 72, 311, 563, etc.). Auerbach also knows, however, that much of the time such abrupt communications with the real do not occur at all: we live in reality but rarely commune with it. And that is most likely why when such moments do occur they warrant the name *tragic*—for they signal their own self-consuming fragility, and their own passing.[32]

---

[31] *Dante* (n. 5 above) 2, 156 (*sinnlich evident*) and 178 (sensuous and historical evidence [*Evidenz*]); "Montaigne the Writer": "It is luminously obvious in his writing" (*Es strahlt von Evidenz*); "Romanticism and Realism." *Evidenz* has a strong empirical flavor, and is not far removed from the idea of visible or tangible proof.

[32] Cf. also the end of "Frate Alberto" in *Mimesis* (n. 14 above) on the tragic realism of Dante and its ephemerality (231).

This is where Auerbach's most famous but possibly least understood contribution to the history of style comes into play. For such moments of communication with the real are also marked by a convergence of high and low styles (*Stilmischung*), which is not simply the formal rupture of the classical separation of styles (*Stiltrennung*),[33] but the shattering of style as a meaningful criterion of anything at all: sublimity is unearthed in the depths that suddenly open up in the realm of the everyday, as the expressions of a passionate subject who is firmly located in space and time here on earth, be this in a saint like Paul or a realist like Balzac.[34] Such moments are "tragic," because tragedy is what results whenever the "forces of individualism, historicism, and lyricism" "r[i]se up against the past as with a common will to embrace the world in all its concrete immanence and to experience the world's spirit through its living body" ("Romanticism and Realism").

Where the secularized self leaves us today, in Auerbach's present, is utterly unclear. But it is only in the face of such uncertainty that the ethical substance of human action can ever be located—a point that tellingly arises out of his interpretation of Dante.[35] Ethics thereby replaces religious morality for Auerbach, even as it remains informed by the deepest urges—and hence, too, the "tragic paradoxes"—of a "dwindling faith."[36] Loss, yearning, despair, and horror are the darker hues of reality so viewed; clear-sightedness and a reassuring sense of life's impregnable value are its brighter aspects. On balance, Auerbach's temperament is one of understated optimism. Uncertain though the progress of history may be, change over time is not random but has a logic. History progresses, not inexorably forward, but recuperatively, whereby each successive step becomes possible only thanks to what came before it, like a glacier that collects and clears rubble as it edges forward. In this way, history *redeems itself*, not providentially, but through its own momentum. (Such moments are often signaled by Auerbach with the phrase, "Y

---

[33] On the classical schema, there exist three styles (high, middle, low), each assigned its own proper domain and often genre of application.

[34] Though Auerbach does not mention it, a good metaphor for this experience of sublimity in the everyday is given by Lucretius in *On the Nature of Things* 4.414–19, where he describes a puddle of water spanning the cracks in the pavement of a street, into which is cast the reflection of the heavens above, "so that you seem to look down on the clouds and the heavens, and you discern bodies hidden in the sky beneath the earth, miraculously (*mirande*)."

[35] See his essay on the occasion of the 1921 Dante jubilee, though the same idea underlies the whole of his interpretation of Dante: "Particularity is all-decisive. Character and fate are one, and the fate of the autonomous self lies in its freedom of choice. The self was created by God in all of its particularity, but the freedom to decide is left entirely up to the self" ("On the Anniversary Celebration of Dante," here Chapter 9). See, too, Emily Apter, *Against World Literature: On the Politics of Untranslatability* (London: Verso, 2013) 201, on Auerbach's "ethical realism."

[36] The process is organic: the one attitude grows out of the other. Cf. *Das französische Publikum* (n. 4 above) 50–53. For the phrase "the tragic paradoxes of a dwindling faith," see Fitzgerald, *Enlarging the Change* (n. 10 above) 17.

would be unthinkable without its predecessor X.") And as humanity accumulates lessons from its own historical struggles, it learns pragmatically—in its habits, its body, its thought, and its culture—what the meaning of history is (see, e.g., "Dante and Vergil").[37] It also learns to take responsibility for its own outcomes. Indeed, it is through this awareness of history, or rather of the course of events that reach into the present, that the nature of experience acquires a depth and meaning of its own, even if such coordinates continue to be measured, whether out of ingrained habit, wistfulness, or instinctual need, against the idea of transcendental meaning. In tracing the rise of historical consciousness, Auerbach is at the same time tracing something like the historical grounding of autonomous—in Vico's sense, man-made—ethical consciousness and human agency.

From Vico,[38] Auerbach learned all this, and he learned something else too, something that he could never have divined from Hegel alone. He learned that history is fraught with danger, and that coming to grips with history means more than simply being alive to one's own historical place and circumstances—being located in a particular place and in a particular time, as he repeatedly puts this in his writings—but also knowing how to confront the potential for violence that history inevitably reveals. A potential of this kind followed like a structural law from Vico's view of historical evolution, at the root of which he posited a natural, primitive creature, the *Urmensch*, as Auerbach calls him, who lived in a radically divided state—in a state of immediate sensuous contact with the world, but also surrounded with the offspring of his own fantastic imaginings. Everything known to subsequent civilization—from law, religion, and government to familial relations and poetry—was first established in this wild initial state of humanity, "which is marked by *incomparable cruelty*" and by an absence of "human tenderness" ("Vico and Herder"). Auerbach lavishes page after page on Vico's retrojected fantasy of a quasi-Golden Age, both in this same essay and in others. What

---

[37] Thus, that most "un-Christian" of thinkers, Michel de Montaigne, whose personal reality is rooted in his own immediate body, derives this very premise from the religion he repudiates conceptually and pragmatically: "Montaigne's unity of mind and body has its roots in Christian-creatural anthropology. . . . It is the basis of his realistic introspection; without it, the latter [sc., his realism] would be inconceivable" (*Mimesis* [n. 14 above] 306; later reiterated on p. 310). Similarly, *Gesammelte Aufsätze* (n. 10 above) 290 (regarding Baudelaire); "The Philology of World Literature." In this way, history comes to consist in a chain of conceptual dependencies for Auerbach. These same dependencies are also what render Auerbach's literary histories so unique, and so uniquely coherent.

[38] And probably also from Troeltsch. See *Der Historismus und seine Probleme* (n. 12 above) 15 and 79–81 (and *passim*), insisting that history must move forward into the area of ethics, the first step being a critical and self-critical philosophy of history. At the end of the day, history in its evolved form amounts to a blend of "historical realism" (ibid. 464–649) and ethical inquiry (*passim*) combined into one.

was the attraction? The answer lies in Auerbach's largest understanding of Vico's historical project, beginning with Vico's own attraction to this era.

Vico's obsessive interest in prehistory had to do, Auerbach claims, with his need to construct an alter ego to modern history out of which he could build up his concept of the civilizing process and the historical superstructure to come. There is a certain intellectual probity to this kind of foundationalism, which Auerbach openly admires. Vico's bold willingness to confront a true "other" to the enlightened present further distinguished him from the German Romantics, and from Herder in particular, who was at most prepared to contemplate some idyllic creature that represented an earlier and nobler version of the modern self (ibid.; see also "Vico's Contribution to Literary Criticism" and "Vico and Aesthetic Historism," here Chapters 1 and 4).

Vico's opening gambit—his postulate of poetic primitive creatures—did more than merely wipe the slate of culture clean. It cast culture in a very particular light. It meant, first of all, that for Vico civilization arose out of primitive fantasy, sheer imaginings, and poetic fabrications, which were at the same time a basic response to fear and which preserved a strong element of brutality. Divinity was the most potent poetic construct of early mankind, and its most immediate response to a fearful world: "Their fantastical sense of divinity, which is completely bound up with sensible ideas, creates a god for every act of existence, which is to say a personified institution, the concept of an imagined person, the *universale fantastico* [imaginative universal]" ("Vico and Herder"). Civilization, by contrast, is the history of the gradual stripping away of these earliest attributes: once the enlightened age is reached, nature is no longer alive, mankind has lost its poetic connection to reality, and the imaginary has faded into conceptual abstraction. A problem not dealt with by Vico is how he can cling to his faith in a providential god, as he manifestly wishes to do, if his god could turn out to have been no more than a residue of the earliest *universale fantastico* that Vico's own theory brings to light—in other words, a man-made product like every other element of human history. Auerbach noticed this and other tensions in Vico's theological historicism, and we will come back to these issues below.

As for the question why Auerbach dwells so insistently on the earliest moments of Vico's world history, the answer must be in part that he is drawn to the historical trajectory that Vico maps out (and which Auerbach retraces in his own way), and in part because he found the role that Vico assigned to the poetic imagination immensely attractive: history works through the poetic imagination as much for Auerbach as it did for Vico. But there are also differences. Auerbach does not "speculate in a fantastical way" as Vico did about mythical prehistory. And Auerbach's view of the imagination is more refined, and more compatible with modern impulses: Montaigne, Baudelaire, and Woolf are as involved as any of Vico's primitive creatures in imagining and in this way creating their respective realities and the kinds of subjectivities that could inhabit them, whether their own or those of the readers they render possible through their writings. Indeed, Vico's own history is the product of an overactive imagination, as Auerbach is the first to acknowledge (just as Vico would be the last to do so).

And so, while Auerbach stood at several removes from Vico's fantastical "drama of history" and could be critical of its various mistakes (which he found "often enough quite grotesque"), he also learned to extract certain virtues from it, even from its most fantastical core. A number of the attributes of Vico's primitive creatures were too precious to abandon to prehistory. Auerbach extended their reach into modernity: the primacy of the sensuous, the concrete, the immediate, intuition, vitalism, and so on. Similarly, the role that the inventive mind enjoyed for Vico must for Auerbach lie at the center of any conception of the human, as must the mechanisms that set this same imagination in motion: its fears, its shames, its most primitive urges, its capacity for untold violence, all of which form an essential part of Vico's historical drama. Which brings us to the third and final attraction that Vico's fantasy of prehistory held for Auerbach: its incontestable psychological realism, which Auerbach shrewdly reads out of Vico's *own* imagination. Vico's view of primitive mankind exposes deep vulnerabilities in his own thinking, some of which he may have been unaware of, and others of which he knowingly shared with his primitive forbears.

As proof of this last point, we might compare the final lines of "Giambattista Vico und the Idea of Philology" (1936, here Chapter 3), which are exemplary in setting Auerbach's vision of history apart from the mere grasp of historical facts, but also from some harmless and pretty form of secular humanism:

> It bears remembering that Vico did not understand what he took to be common to all people as in any way a matter of education or progressive enlightenment. Rather, what all human beings hold in common is the entirety of historical reality, *in all its greatness and its horror*. Not only did he see historical individuals in their totality; he also saw that he was himself a human being and that it made him human to understand them. But Vico did not create the human race in his own likeness; he did not see himself in the other. Rather, he saw the other in himself. He discovered himself, as a human, in history, and the long buried forces of our common nature stood revealed to him. This was Vico's humanity, something *far more profound—and far more perilous*—than what we normally associate with the word. Nevertheless—or, perhaps, precisely for this reason—it was Vico who discovered our common humanity, and held it fast. (emphasis added)

Vico's brutish *Urmenschen*, in other words, lay at the root of his, and our, civilization, as its deepest and ever-present substratum, and in all its terrible potential for creation and destruction. Written as they were in 1936, these lines cannot help but resonate with the particular horrors that surrounded Auerbach at the time. He may have embraced humanism (*das Allgemeinmenschliche*, "the common elements uniting humans") as a key to grasping the problems of mankind, but he was never deluded by its promises.

Why Romance Philology, and Why the Christian Tradition?

One of the abiding puzzles in Auerbach's life is the question why he was drawn to Romance philology at all, and not, say, to German, never mind classical, philology. The essay "Vico and Herder" from which we set out contains the germ of an answer. In it, Auerbach seeks to differentiate the two roots of modern historical inquiry: the one northern, Romantic, idyllic, and founded on "the pantheism of nature," the other southern, at once systematic and intuitive, relativizing and particularizing, and humanistic; the one cherishing national consciousness (*Volksgeist*), national sentiments (*das Völkische*), and questions of race (*die Rassen- und Bodenfrage*, as he put it in 1924 ["Vorrede" 36]), the other indifferent to such impulses, to the pulls of essentialism of all kinds, to the abstract and the vaporous; the one German, the other Mediterranean and Italian.[39] The "and" of the title ("Vico and Herder") veils an unbridgeable contrast, and indeed the historical perspective the essay assumes is itself Vichian.

Other essays on similar themes ("Giambattista Vico and the Idea of Philology" [1936, here Chapter 3], "Vico and the National Spirit" [1955, here Chapter 5], "The Idea of the National Spirit as the Source of the Modern Humanities" [ca. 1955, here Chapter 6]), and "Vico's Contribution to Literary Criticism" [1958, here Chapter 1]) attest to Auerbach's enduring affinities with Vico, whose *New Science* (1744) he translated into German in the early part of his career, but also to his guarded views about German Romanticism. In fact, in the preface to his 1924 abridged translation, Auerbach already sounds many of these same themes, and at times he paints Vico in intriguingly Zarathustran hues,[40] even as he recognizes Vico's several contradictions and limits, including one monumental peculiarity. For all his providential-

---

[39] In the same spirit, Auerbach abruptly dismisses accounts of literary history based on "racial theory" in his dissertation from 1921 (*Zur Technik* [n. 8 above] 50).

[40] Thus, Vico towers over history like a "giant," given the "capaciousness and reach" of his vision and the "incomprehensible" and "inhuman" nature of his god, who is "not a product of methodology, not dreamt up, not a postulate, but a living myth. . . . More fiercely ardent than all the others [viz., his "domestically tame" successors, from Herder and the German Romantics to Hegel], Vico stands alone in the icy air of a glacier, while over him arches the immense baroque, vault-shaped horizon of the heavens" ("Vorrede" [n. 9 above] 30–31, repeating verbatim his first brief foray into Vico ("Giambattista Vico" [n. 29 above] 252).

ism, Vico's thought had one "astounding, practically incomprehensible" gaping "hole"—it both failed to locate Christ's Incarnation at the fulcrum of history, and it lacked a crowning moment of fulfillment, a final Judgment Day that could serve as a self-benediction to the historical processes that his *New Science* so laboriously mapped out. Instead, after reaching a zenith of enlightened rationality, it ended on a sour note of barbarism and degeneration, and then lapsed into eternal recurrence: the cycle of world history started all over again. This was perhaps the one loophole Auerbach needed in order to adapt Vico's methods to his own theory of historical processes and historical understanding. Vico's history showed itself to be un-Christian (not governed by the Christian dispensation), and ultimately to be (all too) human.[41]

So why, then, did Auerbach champion Vico over Romance philology? And why did he opt for Mediterranean subject matter to the exclusion of any other? The answer is all but standing before us. Romance philology as it was practiced in Germany, and indeed in Europe as a whole, was deeply imprinted by German Romanticism. And Auerbach was constitutionally unsuited to this kind of disciplinary straitjacket and its underlying assumptions. Vico offered him a methodological alternative and a philosophy he found it expedient to incorporate selectively, not wholesale, into his own evolving ways of construing the world. And yet for all his admiration of the Neapolitan thinker, Auerbach nevertheless remained steeped in German habits of thought, as he was the first to admit (most memorably, in his "Epilegomena to *Mimesis*"). As it happens, there was a radical strain that ran through German intellectual life from at least the eighteenth century onward. And while it may not always be apparent, Auerbach was at bottom a staunch adherent of this tradition, as the Nietzschean overtones audible in his 1924 preface ("Vorrede") to Vico and elsewhere remind us. Many of these elements in Auerbach's thought have yet to be untangled and evaluated for what they are.

So much for Auerbach's disciplinary style. As for why he preferred the subject matter of Romance philology to, say, classical or German philology, the answer is to be found partly in a certain resistance to things German, a resistance that had figured in the shaping, if not the founding, of Romance philology in Germany (Vossler, Curtius, and Spitzer were overt Francophiles and critics of German parochialism)—which is not to deny that the classics and Romance philology had common disciplinary and methodological roots, or that either field was by any means innocent of German chauvinism,

---

[41] "Vorrede" (n. 9 above) 37–38; and see n. 29 above. David L. Marshall (*Vico and the Transformation of Rhetoric in Early Modern Europe* [Cambridge: Cambridge University Press, 2010] 64) takes Vico's idea of *provvedenza* in the *New Science* to be "not so much a structure outside of time as a part of the structure of time itself," and even "an imaginative capacity." So did Auerbach, eventually: "provvidenza come fatto storico," in Besomi, *Il carteggio Croce-Auerbach* (n. 20 above) 29.

nationalism, or racism.[42] Consequently, Auerbach chose the path of neither a well disciplined Romance philologist nor a classical or German philologist, but rather that of a philologist in a more difficult and radical sense, a philologist who took as his object the world at large, while waging his own quiet campaign against intolerance in the highly politicized and increasingly toxic trenches of the contemporary German academy.

A similar question might be asked about Auerbach's life-long engagement with the Christian traditions of the West, and here things are a bit more complex. To begin with, his interest lay not in the Christian tradition *per se*, but in the Judaeo-Christian tradition as a whole, which was multifaceted and above all multilayered (as he kept emphatically insisting).[43] Second, Auerbach's interest was historical and historicizing: he was not interested in tracing the evolution of Church dogma for its own sake, but in bracketing that dogma with its historical determinants (after the fashion of Troeltsch). Indeed, his view of historical analysis was premised on "a maximum of *freedom* from preconceptions about the world and all other dogmatic commitments," as he stirringly wrote in 1951, recapping his beliefs of the last three decades (compare *Zur Technik* 46, where he declares that the mimetic objects he is tracking in that study are not "example[s] of a dogma but image[s] of the world"). "To be sure," he resumed, "such freedom is not easy to gain or to keep. . . . [It] requires self-criticism and fearlessness far more than a worldview [*Weltanschauung*]. But in historical inquiry, even the greatest and most cherished forms with which individuals have sought to express some absolute truth become a threat to one's judgment the moment one subscribes to them."[44] Third, the Judaeo-Christian heritage afforded Auerbach a far broader cul-

---

[42] See Frank-Rutger Hausmann, "Auch eine nationale Wissenschaft? Die Romanistik unter dem Nationalsozialismus," *Romanistische Zeitschrift für Literaturgeschichte* 22 (1998) 1–39; 261–313 for an excellent account, followed up by his massive study, *Vom Strudel der Ereignisse Verschlungen: Deutsche Romanistik im "Dritten Reich"* (Frankfurt am Main: V. Klostermann, 2000).

[43] This has misled some scholars into locating a crypto-Christian or culturally Christian tendency in Auerbach. Contrast Kuhn's closing remarks in "Literaturgeschichte als Geschichtsphilosophie" (n. 22 above) 248, which are spot on: "[Auerbach's] analysis of style, which he in no way thought of in Christian terms, is nevertheless conceived in so Christocentric a fashion that it appears to be on the verge of transforming into a Christological literary history. This, however, is an illusion."

[44] *Vier Untersuchungen* (n. 3 above) 10–11, emphasis added. Even here the influence of Troeltsch can be felt. See, e.g., *Der Historismus und seine Probleme* (n. 12 above) 15, contrasting history and ethics on the one hand and religious dogma on the other, while the idea of absolute truth recalls Troeltsch's 1912 critique of the same in *Die Absolutheit des Christentums und die Religionsgeschichte*. In the same passage from *Vier Untersuchungen*, Auerbach defends relativism (perspectival interpretation) as a *sine qua non* of historical inquiry and as compatible with truth: "Obedience to truth does not mean forgetting how very susceptible to interpretation truth's commands and dictates are. Quite the contrary, [recognizing] this [susceptibility] is, I believe, the only form of obedience that *is* commensurate with truth" (11). "Obedience" (*Gehorsam*) has ominous overtones in the aftermath of the Second World War. See also chapter 1, "Vico's Contribution to Literary Criticism" (this volume).

tural and historical scope than either classical or German philology would have afforded him alone. His ultimate object, after all, was nothing less than the changing fate and reality of the European subject across the millennia. Finally, there is the peculiar way in which Auerbach set about exploring the history of this heritage—which is to say, through its deepest underlying paradoxes and tensions, and the ways in which these were both internalized and given literary expression.

Dante once again provides a key, as the essays reproduced in this volume repeatedly attest. In "Dante and Vergil" (1931) Auerbach examines the ambiguous attractions that a pagan figure like Vergil could exert on a Christian poet like Dante. Vergil occupies the same paradoxical place in Dante's poetry and in the popular imagination as the peculiar "double position" held by Rome "as the traditional seat of worldly empire on the one hand, and as the seat of the Papacy on the other." The medieval way of resolving this contradiction was to transform Vergil into "a kind of pagan prophet and crypto-Christian, or at least an inspired, if unwitting seer of God's truth"—a *figura* betokening a future fulfillment, in other words—a reputation that Auerbach declared was unearned: it was all a "pious error." A second essay, "The Discovery of Dante by Romanticism" (1929), reaffirms Auerbach's reading of the *Divine Comedy* in his book of the same year, and refocuses its central paradox again: "The all-encompassing crux of the poem's significance is this: our earthly and historical world in its true and eternal form is a manifestation of God's judgment." Auerbach goes on to quote Hegel, who is one of the inspirations behind this reading, and who observed, in a beautifully poetic way, how Dante in essence freezes, in eternal life, the figures of this world in their eternal life on the other side of things:

> In this way the poem comprises the entirety of objective life: the eternal condition of Hell, Purgatory, and Paradise; and on this indestructible foundation the figures of the real world move in their particular character, or rather they *have* moved and now in their being and action are frozen and are eternal themselves in the arms of eternal justice. While the Homeric heroes have been made permanent in *our* memories by the muse, these characters have produced their situation for *themselves*, as individuals, and are eternal in themselves, not in our ideas.

In other words, the *Divine Comedy* is an "*objective*," because objectifying, work that "probes deeply and dispassionately into the essence of the *secular world*"—so Auerbach, rephrasing Hegel now.

Once again, Auerbach shows himself to be the consummate student, not of philosophy or philology, and not even of the history of mentalities, but of something utterly unexpected—the contortions and psychopathology of the Western soul, and above all the Christian soul. This is another way of describing Auerbach's vision and the ultimate reach of his project. Each of his books and essays contributes to this larger design. Each turns on a singular, irreproducible puzzle about a given author or problem that Auerbach sets out to identify, in a quietly provocative way, and then weaves into the logic of his analysis. His provocations are always understated, and so one has to listen attentively to spot them. Once one does, the depths to which Auerbach's thinking plumbs will consistently surprise a reader. At the end of the day, Auerbach will emerge with the distinction he deserves, as one of the more consistently profound and breathtaking cultural thinkers of the twentieth century. We are only now in a position to begin to appreciate what his thought has to offer.

Passionate Subjects

As part of his self-appointed mission to diagnose the psychopathology of the modern soul, whether Christian or secular, Auerbach was particularly concerned to uncover something like a history of the passions and emotions. Indeed, legible in the very emergence of the passions as instruments of affection and self-affection (including self-communication) is a history, Auerbach believes, that says a great deal about the emergence of the person as an autonomous category, responsible for her own inner integrity and well-being, and on the basis of which she could, and still can, enter into ethical relations with others. A series of essays are devoted to tracing this emergence.

"*Passio* as Passion" (1941, here Chapter 14) offers the broadest account, one that will be familiar to readers of Pierre Hadot and Michel Foucault. Auerbach's insights bear more than a passing resemblance to theirs, not least because he was so closely attuned to the formation of subjective habits and identities (*habitus*). As in "*Figura*," the 1941 essay is outwardly concerned with the vicissitudes of a single term—*passio*—as it enters into the modern lexicon under different guises (feeling, sentiment, passion, emotion). But with each stage comes a conceptual transformation and a corresponding behavioral transformation. Other essays examine more individuated cases, for instance "Racine and the Passions" (1927, here Chapter 18), "Marcel Proust and the Novel of Lost Time" (1927, here Chapter 13), and "Montaigne the Writer" (1932, here Chapter 16). Rousseau also belongs to this gallery, but he represents the special case of someone who, as we have seen, is not so much produced by the inner turmoil of social feeling as he is torn apart by it.

Tellingly, Auerbach was drawn to the riveting personality of Michel de Montaigne, both in his essay of 1932 and in a later chapter of *Mimesis* entitled "L'Humaine condition." What he found in Montaigne was the pulsating vitality of an individual who seemed in his writings to be still living and breathing, but also a glimpse into the origins of modern (or at least post-Dantean) individuality: a subject who was free, autonomous, self-dictating, rooted in the present, in himself, his circumstances, and his earthly existence—a subject who was defiantly secular, un-Christian, mundane, and even materialistic. Montaigne is the first modern author because he was the first to write for a lay public, a reality that had no prior existence: he created it himself.[45] In doing so he made himself into the first lay writer of all time, and in this way invented a sociological category that would endure into Auerbach's present in the guise of the journalistic writer, the man of letters, and ultimately "the voice of the world."

The worldly character of Montaigne's writings is everywhere to be felt—in his concreteness, which can be frank if not "horrifying," in his bravery in the face of life's ills and the final prospect of death, in his awareness of his body and not only his mind, and above all in his sheer enjoyment of life. And so, Auerbach concludes in a memorable phrase, Montaigne's "*Essays* are a *symptom* of his existence." Montaigne's existence consisted in what was "given" to him in at least three ways: in the phenomenological sense of the data of experience, in the historical sense of the circumstantial and the contingent, and in the ethical sense of a gift. Finally, "the spirit of the *Essays* is thoroughly un-Christian." As Montaigne writes in his essay on experience, "those transcendental humors frighten me" (a line that is quoted in *Mimesis*, not in the essay). Montaigne, after all, is identified in the very first line of the 1932 essay as "the son of a father from the region of Gascony and of a mother who was a Spanish Jew."[46] And if Montaigne was the first modern subject, self-scrutinizing, self-absorbed, and pitched on "the very edge of the abyss," then surely Proust is the last, at least in Auerbach's survey of literary selves: a decadent, stifling, monomaniacal writer who despite his self-imposed quarantine—his bedroom is his world, and it opens only onto the world of his memories—proves how powerful this human world truly is, and who exemplifies what Auerbach in "Marcel Proust and the Novel of Lost Time" (written in 1925 and published two years later) calls "the pathos of the earthly course of events, a real, ever-flowing, inexhaustible pathos that at once oppresses and sustains us without end." The use of "us" is worth noting. Auerbach's writings are never entirely dispassionate. They merely appear to be at times.[47]

---

[45] The appeal made to the broad public for the first time by Dante through his vernacular, which henceforth became the "mainstay" of the new European culture (*Dante* [n. 5 above] 77; cf. *Literary Language and Its Public* [n. 6 above] e.g., 312–14), was evidently to a different kind of readership (it was, *inter alia*, not distinctively lay). If Montaigne's achievement could not have been possible without Dante's precedent, as was noted above, Montaigne is in turn effectively *completing* Dante's project (*Mimesis* [n. 14 above] 306–308). Cf. also "Racine and the Passions": "the audience [lit., "the public"] emerged as an entirely new sociological category."

[46] A bold remark given the circumstances; cf. n. 54 below. For relevant background and discussion, see Frank-Rutger Hausmann, "Michel de Montaigne, Erich Auerbachs *Mimesis* und Erich Auerbachs literaturwissenschaftliche Methode," in *Wahrnehmen Lesen Deuten* (n. 1 above) 224–37.

[47] Compare Fitzgerald, *Enlarging the Change* (n. 10 above) 31, who notes both the passion and its truest object: "[I]t was part of Auerbach's passion: 'to make understandable the immediate human thing.'"

Racine—the subject, or rather analytical object, of "Racine and the Passions" (1927)—presents another set of symptoms that are uniquely his own. One might have thought that with Racine Auerbach had finally touched the heart of French Classicism and therefore the epicenter of his field (the French having always served as the most ambivalent of rivals to the Germans, at least since Goethe). But nothing could be further from Auerbach's mind, who takes an unexpectedly contrarian view of this playwright. Dissenting once more from the opinion of his distinguished mentor Karl Vossler, who saw in the poet's extreme Protestantism a rejection of "all earthly concerns in favor of the eternal world beyond," Auerbach argues for a more complex reading, one that firmly resituates Racine in the world he inhabited. Racine's theater *stages* the conflict between Christianity and secular art, a battle that is waged over the place, precisely, of the passions—for example, love. Does theater incite or subdue the passions? What is its role in spiritual, moral, or religious terms? This was the burning question of the day. For Racine's answer Auerbach looks to the poet's own dramaturgy and finds a decisive reply: there one witnesses "neither a Christian drama nor even a human one," not even a drama in a classicizing vein, but rather "a fierce clash of instinctual forces"—no "Protestant greatness of soul," but a "canniness" and "rashness" of decisions taken, a "violence of desires," a madness and "autonomy" of passions, and "instincts for *life*." The result is an enthralling tragic sublimity, intensified by a good dose of Old Testament terror, as in Racine's masterpiece from 1691, *Athalie*:

> Displaying not even a trace of the traditions of a living essence of Christianity, the play is based on a horrific chapter of the Old Testament that has been dragged out of its dark corner into the light, a chapter that becomes no more humane just because one of the parties to the struggle is in the right. In *Athalie*, God is Lord not because he is good, but because he is sovereign. *There is no redemptive moment.*

Jewish Philology

Reading these last lines, one cannot help but be reminded of the opening chapter of *Mimesis*, with its terrifying glimpse of the Old Testament Yahweh at his most indomitable and formidable. In that essay Auerbach foregrounds the binding of Isaac episode as one of the foundational scenes of Western literary mimesis—a gesture that is both arresting and puzzling in the extreme, until one considers the realities with which Auerbach was being confronted at the time. *Mimesis* quite plainly bears the scars of the particular circumstances of its composition: it is in more ways than one a book written in the teeth of a German nation derailed by fascism, Nazism, and Lutheranism gone rabid.

The binding of Isaac was one of several Old Testament scenes that had been explicitly banished from schoolrooms across Germany by the fanatical German Christian sect of the Protestant Church.[48] The episode smacked all too much of another sacrifice which it had been held to prefigure at least since Tertullian (*Against Marcion* 3.18), that of Christ by the Jews (see "*Figura*" and "Typological Symbolism"). It recalled too vividly medieval blood libels. And in any case, the *whole* of the Jewish Old Testament was being discredited in many of the same quarters as a falsification of spiritual truth. Why, then, did Auerbach choose to foreground this one text?

The answer ought to be self-evident. Given this contemporary background to which several explicit allusions are made throughout *Mimesis* (some of which were muted in the English translation after the War), it is legitimate to see another side operating in Auerbach's much enlarged view of philology, both in *Mimesis* and earlier. Well beyond a love of words, a love of history, or even an earthly, worldly philology, Auerbach is pressing philology in the direction of something utterly unheard: a new resistant, if implicit, *Jewish* philology, one that carries out its work in the name of everything that the traditions of Vico, Montaigne, the Enlightenment, historicism, and the philosophy of life on this earth had to offer.[49] Some, though not all, of Auerbach's colleagues risked taking public stances against the rising tide of anti-Semitism under the Third Reich, as Vossler did in speeches and in an activist Jewish periodical during the mid-1920s (*Der Morgen*),[50] or as Curtius did with his strident but rather muddled pamphlet of 1932, *Deutscher Geist in Gefahr* (German Spirit in Danger).[51] Even Spitzer bravely published a wartime polemic, *Anti-Chamberlain: Observations of a Linguist on Houston Stewart Chamberlain's "Kriegsaufsätze"* [War Essays (1914)] *and on the Evaluation of Language in General* (1918), which, though not specifically directed against anti-Semitism, nevertheless took direct aim at Chamberlain's facile linking of race and language, and eviscerated it from

[48] See Doris L. Bergen, *Twisted Cross: The German Christian Movement in the Third Reich* (Chapel Hill: University of North Carolina Press, 1996); Susannah Heschel, *The Aryan Jesus: Christian Theologians and the Bible in Nazi Germany* (Princeton: Princeton University Press, 2008).

[49] See James I. Porter, "Erich Auerbach and the Judaizing of Philology," *Critical Inquiry* 35 (Autumn 2008) 115–47; and "Auerbach, Homer, and the Jews," in *Classics and National Culture*, Susan Stephens and Phiroze Vasunia, eds. (Oxford: Oxford University Press, 2010) 235–57.

[50] Vossler, "Reine Sprache—reine Rasse" [Pure Language—Pure Race], *Der Morgen* 1.5 (December 1925) 574–77; "Jüdische Herkunft und Literaturwissenschaft" [Jewish Origins and Literary Study] *Der Morgen* 2.5 (December 1926) 427–30; for some of his speeches, see Vossler's *Politik und Geistesleben: Rede zur Reichsgründungsfeier im Januar 1927 und drei weitere Ansprachen* (Munich: Hueber, 1927).

[51] Curtius's pamphlet is muddled not least for its wavering stances toward the Jewish question and toward German nationalism.

the detached perspective of a trained linguist.[52] On the other hand, simply to insist on the probity of humane and humanistic study carried a polemical charge in these sensitive times, when the mere choice of a research agenda could no longer be innocent.[53] As an acculturated Jew, and more of a scholar than a public intellectual, Auerbach was bound to address the turbulences of his day in less demonstrative ways than Spitzer, Vossler, and Curtius did, but he was never uninvolved.[54]

Once this historical background is grasped, statements like the following from "*Figura*" (here Chapter 7) fall into place: "It was in this struggle with those who despised the Old Testament and wanted to drain it of its meaning—namely, "those who wanted either to eliminate the Old Testament entirely or to interpret it in a strictly abstract and allegorical way"—that the method of historically real prophecy [i.e., the figural method] again proved itself." Auerbach's resistance to Christianity, or, if one prefers, his tracking of Christianity's resistance to itself and to its own mission in the world—its de-Christianization from within—is evident wherever he discusses the Judaeo-Christian heritage (his preferred phrase in *Mimesis* is in fact "Jewish-Christian": *jüdisch-christlich*),[55] which upon closer inspection presents an

[52] A peculiarity of Spitzer's analysis is that in disconnecting race and language he indirectly supported arguments for Jewish assimilation (*Anti-Chamberlain: Betrachtungen eines Linguisten über Houston Stewart Chamberlains "Kriegsaufsätze" und die Sprachbewertung im allgemeinen* [Leipzig: O. R. Reisland] 31), a position he adopted in his own life in response to the stigma of Judaism he too had to endure (for biographical details, see Gumbrecht, *Vom Leben und Sterben der großen Romanisten* [n. 7 above] 72–151). A further example of resistant philology is Victor Klemperer's *LTI* [Lingua Tertii Imperii]: *Notizbuch eines Philologen*, which could not appear until after the war (1947). See further Emily Apter, "Global *Translatio*: The 'Invention' of Comparative Literature, Istanbul, 1933," *Critical Inquiry* 29 (Winter 2003) 253–81; here 273–74.

[53] Compare the contrasting ways in which Gothic architecture, the visual counterpart in stone of Dante's poem (cf. *Dante* [n. 5 above] 20), was approached by German-Jewish and compromised non-Jewish German scholars during the same period, each following radically different agendas (Jaś Elsner, "A Golden Age of Gothic," in *Architecture, Liturgy and Identity: Liber Amicorum Paul Crossley*, Zoë Opačić and Achim Timmermann, eds. [Turnhout: Brepols, 2011] 7–15).

[54] A case in point is a still unpublished letter of 1932, in which Auerbach resolves henceforth to boycott the prominent academic journal *Deutsche Vierteljahrsschrift für Literaturwissenschaft und Geistesgeschichte* after its editor, Erich Rothacker, had "so openly declared his allegiance to the Nazis" by affirming that Jews should be removed from their posts at German universities (letter to Ludwig Binswanger, October 28, 1932; quoted in German in Peter Jehle, *Werner Krauss und die Romanistik im NS-Staat* (Hamburg: Argument-Verlag, 1996) 237, n. 39, and in English in "Scholarship in Times of Extremes: Letters of Erich Auerbach (1933–46), on the Fiftieth Anniversary of His Death," Martin Elsky, Martin Vialon, and Robert Stein, eds. and trans., *Proceedings of the Modern Language Association* 122.3 [2007] 758 n. 7). It was a painful decision, for as Auerbach adds, "I am admittedly doing more harm to myself than to him, for there is no other journal of the same caliber." The publication of his essay on Vico, submitted a year and a half earlier, was already underway at the time, and Auerbach broke off communication with Rothacker the next year, once Rothacker's wish came true.

[55] Cf. "Fortunata," in *Mimesis* (n. 14 above): the mingling of styles that is found in Peter's denial of Christ (Auerbach here follows the Gospel of Mark) "was rooted from the beginning in the

unstable hyphenation of two religious traditions. It is this, first of all because Christianity turns out to be, as it were, *inwardly* hyphenated, torn by its attachments to both the Here and the Beyond, to the flesh and the spirit, to the historical evidence of its own events and the promise of a future salvation, but above all because Christianity cannot rid itself of its Jewish origins.

Figural interpretation is a case in point: the key to this method, according to Auerbach, is the oddity of its logic—that in order to ground its fulfillment in the redemptive future it must anchor itself in the actual historical past. Figural interpretation is thus forever doomed to be self-erasing in its aspirations, because it marks everything that it touches with indelible ink, and above all what it most wishes to efface. The Old Testament was ironically *secured*, not erased, by the figural reading of it, as was earthly, worldly history itself. It is allegory, not figural interpretation, that seeks to eliminate the Old Testament through the work of abstraction and mystification. Figural reading grounds the Old Testament again in historical reality. And so, Auerbach's favoring of figural reading over allegorical interpretation has to be understood in this same light: as an insistence on the historical relevance of the Old Testament, which was being erased at the very moment that he was writing his essay.

All this is perfectly intelligible in the shadow of the catastrophes leading up to "*Figura*," which was composed in 1936–37 and published in 1938, and then *Mimesis*, composed between 1942 (the date of the first, foundational chapter on Homer and the Old Testament) and 1945. But what about an essay like that on Racine, which dates from 1927? Or Auerbach's 1921 dissertation, *On the Technique of the Early Renaissance Novella in Italy and France*? This last work displays all the themes we have witnessed so far, whether in their full or embryonic form: this-worldliness, earthliness, historicity, life lived in its rich and sensuous panoply, "passionate observation of earthly [and "secular"] life," mimesis (understood as the riveting image of the foregoing in all their throbbing actuality), and so on. Indeed, Auerbach's very choice of his dissertation theme was designed to exhibit these features in their purest form.

The operating thesis of that work, announced in its opening paragraph, is that "the subject of the novella is invariably society itself, and for that reason its object is the form that *life here on earth* [lit., this-worldliness] assumes as a whole. . . . *The novella stands unremittingly in the very midst of time and place*; it is a piece of history itself." From this premise follows, of necessity, the novella's formal realism: "it must be realistic, inasmuch as it accepts the foundations of empirical reality as a given, [and is] *not founded upon metaphysics*"—in other words, theological notions (1). Put all this together

---

character of Jewish-Christian literature," etc. Auerbach in fact grounds his theory of tragic realism and stylistic fusion in the Old Testament (ibid. 18–19, 22), not in the New Testament, as is widely assumed.

with the telltale phrase "Western reality" (39) and you have Auerbach's future masterpiece, *Mimesis*, with its thesis of realism as a symptom of *this*-worldly consciousness in the West, effectively preempted here in 1921. Moreover, the object of this early study is a world that has already undergone the work of "de-Christianization,"[56] arguably the most prevalent theme in Auerbach's writings, whether it is named or merely implied. Its most explicit occurrences happen to coincide with the twilight years of Auerbach's career as a professor at Marburg ("Rousseau" [1932] and *Das französische Publikum* [1933] 46–53), when his chair was increasingly endangered.

Is this a mere coincidence? I doubt that it is. Auerbach self-identified as a Jew throughout his career. One need only consider the *curriculum vitae* in narrative form (*Lebenslauf*) that he appended to his 1921 dissertation, in which he named the fateful paradox of his origins: "I am Prussian and of the Jewish faith." Whenever Auerbach stepped into a department of Romance Philology, he knew exactly on which side of the religious divide anyone stood (his correspondence amply testifies to this). And religion was a matter of racial extraction, of *Herkunft* and *Abkunft*, as everyone around him was all too painfully aware at the time.[57] Auerbach was indeed an exilic scholar, but not only when he emigrated to Istanbul and then the States. On the contrary, he led a life of internal exile from his earliest studies onward during one of the most turbulent eras in modern history.

Auerbach was a Jewish philologist who happened to be German. But he was also a practitioner of a special kind of philology, one that could be called earthly, inner, worldly, and even Jewish: it is a philology that celebrates the richness of this-worldly life at the expense of otherworldly abstractions, history over eschatology, lived experience over what has never passed before the senses. He thought in the largest possible terms, but in a subtle and supple way, and with a modest, unassuming, and generally understated voice

---

[56] Cf. *Zur Technik* (n. 8 above) 38: "The world [together with its "wealth of sensual events" and of "life"], so long neglected, had turned away from men just as they had turned away from it"—until the Renaissance novella rediscovered this world once again. That is why the novella can be said to offer up not "dogma," but an "image of the world" (46). Tellingly, Auerbach abruptly dismisses accounts of literary history based on "racial theory" in the same work (50).

[57] Compare Vossler's monitory lecture of 1926, "Jüdische Herkunft und Literaturwissenschaft" [Jewish Origins and Literary Study], n. 50 above. For some of the relevant biographical evidence pertaining to Auerbach, including his correspondence, see Porter, "Erich Auerbach and the Judaizing of Philology" (n. 49 above), for example the following: "At Marburg [sc., the university] I am completely surrounded by people who are not of our origin (*unserer Herkunft*)" (letter to W. Benjamin of October 1935 in Karlheinz Barck, "Fünf Briefe Erich Auerbachs," *Zeitschrift für Germanistik* 6 [1988] 689–90). To this one may now add certain details from Auerbach's asylum papers mentioned in n. 18 above, not least his answer to a questionnaire concerning, *inter alia*, his religious affiliations, to which he replied, "Ich gehöre der jüdischen Religionsgemeinschaft an" [I belong to the Jewish religious community]. A fateful document, it is dated September 1935 (one month prior to his removal from the university) and lists his permanent address as Marburg.

(though he was also a master of the muted crescendo).[58] Auerbach's view of historical reality, with its plunging verticalities and relentless horizontal forward motions, is full of terror, and of beautiful potential as well. It is hoped that the essays gathered together here, brought to life in new translations and largely for the first time, will help to win readers over to the diverse charms of Auerbach's generous view of the world—to his philology not of the word but of the world—and propel future generations on to similar quests of their own.[59]

[58] Compare the climactic final lines of "The Idea of the National Spirit as the Source of the Modern Humanities."

[59] For invaluable comments on earlier drafts, I wish to thank the following: Karlheinz Barckt, Matthias Bormuth, Eric Downing, Jaś Elsner, Tony Grafton, Miriam Leonard, Jane Newman, Maria Pantelia, Stephen Nichols, Martin Treml, Martin Vialon, and Avihu Zakhai, as well as an audience at Johns Hopkins University in September of 2012.

TRANSLATOR'S NOTE

Jane O. Newman

In his essay "Translation as Challenge and Source of Happiness" (originally 2004; transl. 2006), Paul Ricoeur cites Friedrich Schleiermacher on the paradox of translating: the translator both needs and desires to serve "two masters" at once. Schleiermacher describes this doubled task as, on the one hand, "bringing the reader to the author," and, on the other, "bringing the author to the reader." In this model, what the two sides have in common is a refusal to give up mastery. Their shared "resistances" and "pretentions to self-sufficiency" suggest an inability to live under two regimes at the same time.[1]

In the case of Erich Auerbach, the paradoxical task of the translator is even more complex. Properly speaking, neither he nor his multiple readerships were ever really "masters." Rather, they were "subjects" of any number of politically and linguistically over-determined places and discursive regimes in Berlin, Marburg, and Istanbul, for example, as well as in New Haven, Connecticut and State College, Pennsylvania. Auerbach's writing styles followed suit, as did the occasions for and genres in which he wrote, as he moved from the lettered culture of the late Weimar Republic in Germany (whose oracular academic diction was so often the target of Karl Kraus's wrath) to the highly politicized micro-climate of Atatürk's and the new Turkey's Europeanized university culture on the Bosporus, where, along with the host of German-Jewish academics who found safe haven there after 1933, he fell into a slightly archaic micro-idiolect of his mother tongue. After the war, Auerbach arrived in the U.S., where he and others gladly slipped into their new role as learned émigré scholars, Cold War America's inheritance from an "Old World" no longer able to care for its heritage. There he learned to converse and lecture (and eventually also publish) in English in a manner that in many ways corresponded to this image, using an English that was, moreover, not so very unlike the quite cultivated language most readers of Auerbach are now accustomed to hearing him "speak" in Ralph Manheim's and Willard R. Trask's translations of texts originally written in German from approximately these same years. Manheim's and Trask's refined and urbane Auerbach sounds

---

[1] In Paul Ricoeur, *On Translation*, Eileen Brennan, trans. (London and New York: Routledge, 2006 [orig. 2004]) 4–5.

quite a bit like the impassioned global citizen-scholar whose voice we hear in Edward and Maire Said's famous 1969 translation of "Philology and *Weltli-teratur.*" Ironically, of course, it was Said who in his later essay, "Secular Criticism" (1983), made Auerbach a kindred exilic spirit and critical minority consciousness, a postcolonial voice *avant la lettre*.

Given these several transformations, interpretations, and politicizations of his language, translating Auerbach is something of a balancing act. Each text is itself the site of interlocking languages, histories, and styles, as is the linguistic site occupied by the translator. Translating thus involves looking in multiple rearview mirrors at once while also trying to keep one's eyes on the road.

I have tried to capture Auerbach's insights into the way literary texts themselves work and his methodological interventions into how we read them as accurately as possible. While the majority of the essays gathered in this volume appear in English here for the first time, others will be familiar to English-language readers from earlier translations. In some of these cases, I found it necessary to offer alternatives to those translations. I rendered the Saids' "Philology and *Weltliteratur*" with the grammatically more accurate "The Philology of World Literature," for example, because the issue that Auerbach is exploring in this famous essay is philology (a venerable subject) as the most appropriate way to think about "world literature" in particular (a subject of considerable interest today), and not philology as something we are meant to think about separately from that literature or in a more abstract way. Likewise, I have translated *Realprophetie*, one of the central concepts of the essay "*Figura*," with "historically real prophecy" (rather than with Manheim's "phenomenal prophecy," which might be misleading for today's readers if "phenomenal" is read as an adjective indicating "extra special" or "unique," or even in association with phenomenology) since, in that essay, Auerbach is drawing on this technical term from nineteenth-century theology to refer to the *realia*, the historical phenomena, of this world. I was not shy, however, about consulting existing translations whenever they were available (whether by Manheim, the Saids, or Martin Elsky). For, as Stanley Corngold observes in the introduction to his elegant new translation of Goethe, there is no point in needlessly seeking to provide an original translation when one's own translation happens to accord with the translation of one's predecessors, or when an earlier translation is more apt than one's own, simply for the sake of being different.[2] I am grateful, then, for the good work done by earlier Auerbach translators (and I predict there will be subsequent Auerbach translators too), and I have varied their formulations when I found it necessary to do so in order to capture Auerbach's thoughts in more apt ways. In several

---

[2] "Translator's introduction," in Johann Wolfgang von Goethe, *The Sufferings of Young Werther*, Stanley Corngold, trans. (New York: W.W. Norton and Company, 2012) 13–14.

cases, I have also silently corrected and supplemented previous translations where sentences were left out or words and references misunderstood. I did not, however, go to great lengths to "improve" upon them when they were already, in my view, as good as it gets. Finally: When they were available, I used existing translations of the myriad texts from which Auerbach quotes, occasionally altering them slightly to align the quotes with the English version of Auerbach's claims. When such translations of his source texts are not noted, the translations are my own.

One final remark: Auerbach's essays on philology, Vico, figural interpretation, and literary history are the most complex of his writings in German. In these, his lengthy sentences and repeated attempts to use different words (or the same words differently arranged) to clarify his thoughts, made it necessary to break up sentences and occasionally restructure them in ways that render the English less opaque than the original (although also, for this same reason, a bit more halting than the original). When Auerbach reads primary texts of literature or philosophy (Dante, Montaigne, Racine, Pascal, and Rousseau), his diction is less complex, his sentences less involved. It is almost as if he is having a conversation with an equally learned colleague over a late afternoon coffee, leaning forward and patiently explaining what he sees in a text, what moves him about it, and what he hopes will move his interlocutor in turn. In these cases, I tried to reproduce what I perceived to be his characteristic rhythms so that readers may join in.

I am grateful to Jim Porter, as well as to a whole host of fellow scholars and students in the U.S. and in Germany, who helped out with technical terms and proposed many useful amendments. Jim especially went over the translations with a classicist's care (I mean this as highest praise). Since it would be terribly confusing to acknowledge my colleagues separately every time one of their challenges or alternative formulations found its way into these translations, let me declare here my general gratitude for mistakes spotted and suggestions made. I thank them all. The infelicities and errors that remain are of course my own.

PART I

History and the Philosophy of History

Vico, Herder, and Hegel

1

Vico's Contribution to Literary Criticism

I begin with Vico's historical epistemology. This originated from his opposition to Descartes' geometrical method, and it is based on the principle that there is no cognition without creation; only the creator knows what he has created himself. Thus, the physical world (*il mondo della natura*) has been created by God; therefore only God can understand it. But the historical or political world, the world of mankind (*il mondo delle nazioni*), can be understood by men, because men have made it. Even the earliest and most primitive forms of human thought and action are to be found, or rediscovered, within the potentialities (Vico says *modificazioni*, "modifications") of our own human mind, so that we are able to understand them. By this theory, Vico sought to provide an epistemological foundation for his vision of the earliest civilization, of the first forms of society, and the poetic or ritualistic beginnings of human thought and expression. It is true that this theory of cognition leads to certain difficulties and at least apparent contradictions within his own system; but that need not concern us here. Such as he expressed it, Vico's idea is probably the first methodical theory of the understanding of history; moreover it is, if not the justification, at least the recognition of an important fact which is evident at almost any moment of our practical life: viz., that we understand and judge historical events, or even human actions in general, be they private or political, in a special and immediate way, according to our own inner experience, seeking "to find their principles within

Reprinted from Auerbach's English original (1958) as reprinted in his 1967 Gesammelte Aufsätze *(see Appendix: Original Publication History of the Essays in This Collection) with minor editorial changes in punctuation and orthography. Auerbach prefaced his 1967 reprint with these words: "The following paper is part of an essay on method, serving as an introduction to a forthcoming book on* Literary Language and Literary Public in Latin Antiquity and the Middle Ages. *This study, accordingly, will enumerate and describe certain ideas in Vico's philosophy which are important for my own concept of criticism." In point of fact, Auerbach made numerous changes in the published introduction to this posthumous work, the title of which was also revised. Slight editorial changes have been entered in brackets. The reader should note that by "Romanticists" Auerbach means "Romantics."—Ed.*

the modifications of our own human mind." Since Vico's time, more rigidly scientific methods have been developed for the observation and classification of human behavior. But they have not shaken the confidence in our spontaneous capacity of understanding each other by our own inner experience; indeed, their results have provided this capacity with new categories of judgment. Moreover, for historical events, and in general for events and situations which cannot be subjected to the special conditions of scientific experimentation, the new scientific methods are inapplicable in their rigid and exact form. Therefore, the interpretation of historical events (the word "historical" is used here in a very large sense, which shall soon be defined) remains a matter of "understanding" or "finding within the modifications of the mind" of the interpreter. Of course, historiography has its exact aspect (which I should prefer to call scholarly rather than scientific), viz., the exploration and exact transmission of the facts and documents. There are, moreover, certain rules of interpretation, established by learning and experience, which cannot be transgressed; but beyond these limitations, the interpreting, understanding, and combining activity of the historian is nearer to art than to science. It is an art working with scholarly material.

But there is another aspect of Vico's theory of historical cognition: he enlarges the meaning of history to such an extent that it comprehends the whole of social life. His term *il mondo delle nazioni* includes not only political history in its specific sense, but also history of expression, of language, of script, of the arts, of religion, of law, [and] of economics, since all these parts of human activity originate from the same conditions, i.e., the specific state of the human mind at a given time. The understanding of one of these parts of human activity at a certain stage of the development necessarily provides the key for the understanding of all the other parts. Indeed, there exists for Vico an "ideal eternal history": a tripartite model structure of the historical course, constantly recurring in eternal cycles, and which must be understood in its entirety. But his main effort of understanding is concentrated on the early stages of the evolution, because these are the most difficult to understand; the utmost mental energy is required to rediscover in the modifications of our own entirely rationalized mind the principles of the early forms of civilization, governed by instinct and imagination. And in explaining the unity of the various kinds of human activity represented during these early periods of civilization, Vico has expressed, with unequalled grandeur and consistency, the modern idea of "style." It has been recently said that Vico has little meaning for aesthetics or criticism, and that he is rather a philosopher of history, or a sociologist, than the founder of aesthetics. Indeed, Vico did not create a particular system of aesthetics, but a world into which this fits. His starting point, however, is criticism of the forms of human expression, of language, myth, and poetry (*una nuova arte critica*).

There is only a small step from Vico's theory of cognition to this "historicism." He lived in a period which showed little interest in the study of historical development and had even a tendency to be hostile towards history. History seemed to have produced a great variety of civilizations, most of them based on obviously unreasonable institutions and absurd beliefs; their variety led to continuous struggles and subjected mankind to stupidity and misery. Most enlightened thinkers, therefore, were inclined to reject all the various historical forms, and to oppose to history's arbitrary variety the concept of true or original or uncorrupted absolute human nature, which had to be reestablished. In sharp contrast to these trends, Vico says that man has no other nature than his history. One of his most important axioms (*Scienza Nuova* §147) runs as follows: *Natura di cose altro non è che nascimento di esse in certi punti e con certe guise, le quali sempre che sono tali, indi tali e non altre nascon le cose.* [The nature of [human or historical] things is nothing else but their coming into existence at certain times and under certain conditions. Whenever times and conditions are the same, things come into existence in the same way and not otherwise.] The first part of his sentence ("the nature of [human or historical] things is nothing else but their coming into existence at certain times and under certain conditions") establishes historical relativism or perspectivism, a changing nature; and in the second part ("whenever times and conditions are the same, things come into existence in the same way and not otherwise") this historicized nature is subjected by Vico to laws. In many passages of the *Scienza Nuova*, the word *natura* means "historical development"; what all peoples have in common, their nature, is nothing but the regular course of their history, *il corso che fanno le nazioni*; this nature common to all of them, *la natura commune delle nazioni*, is the subject of the *New Science*.

According to Vico, this natural course of history has been ordained by Divine Providence which, it is true, works exclusively within history, not from without. Still, it is Divine Providence; each of the stages of historical development is necessary, perfect in itself, and good; the whole of human history is a permanent Platonic state, in spite of the continual change. Vico's form of historical perspectivism is almost exclusively normative and diachronical; he is much less interested in the individual genius of the particular peoples than were his pre-Romantic and Romantic successors. Therefore, his historicism could not be as easily and immediately utilized for historical philology as happened with the ideas of Herder and the later German Romanticists who used historical perspectivism for the study of the different national civilizations and literatures. Vico does not deny variants within his system, and he was the first to formulate the concept of folk genius as a general phenomenon of early poetry. But his main interest belongs to the general norms to be found in the development of all civilizations. His historicism is mainly concerned with the description of the different stages which all peoples have to pass through; these stages, in their temporal succession, are to be understood as resulting from certain conditions, each of them, in its own way, being a temporal and transient expression of eternal Divine Providence, and therefore perfect.

Thus, together with the concept of style, historicism was being created; it is, as I believe, the "Copernican discovery" in the field of historical studies. In fact, its influence became enormous when it was made generally accessible by the activity of the Romantic critics. The whole labor of research into early and foreign civilizations done since the beginning of the nineteenth century was and is based on a historicist approach; and dogmatic precepts and judgments in historical or aesthetic matters according to fixed rules of beauty, such as were usual until the neoclassical period inclusively, have become obsolete; no one would condemn a Gothic cathedral or a Chinese temple as ugly because they are not in conformity with classical models of beauty or consider the *Chanson de Roland* as a barbaric and ugly monster, unworthy of being compared to the civilized perfection accomplished in Voltaire's *Henriade*. Our historicist way of feeling and judging is so deeply rooted in us that we have ceased to be aware of it. We enjoy the art, the poetry, and the music of many different peoples and periods with equal preparedness for understanding. Indeed, those early and primitive civilizations, which Vico had so much difficulty in understanding, seem to us particularly attractive. The variety of periods and civilizations no longer frightens us—neither the critics and historians nor an important, continually increasing part of the general public. It is true that perspectivist understanding fails as soon as political interests are at stake; but otherwise, especially in aesthetic matters, our historicist[1] capacity of adaptation to the most various forms of beauty is almost boundless; we may make use of it more than once within a few hours or even minutes, during a visit to a museum, in a concert, sometimes in the movies, or leafing through a magazine, or even looking at travel agency advertisements. That is historicism, just as in Molière's *Bourgeois Gentilhomme*, Monsieur Jourdain's everyday language, to his great surprise, turns out to be prose. Most of us are as little conscious of our historicism as Monsieur Jourdain is of his prose.

In recent decades several famous and influential literary critics have tried to establish descriptive and dogmatic categories of judgment, but even they have been unable to achieve the marvelous precision of certain great prehistoric critics, who knew exactly which genres of works of art existed, what kind of style and rules belonged to each of them, and in general the nature of the beautiful and the ugly. But the tendency to forget or to ignore historical perspectivism is widespread, and it is, especially among literary critics, connected with the prevailing antipathy to philology of the nineteenth-century type, this philology being considered as the embodiment and the result of

---

[1] Here and below, "historicist" has been substituted for Auerbach's "historistic."—Ed.

historicism. Thus, many believe that historicism leads to antiquarian pedantry, to the overvaluation of biographical detail, to complete indifference to the values of the work of art; therefore to a complete lack of categories with which to judge, and finally to arbitrary eclecticism. The truth is that one needs to know all the facts which may contribute to the understanding of a work of art; if many scholars, carried away by specialization, have forgotten the aim which specialization serves, this constitutes no objection to a philosophy of which, they, unfortunately, have lost sight. Evidently, the collection of small biographical details and attempts to relate all the writings of a poet exactly and literally to facts of his life are very naïve and often ridiculous. But it seems to me that, by now, there has been enough criticism and parody of this kind of ineptitude. The simple fact that the work of a man is a fruit of his existence, an existence which once was here and now; that therefore everything one finds out about his life may serve to interpret the work—this should not be neglected merely because naïve and overspecialized scholars without sufficient inner experience made bad use of it.

Above all, it is wrong to believe that historical relativism or perspectivism makes us incapable of evaluating and judging the work of art, that it leads to arbitrary eclecticism, and that we need, for judgment, fixed and absolute categories. Historicism is not eclecticism. It is a difficult and infinite task to understand the particular character of historical forms and their interrelations—a task requiring, apart from learning and intelligence, a passionate devotion, much patience, and something that may well be called magnanimity: a state of mind capable of recreating in itself all varieties of human experience, of rediscovering them in its own "modifications." Each historian (we may also call him, with Vico's terminology, a "philologist") has to undertake this task for himself, since historical relativism has a twofold aspect: it concerns the understanding historian as well as the phenomena to be understood. This is an extreme relativism; but we should not fear it.

Since the historian does not leave the world of mankind to which he belongs, he may well hope that this understanding can seize its human object, and that others will understand his understanding. And his work connects him so firmly with human existence that there can be no eclecticism in his approach, if one understands by this word passive pleasure and capricious choice. In performing such a task, the historian does not become incapable of judging; he learns what judging means. Indeed, he will soon cease to judge by abstract and unhistorical categories; he even will cease to search for such categories of judgment.

That general human quality, common to the most perfect works of particular periods, which alone may provide for such categories, can be grasped only in its particular forms, or else as a dialectical process in history; its abstract essence cannot be expressed in exact significant terms. It is from the material itself that he will learn to extract the categories or concepts which he needs for describing and distinguishing the different phenomena. These concepts are not absolute; they are elastic and provisional, changeable with changing history. But they will be sufficient to enable us to discover what the different phenomena mean within their own period, and what they mean within the three thousand years of conscious literary human life we know of; and finally, what they mean to us, here and now. That is judgment enough; it may lead also to some understanding of what is common to all of these phenomena, but it would be difficult to express it otherwise than as a dialectical process in history; and that is what Vico tried to do.

In his historical way he succeeded in describing the essence of poetry. The starting point is his belief that poetry represents the natural and all but exclusive kind of human experience and expression in the early stages of development. At that time, reason is still undeveloped; the sensuous experiences produce powerful instincts and passions; concrete images are their adequate expression. This opinion that poetry was the natural language of primitive men Vico has in common with Herder and the early Romantics influenced by Rousseau; but while these later writers considered the original state of mankind to be one of natural freedom, without laws and institutions, in striking contrast to the laws, conventions, and rules of rationalized society, Vico's primitive imagination has a political function: it leads mankind to the foundation of society, and creates institutions more severe and ferocious, boundaries more narrow and insurmountable than any civilized society can possibly achieve. Primitive men create myths which they themselves believe (*fingunt simul creduntque*); these myths originate from their violent passions, but they give to their life some frame and order. They are concrete symbolizations of the forces of nature, of the ritual believed to be suitable to conjure these forces and to render them propitious, and of the institutions and ceremonies based on that ritual. They are not "feelings," they are forms of thought, even forms of universal concepts or generalizations, but concrete and created by imagination; Vico calls them *universali fantastici*; these are, according to him, the material of poetic expression.

Vico does not develop his ideas in opposition to neoclassic rhetoric, as did Herder and the other Germans; on the contrary, he developed them from the rhetorical tradition. He was himself, for the greater part of his adult life, a professor of rhetoric. He considers the rhetorical figures to be residues of primitive, concrete, imaginative and "realistic" thinking, when man believed [he was able] to grasp the things themselves, in their thoughts and words; but in rational and unpoetic modern life, the once truly meaningful symbols had come to be mere ornaments. In modern attempts to define the essence of poetical expression, critics have returned to the terminology of traditional rhetoric, and they borrow certain rhetorical terms (especially the word "metaphor") in order to express that inexpressible thing, at the same time general and concrete, which is the center of poetry. Vico called this *universale fantastico*.

By formulating such ideas in the 1720s, Vico freed the theory of poetry from all the neoclassical criteria referring to technicalities and questions of exterior form; he destroyed neoclassical dogmatism; and he recognized poetry as an autonomous form of human self-orientation and self-expression. Indeed, he believes that poetry in the primitive periods is always rhythmical. But this is not its essence; its essence is the *universale fantastico*, the concrete and sensuous expression of general conceptions. Vico believes that true poetry, based on instinct and imagination, was limited to the early stages of human development, since later on the development of reason necessarily impoverishes the productivity of imagination. This prejudice about the poetic superiority of the early stages of human development was also entertained by Herder and his Romantic successors, and continued to influence the leading philologists in the nineteenth century. It was very fertile, producing some of the most important ideas of modern criticism: the folk genius, the poetic symbol, and the distinction between poetic or evocative expression on the one hand, and ordinary language of communication on the other.

All these ideas were already expressed by Vico, in very original and vigorous formulas. But, of course, the opinion that only primitive or prehistoric civilizations are capable of producing poetry is a prejudice: the dialectic relation between imagination and reason is not a purely temporal succession, and the two do not exclude each other; very often they collaborate, and reason may well enrich imagination. Vico was not entirely unaware of this, and he acknowledges that his tripartition of the ages of mankind has no absolute validity, for example when he says that "poetic speech continued for a long time into the historic period, much as great and rapid rivers continue far into the sea, keeping sweet the waters borne on by the force of their flow" (*New Science*, §412, Bergin and Fisch, trans.). Still, for Vico, it is antipoetic rationalism that prevails in later periods, and true poetry exists, in his opinion as well as in the opinion of many Romantic critics, only in the earliest periods of mankind, which he calls the age of the gods and the age of the heroes.

In his treatment of these periods we have the most conspicuous example of the all-embracing unity of Vico's vision. In these periods, all kinds of human activities and thoughts were poetic. The metaphysics of these primitive men, their logic, their ethics, their laws, their politics, [and] their economy were all poetic, i.e., inspired by a religious and ritualistic imagination expressing itself in concrete poetic formulas (*universali fantastici*). And the science which explores the contents of their beliefs by the interpretation of documents is called by Vico philology. Thus philology is enlarged to such an extent that it comprehends all the historical humanities including history of law and economy; it becomes almost identical with the German term *Geistesgeschichte*.

But the peculiar character of Vico's idea of philology can best be grasped by using his own terms. He opposes philology to philosophy. It is the task of philology to explore what the peoples believe to be true at each stage of their development (although this is only the outcome of their erroneous and limited knowledge), and what therefore serves as a basis for their actions, institutions, and expressions; this he calls *certum* ("the certain," or "the established"); the *certum* is subject to historical change. Philosophy, however, explores unchanging and absolute truth, *verum*. Now, in Vico's work we are not allowed to see this unchanging or absolute truth which never appears in history. Even the third age of men, the age of fully developed reason, does not contain truth; it too is only one stage of history, unavoidably subject to decadence and relapse into barbarism. The Platonic *verum* which is partly realized in every age, since every age is one of its aspects, is not contained in any of them. Only in the entirety of history is there truth, and only by the understanding of its whole course may one obtain it. Thus the truth for which philosophy is searching appears to be linked with philology, exploring the particular *certa* as well as their continuity and connection. This connection, the whole course of human history, *la commune natura delle nazioni*, is the subject of Vico's work, which therefore may be called a philosophical philology as well as a philological philosophy[2] — dealing exclusively with mankind on this planet.

This is Vico's idea of philology, which I learned from him.

---

[2] "A philosophical philology as well as a philological philosophy" has been substituted for Auerbach's "as well a philosophical philology as a philological philosophy." —Ed.

2

Vico and Herder

The majority of you, as students of the humanities, are pursuing history, be this the study of change in political and economic spheres or the history of language, writing, or art. The fundamental conviction that underlies this kind of study is that there *is* something called history that is more than just a string of events, and that the events that occur in the realm of human acts and human tribulations do not do so in isolation and without any connection to one another, the sum of them being nothing more than their accumulation over the course of time. Rather, the wealth of events in human life, which unfold in earthly time, constitutes a totality, a coherent development or meaningful whole, in which each individual event is embedded in a variety of ways and through which it can be interpreted. Interpretation is thus in principle only possible on the basis of an understanding of the entire course of human history to which—again, as a matter of principle—the future also belongs. But because this kind of perfect understanding is entirely impossible for the future, and for the most part equally impossible for the past, we must often be content with feeling our way toward some sense of the plan that shapes the entire historical continuum. We do this on the basis of evidence provided to us by no more than just a small piece of the past upon which documents of all kinds shed just a bit of light. This feeling, or intuition, must nevertheless remain speculative in nature, maintained as it is by an a priori trust in the fact that such a plan does exist and that it can be apprehended—if not clearly and in its entirety, then at least in these small bits of its realization. It is on the basis of this kind of intuition, often derived unconsciously in the way I have described, that we interpret historical figures and events. That we do so is the result not just of scholarly but also of practical and ethical needs. For, whenever and wherever we engage with life in its details, it is undeniable that we and those close to us experience injustice on a daily basis. To be able to bear with equanimity what happens both generally and to us personally we need to have an intimation of a plan for the sake of which and in the light of whose fulfillment chaos becomes a matter of order.

This idea of history as a meaningful whole, an idea that we consider valid today, is actually quite recent. In a world unified by the Christian worldview, the whole had meaning as a result of God's plan, or Divine Providence. This plan was impossible for men to comprehend, since, as the Lord says, My thoughts are not your thoughts, My ways are not yours. In such a world, the interpretation of history was possible only by means of a revelation about the ways of Providence; it was a revelation that came historically in the person of Christ and textually in the prophecies of Scripture. The Christian interpretation of history is thus an interpretation of the historical revelations of Holy Scripture. Admittedly it often overstates its case in the explication of individual biblical passages—although it does so quite a bit less often when it aims at a philosophical explanation of history than when its aim is to interpret particular individual events. The real power of the Christian interpretation of life thus neither lay nor lies in the horizontal reading of history's unfolding, but rather in investing the individual human life with significance in a vertical scheme. In this scheme, the short span of our lives on earth is conceived of as a kind of spectacular trial, with a verdict of either eternal damnation or eternal salvation handed down at the end of the show. Here, the forces that drive history are not held to work immanently within the historical world. Instead, they are transcendent, which is to say outside and independent of history. We call this Providence. In the Christian model, the actual historical process—and trial—occurs in the space between God (or Providence) and the individual human soul. Regardless of the vexed and problematic question of how power is distributed between these two (this has been and continues to be a matter debated from a vast array of perspectives), the Christian interpretation of history knows no role for immanent historical forces that are distinct from the actions of the individual human being.

With the rupturing of the unified Christian world in Europe came the collapse of any way of endowing human life with transcendental significance. Initially nothing took its place. Rather, a way of thinking inimical to history emerged. The hope—and belief—was that the past could be discarded, the world constructed anew, the slate swept clean of the agony of tradition and the earthly world remade in an orderly fashion in accordance with the principles of natural reason. That history existed as a meaningful whole was thus either directly or implicitly denied. Only when civilizing human reason created order out of events—and this could occur only during the high points of civilization—would such an order have any purpose; otherwise, it was meaningless and to be scorned. One ought not to concern oneself with the barbaric constructions produced by an uncivilized era such as the Middle Ages. Models existed for every form of human activity, an idealized and perfected version for any specific genre, and everything produced in that genre would be measured against this ideal. The *Song of Roland* (which was of course not yet known at the time) would be nothing more than an imperfect early stage of the *Henriade*. Thus one could not profitably occupy oneself with this work. Even those movements that began in the Renaissance and found their high point in Rousseau, movements that were markedly hostile to anything that had to do with culture or civilization, were opposed to history. They were interested in the utopia of a Golden Age, not in what was historically past. Even works concerned with the theory of history did not look for a totality in history, but rather for individual methods and schematic models. Even the defenders of the idea of Christian Providence got caught up in the hostility to history endorsed by their adversaries and made Providence the handmaiden of rational progress.

It was only when opposition arose to this anti-historical frame of mind that there emerged the modern notion of history as an immanent and meaningful totality. This happened mainly in England and Germany, but was most successful in Germany. Hinted at by Johann Georg Hamann beginning in the 1760s, this understanding of history first acquired a methodology with Herder. It went on to achieve its highest philosophical expression in Hegel's work, on the one hand, and the foundations for its practical application among the Romantic scholars, on the other. My own discipline, Romance philology, is one of the smaller branches of Romantic historicism; it is capable of experiencing, if only fleetingly, all of the Romance traditions together as a single, meaningful whole.

Herder was the first to systematize this concept of history for modern scholarship, as I said. But today—and in spite of the title of my talk—I will be speaking less about him than about Vico, using Herder only as the backdrop for Vico's discoveries. Herder experienced the concept of a completely coherent system of meaning and thus of the immanent development of world history as a result of confronting thousands of challenges, contradictions, and reversals. His point of departure, which became decisive for all of German historicism, was his own personality. He projected onto history his own curious disposition as well as needs like the ones he himself felt, which were the product of his acute sense of humanity combined with an ability to feel emotions deeply. We can observe numerous themes and influences that are common to both his person and his image of history and that often overlap: a belief in a pantheistic world imbued with emotion (this is clearly directed against the sterile rationality of the Enlightenment), and, associated with it, a profound love for everything associated with nature and with everything nature-like, everything that develops on its own, in other words, without following any artificial norms. In the sphere of history, finally, Herder was captivated by everything that was original, on the one hand, and everything that was associated with the idyllic and the patriarchal, on the other. But he also espoused a third position in addition to those associated with pantheism and naturalness, a position that was also often antithetical to them—namely, a somewhat vague and fanciful notion of the noble reason of human beings and of their ethical and aesthetic dignity: the ideal of humanity. This idea of a pantheistic world of feeling was the source of Herder's view of history not only as the realization of God's thought, but also as an immanent development in the world, with every age containing within itself a unique aspect of the divine and thus complete in itself. All of this was directly opposed to Enlightenment beliefs in progress and abstract perfectibility and revolutionary in initiating an entirely new way of understanding not only the Middle Ages, but other epochs as well. The aridness of mind and of ways of analyzing history that were full of abstractions and quantifying categories alien to it was replaced with a feeling for things and a desire to empathize with and thus to enter into the spirit of an age and its language and poetry. Herder was the first to discover, through the notion of a world inhabited by feeling in the place of God, and thus through the idea of a spiritual totality that had become so important for German historicism, that language, in its essential nature, belonged entirely to human beings and was a property of their overall intellectual make-up. In this way he replaced the Enlightenment understanding of language as an ability that had been added on to the finished product of humanity after the fact, so to speak, with a belief in a linguistic signification that was more than a matter of arbitrary nominalism, but also more than merely brutish in origin. Rather, he explained that the origin of language lay in a specifically human form of rational sensuousness that was the result of our nature as creatures of sound, who, in responding to cognitive instincts very different from those of animals, reproduce the material impressions of the world in the sounds we make. Herder's affection for everything natural, nature-like, patriarchal, and idyllic also made it possible for him to conceive of the *Volk* as a genetic individual, which is to say as a non-rational, organic, even plant-like entity. He believed in the idea of a national spirit (*Volksgeist*) which taught that everything that is produced in the life of the *Volk* can be said to be derived from a national essence that is entirely its own and unique. All customs, art, language, and literature are emanations and expressions of this spirit. All of this is bound up in Herder with a profoundly unpolitical attitude. For him, law and the state are—unlike the nation and the family— necessary evils: they are artificial and brutal. Also alien and inimical to him is all pursuit of power, *raison d'état*, politics, and war. Here we can see the origins of German historicism in the idyllic feeling for nature—but also the danger that it will in the end amount to nothing more than a folkloristic version of local history. Finally: The third plank in his platform, namely, the idea of humanity, must have permitted him to sense what was specifically human about the history of the human race. It was, however, vague and variable and forced him to adopt an almost Rousseau-like idealization of an original human being like the one developed in natural law theory, on the one hand, and to embrace moralizing value judgments, on the other. He condemns everything that makes him uncomfortable, including everything that is callous, political, and cruel, and presumes a world-historical condemnation of these same facts and events too, often on quite flimsy grounds. He creates a concept of Nemesis that differs from its ancient counterpart in its extremely pathos-laden moralizing tone, a tone that Schiller then inherits in his slogan about world history being the Last Judgment of the world.

As innovative and creative as it was, Herder's system was also a product of its time. Its moment had come, and he adopted it gladly. Leibniz, Shaftesbury, and Rousseau had preceded him, Hamann's powerful aphorisms had reached his ear, and Shakespeare had kindled his sense of dramatic historicism. Yet he alone out of thousands of other youths responded to their calls with the correct password. This testifies to his genius. And yet, when he pronounced this word, many answered, almost as if they had been waiting for him. Seizing on his thoughts, they then aggressively took them much further than Herder himself had imagined. By the time he was an old man, he had been utterly surpassed, left behind by the very individuals on whom he had once made such a decisive impact. He knew very little about the one precursor who, fifty years earlier, long before Rousseau, indeed even before Montesquieu, and also with no knowledge of Shakespeare, in the midst of an entirely uncomprehending milieu, and completely on his own, had had similar thoughts—this despite his isolation and in the absence of any anticipatory movements or support by a band of like-minded young men. This man was Giambattista Vico (1668–1744), the poor son of a bookseller in Naples who, quite late in life, became a professor of Rhetoric and was then appointed court historiographer. Vico was never able to advance professionally beyond lowly positions. He remained a kind of schoolmaster who also acted as the court eulogist to the late Baroque autocrat of the Kingdom of Naples. His principal work, the *New Science*, did not appear until 1725, when he was fifty-seven years old. A second, fully revised edition appeared in 1731, and he continued to work on it throughout his life, dying in 1744, just as the final edition went to press.

We can see the difference between the two men already in the external details. Herder was from the North. A high-spirited and noble young man who associated with other noble youth, he was both literally and figuratively peripatetic, an individual who undertook many journeys both in fact and in his thoughts and deeds. But he squandered these thoughts and his strength in the hot enthusiasm of youth. By contrast, Vico was a Southerner, a little-known professor, respected and esteemed by only those few who valued his learnedness. "Wide open eyes, gaunt, a cane in his hand"—that was how he was described by a contemporary satirist. He basically wrote only one book (for the earlier works were merely preliminaries to it). And this book, on which he worked with single-minded tenacity until the day he died, contained only a single idea. This idea branched out of course in so many different directions that new trestles were always necessary to adequately support its expression. But the most important difference was that Vico was alone.

No one had prepared the way for him, there was no one on whose work he could build, no one to respond to the questions he asked. A superficial and late form of Cartesian rationalism dominated the learned world in Italy in the years when he began his work. Viewing his project through the lens of deductive and mathematical natural philosophy, the exponents of the Cartesian system despised it, regarding history as unscientific and incompatible with the mathematical method. As for Herder: the late Enlightenment, which engaged with history, if in a quite unhistorical way, had prepared the way for him. He had no trouble finding legitimation for his enterprise even in this apparent opponent. Vico, on the other hand, took decades to satisfy his unruly methodological conscience and to establish an epistemological foundation for historical study. In fact, he never really attained methodological clarity. When he was sixty years old, he was still trying to prove his *New Science* on the basis of geometrical principles.

Ultimately, Vico at least found a way out of the constraints of the single-minded dominance of the natural sciences that characterized the Cartesian approach by which he had been so deeply influenced. He did so by means of the same skeptical and agnostic argument against the Cartesian faith in reason that others before him had already espoused—namely, that one can only know what one has created oneself. Because God created nature, only He is capable of knowing it. Out of this rich and ambiguous claim, Vico developed a conclusion that was his very own. History is created by human beings, he argued. And so, while we may not be able to understand nature, we can understand history. Just as God is in nature, humans create history. This is why, Vico claims, proofs of His work are themselves divine and "must fill you, my reader, with divine joy, for, in God, understanding and doing are one and the same thing." On the basis of this logic, Vico was able to declare the priority of the historical, or human, sciences over the natural sciences— but without ever really fully realizing how problematic the claim had to be, particularly for him. For to what extent do we in fact create our history? In his understanding of history, for example, it is precisely Divine Providence that plays the decisive role; human beings are often just blind tools. Providence of course does function for him within and not beyond history, as a historical fact or common understanding of the human race. But Vico's claim remains highly problematic all the same, for human beings can never be creative in the conscious, complete, and knowing way attributed to God. The earthly subject of historical knowledge thus remains obscure. Vico was nevertheless able to reassure himself with this formulation, for it contained at least the basis of a presciently empathetic understanding of history that human beings could more or less assume on the basis of the fact that they were human. And he considered this basis sufficient for the plan that he had designed and used to organize his great discoveries—his plan, that is, to describe an eternal and ideal history "according to which the histories of all nations must play themselves out in time, in their rise, progress, circumstances, decline, and end"—or, put in a more modern way, a morphology of history as a philosophy of history. He carried out this plan on the basis of the one main discovery that he had made, and thus became, by virtue of this discovery, the first and perhaps most perfect interpreter of the dialectic of Becoming in history. He was also the founder of aesthetics as the science of precognitive expression, the first to understand Homer and Dante again. He revived and reestablished the myths of recurrence, world cycles, and eternal rebirth, and foresaw all of today's ethnological problems and, applying his fanciful intuition, interpreted them brilliantly. Vico was, finally, the founder of the theory of class conflict (insofar as it was possible to formulate such a theory before the rise of modern capitalism). His one central discovery, which made all of this possible, was his completely new vision of primitive humans and of their language, their poetry, their customs, and laws. Vico made this discovery at a time when natural law and contract theory were in full bloom, a period dominated by Cartesian rationalism that saw in the savage either an innocent child or a beast. And he did so in Naples between 1700 and 1725, without the least bit of ethnographic information and based only on his complete knowledge of the works of antiquity and of Roman law. He thus derived his knowledge of the essence of primitive humanity from his interpretation of ancient myth, law, and poetic texts alone.

Vico discovered that, in the early days of culture, human beings were neither innocent and naturally tranquil beings nor raging animals driven by the instinct for self-preservation. Rather, they were lonely and fearful creatures, terrified by the chaos of a mysterious and for that reason harrowing nature. Their first sounds were cries of fright as they attempted to banish their fears. Theirs was not the calculating practical reason of civilized men. They had only their senses and imagination. Primitive humans were thus children rather than novice or imperfect versions of hoary old men. He discovered that these primitive humans, rich in sensation and fantasy, endowed the powers of nature with personalities and, seeing in them magicians or gods who make their will manifest to humanity in lightening, thunder, and storms, tried to interpret that will and to placate the gods' desires in rituals and ceremonies that were thoroughly fantastical and formulaic—and entirely irrational. Vico claimed that primitive humans created their lives as a form of poetry in these first rites and that these ceremonies, formulaic and poetic, became the origins of customs and law. As a pious Catholic, Vico hewed closely to the story of Creation in all of this. Excluding from this story the Jews, whom God had given the special privilege of revelation, he declared that, following a brief detour, things began to develop naturally after the Flood. The tribes of the sons of Noah freed themselves from the religion of their father and lived in bestial anarchy and promiscuity in the great forests of the earth. After several centuries, during which there were no storms because the earth was still too moist, the first lightening strikes, driving terror and shame into the hearts of this wild and undisciplined race. In this flash of lightning, humans catch their first glimpse of divinity, Jupiter, who exists for all nations under a different name. Fear and humiliation, the powerful result of that first flare, cause them to hide. Some abandon the nomadic life and its anarchy and seek out caves, linking domicile and sexual intercourse to a specific place and specific ceremonies. Their fantastical sense of divinity, which is completely bound up with sensible ideas, creates a god for every act of existence, which is to say a personified institution, the concept of an imagined person, *universale fantastico*. The gods are beings like themselves, only more powerful. They live on the lofty peaks of mountains, and it is the humans' duty to attempt to divine their will in strange, cultish ways. A settled form of existence generates the first social institutions: marriage, a stable family, patriarchal power over children, the burial of the dead. It also forces them to cultivate the untamed forest, which they clear with fire. (Vico interprets the deeds of Hercules as the first social institutions, and the battle with the Nemean lion in particular as the clearing of the woods.) At first, the language of these early humans consists of inarticulate, even dumb and only material signs; later, it becomes differentiated onomatopoeia and is then enriched through metaphorical transpositions. Their physical dimensions resemble those of giants, with an initial enormity produced by their unrestrained, lawless power that only gradually adjusts itself to natural human proportions. The formalized rituals that determine the lives of these humans distinguish them from those who still roam about aimlessly. They thus consider themselves "chosen" and call themselves the sons of those who are buried beneath the earth, the sons of the earth, giants, and heroes. The rationality of the later civilized ages is foreign to them, as is human tenderness, equal justice for all, and the use of language to communicate or converse. They exist to perform the magic of a cult bound up with sensuous formulas, and for them justice is the formal fulfillment of rites and is marked by incomparable cruelty. Prudence means divination and inquiring into the will of the gods, moderation consists in monogamy, and power equals absolute control of the family, for the father is their priest: he alone can interpret the will of the gods and thus, only he can determine the law. It is an age of gods, of poetry, a golden age, since the first gold is the grain that springs from the earth. Harvests give rise to the telling of time. Hercules, the symbol of the giants' patriarchs, is the founder of the Nemean Games.

The second, or heroic, age begins with the nomads. Bereft of gods, living without rules, and plagued by the rigors of nature, they conceive a desire to partake of the culture of the heroes and thus turn to them and beg for protection. This is granted to them. But they do not participate in religion or the holy rites, and thus do not own property, marry, or bury their dead. With no standing before the law, their children cannot be legitimate. They become servants, *famuli*, and a part of the family of the hero, who rules over them firmly and ruthlessly, as if over things. They are his field hands. The history of the heroic age now becomes the history of the battle of the *famuli* to acquire legal personhood and equality before the law, for which they must fight every step of the way by rebelling. It is thus that feudal law evolves. The *famuli*-farmers rise up and demand a part in the rituals and in ownership. (The two are inextricably intertwined. Without a legitimate marriage, there are no legitimate children and thus no rights of inheritance; without participation in the formal ceremonies, no property can be owned.) What they then initially attain is the *de facto*—but not *de jure*—ability to own property; they thus remain vassals. In the meantime, the heroes close ranks in the class struggle against the *famuli* and begin to form the first strictly aristocratic republics, the heroic states. The one who eventually becomes king is a *primus inter pares*, the leader of his estate, but not a monarch. The *famuli* also begin to join together, however (*famuli* of the heroes—unite!). Class struggle begins between the patricians and the plebeians. Little by little, the former give up their longstanding, hard-and-fast rules that are bound to material forms (these were the rules that had given them a monopoly over the cult and thus over the law), and the latter, the *famuli*-plebeians, demand the same natural and rational rights for all.

The victory of the plebeians means the beginning of the third age, the bourgeois age of reason. Here, a consciousness of the natural equality of all men reigns supreme. Sensuousness loses its power and imagination becomes impoverished. Reason—together with abstraction, philosophical religion, and justice—begins to adjudicate even-handedly on the merits of individual cases, and people are liberated from set ways. All this provides the foundation of the democratic republics. Soon, however, material interests begin to make a mockery of the laws. The interests of the individual no longer coincide with the interests of the state as in the class-based republics of the heroic age. Self-interest gives rise to chaos and a struggle of all against all. A single individual always triumphs, and it is he who founds the enlightened and impersonal absolute monarchy (Augustus). This is the high point of civilized behavior. But it does not last long. Soon reason and sybariticism are out of control, along with luxury, arrogance, atheism, and there is a relapse into barbarism. Culture declines, new barbarian nations appear, and the cycle begins once again, with heroes, formal ceremonial cults, the *famuli*, and fiefdom. This is the cyclical recurrence, the *ricorso*. Vico describes the process in his discussion of the Middle Ages, but he conceived of it as recurring again and again in all ages and for all time.

It is clear that the actual point of departure for this grand concept of history is Vico's new concept of the primitive human being and his idea of that creature's poetic nature. But this poetic nature is not noble, idyllic, and humane; it is not the kind of nature that Herder, grounding it in his own personality, posited for humanity. It was in no way like what could be imagined by analogy with a cultivated and educated individual. It was not an ideal type devised according to the standards of Herder's own century, let alone a purer and more vital version of such an ideal. Rather, Vico meant something alien, untamed, a humanity not at all like the sort we associate with the people of civilized eras. His primitive humans were conceived of as the exact opposite of everything offered to Vico by his own time. When he loved and stood in awe of his creation, it was something foreign that he loved, not a projection of what he desired. Vico had this advantage over Herder, namely, that he was not a proud, self-important personality for whom the entire universe reflected back nothing more than an image of himself. Rather, he was a modest and unselfconscious scholar. He may have often relied on his own fantasy, but it was an objective fantasy that allowed him to reanimate the figures passed on to him by the past. Capable of abandoning himself entirely to things, he speculated in a fantastical way, but did so from the perspective of the things rather than from his own vantage point. It was thus that he alone of all scholars before the nineteenth century (who actually had a much easier time of it, since the quantity of historical and ethnological material available was by then far more manageable) was able to understand the historical world as an objective totality not infected by anything of the spirit of his own time. In spite of all his individual mistakes (and these are often enough quite grotesque), Vico's constructions contained nearly all the elements of later discoveries. He did not make these discoveries one at a time. Rather, as I have said, it was the objective totality of the history of the human race and its origins that revealed itself to him; the specifics were a by-product. At the center lay the figure of the primitive human being, a creature without reason but endowed with the gifts of imagination and sensuousness, who initially created his gods out of the chaos of nature and then, out of fear of these gods, formed the cults whose fantastical formulas were capable of conjuring them. Out of these cults emerged the first institutions of civilization. Everything else followed: the origins of law and of language, of poetry and of industry and commerce, and of states. All of these things began in and with the "poetic," that is, in the fantastic, sensuous, and formalistic nature of the first human being.

Law was a part of this primitive theology. The first man who founded a family, and thus established hearth, altar, and ceremonial rites, was the absolute master in his realm; he was king, judge, and priest at once, the only being who was deemed a person before the law. All of his actions were thus fully invested with the same symbolic formalism that he believed he could use to conjure up the gods. The gods themselves made all the decisions, which then became visible in the sacred trial of single combat, in the interpretation of sacrificial acts or oracles, or in the magical ceremonial acts of conjuring. Even as the first legal arrangements were agreed upon by and between the heroes, they were linked to both sensuous metaphors and strict forms. When a piece of farmland was to be transferred into another's possession, for example, it was handed over from one person to the other with specific ceremonies and specific words. It was in this entirely brilliant way, which could not possibly have been conceived of before 1720, that Vico interpreted ancient Roman law as a "serious poem." It was this poetic (we would say, metaphorical and formulaic) law, in which the sensuous formula meant everything and the individual facts and desires motivated by individual interest counted for nothing, that continued to hold sway in the heroic republics for a long time. Those who became subject to the formula could under no circumstances free themselves from it. A single misspoken word invalidated the binding nature of the legal decision. Only gradually, with the social advancement of the *famuli* and the recognition of the natural person as a legal entity did the law become a matter of material settlement in accordance with individual interests. Civil law was hardly imaginable in these earlier stages of culture.

The language of this culture was poetry, not as arbitrarily assigned signifiers of objects, however, but the objects themselves, initially represented by dumb signs, then by onomatopoeia, and finally by means of sensuous analogies. The surrounding world became animated and personified in ways that were intimately connected with religion. The language consisted entirely of onomatopoeia and images. Vico discovered that metaphors and tropes, the artful forms of figured expression that were still flourishing during his time (albeit in completely nominalist form), were the last remaining trace of the sensuous language of the primordial era. He also discovered that humans had possessed a rhythmic language, verse, before they had prose. Herder described poetry as humanity's first language. But he was thinking of Ossian and folk songs. Vico imagined, rather, the fantastical-formulaic texts of the primitive conjurers. He did not know the most famous examples, since they became available to scholars only much later—for example, the pre-medieval German magic spells or ancient Roman songs like the *carmen Arvale* or the *carmen Saliare*.

This culture existed to produce its poetry—which was also its history. Every word that primitive humans spoke was poetry, and all of their poetry was true speech. True here does not mean that the individual events of which they gave an account had actually happened in the way they said it had; they were hardly able to grasp facts as such. Rather, what they said was true insofar as the fables and myths they composed were not meant as beautiful lies, as was the case with poets who came later, but were composed instead as the true form of their life, which they were not able to comprehend or categorize in any other way than as myths. For they could not endow their lives with order using abstractions such as intelligence, courage, beauty, and love. They could see only figures in whom events and characteristics were one, and so they created fantastic universals, or poetic characters. Jupiter was one such figure, the highest thunder god; Hercules was the poetic character of the hero who founded a race. Any one of us who is capable of interpreting their myths correctly will find revealed in them the political history of primitive times. Let us take, for example, the myth of Cadmus: Cadmus slew the great dragon (the dragon being a symbol of the earth and power). This means that he subdued the earth by clearing it. He then sowed the dragon's teeth (a lovely metaphor, Vico comments, for plowing). Armed men emerged from the furrows and fought. These are the battles between the estates—in the heroic-age republics, between the heroes and the *famuli*—with the furrows signifying the consolidation of the estates. Finally, Cadmus metamorphosed into a snake, a serpent, a *draco*. This signifies the establishment and laying down of the stern, heroic law (it was *Draco* who, among the Athenians, wrote the laws in blood). The myth of Cadmus thus contains several centuries of primitive history. Works such as Homer's poems likewise contain numerous centuries of the mythic history of primitive times. Homer himself never existed, being himself a poetic character. His two epics provide a treasure trove of the ancient natural law of the peoples of Greece, with both ancient and later pieces jumbled together in various layers. Their compilation and editing did not occur until a much later time when no one understood any longer their original mythic sense. It was thus Vico who, for the first time, conceived of the theory (albeit in a much more generous and philosophical way than his successors) that Wolf established for Homer, Lachmann for the *Song of the Nibelungen*, and Gautier and Paris for the old French epics. For him, it was of course not a matter of a purely poetic, aesthetic, or folkloric understanding of the folk songs, in which the poetic sensibility of primitive times romped about, cutting playful capers. For him such poems were more substantial, more concrete. Law and poetry, sociology and theology, all intertwined, were embedded in them. Vico also anticipated another, related thought, one that his successors during the Storm and Stress movement and during Romanticism came upon only much later, namely, the notion of the primacy of poetry in primitive times. Of course he was much more radical than they were. For him, it was only the primitive era that, in its fantastic metaphoricity, was poetic. Its men were poets in their very essence and could not be anything else. The men of the enlightened periods of reason were in turn necessarily unpoetic. For them, the consciousness of the meaning of a word had faded, Vico claimed, and nature was no longer alive; the only concepts that brought order were abstractions. He wrote all this, let us remember, at around the time when the Regency style dominated in France and during the Enlightenment. And he is not merely anticipating Herder and the Romantics. He did more than just rediscover Homer, the Middle Ages, and Dante. Rather, he conceived of the world history of the intellect in a formal way, as a philosophy of the development of Spirit. It was not until Hegel that the basic outlines of this development were discovered once again. Of course the Vichian drama of history—with its mythical primitive times, its development by means of class struggle, its movement through the ages of reason and decline, and its cyclically patterned eternal recurrence—is, in the first place, remarkable as the very antithesis of the political-philosophical theories of natural law or of the Enlightenment, which were entirely mechanistic and atomistic. One thinks here of More, Hobbes, Grotius, Montesquieu, Voltaire, and Rousseau. But Vico is not at all adequately explained when he is represented as a predecessor of the German historical school, and even less so when one or the other scholar of the late nineteenth century lays exclusive claim to him as a precursor. This is as foolish as if one were to celebrate Leibniz as the precursor of Ernst Haeckel. But Vico was also not the precursor of the far greater and more far-flung tradition of the Romantic historical school that includes Herder or Savigny, Grimm, or Adam Müller. It is not by chance that they were unfamiliar with his work, for the crucial phrase *Volksgeist* (national spirit), so significant for all of them, was not one he used. Neither his situation in the absolutist Kingdom of Naples nor the times, around 1720, were conducive to such an idea, and it would also have been unlikely that a man of Vico's nature would have entertained it. In spite of the ways his thought was informed by ideas of organicity, historical rootedness, and evolution, he was not one to thrust himself into a welter of empirical details about particular nations. He was also not a patriot, and any obsession with the self or with folklore as the Romantics understood it was alien to him. He had no interest in the home as a domestic refuge, and he felt no sense of idyllic pleasure at the thought of all that was beautiful and noble in the human race. Rather, an insignificant schoolmaster, he was caught somewhere between being in awe of and being terrified by the primitive giants to which his imagination had given birth. And yet, it was not for their sake that he had written his book. It was not human beings, but rather God and His role in providential history that were Vico's concern. His interest in immanent historical forces thus differed from the interest shown by his successors. For Vico, there was still Divine Providence, and it remained transcendent, unmoving, and eternal. Even though he was the first to believe in the divinely ordained perfection of the earthly world in each of its ever-changing succession of forms, for Vico, God was not of this world, but rather above and beyond it. This world, as it exists at any given time, is the expression of His eternal and everlasting will—an expression that is perfectly adapted and specific to that time, to be sure, but also one that passes into oblivion with time itself.

3

Giambattista Vico and the Idea of Philology

A triumphant Vico bestowed the title the *New Science* on his book, which undertook to explore what all races and nations share. The first edition appeared in 1725, the final one in 1744, the year of his death. It was his life's work. The first traces of his thought on the subject had already surfaced earlier in his *De constantia philologiae*[1] (1721), where he furnished the first chapter with the heading "Nova Scientia tentatur" [in which a new science is attempted].[2] Later, in the last edition of the *New Science*, he proudly wrote in the conclusion: "Hence we could not refrain from giving this work the enviable title of a *New Science*, for anything else would defraud it unjustly of the rightful claim it has over an argument so universal as that concerning the common nature of nations...."[3]

But by characterizing his work in this way, Vico signaled not only pride and the excitement of discovery. Beneath the surface, there lies hidden also a certain unease. What exactly was this "new science"? Was there any existing discipline to which it belonged, or would he have to invent a new name more appropriate for this field of study? Later thinkers employed various names for it: for Michelet, it was the "philosophy of history," for Croce, "the philosophy of spirit." Breysig and his followers would probably prefer "historical

---

[1] The text appears as the *pars posterior* of *De constantia iurisprudentis*, which can be found in Ferrari's complete edition of Vico's works: *Opere di Giambattista Vico*, 6 volumes (Milan 1835–37; second edition: Milan 1852–54); hereafter I cite the second edition as *Opere*. Quotations from the *New Science* are from Nicolini's editions: *La Scienza Nuova Prima* (Bari 1931), cited hereafter as *SNI*, and *La Scienza Nuova giusta l'edizione del 1744* (Bari 1928), 2 volumes, cited hereafter as *SN*. I cite my own translation of the *New Science* as *NW*: Giambattista Vico, *Die Neue Wissenschaft* (Munich 1924; now Berlin/Leipzig). *SN* and *SNI* are cited according to paragraph (*capoverso*). [Citations from the *New Science* here follow Giambattista Vico, *The New Science of Giambattista Vico. Unabridged Translation of the Third Edition (1744) with the Addition of "Practice of the New Science,"* Thomas Goddard Bergin and Max Harold Fisch, trans. (Ithaca and London: Cornell University Press, 1984), cited in square brackets as *New Science*, followed by page number. On occasion, the Bergin and Fisch translation has been altered to follow Auerbach's text. —Trans.]

[2] *Opere* 3, 223.

[3] *SN* 1096; *NW* 420 [*New Science* 415] [Translation altered. —Trans.]

science," and some of our own contemporaries would almost certainly favor something like "the foundations of political theory." Vico himself never provided an answer to this question. Or, perhaps better, he gave far too many answers, but never a unified and comprehensive one. Instead, time and again he offered new definitions of his intentions and enumerated the various points of view (*aspetti*) from which his work should be considered. These he assembled in the chapter entitled, "Corollaries Concerning the Principal Aspects (*Aspetti*) of this Science."[4] In it he explained that the *New Science* is: (1) a rational account of the impact of Divine Providence on history (*una teologia civile ragionata della provvedenza*); (2) a *filosofia dell'autorità* (a philosophy of the origins of property (here, he uses *autorità* following its use in the Roman Twelve Tablets, where it refers to the "origin of property")[5]; (3) a history of human ideas, especially in their nascent stages, when they were irrational and fantastical; and (4) a philosophical critique of the very most ancient traditions handed down to us by the *autori delle nazioni medesime* [the founders of the nations themselves] (cf. n. 5 for the meaning of *autori*). Here Vico combines his critique with a polemic against scholars who never focus their critical work on anything other than the *scrittori*, or writers, who emerged only later, in the twilight, so to speak, of the development of nations. Aspect (5) he describes as the point of view of ideal, eternal history, which is to say the eternal and ideal plan of historical development that governs the histories of all individual nations as those histories unfold in time. Aspect (6) is the natural law of nations. Here Vico polemicizes against Grotius, Selden, and Pufendorf, who in his opinion either ignore Providence entirely or understand it too mechanistically; Vico instead argues that, for the pagans, Providence in fact worked through the *lumen naturale* [natural light of reason] or the *sensus communis* [common sense]. This allowed them a perhaps initially rough and inaccurate, but nevertheless stable understanding of themselves, and in turn permitted the establishment of a fixed rule of law that, in each case, was apposite to the stage of development (the *natura*) of the respective epochs.[6] Vico could thus claim that, as he writes elsewhere, there is only one

---

[4] *SN* 385ff.; *NW* 160ff. [*New Science* 121ff.]

[5] Vico uses the terms *auctor* and *auctoritas* in many different ways and with many different meanings, which he connects with one another in speculative ways: the origin of property and the oldest tradition and, finally, the legally binding nature of this tradition, thus "authority." The obligatory factor is derived from the fact that the "heroic fathers," the "fathers" of Vico's "heroic age," were at once the "founders" (*auctores*) of property and the "founders" (*auctores*) of nations (*Völker*), the creators of tradition and for this reason also the first givers of law. Cf. *SN* 7, 350, 387, 392, 411, 490, 638, 942–46, 1073–74, and 1436.

[6] This is in fact the meaning of *natura*. Vico writes: *natura di cose non è altro che nascimento di esse in certi tempi e con certe guise, le quali sempre che sono tali, indi tali e non altre nascon le cose* (*NW* 81; *SN* 147 [*New Science* 64: The nature of institutions is nothing but their coming into being at certain times and in certain guises. Whenever the time and guise are thus and so, such and not otherwise are the institutions that come into being]). Here, the concept of nature becomes

ideal state (as imagined by Plato); it is eternal, but it is also always becoming, developing, in new ways.[7] And aspect (7): The final aspect, or way, of considering his work is to call it a science of the beginnings of world history.

In addition to these very diverse *aspetti* (which intersect with one another in what are clearly equally as diverse ways), Vico used still other phrases (many of them) to describe the nature, project, and method of his *New Science*. For example, he calls it a science of the human race, or of the historical world (of the *mondo civile* as opposed to the *mondo naturale*), and frequently declares that its main purpose is to be a philosophical critique of philology that will finally make it possible for philology to become scientific.[8] Here he favors calling the method he uses a new critical art, *una nuova arte critica*,[9] but at one point he also calls it a rigorous analysis of human thoughts about what is both necessary to and useful in the communal life of the human race, thoughts that are, he claims, the eternal sources of natural law.[10] He instinctively identifies this notion of rigor with the geometrical method of his intellectual antipode, Descartes, from whom he was in fact never able to free himself entirely (even the final edition of the *New Science* aspires to providing geometric proofs), this in spite of how ill-suited the latter's approach was to his own task and to his particular caliber of mind.[11] Elsewhere Vico emphasizes with the pathos that is peculiar to him the extent to which everything

---

completely historical while nevertheless also remaining a matter of nature. This can be so for Vico because for the human race (which is Vico's sole concern) there exists a stable nature, which is the *sensus communis* in which the course of history as the *storia ideale eterna* is contained; this is the *comune natura delle nazioni* (the common nature of nations [the human race]). Cf. *SN* 242 on the historicization of the concept of nature: *La natura de' popoli prima è cruda, dipoi severa, quindi benigna, appresso dilicata, finalmente dissoluta* [*New Science* 79: The nature of peoples is first crude, then severe, then benign, then delicate, finally dissolute], or *SN* 246: *I governi debbon essere conformi alla natura degli uomini governati* [*New Science* 79: Governments must conform to the nature of the men governed]. Here, Vico is concerned with the development of governmental forms of a single nation, or people, in time; *natura* may thus be translated as "stage of development." See also *SN* 677, where the term *la natura civile* means "the essence of historical development." [Cf. *New Science* 256, where the translation given for *natura* is "civil nature." —Trans.] Likewise *SN* 445, *varie diverse nature* [*New Science* 148: many different customs.]

[7] *SN* 1097 [*New Science* 419].

[8] *Opere* 3, 232: The philosophers were the ones who should have undertaken to promote this project *ut viderent an Philologiam ad Philosophiae principia revocare possent* [so that they might discover whether they would be able to recall philology to the principles of philosophy]. See further *SN* 7 [*New Science* 6] and *SN* 390 [*New Science* 123].

[9] *SN* 7, 143, 348, but also already in *SNI* (208).

[10] *SN* 347 [*New Science* 103–104].

[11] *SN* 349 [*New Science* 104–105]. Vico's philosophy finds its point of departure in the thought that geometrical truth consists in the arbitrary positing of its elements (points, lines, and so on). Only that which men themselves create can be understood by men. He then attempts to extend this principle to the study of history, for history, unlike nature, is created by man. On this topic, see the first chapter of B. Croce, *La filosofia di G.B. Vico*, 2nd ed. (Bari 1921; German translation: Tübingen 1927).

can be achieved by his book all at once: with one fell swoop, he asserts, it creates the philosophy of the human race and the universal history of nations; later he claims that the *New Science* provides a history of thought, a history of morality, and a history of all human achievements all in one breath.[12]

Vico's *New Science* does in fact do all these things. But even though one quickly senses that these many labels, aspects, and definitions share a great deal, it is not easy to state exactly what that is. A plethora of modern words come to mind, including "philosophy of history," "intellectual history," "philosophy of mind," the "morphology of world history," and "philosophical anthropology." But these are all too vague and imprecise. My project here is to determine to which discipline Vico's work belongs. I will begin by asking what is new about and intrinsic to his discovery and what method he used to invent, develop, and depict it. The text itself provides unambiguous answers to questions such as these.

The most important of Vico's discoveries—and the one out of which all the rest, and the project as a whole, unfold—is his insight into the early stages of men as social beings. Living in the midst of an age of rational utopias and breathing the air of the early Enlightenment, he was the first to come up with a concrete idea of the intellectual make-up of the people we today call "primitives." The theoreticians of Vico's time considered the primordial age of the human race to have been either a condition of paradisiacal innocence or an inchoate war of all against all based on the drives. Neither view ascribed to the people of that age any genuine conceptual apparatus. Vico, however, conceived of a *universale fantastico*, the principle of a form of intellect that, while lacking the logical powers of understanding, was nevertheless all the richer for its ability to be moved by the senses, to shape these sensory impressions, and to give them imaginative form. Primitive people used these, their immense imaginations, he claimed, to animate the nature that surrounded them, personifying its forces and exploring its demands, and thus created for themselves a world and a way of life that were entirely fantastical, but also strictly and formulaically sacred at the same time. This is the discovery that lies at the heart of Vico's entire project and that provides, first and foremost, the very architecture of his history of the world. This history begins with the Cyclopean patriarchs of the familial state, who were the priests and judges for their families, their slaves, and their property, as well as their absolute masters. It then proceeds through the period of class struggle and the development of feudalism and the aristocratic republics to the gradual dominance of human reason, which guarantees fairness and is founded on a belief in the equality of all men. The next stage is the development of modern civilized modes of behavior in the democratic and monarchical states, and then,

---

[12] See *SNI* and the title of Book Five, as well as *SNI* 23 and 90; also *SN* 368 [*New Science* 112].

beyond that, comes a new decline into a second age of barbarism. The ever recurring cycle then begins again.

All of Vico's insights followed from his initial discoveries about primitive men, including his ideas about language, poetry, and law, as well as about political theory and economics. His theory of language was based on his understanding of the way in which the language of primordial peoples represented things themselves. To name and express something was to take possession of it by means of *una lingua che naturalmente significasse* (a language that signified naturally), or even a *parlare fantastico per sostanze animate* (a fantastic way of speaking by means of animated substances). His aesthetics analyzed the "divine" and "heroic" age, when those who were "by nature" poets lived their daily lives as "earnest poetry."[13] The sources of his concept of the law were the sacred legal formulas of the heroes, and his political theory and economics were derived from the establishment of the principle of private property by the heroic patriarchs and from their ability to clear the land, to cultivate the soil, and to subjugate the anarchic barbarians, after which came the gradual development of feudalism. Vico's brilliant analysis of the symbolic forms of human expression is conducted in the same way. He bases it on his discovery of primordial religion and the primitive conceptual forms whose *volgar metafisica* (popular metaphysics) led to the creation of myths and poetic figures. His discovery of what later so famously came to be called the *Volksgeist* (national spirit) emerged in this same way, namely, out of his description of the ways in which myths developed in these early times.[14] Finally, it was by looking into the natural impact of Providence on primordial peoples (that is, the way Providence led them to behave in a civilized manner by means of their natural predispositions and habits) that Vico arrived at the insight that was the crowning achievement of his work: the idea that Divine Providence does not produce its effects by means of miraculous interven-

---

[13] For Vico, to be poetic meant the same thing as being sensuous and imaginative, and the opposite of being rational or well planned. Yet, it did not signify modern lyricism or poetic rapture, for the imagination of primordial poetic men is at once strict, formulaic, metaphorical, terrifying, and epic-historical. Their poetry was history as it appeared to them to be true, and their metaphors were not pretty paraphrases but, rather, the thing itself as it became sensuously perceptible to them in material form.

[14] The poetic *Volksgeist* can first be found where Vico speaks of "Homers" (*SN* 873ff). Homer was not an individual person, but, rather, a *carattere eroico d'uomini greci, in quanto essi narravano, cantando, le loro storie* [*New Science* 323: a heroic character of Grecian men insofar as they told their histories in song], and these blind "Homers" possessed extraordinarily strong memories: *ne sostentavanola vita con andar cantando i poemi d'Omero per la città della Grecia, de' quali essi eran autori, perch' erano parte di que' popoli che vi avevano composte le loro storie* [*New Science* 324: [these rhapsodes] sustained life by singing the poems of Homer throughout the cities of Greece, and they were the authors of these poems inasmuch as they were part of these peoples who had composed their histories in the poems].

tions from the outside; rather, it works within history. Providence is, then, a historical fact.

So conceived, this was what was new and true about Vico's science: he discovered the form the human intellect took during the early stages of civilization. Now we must answer the second question: What method did he deploy to make this discovery and then to develop and explain it? This question is as easy to answer as the first. His method consisted in the interpretation of myths, the most ancient linguistic and legal monuments, and the very earliest poetry. He was most fond of calling this approach the *nuova arte critica sopra gli autori delle nazioni medesime* (the new critical art on the authors of similar nations). It was indeed a new critical art and it took as its object of study what it discovered among the authors of the nations themselves, which is to say, what he found in the oldest monuments testifying to human life that were available to him. For, in Vico's time, there were neither prehistoric nor early oriental materials to be had. Ethnographic information about primitive peoples was equally inaccessible; even the Middle Ages were nearly unknown. It is and will continue to be a mystery worth pondering how a man of Vico's intellect was able to arrive at such creative insights in the face of this paltry evidence. He gleaned nearly everything that he used from the data provided to him by classical philology as it was practiced during the late Baroque. His was thus a new critical art. Although this, too, is still much too broad a term, it nevertheless gives us a clue how we might define the category into which his "new science" could be placed. And the nature of this category becomes even clearer when Vico repeatedly declares that he will practice his new critical art on the primordial founders of nations and not, as scholars ordinarily do, by reading the texts of the *scrittori*, the writers, who appeared many thousands of years later, long after the deeds and ways of thinking of the founders had been distorted by being handed on from one generation to the next and there was no longer anyone who understood what they meant.

From this statement we learn what his version of the critical art ought *not* to be—and thus what it actually is. The learned critique of texts is what we call interpretation, or hermeneutics; it is part of philology. It is thus philological methods that Vico uses to consider the oldest monuments of language, religion, poetry, and law. His book in fact teems with these kinds of readings— which are of course often quite speculative and fantastical. He does write, however, that his "art" is a new one and that he invented it only with great difficulty. He also often calls it metaphysical or philosophical. "To discover the way in which this first human thinking arose in the gentile world," he writes in his chapter on method, "we encountered exasperating difficulties which have cost us the research of a good twenty years. [We had] to descend from these human and refined natures of ours to those quite wild and savage natures, which we cannot at all imagine and can comprehend only with great effort."[15] It is completely obvious what this difficult, philosophical *novum* was, namely, the age-old hermeneutical problem of understanding. Here, the case is particularly unusual and extreme: a man of the early eighteenth century is trying to understand the essential nature of the primitive human race! At one point, when Vico is discussing how to understand the way these primitives understood nature, he makes the following remarkable claim:

> But the nature of our civilized minds is so detached from the senses, even in the vulgar [the *Volk*], by abstractions corresponding to all the abstract terms our languages abound in, and so refined by the art of writing, and as it were spiritualized by the use of numbers, because even the vulgar know how to count and reckon, that it is naturally beyond our power to form the vast image of this mistress called 'Sympathetic Nature'. Men shape the phrase with their lips but have nothing in their minds; for what they have in mind is falsehood, which is nothing; and their imagination no longer avails to form a vast false image. It is equally beyond our power to enter into the vast imagination of those first men, whose minds were not in the least abstract, refined, or spiritualized, because they were entirely immersed in the senses, buffeted by the passions, buried in the body. That is why we said above that we can scarcely understand, still less imagine, how those first men thought who founded gentile humanity.[16]

But Vico overcame these difficulties. And he did so by means of a theory that very nearly represents a final, ingenious solution to the core problem of hermeneutics. This new critical art is based on the *senso comune*, the common sense, of all people, and thus on that which all of humanity has in common.[17] It is a "judgment without reflection," a natural predisposition for specific forms of life and developmental paths, instituted in equal measure by Divine Providence in all individuals and nations. The essential characteristics of the individual stages of growth in the development of civilization are thus everywhere the same, untouched by all the differences caused by natural variation. They are, in other words, not transferred from one nation to another, not imposed upon or taught to individuals or nations from

---

[15] *SN* 338; *NW* 131 [*New Science* 100]. Cf also *SNI* 40: *cosi noi, in meditando i principi di questa scienza, dobbiamo vestire per alquanto, non senza una violentissima forza, una si fatta natura (der Urmenschen), e, 'n conseguenza, ridurci in uno stato di somma ignoranza di tutta l'umana e divina erudizione, come se per questa ricerca non vi fussero mai stati per noi nè filosofi nè filologi.* [It is thus that we, in considering the principles of this science, are obliged to very violently take upon ourselves a different attire [so to speak], and, as a result, to lower ourselves to a level of total ignorance of all knowledge, both human and divine.] Later, in *SN* 34, he identifies the discovery of the structure of man's primal language (*Ursprache*), the *caratteri poetici* (the poetic characters), as especially hard, indeed as the main difficulty, which cost him many years. This discovery is, as he writes, the *chiave maestro*, the master key, of his *New Science*.

[16] *SN* 378; *NW* 155 [*New Science* 118].

[17] *SN* 137–46; *NW* 78ff. [*New Science* 62–64].

without. Rather, every group and every nation develops them spontaneously from its own inner resources. When different nations came into contact with one another as the result of war, diplomacy, treaties, or commerce, they discovered that they—and thus all of humanity—held natural law in common. The *senso comune* is thus not derived from reason. Rather, it is a matter of instinct and habit, in other words, a predisposition. The traditions, laws, and institutions that arise from it are thus not philosophical truths (*verum*). Rather, they are conventional and humanly willed institutions (*certum*), or also *autorità dell'umano arbitrio* (authorized by human will).[18] It is this *certum* that is the object of hermeneutic philology, and this is what Vico calls his *nuova arte critica* (new critical art). This is why the *lingua mentale comune* (common mental language) is one of his favorite ideas. Here he assumes an inner language common to all human beings, such that the different individual languages are merely so many different "aspects" of a common inner tongue. The idea is an intensely Platonizing one that was first developed in the original edition of the *New Science*. There Vico even proposes designing a dictionary for this language on the basis of the various terms one could use to designate the patriarchs in the constitutions of the heroic family-state. The final edition of the *New Science* likewise contains frequent allusions to this common tongue and sees it exemplified in the different forms but compatible meanings that proverbs have across different nations. This common inner language is the *koinē*, or vernacular, of all of humanity, and is the "proper language of this science."[19]

For what all humans share, the *sensus communis generis humani*, is not restricted to any one prevailing individual stage of human development. Rather, all of these stages are already given simultaneously in the human mind, at least potentially. We can recognize what we have made and only what we have made. But the historical world *is* the work of human beings, even if they at times produced it unconsciously, as the blind instruments of Providence. Human beings shape the historical world themselves and it is their own; in it, they can observe both the providential plan and themselves and their own history too. In this way, the *sensus communis* becomes not just the objective principle of a historical development in which everything is

---

[18] *SN* 138, 350. The distinction between *verum* and *certum* is not the same as that between *physis* and *thesis*, because for Vico "reason" and "nature" do not coincide. What is *certum* is given by nature, even more directly than reason.

[19] Cf. *SNI* 42 and 387; *SN* 161ff. The crucial passage may be found in *SN* 161: *E necessario che vi sia nella natura delle cose umane una lingua mentale comune a tutte le nazioni, la quale uniformemente intenda la sostanza delle cose agibili nell'umana vita socievole, e la spieghi con tante diverse modificazioni per quanti diversi aspetti possan aver esse cose; siccome lo sperimentiamo vero ne' proverbi* [*New Science* 67: There must in the nature of human institutions be a mental language common to all nations, which uniformly grasps the substance of things feasible in human social life and expresses it with as many diverse modifications as these same things may have diverse aspects. A proof of this is afforded by proverbs . . .].

in tune with itself. It also becomes the subjective foundation of how to understand history and thus of the kind of philological hermeneutics in which Vico was engaged.[20] This is the idea that unites his entire book, namely that the stages of human development do not follow one upon the other merely out of expediency; rather, they co-exist and are always co-present in and as a structure of the human mind. Thus, when they reach fulfillment, one after the other, in the very highest stage of human civilization, which is at the level of fully developed reason, it takes no more than an act of intense self-reflection to grasp them in their remotest origins. This is also the case in the unfolding of history on the empirical level. Here, too, the stages do not succeed one another in any tidy way. Rather, at any given point, each successive stage retains a great deal from the stages that went before. How this works becomes clear when Vico writes that "the traces of the (very earliest, sensuous and real) poetic speech [which our poetic logic has helped us to understand] continued for a long time into the historical period, much as great and rapid rivers continue far into the sea, keeping sweet the waters borne on by the force of their flow."[21] Just a bit further on, he goes so far as to write: "To enter now upon the extremely difficult [question of the] way in which these three kinds of languages and letters were formed, we must establish this principle: that as gods, heroes, and men began at the same time (for they were, after all, men who imagined gods and believed their own heroic nature to be a mixture of divine and human natures), so these three languages began at the same time, each having its letters, which developed along with it."[22] And yet, it is the inner simultaneity of world history in the conscious individual that is far more frequently a matter of concern to Vico than this kind of empirical overlapping of the individual stages of history. He expresses it this way in the chapter on method: "Indeed, we make bold to affirm that he who meditates this Science narrates to himself this ideal eternal history so far as he . . . makes it for himself[,] . . . because this historical world has certainly been made by men, and its essence must therefore be found within the modifications of our own human mind. . . . [H]istory cannot be more certain than when he who creates the things also narrates them."[23] The founding assumption of the *New Science* is the idea that the inner human essence of the history of nations

[20] *SN* 331; *NW* 125 [*New Science* 96. Cf. above, p. 25, n. 5].

[21] *SN* 412; *NW* 176 [*New Science* 132]. [In German, Auerbach renders the original Italian somewhat differently from the quotation as it is given here from Bergin's and Fisch's *New Science*. —Trans.]

[22] *SN* 446; *NW* 192 [*New Science* 149]. Shortly before, at *SN* 445, Vico writes that the richer languages are in heroic styles of speaking (that is, in real, material idioms derived from the original tongue, the *Ursprache*), the more beautiful they are, because they are more expressive, and thus truer and more accurate.

[23] *SN* 349; *NW* 139 [*New Science* 104]. [Bergin and Frisch translation slightly altered to follow Auerbach's quote. —Trans.]

(*Völker*) and of the entire human race is what permits us to understand this history as a possession that we have made ourselves. This is the substance of what he calls the *sensus communis generis humani*. Trusting that this is true makes it possible for Vico to deploy his new critical art in the interpretation of the most ancient monuments, which is a philological task.

As noted above, Vico likes to call his art "philosophical." He offers two kinds of evidence to support the majority of his claims, one which he calls philosophical, the other philological. But at the heart of all of them lies the explication of documents such as the Homeric texts, the Twelve Tablets, and so on, as well as the interpretation of myths. His critique is philosophical insofar as it follows the principle warrants of philosophy detailed above and also insofar as it produces philosophical and anthropological results. But this is in fact philology. Even in those places, such as the chapter on method which we have already cited several times, or in the section of Book Three where he discovers the true Homer,[24] and even in those places where Vico distinguishes between philosophical and philological evidence (and mostly unclearly at that), the philosophical evidence consists entirely of historical and theoretical findings that he had arrived at through earlier hermeneutic and philological work. This is a philosophically informed philology, to be sure. Indeed, it is philology in the broadest sense of the term. Yet it follows the definitions of philology that Vico has just penned himself, and thus corresponds to them exactly and in every way.

Vico had defined philology in a generous-minded fashion already in his *De constantia philologiae* (On the Immutability of Philology): *Hinc nos si non felici, certe pio ausu de Principiis Humanitatis, cuius studium philologia est, . . . dissere . . . decrevimus* [Hence, if not with successful, then at least with pious daring, we have resolved [in this book] to examine the beginnings of humanity, the study of which is philology]. With this we have the whole of Vico. The context makes it clear that he is using the word *humanitas* here to mean not what late humanist philology would have had it mean, namely the *humaniora*, the humanities or human sciences, but more precisely humanity.[25] He also already lists here all of the disciplines that he includes in philology, which we then find in all of his later work. "To the group in which we include those whom we call philologists," he writes in the 1725 edition of the *New Science*, "belong poets, historians, rhetoricians, grammarians, whom we usually refer to as *eruditi*."[26] That he takes this claim seriously soon becomes

---

[24] *SN* 338ff.; *NW* 130ff. [*New Science* 100ff.] Also see *NS* 810ff.; *NW* 326ff. [*New Science* 313ff.]

[25] See *Opere* 3, 233. The beginning of the first chapter is worthy of attention. See 223: *philologia . . . sermonis studium et cura . . . Sed cum rerum ideae quibusque verbis [appictae] sint, ad philologiam in primis spectat tenere rerum Historiam.* [Philology . . . (is) the study of and attention to speech. . . . But since the ideas of things are portrayed with particular words, it (philology) seeks in the first place to represent the history of things.]

[26] *SNI* 32 and 34.

evident when he names Homer to the position of the father of all of Greek learning. Legal scholars also belong to the ranks of the philologists as they too study the science of the *certum*. In the final edition of the *New Science*, Vico repeatedly enumerates everything that is included in philology's compass, this time with even more fervor, as here it is linked to a comprehensive overview of his subject: "Philology [is] the doctrine of all the institutions that depend on human choice; for example, all histories of the languages, customs, and deeds of peoples."[27] Or: "Philosophy contemplates reason, whence comes knowledge of the true (*la scienza del vero*); philology observes that of which human choice is the author (*l'autorità dell'umano arbitrio*), whence comes consciousness of the [historically] certain (*la coscienza del certo*)."[28] Juxtaposing each of these definitions (and not just the final one) to a definition of philosophy, he demands each time that philology become thoroughly philosophical. He has done this in his *New Science*, he declares, and was able to do so with the assistance of the new critical art: "[With the help of] a new critical art . . . concerning the authors of these same nations . . . philosophy undertakes to examine philology . . . and invests it with the form of a science by discovering in it the design of an ideal eternal history."[29] It is by means of philology that history's eternal design can be discovered. Philology's object of study is the *autorità dell'umano arbitrio* that is the source of all human institutions, the *certum*. This choice, or will (*arbitrium*), is nevertheless determined by the *sensus communis generis humani* (the common sense of men). It is for this reason that it can be known.[30] Here the argument has come full circle and is complete.

It would thus be entirely justifiable to consider the *New Science* as a work of philology, indeed, as the first work of the hermeneutical philology that, by the nineteenth and twentieth centuries, was well ensconced and had an important job to do (even if it was of course often called by another name). Vico was the first to base this kind of philology on a belief in what was common to all human beings. For him, the human was the *sine qua non*. Later scholars were often concerned with individual epochs, nations, movements, or figures. But they preserved the image of the human being. They had to do so if they were not to sacrifice their hope, their belief, in the possibility of understanding their human object of study—and thus, in the end, also themselves. It is in this sense that we can understand philology as the epitome of the science of the human, insofar as all humans are historical beings. Philology includes all the disciplines that take this as their subject (including

[27] *SN* 7; *NW* 48ff. [*New Science* 6].

[28] *SN* 138–39; *NW* 78 [*New Science* 63].

[29] *SN* 7; *NW* 48ff. [*New Science* 6]. [In German, Auerbach quotes Vico's text in a sequence different from that of Bergin and Fisch in their *New Science*. Here, the square brackets indicate where Auerbach's German differs from Bergin's and Fisch's English translation. —Trans.]

[30] *SN* 141 [*New Science* 63].

the discipline of history narrowly defined). Its very possibility consists in the assumption that people are able to understand one another and that there exists a world of and for humanity that is common to us all, to which we all belong, and thus to which we can all gain admission. Without a belief in this world there would be no science of the human race in history, and thus no philology. It bears remembering that Vico did not understand what he took to be common to all people as in any way a matter of education or progressive enlightenment. Rather, what all human beings hold in common is the entirety of historical reality, in all its greatness and its horror. Not only did he see historical individuals in their totality; he also saw that he was himself a human being and that it made him human to understand them. But Vico did not create the human race in his own likeness; he did not see himself in the other. Rather, he saw the other in himself. He discovered himself, as a human, in history, and the long buried forces of our common nature stood revealed to him. This was Vico's humanity, something far more profound—and far more perilous—than what we normally associate with the word. Nevertheless—or, perhaps, precisely for this reason—it was Vico who discovered our common humanity, and held it fast.

4

Vico and Aesthetic Historism

Modern critics of art or of literature consider and admire, with the same preparedness for understanding, Giotto and Michelangelo, Michelangelo and Rembrandt, Rembrandt and Picasso, Picasso and a Persian miniature; or Racine and Shakespeare, Chaucer and Alexander Pope, the Chinese lyrics and T. S. Eliot.[1] The preference they may give to one or the other of the various periods or artists is no longer imposed upon them by certain aesthetic rules or judgments dominating the feelings of all our contemporaries, but such preferences are merely personal predilections originating from individual taste or individual experiences. A critic who would condemn the art of Shakespeare or of Rembrandt or even the drawings of the ice age primitives as being of bad taste because they do not conform to the aesthetic standards established by classical Greek or Roman theory would not be taken seriously by anybody.

This largeness of our aesthetic horizon is a consequence of our historical perspective; it is based on historism; i.e., on the conviction that every civilization and every period has its own possibilities of aesthetic perfection; that the works of art of the different peoples and periods, as well as their general forms of life, must be understood as products of variable individual conditions, and have to be judged each by its own development, not by absolute rules of beauty and ugliness. General and aesthetic historism is a precious (and also a very dangerous) acquisition of the human mind; it is a comparatively recent one. Before the sixteenth century, the historical and geographical horizon of the Europeans was not large enough for such conceptions; and even in the Renaissance, the seventeenth and the beginning of the eighteenth

[1] This paper was read at the convention of the American Society for Aesthetics in Cambridge, MA, on September 1, 1948.

Reprinted from Auerbach's English original (1949) as reprinted in his 1967 Gesammelte Aufsätze *(see Appendix: Original Publication History of the Essays in This Collection), with minor editorial changes in punctuation and orthography. The reader should note that by "historism" and "Romanticists" Auerbach intends the more common equivalents "historicism" and "Romantics."—Ed.*

century, the first moves towards historism were overbalanced by currents which worked against it; especially by the admiration of Greek and Roman civilization, which focused the attention on classical art and poetry; these became models to be imitated, and nothing is more contrary to aesthetic historism than imitation of models. It promotes absolute standards and rules of beauty, and creates an aesthetic dogmatism such as was admirably achieved by the French civilization of the Louis XIV period.

Besides this there was another current in the sixteenth and seventeenth centuries acting against historical perspective: the revival of the ancient concept of absolute human nature. The sudden enlargement of the horizon, the discovery of the variety and relativity of human religions, laws, customs, and tastes which occurred in the Renaissance, did not lead, in most cases, to historical perspective, that is to say to an attempt to understand them all and to acknowledge their relative merits; it led, on the contrary, to the rejection of all of them, to a struggle against the variety of historical forms, to a struggle against history, and to a powerful revival of the concept of true or original or uncorrupted absolute human nature as opposed to history. History seemed to be nothing but "the actions and institutions of men," arbitrary, erroneous, pernicious and even fraudulent. The worthlessness of such institutions seemed to be proved sufficiently by their variety; and the task of mankind seemed to be to replace them all by absolute standards according to the law of nature. There were indeed very different opinions about the nature of this nature; between those who identified human nature with the primitive uncivilized origins of mankind, and those who, on the contrary, identified nature with enlightened reason, there were all kinds of shades and gradations. But the static and absolute character of this human nature, as opposed to the changes of history, is common to all these theories of human nature and natural law. Montesquieu introduced a certain amount of historical perspective by his explanation of the variety of human forms of government by climate and other material conditions; with the ideas of Diderot and Rousseau, the concept of general and of human nature became strongly dynamic; but it was still a nature opposed to history.

Aesthetic historism, followed by general historism, practically originated in the second half of the eighteenth century, as a reaction against the European predominance of French classicism; the pre-Romantic and Romantic currents created it and spread it all over Europe. The most vigorous impulse came from Germany, from the so-called Storm and Stress group of the 1770's, from the first works of Herder and Goethe and their friends; later from the Schlegel brothers and the other German Romanticists. Herder and his followers started from the conception of the original folk genius as the creator of true poetry; in strong opposition to all theories which based poetry and art on highly developed civilization, good taste, imitation of models, and well-defined rules, they believed that poetry is the work of free instinct and imagination, and that it is most spontaneous and genuine in the early periods of civilization, in the youth of mankind, when instinct, imagination, and oral tradition were stronger than reason and reflection, when "poetry was the natural language of men"; hence their predilection for folk songs and folk tales, their theory that ancient epic poetry (parts of the Bible, Homer, the epic poetry of the Middle Ages) were not consciously composed by individuals, but had grown up and were synthesized unconsciously from many anonymous contributions—songs or tales—originating from the depth of the folk genius; hence finally their conviction that even in modern times true poetry can be reborn only from a return to its eternal source, the folk genius, with its unconscious and instinctive development of traditions. These men conceived history, not as a series of exterior facts and conscious actions of men, not as a series of mistakes and frauds, but as a subconscious, slow, and organic evolution of "forces," which were considered as manifestations of the Divinity. They admired the variety of historical forms as the realization of the infinite variety of the divine spirit, manifesting itself through the genius of the various peoples and periods. The divinization of history led to an enthusiastic research into the individual historical and aesthetic forms, to the attempt to understand them all by their own individual conditions of growth and development, to a contemptuous rejection of all aesthetic systems based on absolute and rationalistic standards.

Thus, the pre-Romantic and Romantic movement was practically the origin of modern historism and of modern historical sciences: history of literature, of language, of art, but also of political forms, of law, and so on, conceived as an organic evolution of various individual forms. The origin of modern historism is, therefore, closely linked with the pre-Romantic and "Nordic" admiration for primitive and early forms of civilization, and, of course, strongly influenced by Rousseau's concept of original human nature; the origins of mankind are conceived with a certain idyllic, lyrical, and pantheistic connotation. But, whereas Rousseau's concept was, on the whole, revolutionary—nature directed against history, because history was responsible for the inequality of men and the corruption of society—the Romanticists introduced the conception of natural and organic evolution into history itself; they developed an evolutionary conservatism, based on the traditions of the folk genius, directed as much against the rationalistic forms of absolutism as against rationalistic tendencies towards revolutionary progress. Their organic conservatism resulted from their prevailing interest in the individual roots and forms of the folk genius, in folklore, national traditions, and the national individuality in general. Although this interest was extended to foreign national forms in the literary and scientific activities of the Romanticists, it led many of them, especially in Germany, to an extremely nationalistic attitude towards their own fatherland, which they considered as the synthesis and supreme realization of folk genius. Contemporary circumstances and events—the political disaggregation of Germany, the French Revolution, Napoleon's domination—contributed to the development of such feelings.

Now, it is one of the most astonishing facts in the history of ideas that very similar principles had been conceived and published half a century before their first pre-Romantic appearance by an old Neapolitan scholar, Giambattista Vico (1668–1744), in his *Scienza Nuova* which appeared first in 1725—by a man totally ignorant of all the atmospherical conditions which, fifty years later, fostered and promoted such ideas. Shaftesbury's and Rousseau's influence, the vitalistic trend of certain eighteenth century biologists, French and English poetry of sensibility, the cult of Ossian, and German pietism—all these influences and movements which created the pre-Romantic *milieu* developed long after Vico's death. He did not even know Shakespeare; his education had been classical and rationalistic, and he had no opportunity to become interested in Nordic folklore. The Storm and Stress movement was specifically Nordic in its aspect: it originated in a *milieu* of youthful liberty, it was promoted by a whole group of young men bound together by the same enthusiastic feelings. Vico was a solitary old professor at the University of Naples, who had taught throughout all his life Latin figures of speech and had written hyperbolical eulogies for the various Neapolitan viceroys and other important personalities. Nor had he any appreciable influence upon the pre-Romantic and Romantic movements. The difficulties of his style and the baroque atmosphere of his book, an atmosphere totally different from Romanticism, covered it with a cloud of impenetrability. Even the few Germans who, in the second part of the eighteenth century, happened to see it and to turn over its leaves—men like Hamann, Friedrich Heinrich Jacobi, and Goethe—failed to recognize its importance and to penetrate to its leading ideas.

It is true that the continuous efforts of modern scholars to establish a link between Vico and Herder have finally met with some success, since Professor Robert T. Clark has made it very probable that Herder was inspired, in some of his ideas concerning language and poetry, by the notes to Denis's German translation of Macpherson. Denis had appropriated these notes from Cesarotti, an Italian translator of Ossian who was well acquainted with the corresponding ideas of Vico.[2] Professor Clark's discovery is certainly interesting and important, but such a casual, indirect, and incomplete contact—Herder did not even mention the name of Vico, which meant nothing to him—is almost tragically incongruous with the general importance Vico should have had for the pre-Romantic and Romantic writers. He should have been one of their acknowledged and admired forerunners just as, or even more than were Shaftesbury and Rousseau. But even in Vico's own country, in Italy, nobody really understood his ideas. To put it in the words of Max Harold Fisch, in

[2] Robert T. Clark, Jr., "Herder, Vico and Cesarotti," *Studies in Philology* 44 (1947) 645–71.

the excellent introduction to his (and Thomas G. Bergin's) recent American translation of Vico's *Autobiography*: none of those "who borrowed this or that from Vico in the pre-revolutionary period was able to free himself altogether from the prevailing rationalist temper, to grasp Vico's thought as an integral whole, or even to place himself at its living center."[3]

Vico arrived very late at the maturity of his ideas. Neither the Epicurean tendencies of his youth nor the Cartesianism which prevailed in Naples during his later life, which he opposed passionately without succeeding in freeing himself from its powerful attraction—nor, finally, the rationalistic theories of natural law—were a favorable background for his approach to history. Throughout a great part of his life, he tried to find an epistemological base for his ideas, against the Cartesian contempt of history. He was in his fifties when he finally succeeded in finding a form for his theory of cognition which satisfied him, and even filled him with enthusiasm. In this ultimate form, the theory says that there is no knowledge without creation; only the creator has knowledge of what he has created himself; the physical world—*il mondo della natura*—has been created by God; therefore only God can understand it; but the historical or political world, the world of mankind, *il mondo delle nazioni,* can be understood by men, because men have made it. I have no time now to discuss the theological implications of this much-debated theory, considered in its relations with Vico's conception of Divine Providence. For our purpose, it is sufficient to stress the fact that Vico had achieved by this theory the predominance of the historical sciences, based on the certitude that men can understand men, that all possible forms of human life and thinking, as created and experienced by men, must be found in the potentialities of the human mind (*dentro le modificazioni della nostra medesima mente umana*); that therefore we are capable of re-evoking human history from the depth of our own consciousness.

The impulse to this theory of cognition was given to Vico undoubtedly by his own historical discoveries. He had no scientific knowledge of primitive civilizations, and a very incomplete and vague knowledge of the Middle Ages; he was supported only by his scholarship in classical philology and Roman law. It is almost a miracle that a man, at the beginning of the eighteenth century in Naples, with such material for his research, could create a vision of world history based on the discovery of the magic character of primitive civilization. Certainly, he was inspired by the theories of natural law, by Spinoza, Hobbes, and especially by Grotius; or better, he was inspired by his opposition to their theories. Still, there are few similar examples, in the history of human thought, of isolated creation, due to such an extent to the particular quality of the author's mind. He combined an almost mystical faith

---

[3] *The Autobiography of Giambattista Vico*, translated from the Italian by Max Harold Fisch and Thomas Goddard Bergin. (Ithaca, NY: Cornell University Press, 1944) 64.

in the eternal order of human history with a tremendous power of productive imagination in the interpretation of myth, ancient poetry, and law.

In his view, the first men were neither innocent and happy beings living in accordance with an idyllic law of nature, nor terrible beasts moved only by the purely material instinct of self-preservation. He also rejected the concept of primitive society as founded by reason and common sense in the form of mutual agreement by contract. For him, primitive men were originally solitary nomads living in orderless promiscuity within the chaos of a mysterious and for this very reason horrible nature. They had no faculties of reasoning; they only had very strong sensations and a strength of imagination such as civilized men can hardly understand. When, after the deluge, the first thunderstorm broke out, a minority of them, terror-struck by thunder and lightning, conceived a first form of religion, which modern scholars would call animistic: they personified nature, their imagination created a world of magic personifications, a world of living deities expressing their might and their will by the natural phenomena; and this minority of primitive men, in order to understand the will of the deities, to appease their wrath and to win their support, created a system of fantastic and magic ceremonies, formulas and sacrifices which governed all their life. They established sanctuaries at certain fixed places and became settled; hiding their sexual relations as a religious taboo, they became monogamous, thus founding the first families: primitive magic religion is the base of social institutions. It is also the origin of agriculture; the settlers were the first who cultivated the soil. The primitive society of isolated families is strongly patriarchal; the father is priest and judge; by his exclusive knowledge of the magic ceremonies, he has absolute power over all the members of his family; and the sacred formulas according to which he rules them are of extreme severity; these laws are strictly bound to the ritual wording, ignoring flexibility and consideration of special circumstances. Vico called the life of these primitive fathers a severe poem; they had huge bodies, and called themselves giants, *gigantes,* sons of the Earth, because they were the first to bury their dead and to worship their memory: the first nobility. Their conceptions and expressions were inspired by personifications and images; the mental order in which they conceived the surrounding world and created their institutions was not rational but magic and fantastic. Vico calls it poetic; they were poets by their very nature; their wisdom, their metaphysics, their laws, all their life was "poetic." This is the first age of mankind, the golden age (golden because of the harvests), the age of the gods.

The development from the first to the second, the heroic age, is mainly political and economic. Stationary life and family constitution had given to the minority of settlers a superiority of wealth, material power and religious prestige over the remnant of nomads, who finally were obliged to have recourse to the families of the fathers for protection and better living conditions; they were accepted as labor-slaves, as dependent members of the family of the first fathers or "heroes"; they were not admitted to the ritual ceremonies, and consequently had no human rights, no legal matrimony, no legitimate children, no property. But after a certain time the slaves or *famuli* began to rebel; a revolutionary movement developed, religious as well as social, for participation in the ceremonies, in legal rights, and property. This movement obliged the isolated fathers to unite for defense, and to constitute the first communities, the heroic republics. They were oligarchical states, where religious, political, and economic power was entirely in the hands of the heroes; by maintaining the secrecy and inviolability of the divine mysteries they opposed all innovations in religion, law, and political structure. They preserved during this second period (which still was mentally "poetic" in the sense Vico uses this word) their narrow-minded virtue, their cruel discipline and their magic formalism, still unable and unwilling to act by rationalistic considerations, symbolizing their life and their institutions in mythical concepts and strongly believing themselves to be of a higher nature than the rest of men. But rationalistic forms of mind, promoted by the revolutionary leaders of the plebeians (the former *famuli),* developed more and more. Step by step the plebeians tore away from the heroes their rights and prerogatives. With the final victory of the plebeians begins the third period of history, the age of men, a rationalistic and democratic period, where imagination and poetry have lost their creative power, where poetry is only an embellishment of life and an elegant pastime, where all men are considered as equals and are governed by elastic and liberal religions and laws.[4]

There is no doubt about the striking similarity between Vico's ideas and those of Herder and his followers. The poetical irrationalism and the creative imagination of primitive men are concepts common to both; both say that primitive men were poets by their very nature, that their language, their conception of nature and history, their entire life was poetry; both considered enlightened rationalism as unpoetical. But the concept of poetry, the basic concept, is entirely different. Vico admired his primitive giants and heroes as much as, perhaps even more than, Herder loved and cultivated the folk genius. Their power of imagination and expression, the concrete realism of their sublime metaphoric language, the unity of concept pervading all their life became for this poor old professor the model of creative greatness. He

---

[4]This survey of the first two periods of Vico's *storia ideale eterna* is very incomplete; and for the purpose of this paper, the further development of the third period and the *ricorso delle cose umane* (the theory of the historical cycles) are not necessary. The best sources of information for the English reader interested in Vico's philosophy are the translation of Benedetto Croce's monograph (*The Philosophy of Giambattista Vico*, New York 1913) and Professor Fisch's introduction to the autobiography, quoted in our note 3. There has just been published the first English translation of the *Scienza Nuova* (also by Bergin and Fisch, Ithaca and New York 1948); it is an admirable achievement of a very difficult task.

even admired—with an admiration so overwhelming that it proved to be stronger than his horror—the terrible cruelty of their magic formalism.

These last words—the terrible cruelty of their magic formalism—well illustrate the immense discrepancy between his concepts and those of Herder. Herder's conception of the youth of mankind had grown on the ground of Rousseau's theory of original nature; it had been nourished and inspired by folk songs and folk tales; it is not political. The motive of magic animism is not entirely absent from his concepts, but it does not dominate, and it is not developed to its concrete implications and consequences. He saw the original state of mankind as a state of nature, and nature, for him, was liberty: liberty of feeling, of boundless instinct, of inspiration, absence of laws and institutions, in striking contrast to the laws, conventions, and rules of rationalized society. He would never have conceived the idea that primitive imagination created institutions more severe and ferocious, boundaries more narrow and insurmountable than any civilized society can possibly do. But that is Vico's idea; it is the very essence of his system. The aim of primitive imagination, in his view, is not liberty, but, on the contrary, establishment of fixed limits, as a psychological and material protection against the chaos of the surrounding world. And later on, mythical imagination serves as the base of a political system and as a weapon in the struggle for political and economic power. The ages of the gods and the heroes, with their all-pervading "poetry," are not at all poetical in the Romantic sense, although, in both cases, poetry means imagination opposed to reason. The imagination of the folk genius produces folklore and traditions; the imagination of the giants and heroes produces myths which symbolize institutions according to the eternal law of Divine Providence. In Vico's system the old contrast of natural against positive law, of *physis* against *thesis*, of original nature against human institutions becomes meaningless; Vico's poetical age, the golden age, is not an age of natural freedom, but an age of institutions. It is true that Romantic conservatism also was very fond of institutions slowly and "organically" developed by the traditions of the folk genius—but these were of another kind, and had another atmosphere than the magic formalism of the heroes.

It is easy to show that Vico, long before Herder and the Romanticists, discovered their most fertile aesthetic concept, the concept of folk genius. He was the first who tried to prove that primitive poetry is not the work of individual artists, but was created by the whole society of the primitive peoples [who] were poets by their very nature. In his third book, on "the discovery of the true Homer," long before the German philologist Friedrich August Wolf, he developed the theory that Homer was not an individual poet, but a myth, or, as he puts it, a "poetical character" symbolizing the rhapsodes or popular singers who wandered through the Greek towns singing the deeds of the gods and the heroes and that [the] *Iliad* and *Odyssey* were not originally coherent works, but that they are composed of many fragments from different periods of Greek early history; that they have been transmitted to us in a form already altered and corrupted; but that to those who are able to interpret them, they tell the history of Greek primitive civilization. He thus anticipated the famous Romantic theory of popular epic poetry as a product of the folk genius, a theory which dominated philological research during a great part of the nineteenth century, and which still is very influential.

But Vico did not show any special interest in the folk genius of the different individual peoples. His aim was to establish eternal laws—the laws of Divine Providence which govern history: an evolution of human civilization through different distinct stages, an evolution which would develop again and again, in eternal cycles, wherever men should live. His suggestive analysis of the different periods stresses their individual aspect only in order to prove that they are typical stages of this evolution; and although he occasionally admitted that there exist some variants within the development of the different peoples and societies, the study of these variants would have seemed to him a matter of minor importance. The Romanticists, on the contrary, were chiefly interested in the individual forms of the historical phenomena; they tried to understand the particular spirit, to taste the specific flavor of the different periods as well as of the various peoples. They studied the Scotch, the English, Spanish, Italian, French, German "folk genius" and many others; the understanding of the various organic popular developments was the very center of their critical activities. It was this impulse focused at individual forms of life and art which proved so fertile for the historical sciences in the nineteenth century, and which introduced into them the spirit of historical perspective, as I tried to explain on the first pages of this paper.

In this movement of early European historism, Vico's ideas did not play an important part; his work was not sufficiently known. It seems to me that this is due not only to a casual combination of unfavorable circumstances, but primarily to the fact that his vision of human history lacked some of the most important elements of Romantic historism, and possessed others which could hardly be understood and appreciated in the pre-Romantic and early Romantic period. The slow process of his gradual discovery in Europe began in the 1820's; in the rest of the nineteenth century, his influence still remained sporadic, and many leading textbooks of [the] history of philosophy did not even mention his name. But in the last forty years, this has changed; his name and his ideas have become important and familiar to an ever-increasing number of European and American scholars and authors; the admirable activity of Croce and Nicolini devoted to the edition and interpretation of his work met with considerable and steadily growing success. Some of his basic ideas seem to have acquired their full weight only for our time and our generation; as far as I know, no great author has been as much impressed by his work as James Joyce. There are, as it seems to me, three main ideas which are and may prove to be in future of great significance for our conceptions of aesthetics and history.

First, [there is] his discovery of the magic formalism of primitive men, with its power to create and to maintain institutions symbolized by myth; it includes a conception of poetry which has, undoubtedly, some relationship to modern forms of artistic expression. The complete unit of magic "poetry" or myth with political structure in primitive society, the interpretation of myths as symbols of political and economic struggles and developments, the concept of concrete realism in primitive language and myth are extremely suggestive of certain modern tendencies. By the word "tendencies," I do not allude to certain parties or countries, but to trends of thought and feeling spread all over our world.

The second point is Vico's theory of cognition. The entire development of human history, as made by men, is potentially contained in the human mind, and may therefore, by a process of research and re-evocation, be understood by men. The re-evocation is not only analytic; it has to be synthetic, that is to say, an understanding of every historical stage as an integral whole and of its genius (its *Geist*, as the German Romanticists would have said), a genius that pervades all human activities and expressions of the period concerned. By this theory, Vico created the principle of historical understanding, entirely unknown to his contemporaries; the Romanticists knew and practiced this principle, but they never found such a powerful and suggestive epistemological base for it.

Finally, I want to stress his particular conception of historical perspective; it can best be explained by his interpretation of human nature. Against all contemporary theorists who believed in an absolute and unchanging human nature as opposed to the variety and changes of history, Vico created and passionately maintained the concept of the historical nature of men. He identified human history and human nature, he conceived human nature as a function of history. There are many passages in the *Scienza Nuova*[5] where the word *natura* should best be translated by "historical development" or "stage of historical development." Divine Providence makes human nature change from period to period, and in each period the institutions are in full accordance with the human nature of the period; the distinction between human nature and human history disappears; as Vico puts it, human history is a permanent Platonic state.

The original essay concluded with the words, "This sounds rather ironical in a man who did not believe in progress, but in a cyclical movement of history. However, Vico was not ironical; he meant it in earnest." The 1967 reprint does not contain this final sentence. —Ed.

[5] E.g., *capoversi* 246, 346, 347 of the edition by Nicolini in 2 vols. (Bari 1928).

5

Vico and the National Spirit

It often happens that similar thoughts and intellectual paradigms appear almost simultaneously in different places and yet, entirely independently of one another. We might legitimately suppose that this means that their time has come and that they have spontaneously suggested themselves to a whole range of different people whose experiences and activities nevertheless developed in analogous ways because of the similar circumstances and times in which they lived. Related to one another, even though they have developed independently, such intellectual movements remain isolated from, or even unknown to, one another only with difficulty, at least in modern times. They quickly make contact with one another. The resulting relations may be friendly or adversarial, but they are invariably exciting and mutually enriching.

The case of Vico is much more curious. He articulated his thoughts about language, poetry, and history a full half-century before Herder, yet his ideas often seem so similar to Herder's that they could be mistaken for them, or for the ideas of the Romantics who took up Herder's ideas, and even for Hegel's. Vico was nevertheless all but unknown to Herder and to those among the Romantics who espoused historicism. He only gradually became known after this influential tide of Herderian Romanticism had ebbed—after those who contributed to the approach in a positivist-empiricist way had fundamentally changed Romantic historicism over the course of the nineteenth century (starting around 1820 and continuing through the beginning of the twentieth century). Under such circumstances, it is completely understandable that there were attempts to prove some kind of productive relation between Vico's thought and the thought of the pre-Romantic and Romantic movements. But the relationships that were ascertained turned out to be coincidental and superficial. And if any productive influence did occur, it was equally coincidental, the result of chance encounters, disjointed and indirect, between this or that intellectual intermediary. Vico's ideas thus remained unknown in Germany in the second half of the eighteenth century and we must assume from the very outset that even the most learned detective work bent

on discovering hidden connections will fail to unearth any significant associations, for, if any were there, they would have to be well known and not
buried or out of sight. Herder and his historicist acolytes would have had to
revere Vico and to laud him. Had they known him and found his thought
congenial to theirs, his conceptual universe and vocabulary would had to
have lived on in their work.

An initial explanation for why this was not the case has to do with how
difficult it is to become familiar with Vico and his work. It is not easy to read
one's way into his Italian. Moreover, even in his own country he had not
achieved the kind of reputation that would have brought him to the attention of foreigners—especially to the Germans (who are the foreigners about
whom I am speaking here). Although this explanation seems reasonable, it
is not entirely satisfying. Thinkers involved in the nascent stages of an idiosyncratic intellectual movement always perk up their ears at anything at
all related or congenial to their thought, anything that might confirm and
nurture it or give it a boost. At least one of the many historicizing Germans—
from Hamann to the Schlegels—would have been bound to discover Vico's
intellectual world. But no one did—and this in spite of the fact that opportunities for such a discovery were not entirely lacking. Goethe's divining rod
twitched, for example, when Filangieri pressed a copy of the *New Science* into
his hands in Naples, but not strongly enough to cause him to dig any deeper.

In the end, there is only one explanation for the failure of the two movements to connect, and it is this: the similarities between them are not as intimate or real as they seem. If this is the case, it is entirely predictable and
makes sense that the later movement did not attend to the earlier one, for
there would not have been substantial benefit in doing so. In spite of all their
similarities, Vico and the historicism of the pre-Romantics and the Romantics were fundamentally different. They took root in soils that were as different from one another as were the respective goals they sought to achieve.

There is virtually no idea that is more intimately intertwined with the
roots of German historicism, for example, than that of the national poetic
spirit. Vico provided a model. He too was convinced that poetry was the primordial language of man; for him, the giants and the heroes of the first two
ages of his historical system were poets by nature. In those times, he claimed,
poetry was not ornament, but how men naturally expressed themselves; the
figurative ways of speaking proper to poetry had not yet deteriorated into the
similes, allegories, and highly wrought phrases that took over in times of rational civilization. They still possessed a real and originary pictorial character
because the imaginations of Vico's primitive men were pictorial and linguistically creative. For them, language was not meant to function as a vehicle of
rational communication. Rather, it evoked the sensuous and the fantastic.
He maintained that in those early times, men did not distinguish between
poetry and history since they were only able to perceive and process events

in and as poetry. It was not single individuals who were poets, but rather an entire nation. On the basis of this claim, Vico drew the important conclusion that he articulates in his "Discovery of the True Homer" in the third book of the *New Science*, where he asserts that the Homeric poems were not the work of a single poet, but, rather, the work of all of the Greek peoples who in those poems were writing their own history in and as poetry. Individual parts were composed at different times during the early epochs of Greek civilization and performed by itinerant blind singers. Much later, they were revised, re-interpreted, and compiled, and it is only in this semi-rationalized and thus impure form that we have access to them today. Such speculations contain the seeds not just of Friedrich August Wolf's theories about Homer, but also of the more generally Romantic view of national epics and primordial lyric forms as products of a nation's spirit. These ideas dominated scholarship for a good part of the nineteenth century; this scholarship's effects are still felt by scholars today and will continue to be felt for a long time in the future.

But the materials out of which Vico developed the architecture of his system were completely different from those used by Herder and his successors. He did not yet know anything about Ossian, for example, or about any of the Nordic folk songs. He did not even know Shakespeare. Nearly all of his material was derived from classical philology and Roman law. In spite of some nearly literal correspondences, his tone was thus completely different. Vico's giants and heroes breathed a different air from that of the bards at the dawn of the human race. From the very start, Herder conceived of the primitive origins of poetry, for example, as something free, lyrical, and unconstrained; this prevented him from discovering any firm political profile in the early stages of human society. Like Vico, he sometimes speaks of the horror and fear that the first humans felt and expressed in song—the terrible gods of nature, tribal enmities, and the rugged valor of the heroes. But none of this produced a politics. Everything remained at the level of generality and lyricism, with the whole idea of a primordial poetry dominated by a sense of Ossian-like, folkloristic emotionalism that injected a kind of directionless enthusiasm into Herder's rich conceptual world. If we pursue this impression, we find something even more deep-seated, and it was this that gave rise to his predilection for Ossian and the folk song; namely Rousseau's concept of nature. I am not suggesting that Herder was in full agreement with Rousseau. But it eventually became axiomatic for him that one could think the natural and the primordial together and equate both with freedom; the singing nations of the earliest eras were unmonitored and unpoliced, and Herder does not mention any political institutions. Later, when in his *Ideas*, he—again like Vico—writes of religion as the foundation and beginning of all culture, he conceives of it in terms that lack any effective political and economic focus. Rather, religion is merely that which predisposes people to be humane.

Rousseau wrote long after Vico died and Vico knew nothing of him. He fought vigorously against the older forms of natural law, which endorsed a more static idea of nature than Rousseau (not to speak of Herder) ever envisaged. It is one of the most definitive characteristics of Vico's concept of primitive history that he turns the old opposition of natural and positive law, of *physis* and *thesis*, on its head. Vico's patriarchal giants and hero state-founders lived in a thetic world of positive law. The poetic age, the age of the gods, when the history of the human race actually commences, begins, according to Vico, when the first fathers of the race of giants, moved by magical religious impulses, settle down in one place and start families. Their mores are everything other than "natural," in the way that the natural law theorists or Rousseau might have understood the term. Rather, they are based on institutions that immediately become formal, rigorous, and binding. These institutions were of course products of the imagination rather than of reason, and thus poetic—in Vico's sense. But here poetry is not the same as a spontaneous outpouring of feeling. Rather, it consists in set rituals with strictly defined ceremonies that were used to conjure up and appease the forces of divinity. There is no freedom in this kind of primitive poetry, no innocent and uninhibited virtue, no unrestrained rush of human feelings. Vico's giants and heroes rule with harsh discipline, their virtue is political, and their poetic creativity permeates every corner of their world. Every one of their actions, and everything they say—is determined by religious ideas that we would call magical, symbols made real. The result is a system of institutions that may have its origins in the imagination, but that becomes narrowly circumscribed and precisely defined. This is what Vico calls the *certum*, the certain and established, in contrast to philosophical truth as determined by reason. The latter he calls the *verum*. The term *certum* is the exact equivalent of the Greek *thesis*. Even though it is not a product of the rational faculty nor written down, what we are dealing with here is a product of the imagination that has a rigorously defined shape. The system of ritual obligations that ordered legal, political, and economic culture in Vico's early eras belonged entirely to the established, formalized, positive, and institutional realm of *thesis*, rather than to nature as Rousseau and Herder understood it.

Of course, traditional religious motifs appear throughout all early periods of civilizations for Herder too. But they neither dominate his idea of the era in its entirety nor do they produce any form of political organization. Rather, his notion of a spontaneous primordial poetry (which he associates with Ossian and folk song) completely overwhelms the religious elements time and again. For Vico, on the other hand, the poetic imagination of primitive cultures is not associated with any idea of wide-ranging freedoms. Rather, it is bound to the necessity of imposing the fixed order of the *certum* upon the phenomenal chaos of the world and thus functions within and in spite of a kind of conservative ritualistic formalism. Such ideas remind us far more of the hypotheses and scholarly discoveries made by many modern ethnologists and sociologists than of anything associated with Herder and Romanticism. We might add that Vico's "national spirit" is in reality an aristocratic construct. His myths of the poetic age of the gods and the age of the heroes are devised, developed, and defended as institutions by the minority ruling class of heroes who founded the nation. As soon as the people—the original slaves (*famuli*) and later plebeians—become conscious of themselves as such, it is they who appeal to reason to support the cause of freedom against the rigid restrictions to which the imagination of the aristocrats had given birth. A stand-off occurs between the rigidly controlled fantasy of the primordial aristocratic era and the emancipated reason of the democratic Enlightenment. One can imagine analogous (although hardly entirely similar) systems of thought emerging during the later Romantic era, but not until after Rousseau's concept of nature had lost its purchase as a result of the French Revolution.

Here we must add that Vico's system eliminates the conceptual possibility of an original, invariable human nature. Human nature exists *only* as the sum of its historical variations, which are guided by specific providential laws. It is thus a *storia ideale eterna* (eternal ideal history). Vico's terminology varies here (as it does everywhere), to be sure. Sometimes he invests the word "nature" with meanings that he has taken over from others, meanings that, although they make sense each time in the context and can thus be easily understood, do not really fit with his system overall. In his system, and also at many typical individual moments in the *New Science*, the expression "human nature" means no more than the historical development of the human race—and occasionally also a specific moment in this development. Because at every stage of culture, people have a corresponding "nature," there can never be any perfect or ideal form of the state, other than the form of the state that history offers up at the time. World history is always in motion, but this motion is itself an eternal Platonic state.

Here we stumble upon something that is stable amidst all this movement: human development in its three stages and eras is *storia ideale eterna*. Modeled upon the idea of a plan of development determined by Providence, it recurs eternally whenever and wherever human societies emerge and, once the three eras have run their course, the cycle begins again and in the same way. All people and all nations thus follow the same pattern of development— *una comune natura delle nazioni*. This is not to say that Vico would have denied that there are individual nations. He acknowledged variability within the general course of development. But he recognized this variability only insofar as it did not really concern or interest him. *Natura di cose*, he said in the fourteenth Principle, *altro non è che nascimento di esse in certi tempi e con certe guise, le quali sempre che sono tali, indi tali e non altre nascon le cose* [The nature of institutions is nothing but their coming into being at certain times and in certain guises. Whenever the time and guise are thus and so, such and not otherwise are the institutions that come into being (*The New Science of Giambattista Vico*, Thomas Goddard Bergin and Max Harold Fisch, trans. [Ithaca and New York: Cornell University Press, 1948] 64). The first part of this important sentence—the nature of things is nothing other than their birth at a specific time and under specific conditions—provides the foundation for historical relativism, or perspectivism. The second part—when the times and circumstances are a certain way, things always emerge from them in a certain way and in no other—subjects the nature that has become history to a set of laws. Vico's main concern is with these laws and thus with the universal, and he attempts to capture both them and it in an invariable and concrete pattern of development. By contrast, the interest in the national spirit championed by Herder and the Romantics remained an abstraction and was ambiguous when it came to the general development of the human race. They devoted both all their fondest attention and all their concrete research to divining the individual genius of periods and peoples by means of a discriminating hermeneutics. They were successful and extremely influential when they did so, for it was thus that they established the modern historical sciences across the disciplines, in historical linguistics, in the history of literature and the arts, and in the history of law. Vico also distinguished between individual epochs, but he was committed to understanding the character of each one as no more than a specific stage of an ever-recurring process of development. He disregarded the individuation of nations entirely. For the Romantics, the spirit of a nation was individual. This was the essence of its existence. Such an essence is alien to Vico, for there was no way, at the beginning of the eighteenth century and in the Cartesian and, moreover, clerical and absolutist atmosphere of the Kingdom of Naples that a sensuous, or a *self-consciously* sensuous, national consciousness could have emerged. The kind of feelings of loyalty to place or to nature that began to emerge after 1750 in the North were unknown to Vico. Vico harbored no national feelings—or, if he did, it was only of the philological, humanist sort that we see in his text, *De antiquissima Italorum sapientia*. That he was completely indifferent to the idea of the individual nation and the idea of a *Volk* is probably the most important reason why the German Romantics had to remain ignorant of him. His world may have borne great similarities to the world of Herder and the Romantics. But it was filled with an air they could not breathe.

After all, the Romantics also wanted to be the educators of their nation. the *New Science* is nothing but—and cannot be anything but—theory. Its ultimate goal was knowledge alone. By contrast, the Germans of the Storm and Stress movement and of early Romanticism formed a movement. They wanted to have an impact, to educate, to stir people up. Their slogan was no longer Rousseau's "Back to nature!" Rather, it was back to *origins*, to the spirit of the nation and its traditions, to the true sources of poetry and life.

Such pronouncements would have been entirely out of the question for Vico, not only because his personality and position were very different, but also because, according to his theory of history, a self-chosen return to any earlier stage was impossible. He too of course believed that the poetic-imaginative creative powers of the human race had been far greater in earlier times than in the age of rational and civilized behavior. He stood in awe of his poetic progenitors of the heroic age, admired them above everything else, and his opinion of elegant, rationalistic poetry was every bit as damning as Herder's. But he would have considered it meaningless to critique civilization as such, for it was his conviction that people were not at liberty to develop in this or that way according to their whims. To return, in the midst of an age of rational high culture, to the poetry of the primordial heroes and to the original spirit of the nation was not an option, even if, as Vico admits, much of this earlier stage of culture lived on in the peasants and among the lower classes in general. But once a nation reaches the highest stage of civilization, it cannot decide of its own accord to return to an earlier stage. The only way back is an involuntary or necessary one based on the destruction of that higher culture and the reemergence of a new barbarism as part of the eternal recurrence of all human affairs. Vico's history was not teleological; he did not even acknowledge an ideal form of the historical condition. He had no deep-seated sympathy for high culture. Without a doubt, his heart belonged to the primordial poetic-heroic age.

If it is the case, as we have been making every effort to show, that Vico sets no great store by individual nations and thus pays no attention to the idea of a national spirit (at least in terms of the way the Romantics understood it), the question remains: What concept occupies the position in his system that the spirit of the nation occupied for them? What concept allowed him to create a unified idea of the "spirit of the times"? It would seem that for Vico that concept was one immediately identifiable as being rational, even juridical, in origin. It was the concept of consent, agreement, and consensus, of the general agreement of many or even all individuals, which he understood as the *senso comune*. This is not to say that Vico did not broaden this concept in his own way. It originates in the realm of the concrete and the practical and then becomes metaphysical. But Vico's metaphysics remained classically rational, characterized by clarity of form and far removed from the earthy vapors of anything that smacked of the *völkisch*. To clarify what Vico meant by consensus, we must explain both its origins and its function in a wider context.

One occasionally reads that Vico met with opposition from Enlightenment reason—as did the later founders of the philosophy of history in Germany. But rationalism had changed considerably by Herder's day. It had been tempered by empiricism and developments in biology and was no longer Cartesian. Instead, it much more decisively flew the banner of the Enlightenment and had also already been concerning itself with history for a long time.

A series of projects had begun laying the groundwork for a philosophy of history: Montesquieu's attempt to distinguish constitutions from one another on empirical and biological grounds, Voltaire's writings on cultural history, even (and not least) Rousseau's anti-historicism. It is obvious that the special conditions obtaining in Germany were ripe for such projects, since it was there that reflection on the unique personality of the nation and its past had just begun. In Vico's youth, however, and in Italy, Cartesianism still ruled, with its analytic and deductive methods and its privileging of those sciences that were especially appropriate for it, namely mathematics and physics. History and philology were a source of suspicion; they were thought to be of no value. In fact, not even the political theorists of the seventeenth century were really interested in history. They saw in it nothing but a wasteland of errors, the antithesis of nature or reason, or both. Of course, it was at exactly this same time that the Maurists were developing methods of historical source study. Nevertheless, none of the prerequisites existed for the development of a philosophy of history, for an understanding of the laws of human society through historical research. Vico devoted considerable energy and time, indeed, the greater part of his life, to freeing himself from Cartesian influences as well as from the influence of natural law. The breakthrough and expression of his own thoughts required this. But it is not surprising that traces of Cartesianism and of natural law continued to be visible everywhere in his work. Ultimately, and after a long struggle, he finally freed himself from the deductive Cartesian method of epistemology by turning to a variation of the old theological, but also agnosticizing, proposition (which was originally both Neoplatonic and indebted to Avicenna): only the creator can know his own creation. Knowing something that one has not created is impossible. Vico ultimately varied this theorem in a way that was so supremely satisfying for him that he could never speak of it without great excitement. He claimed that God alone created the physical world, *il mondo della natura* [the world of nature]. Thus God alone can know it. But the world of history and politics, *il mondo delle nazioni* [the world of nations], *can* be known by man, since it was he who created it. It must thus be possible to locate the basic principles of history in the formative powers of the human mind (*dentro le modificazioni della nostra medesima mente umana* [within the modifications of our own human mind]) precisely because it is there that historical phenomena find their origins. Whatever we can find in our own nature and also mobilize, so to speak, as a means of understanding human history is that which is common to and universally agreed upon by all men, the *senso comune* [common sense]. This is the source of natural law. And yet, just like human nature or natural law, the *senso comune* is not static. Rather, it is the very embodiment of a process of change that occurs with regularity and according to set rules. But each and every stage of the process, insofar as it is human and man-made, must be capable of being discovered in the human mind. All nations, regardless of the stage of development in which they find themselves, agree about the "unthinking judgment on all that is necessary and useful in human life." With Providence acting as the instructor, men are thus able to establish the *certum* (the certain, the positive, the institutional) in their natural law, even already at those points in their development where they do not possess the enlightened ability to form judgments from reason. Natural law can thus be understood as embodying a unified and substantial whole both at each individual stage of the process of man's development and in the entire course of that development overall.

This theory is extremely speculative. And it creates problems when we consider the relationship between immanence and transcendence because it does not entirely explain the relation between man and Providence in the creation of history. Vico often maintains that Providence works through purely historical and human means in the natural course of events and their unfolding. Here the question poses itself as to why Providence would then still be necessary at all. Modern readers have often posed this question. Vico's idea of Providence as a force that operates on the transcendental plane, but is visible as immanent and in the world, unfortunately no longer really makes sense for us. He often comments on the degree to which the human race is involved in the creation of history by maintaining something along the following lines: unlike Providence, the human race for the most part engages in activity without knowing what the outcome of its actions will be. We must supply what Vico does not articulate here, namely that there must be individual people—in all likelihood only in ages of Enlightenment, after the entire process of development has run its course—who, perhaps like Vico himself, can take care of the business of discovering all of the individual stages in their—and his—own mind, the business, that is, of consciousness and understanding.

In any case, this theory proved very fruitful for Vico. It is also, to my mind, very productive in general. Every time we rediscover history in our own minds, this discovery becomes a moment of self-knowledge, the germ of a theory of historical understanding in a moment of self-knowledge. Synthetic understanding emerges out of one's own experience, from the inside, so to speak, in a way that extra-human matters can never be understood. This is a method that, consciously or unconsciously, we always use. Understanding the facts of human history, in either the past or the present, is not a matter of unmediated observation of empirical data. Rather, we must also evoke those facts in a way that reproduces them, communicating meaning and then testing that meaning against that which we have experienced ourselves. And because everything that is produced by this process of mediation and understanding flows directly out of the experience of the person engaged in the acts of mediation and understanding, there is no way to test it other than by securing the agreement of others who are likewise trying to understand. This is consensus, *il senso comune.*

It is nearly impossible to ignore how foreign this kind of conceptual apparatus is to the *senso comune* of early Romanticism and how different it is from the idea of the *Volksgeist*, the spirit of the nation. Vico's system is derived from legal terminology and rises to a level of purely rational and rarified speculation. Its focus is the universal, not the particular.

All of these reflections come down to the same thing. The similarities between the ways in which Vico thinks, on the one hand, and the ways in which Herder and the Romantics think, on the other, are astounding. And if Vico's frenetic and cluttered baroque periods were not so very different from the youthful agitation that characterizes Herder's style (which is full of exclamation marks), their formulations would often be nearly identical. If one conducts a material history of ideas, and especially if one uses modern terminology in place of the terms that the authors originally used, the essential distinctions can no longer be seen at all. It is nevertheless the case that differences do exist in the points of departure and intentions, differences that throw up a wall between the two worlds of thought that is hard to scale. Rousseau, Ossian, Pietism, and the awakening of the Nordic-German national sentiment created a different set of assumptions from those produced by southern Italian Catholicism, Cartesianism, and natural law. Both Vico and Herder conceived of the unfolding of history in ways that had not occurred to anyone before them. In both cases, these ways were intensively speculative. But the nature of the speculation was different. Vico does his best to approach his subject as rationally as he can. He would have preferred above all else to have been able to write a geometry of history, and it was against his will that intuition and empathy broke through. For him, historical development is structured sociologically, economically, and politically. He attributes no ideal goal to history. What he is looking for are history's eternal laws. Herder, on the other hand, consciously endorses intuition and pursues empathy of a sensuous kind. For him, the structures of development are at once biological and emotional; the ideal of education was also involved on all fronts. His goal is national individuation and the emergence of the spirit of the nation within the framework of a religion of Humanity. What would Herder or the Romantics have said to Vico's idea of an eternal Platonic state, in which individuality—of either the nation or of individual human beings— did not matter in the least? It is just as well, then, that Herder and his supporters paid him no mind.

6

The Idea of the National Spirit as the Source of the Modern Humanities

The idea of a national spirit (*Volksgeist*) involves the claim that poetry is the first language, the mother tongue of the human race, and that it emerges spontaneously out of the depths of the national soul. It is an idea conceived as both universally human and as proper to the traditions of an individual nation. It presumes that when- and wherever a human community becomes conscious of itself as human, poetry emerges as the expression of this consciousness. When- and wherever this happens, poetry takes on a form appropriate to the specific nature and fate of each individual nation. Moreover, this idea applies not only to poetry in the narrow sense of the word, but also to all modes of civilized behavior. For, in those prehistoric times when poetry developed as the original language of the human race, all civilized behavior was poetic: religion, law, political institutions, art—and of course language too, since poetry was humanity's first language. Finally, the idea of a national spirit applies not just to the earliest periods of civilized behavior. Rather, it suggests that a national spirit and its manifestations develop organically alongside both the nature and the fate of a particular nation as long as its development continues in an undisturbed and unhampered way. Yet, according to this theory, some kind of disturbance or interruption, or, at the very least, impairment, occurs almost inevitably in the course of a culture's progress whenever contrived rules and homogenizing rationalistic principles attempt to guide or limit that course. From time to time, these kinds of restrictions even succeed in rendering the culture extinct. Reason, when it is of this calculating, rule-imposing sort, is thus the archenemy of the national spirit, while the most natural flowering of mankind's creative powers, those of the imagination, takes place in prehistoric times, when reason is not yet fully formed. Accordingly, the way to heal and restore a culture that has been undermined by the calculations of reason is to return to its sources, to the national spirit of prehistoric times.

The idea of a national spirit first appeared among those who were involved in the pre-Romantic movements of the eighteenth century as a reaction against the normative aesthetics that dominated at the time, the tendency and taste associated with French Classicism. More generally, it was a reaction against the rationalistic reform movements of the Enlightenment, which considered human nature to be either entirely reasonable or else capable of being brought to heel by the rational will of those who made the laws whenever it was under the sway of irrational powers. We find the first traces of this new understanding of man and history very early on, already in the 1720s, and where one might least expect it, indeed, in a place where all the conditions required for the emergence of an idea like that of a national spirit seemed in short supply, namely, in the late Baroque in southern Italy, in Vico. Soon thereafter the movement can be observed in England (indeed, in a number of locations by the 1750s). Directly following, we find it in Germany in the work of Justus Möser and in the circle around Herder to which Goethe also belonged. Opponents of the French Revolution brought the new idea into a very current form in both England and in Germany. But it was perfected only in Germany, for it was there that the scholarly approach and way of thinking that we now know as historicism emerged. It started with Möser and Herder and then was further developed by poets, critics, philologists, historians, and students of law during the era of the Romantic Restoration (here we think of the Schlegels, Schelling, the Grimm brothers, Savigny, Puchta, and so on). During this period, my own discipline of Romance philology also began to develop as, one might say, a small branch on the great tree of Romantic historicism. It was founded by Friedrich Diez, who had been inspired by Goethe, August Wilhelm Schlegel, and Jacob Grimm. But developments did not stop there. Historical-comparative linguistics and literary studies in general, history as a discipline (as it was just beginning), and historical jurisprudence—all these were the products of historical philology, or, if you prefer, of philology as history. Finally, the philosophy of Hegel perfected historicism. It was a philosophy that discovered in the principles of historicism the dialectical possibility of a history of the present and the future. It was nevertheless also this philosophy that—precisely in perfecting historicism—also began to undermine it in dialectical fashion when it attempted to reshape the irrationality that lay at historicism's very core into a rational system.

The idea of a national spirit dominated the entire nineteenth century. Its impact was most obvious (at least for philologists) in the various theories that emerged regarding the origins of poetry in premodern times, and especially in the Western Middle Ages. All nineteenth-century theories concerning the topic were variations on this idea. Medieval poetry emerged out of the very depths of a nation's traditions, out of its folk songs and legends, in the pre-literate periods and as oral tradition. According to these theories, the written versions preserved for us are the work of relatively late editors who assembled the individual scattered pieces into a whole, all the while adapting the finished product to the needs of their own relatively distinct times and mores. A great deal of the original content was lost as a result. Vico had himself already made the same argument about Homer. For the Romantic and post-Romantic philologists, who were otherwise absolutely devoted to particulars, the subject was a free-for-all of often undisciplined (and occasionally also pedantic) speculation. For, since no one could actually observe the medieval national spirit at work (there was very little evidence of its activity, its dating was unreliable, and its interpretation a matter of debate), there was ample room for conjectures of all sorts. The reaction began to set in around 1900, inspired partly by the ambition to compete with the precision of the natural sciences and partly also by French nationalism—for it seemed that in Europe, the "epic" national spirit meant the *German* national spirit.

In its campaign against the theory of a national spirit, this early form of positivism took as its first and most important target the French *chanson de geste*. The most effective warrior in the campaign was Joseph Bédier, with his important and intellectually stimulating work (he was also an excellent writer). He founded an entire school of thought that persists in France to this day, a school that claims that the *chanson de geste* was a product of the twelfth century and can thus be most adequately explained in terms of expectations proper to that century and as the work of *individual* poets. Seeking to undermine all of the indices that spoke against such ideas, this school considered the precursors hypothesized by the Romantic philologists to be the products of a speculative and unscholarly approach. Soon enough there were of course others who began to express similar ideas about early lyric. Although the ideas associated with Bédier never really caught on among German philologists (and even less among the Spanish), it did succeed in discrediting the expression "national spirit." (Of course the caricature of the idea for which National Socialism is responsible also contributed substantially to this disrepute.) Soon no philologist who thought anything of himself would have dared to have recourse to it—not even those who attacked Bédier's theories with both energy and success.

I do not wish to dwell on this topic here. It goes without saying that Bédier and his followers—but most of all Bédier himself—contributed a great deal to our understanding of the literature of the twelfth century. But he did not disprove the theory of a national spirit. It is absurd to suppose that a great nation would have gone many centuries without a poetry in its own mother tongue. One need only listen to oneself stating the axiom that when there is no evidence for a fact, its nonexistence is proven, in order to understand that this is a fallacy. Happily, evidence is not entirely lacking in this case; indeed, more and more new evidence surfaces all the time. A second fallacy lies at the heart of Bédier's reasoning as well, namely the notion that if a work of art reflects the spirit of the time when it was written down, we may conclude that its subject had never been dealt with before. According to this logic, one might as well conclude from the fact that Goethe's *Faust* clearly mirrors the period around 1800 and deals with problems of that time that neither chapbooks nor puppet shows had ever existed prior to that date. It is obvious that we need to rethink the theory of a national spirit in connection with the origins of medieval poetry and especially of French Provençal poetry. The earlier theories are simply too sentimental, too idyllic, and too purist.

And yet, Bédier and those who came after him are not my concern here. I have only mentioned them in order to explain the suspicion harbored by many philologists about the expression, "national spirit." Recently, and partly as a result of the work of Ernst Robert Curtius, this wariness has prevented even opponents of both Bédier's and Curtius's work from using the term. In my estimation, this must change. The history of the world has seen to it that the idea of a national spirit developed by the pre-Romantics and Romantics awakened an understanding for the individuality of nations and their cultures. That is, hermeneutical perspectivism, on which all historical humanistic disciplines are based, grew out of this idea. This fact explains the origins of the almost automatic expectation we now have of ourselves and of our academic colleagues that we understand the phenomena we study in terms of the specific assumptions of the times and social context out of which they arose. It also explains the fact that we no longer consider the artifacts of foreign cultures to be curiosities, but, rather, variations of a common humanity, each with its own beauty, virtue, vitality, and capacity to evolve organically, to which we must surrender ourselves if we are to be permitted to understand them. This expectation is rooted in the idea of a national spirit as it was entertained among the Romantics and is the fundamental assumption of all of our interpretive work, regardless of the historical object upon which we are focused. It is not enough to say that this hermeneutical perspectivism is decisive only for the work of those in the humanities. It is important for all contemporary Western civilization insofar as its members consider themselves part of the "educated public." And who would not like to belong to this group in some way or another these days?

A great number of our contemporaries who may be counted among the "educated" do not find it in the least bit difficult to admire, in equal measure, the Gregorian chant, Bach, Mozart, and Ravel. They read Aeschylus, Dante, Chinese poetry, Shakespeare, Racine, and Faulkner, and are equally keen to understand them all. They gaze upon Cretan-Minoan fresco paintings, Byzantine mosaics, Gothic sculpture, Dürer, Rembrandt, and Matisse at exhibits—often on the same day and in the same museum. It would never occur to them to think that a Turkish mosque, the temple to Poseidon at Paestum, and the cathedral at Reims might exclude one another aesthetically. The development of various means of transportation and the numerous ways of producing reproductions has of course contributed massively to this tumultuous confusion of cultures. Already in the sixteenth, seventeenth, and eighteenth centuries, however, cultures that were strangers to one another came into contact—some of them over the course of many years—as the result of war, missionary work, and travel. No one would have thought of considering or evaluating them as we do today. Moreover, a broader segment of the population today has developed a more acute understanding of foreign political, economic, and general social relations. Of course, historical understanding comes to a halt as soon as political enmities and corresponding forms of propaganda rear their heads.

I consider the discovery of historical perspectivism based on the idea of a national spirit to be one of the most important events in the history of the humanities. It allowed us to enlarge our understanding of how to orient ourselves in the historical world in ways not unlike those in which Copernicus's discovery allowed us to find our place in the astrophysical world. I have long been amazed that this insight has been known (albeit in a vague way) for so many years—Troeltsch, Croce, and Meinecke all wrote important works about it—and yet has so seldom really been emphasized or brought to our attention. All pre-Romantic humanistic study falls short of being real scholarship (and is in this sense prescientific) because it relies on normative thinking and is narrowly circumscribed. It is certainly true that Renaissance philologists and the Benedictine monks of Saint Maur had already worked out the technical details of how to engage in critical philology and archeology. But without the turn to the idea of a national spirit undertaken by the Romantics, all this would have led only to learned collections of the sort that abounded in the seventeenth and eighteenth centuries and never to an organically integrated history of the human race.

One might easily pose the question why the West—indeed, why the human race in general, so far as I can tell—came so late to a recognition of genetic perspectivism. As superb as the ancient historians and critics of culture were, it is difficult to discern even a hint of such an approach in their work. Even their most lofty achievements remained on the level of morality and the universal. They were never concerned with the individual in any genetic-developmental sense. Over the course of the Middle Ages, the European historical and geographical horizon was entirely too limited to engage in empirically-based historical perspectivism. Nevertheless, it seems to me that a kind of proto-perspectivism can be located in the way the Christian historical imagination organized time as a sequence of epochs running from Original Sin through to the Coming of Christ, and from there to the Resurrection and the Last Judgment. This kind of historical sequencing, thinking in stages, is far less mystical—and much more historically informed—than the corresponding divisions of time that one finds in classical antiquity.

The openness to historical diversity and the impulse toward perspectivism are most pronounced in the Joachimite movements of the thirteenth century, and above all in Dante's *Divine Comedy*. With its focus on eternal salvation (which is also the historical goal of mankind), the entire poem is of course constrained by eschatological norms. Be that as it may, it is nevertheless shocking that genetic perspectivism failed to emerge during the Renaissance. One would have thought that the sudden, powerful expansion of the historical and geographical horizon that began with the Crusades and that lasted up to the Age of Exploration would have opened people's eyes to the historical diversity of our planet and encouraged them to take on a perspectival, individualizing inquiry of the world. Moreover, it was Humanism that for the first time created the practical and empirical possibility of understanding the ages as layered in its idea of a Greco-Roman Golden Age, now long gone, followed by a dark cultural void that separated the present (e.g., Humanist) era from the classical past. The temporal and spatial difference between cultures in fact presented itself as a great problem for the writers of the sixteenth century, and we often find comments in their work that betray a sense of perhaps not quite historical perspectivism, but certainly of historical relativism. Moreover, their historical-geographical intuition was by then, for all intents and purposes, essentially modern. We need only to compare the sweeping historical-geographical breadth we find in Shakespeare with medieval descriptions of foreign cultures composed before 1300. It becomes obvious how superior to the medieval writers Shakespeare's perspectival vision is (in spite of the mistakes he makes in the details). Yet, in spite of this favorable context—and in spite of these fledgling attempts—historical perspectivism was not able to come into its maturity at that time.

Two powerful movements prevented this development. One was the admiration of the Humanists for classical antiquity—to the exclusion of anything else. This led to the notion that only ancient works, indeed, only the culture of antiquity, could be taken as a model. The result was an aesthetics based on imitating these models. And nothing is more antithetical to historical perspectivism than an imitative aesthetics, for it proposes absolute standards of the beautiful and the just and rejects everything that does not correspond to them. This was the origin of the normative aesthetics of French Classicism, which was avowedly anti-perspectival. The other movement that stood in the way of historical perspectivism was almost even more powerful than Humanism, because it was far more widespread. This was the revival of the old conceit of an absolute human nature.

PART II

Time and Temporality in Literature

7

Figura

I. From Terence to Quintilian

Etymologically, *figura* comes from the same root as *fingere, figulus, factor,* and *effigies* and means "three-dimensional shape." The word is first attested in Terence, who in his *Eunuchus* (l. 317) writes of a girl that she has a *nova figura oris* [an unusually shaped face]. The following fragment from Pacuvius (270/1; cf. Otto Ribbeck, *Scaenicae Romanorum poesis fragmenta* [3rd ed. (Leipzig: B. G. Teubner, 1897)] 1:110) dates from approximately the same time:

> Barbaricam pestem subinis nostris optulit
> Nova figura factam. . . .[1]

> (To our spears, she presents a foreign plague,
> fashioned in a new shape. . . .)

It is unlikely that Plautus was familiar with the word. He uses *fictura* twice (*Trinummus* 365, and *Miles Gloriosus* 1189), both times admittedly more to express the *act* of making an image than its result. Later *fictura* occurs only very rarely.[2] But the very mention of *fictura* immediately alerts us to a special feature of *figura*. According to Ernout-Meillet's *Dictionnaire étymologique de la langue latine* (346), *figura* is derived directly from the root and not, as is the case with *natura* and other words that have the same ending, from the supine. Stolz-Schmalz attempted to explain this development as an adaptation of *effigies* (*Lateinische Grammatik*, 5th ed. 219). In any case, this special form of the word expresses something animated and lively, open-ended and playful, and the high elegance of its sound seems to have seduced many a poet.

Translations of Auerbach's sources are cited according to the editions listed in the appendix of this book, with some amendments. Where no published translation is listed here or in the text, the translations are my own.—Trans.

[1] Paul Friedlaender informs me that *barbarica pestis* refers in all likelihood to the stinger of a stingray by which Odysseus was mortally wounded. *Subinis* is uncertain.

[2] It reappears in late antiquity (Chalcidius and Isidore) and the Middle Ages in wordplay involving *pictura*. Cf. E. R. Curtius in the *Zeitschrift für Romanische Philologie* 58 (1938) 45.

It may be mere chance that the two oldest occurrences of the word combine *nova* with *figura*. But even if it is chance, it is significant that they do, for the idea of something that is new and appears for the first time, of something that creates change in things that normally resist change, marks the entire history of the word.

For us, this history begins with the Hellenization of Roman education in the last century before Christ. Three authors played a decisive role: Varro, Lucretius, and Cicero. We can of course no longer say with certainty what they may have taken over from earlier sources that have not survived. However, Lucretius's and Cicero's contributions are so distinctive and also so independent of one another that we must credit them with a high degree of individual creativity in the forging of its meaning.

Varro displays the least such independence. In his work, *figura* sometimes takes on the meaning of "external appearance," even "outline,"[3] as it begins to shed its origin in the more limited concept of a three-dimensional shape. But this appears to have been a general trend (the causes of which I will return to below) in which Varro does not seem to have participated in any particularly noticeable way. He was, after all, a student of etymology and very conscious of the origins of words: *fictor cum dicit fingo*[,] *figuram imponit* (the *fictor* [image-maker], when he says, "*Fingo*" [I shape], puts a *figura* [shape] on the object); *De lingua latina* [On the Latin Language] 6.78. This may be why the word for the most part does have the idea of something three-dimensional about it whenever he uses it in connection with living creatures and objects. Just how much of an impact this idea still had is sometimes difficult to judge. For example, Varro says that when buying slaves, one ought to consider not just their *figura*, but also their qualities. In the case of horses, one ought to attend to their age, in the case of cocks, to their value as breeders, and, in the case of apples, to their fragrance (ibid., 9.93). Of a star, he writes that it has changed its *colorem* [color], its *magnitudinem* [size], its *figuram* [shape], and its *cursum* [path] (as quoted in Augustine, *De civitate Dei* 21.8). Finally, he compares the forked posts of a stockade with the *figura* of the letter "V" in *De lingua latina* 5.17. The term becomes very much less three-dimensional as soon as he begins to discuss the forms of words. In *De lingua latina* 9.21, for example, he writes something along these lines: We have inherited new shapes for containers from the Greeks; why do we then resist taking over from them new forms of words (*formae vocabulorum*), as if these forms were somehow toxic? *Et tantum inter duos sensus interesse volunt, ut oculis semper aliquas figuras supellectilis novas conquirant, contra auris expertes velint esse?* [And do they claim that there is so great a difference between the two senses [sc., sight and hearing], that for their eyes they are always seeking some new

---

[3] Many of the later definitions move in the direction of this meaning; see the *Thesaurus Linguae Latinae* 722.54.

Figura | 67

shapes of their furniture, but they wish their ears to have no share in similar novelties?] Here, we are already very close to the idea that we can also *hear* "figures." It is important, moreover, to know that Varro did not hesitate to use *figura* and *forma* interchangeably to mean "shape." This was, incidentally, quite common, and in doing so, he resembles all those other Latin authors who, because they were not philosophers, did not command the same precise terminology as the specialists. Strictly speaking, *forma* means "mold," in French *moule*. It is thus related to *figura* as the hollow mould relates to the three-dimensional object that it is used to make. We nevertheless seldom find any suggestion of this distinction, at most perhaps in Gellius (*Attic Nights* 3.10.7): *Semen genitale fit ad capiendam figuram idoneum* [Trans: sic; Gellius's text reads: *genitale semen . . . fitque ad capiendam figuram idoneum* (the life-giving seed . . . is rendered fit to take shape)].

As I have already suggested, Varro's real innovation—which then obscured the original meaning of the word—was a grammatical one. He was the first to use *figura* as a grammatical, inflected, and derived form. For him, *figura multitudinis* means "the form of the plural," *alia nomina quinque habent figuras* (9.52) [other nouns have five forms . . .], which means that other nouns have five declined forms. This usage had a significant impact (cf. *Thesaurus Linguae Latinae*, [s.v.] *figura*, III A 2a, col. 730 and 2e, col. 734). *Forma* was also often used in this way, beginning with Varro, but *figura* occurs more frequently and seems to have been preferred by the Latin grammarians. How was it possible that both words, and especially *figura*, whose form so clearly calls its origin to mind, could so quickly take on such a purely abstract meaning? This happened because of the Hellenization of Roman education. Greek had an incomparably richer technical rhetorical vocabulary than Latin, and also a great many words for the concept of form: *morphē, eidos, schēma, typos,* and *plasis,* to name only a few of the most important. As Platonic and Aristotelian vocabulary was expanded in subsequent philosophy and rhetoric, each of these words was assigned its special domain, with a clear distinction between *morphē* and *eidos,* on the one hand, and *schēma,* on the other. The former refer to the form, or idea, that informs matter, the latter to the strictly sensible and perceptible shape of this form. Aristotle's *Metaphysics* (Z 3.1029) is the *locus classicus* for this differentiation; there, he discusses *ousia* [essence] and in this context identifies *morphē* as the *schēma tēs ideas* [the shape of the form]. Aristotle thus uses *schēma* to designate one of the categories of quality that can be perceived by the senses and in combination with *megethos* [quantity], *kinēsis* [motion], and *chrōma* [color], as we already came upon in Varro. The Latin word *forma* came almost automatically to take the place of *morphē* and *eidos,* since it contained the idea of a model from the very start. Even though *exemplar* is sometimes used in this context, we most often find *figura* for *schēma.* And because *schēma* in the sense of "external shape" had become so widely used by the Greeks in their scientific terminology—in grammar, rhetoric, logic, mathematics, and astronomy—Latin always employed *figura* for this purpose.

Thus it happened that alongside—and also taking precedence over—its original meaning of three-dimensionality, shape, *figura* came to signify a far more general concept. First, it designated something that could be perceived with the senses, second, it was a grammatical, rhetorical, logical, mathematical and then, later, even a musical and choreographic form. The original three-dimensional sense is of course never entirely relinquished; *typos* as "imprint" and *plasis* as "three-dimensional shape" were often rendered with *figura* as a result of the word root *fig-*. Indeed, it was against the background of the meaning of *typos* that *figura* came to mean the "imprint of a seal." The metaphor has a lofty history, beginning with Aristotle in *De memoria et reminiscentia* 450a31 (*he kinēsis ensēmainetai hoion typon tina tou aisthēmatos* [the movement suggests some imprint of the thing that is being perceived]), extending through St. Augustine (*Epistolae* 162.4) and Isidore (*Differentiae* 1.528), and down through Dante, who writes *come figura in cera si suggella* [like a figure (stamped) in wax] at *Purgatory* 10.45 and *Paradise* 27.62.[4] Yet, in addition to its sense of three-dimensionality, *typos* was also significant for *figura* because of its suggestion of universality, exemplarity, and law (compare how it appears together with *nomikōs* [legally] in Aristotle, *Politics* 2.7.1341b31). This in turn contributed to effacing the distinction between it and *forma*—which of course had only been a subtle one at best. The association with words like *plasis* intensified the tendency in *figura*—which had probably been there since the beginning, but emerged only gradually—to expand in the direction of "statue," "picture," and "portrait," allowing it to encroach upon the territory of *statua* as well as of *imago*, *effigies*, *species*, and *simulacrum*. Thus, although we can in general say that the Latin *figura* is used in place of the Greek *schēma*, the power of the word, the *potestas verbi*, is by no means spent in this substitution. *Figura* is, moreover, not only occasionally more oriented towards the sense of three-dimensionality; it is also more dynamic and radiates out more forcefully than *schēma*. Of course, the Greek word *schēma* is itself more dynamic than the foreign loan-word *Schema* that

---

[4]In Aristotle (and also already in Plato), *typōi* means "in general," "in broad outlines," and "usually." His formulation—*pachulōs kai typōi* [in broad outline] [Nichomachean Ethics] 1094b20, or *kath' holou lechthen kai typōi* [given broadly and in a general outline] [ibid.] 1101a2—was handed down via Irenaeus 2.76 and Boethius, *Topicorum Aristoteles Interpretatio* 1.1, *Patrologia Latina* 64, paragraph 911B, to French and Italian. Compare Godefroy, s.v. "figural": *Il convient que la manière de proceder en ceste oeuvre soit grosse et figurele* [In this work one ought to proceed in a rough and figural way] or s.v. "figuralement": *Car la manière de produyre / Ne se peust monstrer ne deduyre / Par effet, si non seuelement / Grossement et figuralement* [For one can in effect neither show nor deduce the manner of producing except only roughly and figuratively" —Greban.] In Italian, the meaning of the combination *sommariamente e figuralemente* [summarily and figuratively] appears to have quite quickly no longer been understood. Compare Tommaseo-Bellini's *Dizionario della lingua Italiana*, s.v. "figura" 18.

Figura | 69

we use in German. In Aristotle, for example, the miming gestures that human beings—and especially actors—make are called *schēmata*. It is thus by no means odd to want to associate a sense of dynamic form with the word. It was nevertheless the word *figura*—rather than *schēma*—that developed this element of movement and transformation to a much greater extent.[5]

Lucretius uses *figura* in the Greek philosophical sense in a highly idiosyncratic, free, and significant way. He begins with the general concept of "figure," which can be found in all variations—from the actively three-dimensional (*manibus tractata figura* [a shape handled by hand], 4.230) to the purely geometrical outline (2.778, 4.503). He also takes the concept as it applies to the three-dimensional and visible sphere and uses it to refer to the acoustic realm, as when he writes of the *figura verborum* [the shape of words] (4.556).[6] But the important transition from a "figure" to its imitation, from original to copy, can be best understood when we turn to the passage in which he writes of the resemblance children bear to their parents, the mixing of seed, and matters of heredity. He discusses children who are *utriusque figurae* [images of each both], of the father and the mother and who often mirror back to us *proavorum figuras* [the images of earlier ancestors], and so on: *inde Venus varia producit sorte figuras* [from these Venus brings forth forms with varying lot] (4.1223). Here, we see that the playful association between original [*Urbild*] and copy [*Abbild*] can be captured successfully only in the Latin *figura*. *Forma* [form] and *imago* [likeness, image] are rooted much too firmly in the one or the other register of meaning. *Figura* gives a greater impression of something available to the senses. It is also more dynamic than *forma* and preserves the identity of the original more exactly than *imago*. We must of course also keep in mind, both here and later, especially when we come to the poets, that the three metrical feet of *figura*—regardless of the grammatical case in which the word appears—provide an excellent final foot for a hexameter.[7] Finally, a very special variant of the meaning of "copy" may be found in Lucretius's theory of the forms that peel off from things like thin

---

[5] There are meanings associated with *schēma* that are not found in or that did not have any afterlife in *figura*. Cf., for example, "constitution."

[6] Cf. also the shaping of tones at 2.412–13: *per chordas organici [quae] / mobilibus digitis expergefacta figurant* [which harpers awaken and shape on the strings with nimble fingers].

[7] Accordingly, *forma* appears primarily where only two syllables must be used. Thus, the relationship between the two words is relatively loose and variable, also in Lucretius. Nevertheless, we can find passages in his work where the two concepts are clearly differentiated, as when he speaks of the primal elements: *Quare . . . necesset / natura quoniam constant neque facta manu sunt / unius ad certam formam primordia rerum / dissimili inter se quaedam volitare figura* (2.377–80). [Wherefore . . . since they exist by nature and are not made by hand after the fixed model of one single atom, [they] must necessarily have some of them different shapes as they fly about.] As at 4.9, so here too *formae servare figuram* clearly expresses the well-known relationship between *morphē* and *schēma* that is quite clearly paraphrased by Ernout-Meillet, loc. cit., as *la configuration du moule*. Cf. Cicero, *De natura deorum* [On the Nature of the Gods] 1.90.

sheets of skin (*membranae*) and float about in the air. This is his version of the Democritean doctrine of "film images" (Diels), or *eidōla* [images], which are conceived of in materialist terms. Lucretius calls them *simulacra, imagines, effigias*, and sometimes also *figuras*. It is also in Lucretius that we first find *figura* used in the sense of "dream image," "a figment of one's imagination," and a "shadow of the dead."

These are all very vivid variations on the word. Each of them—original, copy, counterfeit, dream image—went on to become important, and all continue to remain intimately connected with *figura*. But the canniest use of the word is one that Lucretius makes in another context. It is well known that he espoused a cosmogony indebted to Democritus and Epicurus, in which the world consists of atoms. He calls the atoms *primordia, principia, corpuscula, elementa, semina* [first things, constituent principles, atoms, elements, seeds] and, in a general sense, the *corpora, quorum concursus motus ordo positura figurae*[8] [bodies whose clashings, motions, order, positions, [and] shapes] create all things] (1.685, [cf.] 2.1021). Although very tiny, the atoms are both made of matter and have form and can take on an infinite variety of shapes. And so it is that Lucretius also often refers to them as "shapes" (*figurae*), and that, conversely, one can often translate *figurae* with "atoms," as Diels has sometimes done.[9] An incalculable number of atoms are constantly in motion. They careen about in the void, first joining with and then repelling one another, in a dance of figures. But this use of the word does not appear to have survived Lucretius. The *Thesaurus Linguae Latinae* gives only a single passage in Claudian's *Rufinum* (1.17) from the end of the fourth century. Lucretius's most imaginative creation thus remained without any echo in this small field. Yet, of all the authors whose texts I have worked through as part of this project, his innovative contribution is without a doubt the most individually brilliant, if not the historically most important one.

We see represented in Cicero's frequent and extremely supple use of the word all of the versions of the concept of "figure" to which he was introduced in the course of his political, publicistic-rhetorical, legal, and philosophical work. His deployment of *figura* also allows us to catch a glimpse of his kind, excitable, and uncertain personality. For example, Cicero often deploys the word in reference to individuals, occasionally with a tone of pathos, as in *Pro Q. Roscio* 63: *portentum atque monstrum certissimum est, esse aliquem humana specie et figura, qui tantum immanitate bestias vicerit, ut . . .* [it is undoubtedly an unnatural and monstrous phenomenon, that a being of

---

[8] Munro has pointed out that the Democritean-Leucippean formula of *rhysmsos, tropē*, and *diathigē* is contained in the last three of these terms. (Cf. Diels, *Fragmente der Vorsokratiker*, 4th ed., vol. 2 [Berlin: Weidmann, 1922] 22). Aristotle uses *schēma* to capture *rhysmos* (*Metaphysics* 985b16 and 1042b11 and *Physics* 188a22). Lucretius translates the term with *figura*.

[9] I cite several passages here: Lucretius, *De rerum natura* 2.385, 514, 678, and 682; 3.190 and 246; and 6.770.

Figura | 71

human form and figure should exist so far surpassing the beasts in savagery as to . . .]. In the same text (20), he refers to a *tacita corporis figura* [the silent form of a man's body] as the dumb figure whose appearance already betrays the presence of a villain. One's limbs and inner organs, animals, tools, the stars—everything that is perceptible to the senses—have a *figura*, even the gods and the entire universe too. The meaning of things that appear to the senses, of things that have the appearance of something—which is intrinsic to the Greek word *schēma*—is also audible when Cicero writes of a tyrant that he has no more than the *figura hominis*, the shape of a man, or when he says that ideas of the gods as immaterial beings are theories without *figura* and *sensus*, without form and sensible content. It is rare to find a clear distinction between *figura* and *forma* in Cicero's work (see, for example, *De natura deorum* 1.90, and note 7 above). Neither is restricted to the visible or three-dimensional realm. For example, he writes of the *figura vocis* [the figure of the voice], indeed, even of a *figura negotii* [an aspect, or branch, of business]. Most often we read of the *figurae dicendi* [the figures of speech]. Geometric and stereometric shapes naturally also have a *figura*. But the notion of *figura* as a copy is hardly developed at all. To be sure, Cicero writes in *De natura deorum* (1.71) that Cotta, one of the interlocutors, might be able to understand the expression, *quasi corpus* [as if it relates to a body], when it is used of the gods, *si in cereis fingeretur aut fictilibus figuris* [if it related to waxen images of figures of earthenware] and, in *De divinatione* (1.23), that there is a *figura* of a piece of a cliff that is said to be not unlike a little Pan. But this is not really enough, for the *figura* being referred to here is the *figura* of the clay or the rock and not of that which it is supposed to represent.[10] Finally, Cicero uses the word *imagines* (*De divinatione* 2.137)[11] for the Democritean films that detach themselves from bodies (these were already mentioned in connection with Lucretius)—*a corporibus enim solidis et a certis figuris vult fluere imagines Democritus* [Democritus would have it that images emanate from material bodies and from actual forms], and usually refers to images of the gods as *signa* [images, statues] and never as *figurae*. An example of this is his nasty joke about Verres (*In Verrem* 2.3.89). Verres wanted to steal a valuable statue of a god in a Sicilian city, but fell in love with the wife of his host: *contemnere etiam signum illud Himerae iam videbatur quod eum multo magis figura et lineamenta hospitae delectabant* [for he now seemed to despise that statue of Himera because the *figura* and the features of his hostess pleased

---

[10] The transition from the "*figura* of the material" to the "*figura* of the object that is to be represented" occurred only gradually, first among the poets. Cf. (in addition to Lucretius) Catullus 64.50 and 64.265, and Propertius 2.6.133. Velleius Paterculus (1.11.4) uses *expressa similitudine figurarum* [those things that are clear in their resemblance to figures] to mean "portrait-like."

[11] Cf. also Cicero, *Ad familiares* 15.16. Also see, however, Quintilian 10.2.15: *illas Epicuri figuras* [those images of Epicurus].

him much more].[12] In any case, there are in his work never any bold innovations like those associated with the Lucretian basic elements.

It is thus clear that Cicero's contribution lay above all in his having introduced the materialist concept of *figura* into learned discourse and, by adapting it as needed, in having made it useful there. He employed it primarily
in his philosophical and rhetorical works, most frequently in his treatise
on the nature of the gods and, in doing so, strove to define what today we
might call a holistic notion of form. It was not only his well-known ambition to achieve rhetorical *copia* that most often prevented him from being
content just with the term *figura* and drove him instead to spin out strings of
numerous equivalent words aimed at expressing that whole: *forma et figura,
conformatio quaedam et figura totius oris et corporis, habitus et figura, humana species et figura, vis et figura* [form and figure, a certain shape and
figure of the whole face and body, the expression and figure, the human appearance and figure, power and figure], and many more. It is also impossible
to overlook his ambition to create a comprehensive theory of all existing
phenomena; his Roman readership may have been at least partially aware
of this plan. But Cicero was of course little served by either his native gifts
or his eclecticism in the project of either establishing a compelling concept
of form or working it out in detail, and so his project remained ill-defined.
We must be content with the wealth of formulations he collected in so even-
handed a way.

Yet there was something else that was ultimately much more important
for the further development of *figura*, and it was this: Cicero and the author
of the *Ad Herennium* were the first to use the term as a technical rhetorical
expression to designate the *schēmata* or the *charactēres lexeōs*, the three levels of style that are referred to as the *figura gravis, mediocris*, and *attenuata*
in the *Ad Herennium* (4.8.11) and as *plena, mediocris*, and *tenuis* in Cicero's
De oratore (3.199 and 3.212). By contrast, Cicero does not yet use *figura* in
a technical sense to mean the periphrastic or ornamental uses of speech,
which is to say the "figurative" forms of language in the proper sense of the
term, as is clearly pointed out by Vetter, who wrote the article on *figura* in
the *Thesaurus Linguae Latinae* (col. 731.80ff). Cicero was familiar with the
term as it was used in these ways and describes them in detail. But he does
not yet call them *figurae*, as later authors do. Rather, for the most part he
labels these *formae et lumina orationis* [the forms and ornaments of speech],
and so is also being pleonastic here. Moreover, he often uses the expression
figura dicendi [figure of speech]—indeed, mostly *forma et figura dicendi* [the
form and figure of speech]—in a non-technical way to refer simply to a kind
of eloquence and does so both in a general way, when he wants to express

---

[12] Later we find *figura* used fairly often to refer to "statues of gods"; Christian authors use it to
refer to pagan "idols," and also to the image stamped on a coin.

Figura | 73

that there are innumerable kinds of eloquence (*De oratore* 3.34), and in the case of individuals, as when he writes of Curio (ibid., 2.98): *suam quondam expressit formam figuramque dicendi* [he used to give expression to his own peculiar pattern and type of oratory]. Students learning to be orators in the schools, for whom Cicero's treatises on rhetoric soon became canonical, grew accustomed to this association.

By the end of the Republican period, *figura* had thus found a fixed place in both the language of the educated classes and the vocabulary of the philosophers. The possibilities for its use and meaning continued to expand during the first century of the imperial age. As one can easily imagine, it was the poets who were most involved in the playful association between original and copy, and in the shape-shifting and dream images that seem so deceptively real. Catullus already writes in a passage that is characteristic (63.62): *quod enim genus figurae est ego quod non obierim?* [For what kind of human figure is there which I had not?]. Likewise, Propertius (3.24.5)[13]: *Mixtam te varia laudavi semper saepe figura* [Oft did I praise the varied beauty of thy blending charms], or (4.2.21): *opportuna meast cunctis natura figuris* [my nature suits with every form]. We can also find the phrase *mutata figura* [the altered shape] at the beautiful close to the *Panegyricus in Messalam,* where it refers to the power of death to transform the human form. Vergil describes the phantom that tricks Turnus into thinking he is seeing Aeneas before him as *morte obita qualis fama est volitare figuras* [even like shapes that flit, 'tis said, when death is past] at *Aeneid* 10.641. The richest source for the use of *figura* as referring to the shifting of shapes is naturally Ovid. Although he of course never hesitates to use *forma* when he needs a two-syllable rather than a three-syllable word to fill out a verse, it is mostly *figura* that he chooses. He has at his fingertips an astonishing treasure trove of combinations in which the word appears, including *figuram mutare, variare, vertere, retinere, inducere, sumere, deponere, perdere* [of forms being altered, varied, altered, retained, introduced, assumed, shed, and lost]. The following brief anthology gives us an idea of the diversity of his usage:

Met. 1.436: *tellus . . . partimque figuras/rettulit antiquas* [the earth . . . in part restored the ancient shapes]

5.326: *. . . se mentitis superos celasse figuris* [and the gods hid themselves in lying shapes]

8.730: *Sunt[,] quibus in plures ius est transire figuras* [To others the power is given to assume many forms]

11.634: *. . . artificem simulatoremque figurae/Morphea* [(Morpheus) a cunning imitator of the human form]

---

[13] In Propertius and also in Ovid, *figurae* as "shapes" are sometimes transferred to mean "kinds" as opposed to "species." This same development occurred in French: *species-espèce.*

15.253: *ex aliis alias reparat natura figuras* [makes up forms from other forms]

15.172: *animam . . . in varias doceo migrare figuras* [the soul . . . passes into ever-changing bodies]

15.308: *lympha figuras/datque capitque novas* [water give[s] and receive[s] strange forms]

The image of the imprint of a seal may also be found in this delightful passage:

Utque novis facilis signatur cera figuris
Nec manet ut fuerat nec formas servat easdem,
Sed tamen ipsa eadem est. . . . (15.169–71)

[And, as the pliant wax is stamped with new designs, does not remain as it was before nor keeps the same form long, but is still the selfsame wax.]

We also find in Ovid a very clear rendering of *figura* as "copy," as in the *Fasti* 6.278: *globus immensi parva figura poli* [a globe [is] a small image of the vast vault of heaven], and in the *Heroides* (14.l.97), as well as in *Ex ponto* (2.8.64). *Figura* is also used as "letter," as was already the case in Varro: *ducere consuescat multas manus una figuras* (*Ars amatoria* 3.493) [Let one hand be accustomed to tracing many figures] and, finally, as a position in erotic play: *Venerem iungunt per mille figuras* (ibid., 2.679 [They embrace love in a thousand ways [sc., figures]]. Throughout Ovid's work, *figura* is animated, changeable, variable, and prone to deception. Manilius, the author of the *Astronomica*, also uses the word in an artful way. In addition to the meanings already indicated, it occurs in connection with the patterns of the stars and as a "constellation" (he also uses *signum* and *forma* in this way). Finally, we also find the term in Lucan and Statius when they write of a "figure in a dream."

In the work of the architect Vitruvius, we find something that is very different from these writers and from what we will see in the rhetoricians. For Vitruvius, a *figura* is an architectural and three-dimensional shape, or, at most, the copy or outline of such a shape. There is no sense of illusion or transformation here. Thus he does not mean "by simulation" when he writes *figurata similitudine* (7.5.1); rather, he means "by creating a similarity in form." *Figura* can often mean "floor plan," "plan" (*modice* [. . .] *picta operis futuri figura* [the quick depiction of the figure of a future work], 1.2.2); a *universae figurae species* or even a *summa figuratio* is the overall shape of a building or of a human being (he is fond of comparing the two from the point of view of symmetry). In spite of his occasionally mathematical deployment of the word, then, for Vitruvius and for contemporary architectural writers, *figura* (as well as *fingere*) has a very concrete and three-dimensional meaning. Compare Festus (98): *crustulum cymbi figura* [a pastry in the shape

Figura | 75

of a cup];[14] or Celsus (2.3.5f.): *venter reddit mollia, figurata* [the womb gives forth soft shapes]; and Columella (12.15.5): *ficos comprimunt in figuram stellarum floscularumque* [they press the figs into the shapes of stars and small flowers]. The elder Pliny is even more elaborate—also in this detail. Of course he belonged to a different social class and had been educated differently; his work includes every possible shading of the concepts of species and form. The transition from form to portrait can be nicely observed in the remarkable beginning of the thirty-fifth book of his *Natural History* where he laments the decline of portrait painting: *Imaginum quidem pictura, qua maxime similes in aevum propaga[ba]ntur figura[e]* . . . [The painting of portraits, used to transmit through the ages extremely correct likenesses of persons . . .] and a bit later, when he writes of the books illustrated with portraits that Varro had invented a way of producing: *imaginum amorem flagrasse quondam testes sunt* . . . *et Marcus Varro* . . . *insertis* . . . *septingentorum illustrium* . . . *imaginibus: non passus intercidere figuras, aut vetustatem aevi contra homines valere, inventor muneris etiam dis invidiosi, quando immortalitatem non solum dedit, verum etiam in omnes terras misit, ut prasentes esse ubique ceu di possent* [The existence of a strong passion for portraits in former days is evidenced by . . . Marcus Varro [who] . . . inserted . . . portraits of seven hundred famous people, not allowing their likenesses to disappear or the lapse of ages to prevail against immortality in men. Herein Varro was the inventor of a benefit that even the gods might envy, since he not only bestowed immortality but dispatched it all over the world, enabling his subjects to be ubiquitous, like the gods].

The legal literature of the first century contains a limited number of passages in which *figura* means "empty external form," or even "appearance," as in the *Digest* 28.5.70 (Proculus): *non solum figuras sed vim quoque condicionis continere* [to contain not just the formal dimension, but also the actual force of the contract] and *Digest* 50.16.116 (Javolenus): *Mihi Labeo videtur verborum figuram sequi, Proculus mentem* [Labeo seems to me to follow the appearance of the words, Proculus follows their meaning].

But the most significant and far reaching development in the use of *figura* during the first century C.E. occurred when it became a rhetorical term. We find this usage attested in book 9 of Quintilian's *Institutio Oratoria*. The practice of rhetorical figuration is of course older. It was Greek and had been Latinized already by Cicero, as noted above. But he did not yet use the word *figura* in this way, and the intervening years had in any case seen the refine-

[14]In the context of confectionaries, cf. Martial (14.221.1), as well as Festus (129.15: *ficta quaedam ex farina in hominum figuras* [things made of dough in the shape of men]; and Petronius (33.6): *ova* . . . *ex farina figurata* [eggs, which were balls of fine meal]. The confectioner is often considered a sculptor and a decorator; later eras, including the Renaissance, the Baroque, and the Rococo, returned to this sense. Cf. Goethe, *Wilhelm Meister's Apprenticeship* (Book 3, Chapter 7), as well as Creizenach's note in the Jubilee edition, 17: 344.

ment of the technique of figuration as the result of the constant discussion of rhetorical questions. There is no way to ascertain when the word was first used in this way. In all likelihood it was soon after Cicero, as can be surmised from the title of a book—*De figuris sententiarum* (*On the Figures of Periods*)—by Annaeus Cornutus (preserved in Gellius 9.10.5), as well as from the observations and references to it that we find in both Senecas[15] and in Pliny the Younger. That this occurred is not surprising since the Greek word for this process was *schēma*. In general we must assume that the scientific and technical use of the term had developed earlier and more fully than is indicated to us by the texts that have survived. For example, it is likely that one referred in Latin to the "figures of a syllogism" (the term *schēmata syllogismou* was already Aristotle's) quite a bit earlier than in Boethius or in the pseudo-Augustinian *Book of Categories*.

It is in the last section of books 8 and 9 of his *Institutio Oratoria* that Quintilian gives a detailed account of his theory of tropes and figures. The section appears to offer a comprehensive discussion of all earlier opinions and works, and it became foundational for all future efforts of its kind. Quintilian distinguishes tropes from figures. "Trope" is the narrower category of the two and refers only to non-literal uses of words and phrases. The term "figure," on the other hand, refers to every form of speech that deviates from the conventional and most obvious usage. In the case of figures, it is thus not a question of substituting some words for others, as is the case in all tropes. Rather, figures can be formed from words in their proper meaning and in their proper arrangement. Every speech-act, he writes, is in principle something that is formed—a figure. But we use the word only for those forms that are constructed in deliberately poetic or rhetorical ways. This is why one distinguishes between simple (*carens figuris, aschēmastistos*) and figurative (*figuratus, eschēmatismenos*) modes of speech. The distinction between trope and figure proves to be a difficult one to make and Quintilian is himself often undecided whether to associate any particular speech act with the one or the other. Later usage often appears to have determined that *figura* was the generic term that included tropes, and that any non-literal or indirect form

---

[15] There is a passage in Seneca's *Epistolae* (65.7) that is significant in another context; there, *figura* refers to the original, the Idea, a Form in the Neoplatonic sense of an internal model, the forms in the mind of the artist. Here we also see evidence of the comparison—used so often later—between the artist and God the Creator. According to Seneca, the sculptor can find the model (*exemplar*) for his work both in his mind and in the world; either his eyes or his own mind can provide it for him. God, however, contains the *exemplaria* of all things in himself: *plenus his figuris est quas Plato ideas appellat* [. . .] *immortales* [he is filled with these shapes which Plato calls the "immortal ideas."] Dürer remarks: *Dann ein gutter Maler ist inwendig voller Figur* [A good painter is full of figures in his mind]. Cf. Erwin Panofsky, "*Idea*." *Ein Beitrag zur Begriffsgeschichte der älteren Kunsttheorie* (Leipzig: B. B. Teubner 1924) 70.

Figura | 77

of expression would be labeled figurative. Quintilian identifies the following as tropes: metaphors, synecdoches (*mucronem pro gladio, puppim pro navi* [blade for sword, prow for ship]), metonymies (the god Mars for war, Vergil for Vergil's oeuvre), antonomasia (Pelides for Achilles), and many other similar terms. He divides figures into those that concern the meaning or content and those that concern the words in which this content is expressed (*figurae sententiarum* and *verborum*). Under the *figurae sententiarum* he lists rhetorical questions and their answers; the various ways of anticipating objections (*prolepsis*); the feigning of taking a judge or an audience or even an antagonist into one's confidence; *prosopopoeia*, in which one has others—the enemy or a personification of the motherland, for example—speak in their own words; the formal apostrophe; *evidentia* or *illustratio*, the elaboration of an event in a way that makes it more concrete; the various forms of irony; *aposiopesis*, or *obticentia* or *interruptio*, whereby one "swallows" something; feigned regret about something that one has said; and many other similar instances. Above all, he mentions the figure that appears to have been the most important at the time and which was thought to be most deserving of the name "figure," namely hidden allusion in its different forms. Orators had developed a clever technique whereby one could express or insinuate something without saying it directly. This was especially apt in cases where, for political or tactical reasons, or perhaps simply to make a greater impression, something was left hidden or at least unsaid. Quintilian describes the great significance that the practice of this technique had in the rhetorical schools; the students created their own cases, called *controversiae figuratae* [imaginary controversies] in order to perfect and excel in their use of it. As "word figures," finally, he mentions intentional solecisms, rhetorical repetitions, antitheses, homophones, the omission of words, asyndeton, climax, and several other related constructions.

Quintilian's account of tropes and figures, of which I have summarized only the most essential parts here, is studded with abundant examples and very precise investigations of the individual kinds and the distinctions between them. It takes up the majority of books 8 and 9. He develops a complete system, a theory upon which the highest value is placed. At the same time, however, it is likely that among the orators, Quintilian occupied a relatively independent position and was for the most part disinclined—as far as it was possible to take this position at the time—to split hairs. The art of inauthentic, periphrastic, allusive, insinuating, and occlusive modes of speech by means of which a topic was elaborated upon—whether in a decorative, effective, or even insidious way—had reached a level of perfection and versatility in the rhetorical tradition of late antiquity that appears to us to be beyond comprehension, odd, often even foolish. Such ways of speaking were known as *figurae*. The doctrines of figural speech were, as we know, still of great importance in the Middle Ages and the Renaissance. Theorists of style during the twelfth and thirteenth centuries took the text of the *Ad Herennium* as their primary source.[16]

With this, the history of what *figura* meant during pagan antiquity comes to a close. There are several further developments in grammar, rhetoric, and logic.[17] These followed automatically from what I have already said and have in part already been discussed.[18] It was, however, the meaning that the Church Fathers were able to give the word, precisely on the basis of the developments described thus far, that was to become historically significant.

II. *Figura* as Historically Real Prophecy in the Texts of the Church Fathers

The new meaning of the word *figura* peculiar to the Christian world occurs first in Tertullian, where, from the very start, it is used quite frequently. A discussion of several passages will help clarify how this meaning developed.

In the text, *Adversus Marcionem* (3.16), Tertullian writes the following of Hoshea, the son of Nun, whom Moses calls Joshua (cf. Numbers 13:16): . . . *et incipit vocari Jesus . . . Hanc prius dicimus figuram futurorum fuisse. Nam quia Jesus Christus secundum populum, quod sumus nos, nati in saeculi desertis, introducturus erat in terram promissionis, melle et lacte manantem, id est vitae aeternae possessionem, qua nihil dulcius; idque non per Moysen, id est, non per*

---

[16] See here Edmond Faral, *Les arts poétiques du XIIe et du XIIIe siècle* (Paris: Champion, 1924) 48ff. and 99ff.

[17] Ammianus Marcellinus offers a variation worth mentioning; he uses the term to refer to the topography of the battlefield as well as for strategic battle formations and the design of military camps.

[18] A passage occurs in Sedulius, *Carmen Paschale* (5.101–102) in which it is impossible for *figura* to mean anything other than "face," just as it does in modern French: *Namque per hos colaphos caput est sanabile nostrum, / Haec sputa per Dominum nostram lavere figuram* [For our head can be mended by these blows / This spittle washes our face by means of the Lord]. Because *spuere in faciem* [to spit in the face] and *colaphis pulsare caput* [to beat the head with blows] had been mentioned before, the meaning of "face" cannot be doubted here. We must of course consider the need for a three-syllable word, with a long internal syllable in the middle, to end the verse; Sedulius could have been persuaded to use a more general word that was metrically suitable [namely, *figura*] for this reason. In any case, this is the only confirmed ancient example for a Latin *figura* meaning "face" that we have. Jeanneret's suggestion in his *La langue des tablettes d'exécration latines* (Neuchâtel 1918, 109) that *figura* means "face" on the Minturnian Tablet of Curses, is entirely unlikely, simply because of the alignment of *membra* [limbs] and *colorem* [color], which is quite common. As "shape," it belongs to the description of the properties in general and to those parts of the body with which the curses begin; the individual body parts then follow. Jeanneret's claim has been rejected by Wartburg (cf. *FEW*, s.v. "figura" 9). The question is still open in the case of a fragment from Laberius: *figura humana inimico [nimio] ardore ignescitur* [the human figure becomes inflamed by a far more hostile passion]. Cf. Otto Ribbeck, *Scaenicae Romanorum poesis fragmenta, vol. 2: Comicorum fragmenta* (Leipzig: B. G. Teubner, 1898) 344.

Figura | 79

legis disciplinam, sed per Jesum, [id est] per evangelii gratiam provenire habe-
bat [Vulgar Latin for the form: "ought to have happened"], *circumcisis nobis*
petrina acie, id est Christi praceptis; Petra enim Christus, ideo is vir, qui in
huius sacramenti imagines parabatur, etiam nominis dominici inauguratus est
figura, Jesus cognominatus. [. . . and begins to be called Jesus [Jehoshua] . . .
We observe first that this was a figure of him who was to be. Because Jesus
the Christ was going to bring the second people, which are we, born in the
wilderness of [this] world, into the land of promise, flowing with milk and
honey, which means the inheritance of eternal life, than which nothing is
sweeter: and because this was going to be effected not by Moses, not, that is,
by the discipline of the law, but by Jesus, through the Grace of the Gospel,
after we have been circumcised with the knife of flint, that is, the precepts of
Christ—for the rock was Christ—therefore that man who was being set aside
for the similitudes of this mystery was also first established in the likeness
of our Lord's name, being surnamed Jesus [Jehoshua].] Here, the naming of
Joshua-Jesus is presented as a prophetic process that tells in advance of things
to come.[19] Just as Joshua, and not Moses, led the people of Israel into the
Promised Land of Palestine, so too did Christ's Grace—and not the Law of
the Jews—lead the "second people" into the Promised Land of eternal bless-
edness. The man who appeared as the prophetic proclamation of this still
hidden mystery—the one *qui in huius sacramenti imagines parabatur* [who
was being set aside for the similitudes of this mystery]—was introduced
under the *figura* of God's name. The naming of Joshua-Jesus is a historically
real prophecy or a prophetic form of something in the future. *Figura* is something real and historical that represents and proclaims in advance something
else that is also real and historical. The reciprocal relationship of the two
events can be recognized in their accord with or similarity to one another.
Tertullian says in the *Adversus Marcionem* (5.7), for example: *Quare Pascha*
Christus, si non [p]ascha figura Christi per similitudinem sanguinis salutaris
et pecoris Christi? [Yet how can Christ be the Passover except that the Passover is a figure of Christ because of the similitude between the saving blood
of the (paschal) lamb and of Christ?]. Shadowy similarities in the structure
of events or in the circumstances that accompany them are often enough to
make the *figura* recognizable, but it took a commitment to a certain kind of

[19] Joshua is already called "Jesus" in the Septuagint; "Jesus" is a contraction of "Joshua." Cf. the
images in the Vatican Joshua Scroll, which is thought to be a sixth-century copy of the fourth-
century original. I have access only to one page of it in Kurt Pfister's *Die Mittelalterliche Buchmalerei*
des Abendlandes (Munich: Holbein, 1922), where the erection of the Twelve Stones (Joshua 4:20–
21) is depicted. In the text and in the inscription, Joshua is called *Iēsous ho tou Nauē* [Jesus, the
son of Naue], wears a halo, and clearly is meant to suggest Christ. Later depictions of the figure of
Joshua are frequent; cf., for example, Hildebert of Tours, *Sermones de diversis* 23 (*PL* 171:842ff.).
[*PL* refers here and elsewhere to the 221 volumes of the *Patrologia Latina*, Jacques-Paul Migne, ed.
(Paris: Migne, 1844–66)—Trans.]

interpretation to discover it. Examples are to be found in *Adversus Marcionem* 3.17 and *Adversus Iudaeos* 14, where the two sacrificial goats from Leviticus 16:7 are interpreted as signifying the First and the Second Comings of Christ, or in *De anima* 43 (see also *De monogamia* 5), where Eve is said to be a *figura Ecclesiae* [a figure of the Church] based on Adam's identity as a *figura Christi* [a figure of Christ]. *Si enim Adam de Christo figuram dabat, somnus Adae mors erat Christi dormituri in mortem, ut de iniuria* [wounds] *perinde lateris eius vera mater viventium figuraretur ecclesia.* [For if Adam presented a figure of Christ, Adam's sleep was the death of Christ who was to sleep in death that the Church, the true mother of all living things, would likewise be figured by the wounds in his side.][20] I will return below to the question of how the desire to engage in this kind of interpretation arose. Its aim, however, was to read the people and events of the Old Testament as "figures" or historically real prophecies of New Testament eschatology. We must note here that in so doing Tertullian specifically refuses to use figural interpretation to invalidate the literal and historical authority of the Old Testament. He is in fact decidedly disinclined to endorse the possibility of spiritualist encroachments. In no way does he want to understand the Old Testament merely allegorically. Rather, he believes that it was literally and really true. Even in those places where figural prophecy does occur, both the figure itself and what it prophesies are historically real in equal measure. The prophetic figure is a material historical fact and is fulfilled by material historical facts. Tertullian uses the term *figuram implere* (to fulfill the figure; cf. *Adversus Marcionem* 4.40: *figuram sanguinis sui salutaris implere* [to fulfill the figure of his saving blood]) or *confirmare* (confirm, sanction; *De fuga in persecutione* 11: *Christo confirmante figuras suas* [With Christ confirming his figures]). In what follows, I will refer to the two events as the "figure" and the "fulfillment."

Tertullian's emphatic realism in other respects is well known. He understands *figura,* in its most basic sense of "shape," as a part of substance, equating it with the flesh in *Adversus Marcionem* 5.20. Just before this (4.40), he had spoken of the bread used in the Eucharist: *Corpus [suum] illum fecit 'hoc est corpus meum' dicendo, 'id est figura corporis mei'. Figura autem non fuisset, nisi veritatis esset corpus. Ceterum vacua res, quod est phantasma, figuram capere non posset. Aut si propterea panem corpus sibi finxit, quia corporis carebat veritate, ergo panem debuit tradere pro nobis. Faciebat ad vanitatem Marcionis, ut panis crucifigeretur. Cur autem panem corpus suum appellat, et non magis peponem, quem Marcion cordis loco habuit? Non intelligens veterem fuisse istam figuram corporis Christi, dicentis per Ieremiam (11:19): Adversus*

---

[20] Here *figuraretur* means both "would be made" and "would be figured," the latter by blood and water, the Eucharist and baptism. The juxtaposition of the two wounds in Christ's sides continued to be an important theme for a long time. Cf. Konrad Burdach, *Vorspiel* 1.1 (Halle/Saal: Max Niemeyer Verlag, 1925) 162 and 212, as well as Dante, *Paradise* 13.37ff.

Figura | 81

me cogitaverunt cogitatum dicentes, Venite, coniciamus lignum in panem eius, scilicet crucem in corpus eius. [[H]e made it into his body, saying "This is my body," that is, the figure of my body. Now there could have been no figure, unless it had been a veritable body; for an empty thing, which a phantasm is, would have been incapable of figure. Or else, if you suppose he formed bread into a body for himself because he felt the lack of a veritable body, then it was bread he ought to have delivered up for us. It would well suit Marcion's vacuity, that bread should be crucified. Yet why does he call his body bread, and not rather a pumpkin, which Marcion had instead of a heart? For he did not understand how ancient was this figure of the body of Christ, who himself speaks of Jeremiah (Jer. 11:19), "They have devised a device against me, saying, Come and let us cast wood upon his bread, meaning, the cross upon his body."] These stirring lines—and later, the wine, *figura sanguinis* [figure of the blood], is no less powerfully understood, following *Genesis* 49:11 and *Isaiah* 63:1, as a *probatio carnis* [a test of the flesh][21]—give us the very clearest sense of just how material both poles of figural interpretation are for him. In every case, the only spiritual moment is the moment of understanding, the *intellectus spiritalis*, which recognizes the figure in its fulfillment. In *De resurrectione carnis* (19ff.), he writes that the prophets by no means spoke only in images. If they had, we would not be able to recognize the images at all. He also claims that much of what they said must be understood quite literally; likewise, for the most part, the New Testament: *nec omnia umbrae, sed et corpora; ut in ipsum quoque Dominum insigniora quaeque luce clarius praedicantur; nam et virgo concepit in utero, non figurate; et peperit Emanuelem nobiscum Jesum Christum, non oblique.* [And not everything is a shadow, but also a body—such that the marks of the Lord by which He is prophesied are clearer than day; for the Virgin conceived in her womb, not figuratively; and she gave birth to Emanuel, Jesus Christ with us, directly]. Tertullian is also keen to refute those who would *distorquent* [twist] the clearly proclaimed resurrection of the dead as having only *imaginarium significationem* [imaginary meaning]. There are numerous passages of this kind in which he resists the spiritualizing tendencies of contemporary groups. His realism is even more evident in the way he describes the relationship of the figure to its fulfillment. Sometimes the one and sometimes the other appears to be invested with greater concreteness. In the following passage from *Adversus Marcionem* (4.40), for example, the figure appears to be merely a simile, with the servant of God as a lamb: *an ipse erat, qui tamquam ovis coram tendente* [*tondente* —Trans.] *sic os non aperturus figuram sanguinis sui salutaris implere concupiscebat.* [Or not rather that he was [...] as a sheep before the shearer . . . not to open his mouth, and so had that great desire to accomplish the figure

---

[21] *Ita et nunc sanguinem suum in vino consecravit qui tunc vinum in sanguine figuravit* [Thus he now consecrated his blood in wine he who had figured wine in his blood].

of his saving blood]. Elsewhere (5.19), the Law as a whole is juxtaposed to Christ as its fulfillment: *de umbra transfertur ad corpus, id est de figuris ad veritatem* [by being transferred out of shadow into body; that is, from figures into the truth]. In the first example, it appears to be the simile, in the second, the abstraction that endows the figure with a lesser degree of reality. Yet there is no shortage of examples in which the figure seems to be more concrete. We find the following sentence in *De baptismo* (5), in which the pool of Bethesda appears as a figure of baptism: *Figura ista medicinae corporalis spiritalem medicinam canebat, ea* [*ex* —Trans.] *forma qua semper carnalia in figuram spiritalium antecedunt* [This example of bodily healing was prophetic of spiritual healing, by the general rule that carnal things always come first as examples of things spiritual]. But both of them—both the pool and baptism—are real and concrete objects and events, and the only thing that is spiritual about them is the interpretation or the effect—for even baptism is, as Tertullian himself immediately adds (7), something that happens to the body: *Sic et in nobis carnaliter crurit* [*currit* —Trans.] *unctio, sed spiritaliter proficit; quomodo et ipsius baptismi carnalis actus, quod in aqua mergimur, spiritalis effectus, quod delictis liberamur* [So also in our case, the unction flows upon the flesh, but turns to spiritual profit, just as in the baptism itself there is an act that touches the flesh, that we are immersed in water, but a spiritual effect, that we are set free from sins.] We can tell from these examples that even in the cases of the lamb mentioned above, Tertullian was speaking literally rather than metaphorically, and that he regarded the Law not merely as an abstraction but also as more than this, because he also regarded the time of the Law as a historical moment. There are also times when two pronouncements stand in relation to one another as figure and fulfillment as, for example, in *De fuga in persecutione* 11: *Certe quidem bonus pastor animam pro pecoribus ponit; ut Moyses, non domino adhuc Christo revelato, etiam in se figurato, ait: Si perdis hunc populum, inquit, et me pariter cum eo disperde (Exodus 32:32). Ceterum, Christo confirmante figuras suas, malus pastor est, etc. (John 10:12).* [Surely the man who is a good shepherd puts down his life for his sheep, even as Moses claimed when he said that Christ the Lord had not yet been revealed, but was also figured forth in himself: If you destroy this people, he said, you equally destroy me along with them (Exodus 32:32). Besides, Christ, confirming his figures, says: The evil shepherd is, etc. (John 10:12).] But both of these statements are historical events. Moreover, it is less they than Moses and Christ themselves who stand in relation to each other as figure to fulfillment.[22] As indicated above in the example, the fulfillment is often designated as *veritas* [the truth] and the figure, correspondingly, as *umbra* [shadow] or

---

[22] Moses is always a figure of Christ when he crosses the Red Sea, for example, or turns bitter water sweet for baptism. This of course does not mean that, in contradistinction to this figuration, he cannot also figure the Law, as in my first example above.

Figura | 83

imago [likeness, image]. But both—the shadow and the truth—are abstract only in relation to the initially concealed and then revealed meaning, but concrete in relation to the things or shapes that function as the vehicles of the meaning. Moses is no less real and in the world because he is an *umbra* or *figura* of Christ, and Christ, who is the fulfillment, is not an abstract idea, but is rather concrete and in history. The historically real figures are to be interpreted spiritually (*spiritaliter interpretari*), but this interpretation points to a bodily and thus a historical fulfillment (*carnaliter adimpleri*—cf. *De resurrectione* 20)—for at this moment, the truth has become history or the flesh.

Beginning in the fourth century, both the word *figura* and the interpretive method associated with it begin to appear in fully developed form in nearly all of the Latin Church writers.[23] Of course occasionally (as generally became the case in later periods) even ordinary allegory was called *figura*. Lactantius (*Div. inst.* 2.10), for example, interprets South and North as *figurae vitae et mortis* [figures of life and death] and day and night as figures of true and false faith. Yet the Christian reference to foreshadowing and fulfillment immediately became part of the mix: *etiam in hoc praescius futurorum Deus fecit, ut ex iis verae religionis et falsarum superstitionum imago quaedam ostenderetur* [also here, God, knowing the future, causes the image itself to appear in both true religious things and in false superstitions]. *Figura* thus often appears in the sense of "a deeper meaning that suggests something in the future." The sufferings of Christ *non fuerunt inania, sed habuerunt figuram et significationem magnam* [were not meaningless, but rather were powerful figures and had great significance]. In this context, Lactantius is speaking of divine acts in general (4.26): *quorum vis et potentia valebat quidem in praesens, sed declarabat aliquid in futurum* [whose force and power were indeed valid in the present but also announced something in the future]. Tertullian's eschatology is also dominated by this way of thinking. He follows a speculative interpretation that was widespread at the time, reading the six days of the Creation as six millennia that were then almost at an end. The Millenial Kingdom was at hand (7.14): *saepe diximus minora et exigua magnorum figuras et praemonstrationes esse; ut hunc diem nostrum, qui ortu solis occasuque finitur, diei magni speciem gerere, quem circuitus annorum mille determinat. Eodem modo figuratio terreni hominis caelestis populi praeferebat in posterum fictionem.* [We often said that small and unimportant things are figures and foreshadowings of great things, so that this day of ours, which is limited by the rising and setting of the sun, bears the image of that great day which is bounded by the passing of a thousand years. In this same way

---

[23] Cf. Hilary of Poitiers, *Tractatus mysteriorum*, paragraph 1 (*Corp. Vind.* 65.3), cited by Pierre de Labriolle, *Histoire de la littérature latine chrétienne*, 2nd ed. (Paris: Société d'édition "Les Belles Lettres," 1924) 324.

the *figuratio* of man on earth carried with it a story of the heavenly people to come.][24]

Both figural interpretation in general and many of these, its most well-known examples, are commonplace in most authors of this period,[25] as is the opposition between *figura* and *veritas*. But we also occasionally find a more intensely spiritualist, allegorical, and ethical kind of interpretation—for example, in Origen's commentaries on Scripture. There is a passage about the sacrifice of Isaac—this is usually considered one of the most famous examples of realistic figural interpretation—which, in the Latin translation by Rufinus (*Patrologia Graeca* 12.209B—the Greek original has not survived), reads as follows: *Sicut in Domino corporeum nihil est, etiam tu in his omnibus corporeum nihil sentias: sed in spiritu generes tu filium Isaac, cum habere coeperis fructum spiritus, gaudium, pacem.* [Just as there is nothing corporeal in the Lord, so too you perceive nothing corporeal in all these things. But you will give birth to your son Isaac in spirit when you will have begun to have the fruit of the spirit, joy, and peace.] Origen is of course not nearly as abstract in his allegories as is, say, Philo. In his texts, the events of the Old Testament seem alive and of immediate concern to the real reader and to his real life. Only when we consider his beautiful explanation of the three-day journey in Exodus (313ff.), for example, do we sense very clearly that the mystical and the moral far outweigh the strictly historical elements.[26] And another conflict—which was well known within early Christianity and in other contexts too—emerges in the difference between Tertullian's more worldly, historical, and realistic way of interpreting and Origen's more allegorical and moral approach, namely that while some sought to turn the content of the new teachings—and especially the matter of the Old Testament—into something purely spiritual and thus to cause its historical character to evaporate, others desired to maintain its concrete historicity—which was of course deeply meaningful in its own right—in its entirety. In the West, the latter tendency was the unqualified victor, even though the former never really lost its influence—which is already obvious from the persistence of the doctrine

---

[24] Cf. Hilarian, *De Cursu Temporum* (*PL* 13:173.2: *sabbati aeterni imaginem et figuram tenet sabbatus temporalis* [The Sabbath of this world is an image and figure of the eternal Sabbath].

[25] Just how deeply devoted to the custom of this kind of interpretation the authors of the period were can be seen in the only half joking interpretation of gifts that we find in the letters of Jerome (*Epistolae* 44; *PL* 22:480).

[26] Jerome writes polemically of Origen that he (Origen) is *allegoricus semper interpres et historiae fugiens veritatem . . . nos simplicem et veram sequamur historiam, ne quibusdam nubibus atque praestigiis involvamur* [He always interpreted allegorically, fleeing the truth of history . . . let us follow true history and not involve ourselves in any haziness or illusions] (Jeremiah 27:3–4; *PL* 24: 849C). On the relationship of the Alexandrians, and especially Origen, to figural interpretation, cf. A. Freiherr von Ungern-Sternberg, *Der traditionelle alttestamentliche Schriftbeweis* (Halle/Saale: Max Niemeyer Verlag, 1913) 154ff. On p. 160, he writes of Origen: "He did not live in the Biblical realism of Scriptural proof."

Figura | 85

of multiple levels of meaning in Scripture. This doctrine leaves the literal or historical meaning intact, but disrupts its connection with the equally real prefigurative level by inserting other purely abstract interpretations beside or in place of the prefigural ones. St. Augustine played a decisive role in the reconciliation between these two ways of thinking, a compromise in which the dynamic figural interpretive approach was nevertheless ultimately preferred. His spirituality was much too alive and situated in history for him to have been content with anything that was allegorical in a purely abstract way.

That the entire ancient tradition lived on in Augustine is clearest in his use of the word *figura*. It appears in his work as a general concept of form with all of its inherited variants, both fixed and in motion, as an outline, but also in three dimensions and applicable to the world, or to nature in its entirety, or to the individual object. It suggests, along with *forma*, *color*, and the like, the external and the concrete (*Epistolae* 120.10 or 146.3), but also mutability as contrasted with unchangeable essence. It is in this sense that Augustine interprets 1 Corinthians 7:31 (*De civitate Dei* 20.14): *Peracto quippe iudicio tunc esse desinet hoc c[a]elum et haec terra, quando incipiet esse c[a]elum novum et terra nova. Mutatione namque rerum non omni modo interitu, transibit hic mundus. Unde et apostolus dicit: praeterit enim figura huius mundi, volo vos sine sollicitudine esse. Figura [ergo] praeterit, non natura.* [For after the completion of the judgment this heaven and this earth will, of course, cease to be, when a new heaven and a new earth shall begin to be. For it is by the change of substance, not by its utter destruction, that this world shall pass away. Wherefore the Apostle says: "For the form of this world is passing away; I want you to be free of anxiety." It is the form, then, that passes away, not the substance.] *Figura* appears, moreover, as a pagan idol, as a dream figure or vision, and as a mathematical formula. Hardly any of the many uses already familiar to us are missing. But by far the most frequent of all is its appearance as a historically real prophecy. Augustine expressly adopts the figural interpretation of the Old Testament and strongly recommends it for preaching and missionary work (see, for example, *De catichizandis rudibus* 3.6) and himself develops it further in this direction. In his work, the meanings of *figura* pass before our eyes in all of their abundance. Thus, Noah's Ark (*De civitate Dei* 15.27) is a *praefiguratio ecclesiae* [a prefiguration of the Church]; Moses is a *figura Christi* [figure of Christ] in several different ways (for example, *De civitate Dei* 10.6 or 18.11), the *sacerdotium* [priesthood] of Aaron (17.6) is an *umbra et figura aeterni sacerdotii* [the shadow and figure of an eternal priesthood], Hagar the slave (16.11) is a *figura* of the Old Testament, the *terrena Jerusalem* [earthly Jerusalem], Sarah of the New Testament (17.3, *Expos. ad Galatas* 40), the *supernae Jerusalem, civitatis Dei* [heavenly Jerusalem, city of God]; Jacob and Esau (*De civitate Dei* 16.42) *figuram praebuerunt duorum populorum in Christianis et Iudeis* [prefigured the two peoples of the Jews and the Christians] and the anointed kings of Judaea (17.4 [17.10

—Trans.]) *(Christi) figuram prophetica unctione gestabant* [. . . [whom] they represented symbolically in being anointed prophetically]. These are only a very few examples. The entire Old Testament, or at least the important figures and events, are universally interpreted in a figurative way. Even in those places where the hidden meaning of words and prophecies is explained, as, for example, in Augustine's reading of Hannah's song of thanksgiving (I Samuel 2:1-10) in *De civitate Dei* 17.4, the interpretation is for the most part not only allegorical, but also figurative. Hannah's song of praise for the birth of her son Samuel is explained as a figure of the transformation of the old earthly kingdom and priesthood into the new heavenly one, whereby she herself becomes a *figura ecclesiae* [figure of the Church].

Augustine emphatically rejected those who would interpret Holy Scripture in a purely allegorical way and thus also the claim that the Old Testament was more or less a hermetic text that could be understood only by denying any possibility of a literal-historical reading based on common sense. Every believer can come to an understanding of its sublime themes, he maintained, if the task is approached one step at a time. He writes in his *De trinitate (I.2)*: . . . *sancta scriptura parvulis congruens nullius generis rerum verba vitavit, ex quibus quasi gradatim ad divina atque subliiam [sublimia* —Trans.] *noster intellectus velut nutritus assurgeret* [the Holy Scripture, as is apt for the young, did not shun any kind of words through which our understanding could be nourished and rise up gradually to divine and sublime things] and elsewhere (*Sermones* 2.6ff. [2.7 —Trans.]) he explains—with an even more pronounced reference to the problem of figuration under consideration here: *Ante omnia, frater* [*fratres* —Trans.]*, hoc in nomine Domini admonemus et praecipimus, ut quando auditis exponi sacramentum scripturae quae gesta sunt, prius illud quod lectum est credatis sic gestum quomodo lectum est; ne substrato fundamento rei gestae quasi in aere quaeratis aedificare.* [But first and above all, brothers, I must in the name of the Lord to the best of my ability both urge upon you and insist upon one thing: when you hear the hidden meaning explained of a story in Scripture that tells of things that happened, you must first believe that what has been read to you actually happened as read, or else the foundation of an actual event will be removed, and you will be trying to build castles in the air.][27] Following a long-standing tradition, he also understood the Old Testament to be strictly a matter of historically real prophecy; more than others, however, he motivates his claim by greater emphasis on several passages in Paul's letters to which I return below. The observances of the law (*quas tamquam umbras futuri saeculi nunc respuunt Christiani, id tenentes, quod per illas umbras figurate promittebatur* [which Christians now cast aside as so many shadows of the age to come, possessing that which was promised figuratively in those shadows]) and the sacraments

---

[27] Cf. also *De civitate Dei* 15.27 and 20.21 (regarding *Ad Isaiam* 65.17ff.)

Figura | 87

(*quae habuerunt promissivas figuras* [which contained the promised figures]) are the letter—in the sense that their unquestionably embodied and historical reality is revealed and interpreted spiritually by fulfillment in Christ—an act which is no less historical—and, then, as we will see in a moment, is replaced by a new, more complete, and clearer promise. A Christian must therefore behave (14.23): *non ad legem operum, ex qua nemo iustificatur, sed ad legem fidei, ex qua iustus vivit (de spiritu et literra)* [not according to the law of deeds, by which no one is pardoned, but rather according to the law of faith, by which the just person lives]. The old Jews *quando adhuc sacrificium verum, quod fideles norunt, in figuris praenuntiabatur, celebrant figuram futurae rei; multi scientes, plures ignorantes* [when they still prophesied in figures the true sacrifice, which the faithful know, they were celebrating the figure of things to come; they knew many things and were also ignorant of many things as well], *Enarrationes in Psalm.* 39.12. But in their stubborn blindness, the Jews of his day—and in these words we hear the strains of a polemic against the Jews that runs throughout all later arguments of this sort[28]—resisted recognizing that this was the case (*De civitate Dei* 20.28): *non enim frustra Dominus ait Judaeis: si crederetis Moysi, crederetis et mihi; de me enim ille scripsit (Joan. 5: 46): carnaliter quippe accipiendo legem, et eius promissa terrene rerum c[a]elestium figuras esse nescientes* [For not in vain does the same Lord say to the Jews: "If you believed in Moses, you would believe also in me: for it was of me that he wrote" (John 5:46). Now it was by taking the law in a carnal sense and not knowing that its earthly promises are figures of heavenly things . . .]. But this "heavenly" fulfillment is still not complete. We thus see—as in several of the earlier writers, but more pronouncedly in Augustine—that the juxtaposition of two poles, figure and fulfillment, is sometimes replaced by a three-step process: first, the Law, or the history of the Jews as a prophetic *figura* of the coming of Christ; then, the Incarnation, or the fulfillment of this *figura*, which is simultaneously a new promise of the end of the world and the Last Judgment; and, finally, the future advent of these events as the final fulfillment. *Vetus enim Testamentum est promissio figurata, novum Testamentum est promissio spiritualiter intellecta* [The Old Testament, you see, is the promise in figure and symbol; the New Testament is the promise spiritually understood], he writes in *Sermones* 4.9, and even more clearly in *Contra Faustinum* (4.2): *Temporalium quidem rerum promissiones Testamento Veteri contineri, et ideo Vetus Testamentum appellari nemo nostrum ambigit; et quod aeternae vitae promissio regnumque coelorum ad Novum pertinet Testamentum: sed in illis temporalibus figuras fuisse futurorum quae implerentur*

---

[28] A. Rüstow has called to my attention the following lines from a religious Shrovetide play (ca. 1500) by Hans Folz: *Hör Jud, so merk dir und verstee / Daß alle Geschicht der alten Ee / Und aller Propheten Red gemein / Ein Figur der neuen Ee ist allein* [Listen, Jew, remember this and understand that the whole history of the old covenant, together with all of the sayings of the Prophets too, are nothing more than a figure of the new covenant.]

in nobis, in quos finis saeculorum obvenit, non suspicio mea, sed apostolicus intellectus est, dicente Paulo, cum de talibus loqueretur: Haec autem . . . [None of us doubts that the Old Testament contains promises of temporal realities and is called the Old Testament for that reason, and that the promise of eternal life and of the Kingdom of Heaven pertains to the New Testament. It is not, however, my suspicion but the understanding of the apostle that those temporal realities were symbols of things to come, which were fulfilled in us upon whom the end of the ages has come. For when he was speaking of such things, Paul said: All these . . .]. (He then proceeds to quote 1 Corinthians 10:6 and 11.) Although he considers the final fulfillment to be imminent here, it is obvious that two promises are in play, one that, concealed in the Old Testament, is apparently within time, while the other, in the Gospel is— it is stated with clarity—beyond time. Such claims give the doctrine of the fourfold meaning of Scripture a much more intensely realistic and historically concrete character, in that three of the four meanings acquire concrete and interrelated meaning as events, with only one remaining purely moral and allegorical. Augustine explains as much in his *De Genesi ad litteram* 1.1: *In libris autem omnibus sanctis intueri oportet, quae ibi aeterna intimentur* [In all the holy books, however, one ought to note what eternal realities are there suggested]—i.e., the end of the world and eternal life, this is the analogical meaning; *quae facta narrentur* [what deeds are recounted]—the literal, historical meaning; *quae futura praenuntientur* [what future events are foretold]—the figurative meaning in a more narrow sense, as in the Old Testament and the real prophecy of the coming of Christ; *quae agenda praecipiantur vel moneantur* [what actions commanded or advised]—the moral meaning.

Even if Augustine decisively rejects abstract allegorical spiritualism and develops his entire interpretation of the Old Testament out of its concrete reality in worldly historical time, he nevertheless continues to endorse a kind of idealism that removes the concrete event from time as *figura*—even though it also remains entirely real—and places it into the perspective of timeless eternity. Such ideas were implicit in the very fact of the Incarnation. The figural interpretation of history then propounded them directly, and they became visible quite quickly, as when Tertullian writes in *Adversus Marcionem* (3.5) that in Isaiah 50:6, *dorsum meum posui in flagella* [I gave my back to the scourging] (in the Vulgate: *corpus meum dedi percutientibus* [I gave my body to those who beat me]), what is to come is represented figuratively as having already happened, as already past. He adds that for God, there is no *differentia temporis* [distinction of time]. But no one among Augustine's predecessors or contemporaries developed these ideas as subtly and completely as he did. Augustine emphasized time and again the contrast that Tertullian sensed only because of the perfect tense in that sentence, as, for example, in the *De civitate Dei* (17.8): *Scriptura sancta etiam de rebus gestis prophetans quo-*

Figura | 89

dammodo in eo figuram delineat futurorum [the Holy Scripture, even when foretelling things that have already happened, outlines in so doing the figure of future things], or when he observed a discrepancy between Psalm 113 (*In exitu*) and the corresponding story in Exodus (*Enarr. in Psalmos* 113.1): *ne arbitremini nobis narrari praeterita, sed potius futura praedici . . . ut id, quod in fine saeculorum manifestandum reservabatur, figuris rerum atque verborum praecurrentibus nuntiaretur* [we should not suppose that past events only are being related to us but understand that the future is being foretold . . . so that though [the full truth] was held back to be manifested at the end of time, it might be figuratively announced through both events and words long beforehand]. Augustine's view of figures as timeless and belonging to all times is best captured in the following passage (which of course does not refer explicitly to figural interpretation) (*De diversis quaestionibus ad Simplicianum* 2.2.2): *Quid enim est praescientia nisi scientia futurorum? Quid autem futurum est Deo qui omnia supergreditur tempora? Si enim scientia Dei res ipsas habet, non sunt ei futurae sed praesentes; et per hoc non praescientia, sed tantum scientia dici potest.* [For what is foreknowledge if not knowledge of the future? What is the future to God who is above all time? If God's knowledge contains all these things, they are not future to him but present; therefore it can be called not foreknowledge, but knowledge]. Figural interpretation was of great practical use for the missionary work of the fourth century and in the following centuries as well. It was regularly used in sermons and religious instruction, often combined of course with purely allegorical and moral readings. The *Forumulae spiritalis intelligentiae* by Bishop Eucherius of Lyons (beginning of the fifth century), who had been educated in Lérins, is a textbook of figural and moral explications, probably designed for use in schools.[29] From the sixth century we have the *Instituta regularia divinae legis* by Junilius, the Treasurer of the Holy Palatine Hill (*PL* 68), which is a translation of a Greek text influenced by the School of Antioch. The first chapter contains the following teaching: *Veteris Testamenti intentio est Novum figuris praenuntiationibusque monstrare; Novi autem ad aeternae beatitudinis gloriam humanas mentes accendere* [The purpose of the Old Testament is to reveal the New by means of figures and prophecies; on the other hand, the purpose of the New Testament is to illuminate for the human mind the glory of eternal blessedness]. A practical example of how figural interpretation was used in the instruction of the recently converted may be found in the explanation of the sacrifice in the second sermon of Bishop Gaudentius of Brescia (*PL* 20, 855A), in which we discover a perhaps unintended expression of the perspectivism of figural temporality. He writes that the *figura* (which temporally comes first) is not *veritas* (truth), but is rather an *imitatio veritatis* [an imitation of the truth]. We also find a large number of peculiar

[29] *Corp. Vind.* 31. Cf. Labriolle (n. 23 above) 567.

and exaggerated figural interpretations combined over and over again with purely abstract and moral allegories. But the fundamental belief that the Old Testament was a historically concrete prefiguration of the Gospel both in its entirety and in its most important details had become a hard-and-fast tradition by this time.

At this point I want to return once again to my semantic question: How did *figura* acquire its new meaning among the Church Fathers? The oldest texts in the Christian tradition were written in Greek, and the word that is most often used there to mean "historically real prophecy"—in the Epistle of Barnabas, for example—is *typos*. This leads me to suppose—as some of my readers may have already done upon reviewing some of my earlier citations (those from Lactantius, for example)—that it was directly from its general meaning as "formation," "forming," and "shape" that *figura* proceeded to acquire its new meaning. Indeed, the use of the term by the very oldest of the Latin ecclesiastical writers suggests this, as when individuals or events in the Old Testament are often described as being *figuram Christi (ecclesiae, baptismi*, etc.) *gerunt* or *gestant* [providing *or* giving birth to a figure of Christ, of the Church, of baptism, etc.], or when it is stated that the Jewish people in all things *figuram nostrum portat* [bears our *figura*], or that Holy Scripture *figuram delineat futurorum* [outlines the *figura* of future things], and so on. In these cases, we may without hesitation translate *figura* as "shape" or "form." Yet the idea of *schēma*, as it was associated with metaphorical and rhetorical periphrasis, dissemblance, change, and even deception in the pre-Christian poetic and rhetorical traditions, immediately became part of the mix. The opposition between *figura* and *veritas*, between the interpretation (*exponere*) and unveiling (*aperire, revelare*) of figures,[30] on the one hand, and the equating of *figura* and *umbra* and *sub figura* with *sub umbra*, on the other (for example, *ciborum* [of food] or more generally *legis* [of the law], by which it is understood that it is "beneath" the *figura* that something else—something that will happen in the future—lies hidden)—all of these examples reveal that the metaphorical and rhetorical use of *figura* lived on in the new concept of *figura* as "shape" or "form," which is now a *praefiguratio*, except that it had succeeded in moving out of the purely nominalistic realm of the rhetorical schools and of Ovid's half playful myths and into a realm that was both real and spiritual, and thus authentic, meaningful, and a part of existence. The opposition between figures of speech and figures of thought that we saw in Quintilian likewise reappears in the distinction between *figurae verborum* (prophetic words, similes, and so on) and *figurae rerum* (real concrete proph-

---

[30] We also of course find *claudere* [to shut, to block] as a reminder of Isaiah 22:22 and Revelation 3:7. Cf. later Peter Lombard, on Psalms 146:6 (*PL* 191:1276): *clausa Dei* [places made inaccessible by God], "that which God has concealed in the darkness of expression," and the Provençal word *clus*.

Figura | 91

ecies). At the same time, it was on this basis that the scope of the *potestas verbi* [power of the word] had become quite broad. We find *figura* signifying "a deeper meaning" in Sedulius (*Carm. pasch.* 5.348ff.), for example (*ista res habet egregiam figuram* [this thing has an exceptional figure]) and in Lactantius (see above, 454). It can also suggest "deception" or a "deceptive shape," or "form" (Philastrius 61.4: *sub figura confessionis christianae* [under the figure of the Christian faith] "they pretended to be Christian," or Sulpicius Severus, when he writes in his *De Vita beati Martini* 21.1 of the devil: *sive se in diversas figuras spiritalis nequitiae transtulisset* [transformed himself into various figures of spiritual wickedness], or Leo Magnus in his *Epistolae* 98.3 (*PL* 54, 955A): *lupum pastorali pelle nudantes qua prius quoque figura tantummodo convincebatur obtextus* [stripping the wolf of his sheep's skin with which earlier in a figure he was shown to be covered]). *Figura* also suggests an "empty" and "deceptive mode of speaking," an excuse (*per tot figuras ludimur* [we are mocked by such a great number of figures], Prudentius, *Peristephanon* 2.315, or in Rufinus, *Apologia adversus Hieronymus*: *qualibus [Ambrosium] figuris laceret* [with which figures he slandered Ambrose]). It can also mean "speech" or "word" plain and simple (*te . . . incauta violare figura* [I hurt you with an incautious figure], Paulinus of Nola, *Carmina* [Songs] 11.12). We also find it, finally, in versions that it is nearly impossible to translate appropriately: In the poetic text *De actibus Apostolorum* of the sub-deacon Arator in the sixth century (*PL* 68, 2.361, we find the lines: *tamen illa figura, qua sine nulla vetus (i.e., Veteris Testementi) subsistit littera, has melius novitate manet* [but that figure, without which not one letter of the Old Testament exists, now survives to better effect in the New]. And there is a passage from approximately the same time in the poetic writings of Bishop Avitus of Vienne (*Carmina* 5.254; *MG auct. ant.* 6.2),[31] in which he speaks of the Last Judgment: Just as during the slaughter of the firstborn in Egypt, the Lord had spared those houses marked with blood, so may He recognize and spare the faithful marked by the sign of the Eucharist: *tu cognosce tuam servanda in plebe figuram* [know your figure in the people who are to be saved]. Finally, we should note that in addition to the opposition between figure, on the one hand, and fulfillment and truth, on the other, another opposition emerges, namely between *figura* and *historia. Historia,* or also *littera,* is the literal meaning or the event to which it refers; *figura* is the same meaning or event, but seen from the perspective of the future fulfillment hidden within it, and this fulfillment is *veritas,* or truth. *Figura* thus appears as the middle term between *littera-historia* and *veritas* and means approximately the same thing as *spiritus* or *intellectus spiritalis. Figuralitas* sometimes even takes its place, as we can see in the following passage from the *Continentia Vergiliana* of Fulgentius (90.1): *sub figuralitate historiae plenum hominis monstravimus*

---

[31] Cited in the *PL* 59:360D.

statum [we have revealed the entire state of the human race under the figure of history]. *Figura* and *historia* can of course often be used interchangeably; *ab historia in mysterium surgere* [to rise up from history into the mystery], writes Gregory the Great (*Ezech.* 1.6.3). And later, both *historiare* and *figurare* mean "to represent in images" or "to illustrate," although in the first case only in a literal sense, while in the second case also figuratively in the sense of "to interpret allegorically."[32]

Figura is not the only word that is used in Latin to mean historically real prophecy. Often we find *allegoria* and *typus*, words that are taken from the Greek. *Allegoria* in general suggests any deeper meaning, and not just real prophecy. The boundaries are nevertheless fluid, for both *figura* and *figuraliter* often also exceed the domain of real prophecy. Tertullian often uses *allegoria* as nearly synonymous with *figura*, although much less often, and in Arnobius (*Adversus nationes* 5.32), we find *historia* contrasted with *allegoria*. *Allegoria* is also supported by the authority of Galatians 4:24. Nevertheless, *allegoria* is not always to be used as synonymous with *figura*, as it does not include the meaning of "shape" or "form"; one could not write, *Adam est allegoria Christi* [Adam is an allegory of Christ]. By contrast, *typus* takes second place to *figura* only because it is a foreign word, which is of course important, since for those who spoke Latin or, later, a Romance language, *figura* more or less consciously conjured up all of the associations that belonged to the history of its meaning, while *typus* remained only a borrowed, lifeless sign. The following Latin words were used or were considered either in place of or alongside *figura* in the sense of historically real prophecy: *ambages, effigies, exemplum, imago, similitudo, species,* and *umbra. Ambages* [riddle] was discarded as being too pejorative. *Effigies* suggests "copy" and was thus too narrow, and when compared with *imago* [image], moreover, it does not seem to have developed the potential for any broader meaning. The others intersect in various ways with historically real prophecy, but in the end they do not seem to be completely apt. All of them are used on occasion, *imago* and *umbra* most frequently. *Imagines,* standing alone and not in the genitive, was the term used to refer to statues of one's ancestors in Roman homes, for example; the Christians then refashioned it to refer to the images of saints. The history of *imago* and its meaning thus took a different course. In the Vulgate, man was fashioned *ad imaginem Dei* [in God's image]. As a result, *imago* competed with *figura* for a long time—although only when the context made it clear that the meaning of "image" was identical with "historically real prophecy." *Umbra* is testified to and thus authorized by several passages

---

[32] Cf. Du Cange and Dante, *Purgatory* 10.73 and 12.22, as well as Alan de Lille, *De planctu naturae* (*PL* 210:438D). There are many other similar passages that one could find. Amyot says in his *Thémistocle* (52), for example: *La parole de l'homme ressemble proprement à une tapisserie historiée et figurée* [Human speech truly resembles a storied and figured tapestry].

Figura | 93

in the letters of the Apostles (Col. 2:17; Hebrews 8:5, 10:1). It occurs quite frequently, but mostly as a metaphorical version of the concept of historically real prophecy rather than as the thing itself. In any case, none of these words brought together as completely as *figura* did all of the elements of the concept, including the senses of creativity and shaping, of change in an unchanging essence, and of the play between copy and original. It is thus not all that surprising that *figura* became the most commonly, universally, and distinctively used term for historically real prophecy.

III. The Origin of Figural Interpretation and an Analysis

In the previous section we could not help but stray several times from a purely semantic consideration of *figura*. This was because the substance of what the word means in the writings of the Church Fathers had to be explained. Precisely this meaning makes it imperative to investigate its origins in greater detail and to distinguish it from related meanings. We must also assess its historical significance and influence.

The Church Fathers often rely on a number of passages from the earliest periods of the Christian tradition (primarily the letters of the Apostles) for their justification of figural interpretation.[33] The most important texts here are 1 Corinthians 10, especially verses 6 and 11, where the Jews in the desert are referred to as *typoi hēmōn* [figures of ourselves] and where it is written of their fate: *tauta de typikōs synebainein ekeinois* [these things happened to them as figures]. We also find frequent references to Galatians 4:21-31. There Paul uses the example of the contrast between Hagar and Ismael, on the one hand, and Sarah and Isaac, on the other, to explain to the newly baptized Galatians, who, influenced by Judaism, want to be circumcised, the difference between the Law and Grace, the old and the new Covenant, and servitude and freedom, and in so doing, tells the story of Genesis in combination with Isaiah 54:1, interpreting it as a historically real prophecy. See also Colossians 2:16ff., where, when discussing the Jewish dietary laws and holidays, it is said that they are only shadows of what is to come, but the body is Christ, Romans 5:12ff., and 1 Corinthians 15:21, where Adam appears as the *typos* of Christ to come, both times in connection with the opposition between the Law and Grace, as well as 2 Corinthians 3:14, where the veil, *kalumna*, that lies on top of the Scripture when the Jews read it is mentioned. Finally, at Hebrews

---

[33] Allusions that appear to be to historically real prophecies are not entirely absent from the Synoptic Gospels, as when Christ compares himself to Jonah (Matthew 12:39ff. and Luke 11:29ff). The passage at John 5:46 should also be noted. Compared with the Epistles of the Apostles, there are nevertheless only faint similarities here.

9:11ff., the sacrifice of the blood of Christ is represented as the fulfillment of the Old Testament sacrifice performed by the high priest.

These are, as one can see, almost all Pauline passages. That figural interpretation played an important role in missionary work from the very start is clear in several passages in the Acts of the Apostles (for example, 8:32). It would have only been natural, and in need of no further explanation, if the new Jewish-Christians had looked in the Jewish holy books for predictions of the Coming of Christ and for a confirmation of his deeds and had left the interpretations to which they came in this way to become part of tradition. This would have been the case particularly because it was commonly thought that the Messiah would be a second Moses and that redemption through him would be a second exodus from Egypt in which the miracles of the first would be repeated.[34] But an examination of the passages listed above reveals, especially in connection with the overall impact of Paul's teaching, that those Jewish ideas were combined with a way of thinking that stood in the very sharpest of contrasts with the thought of the Jewish-Christians, and that it was only as a result of this way of thinking that these passages took on their particular significance. Those passages of the Epistles that contain figural interpretations were almost all written as the result of the bitter struggle associated with the mission to the Gentiles, and were often downright hostile to and defensive in the face of persecution and attacks by the Jewish-Christians. They were also almost all intended to strip the Old Testament of its normative status and to interpret it as a mere shadow of things to come. All figural interpretation was part of Paul's basic teachings of the opposition between the Law and Grace, between justification by works and justification by faith. The old Law is suspended and replaced, it is merely a shadow, a *typos*. Obedience to it is pointless, even harmful after Christ has brought fulfillment and salvation to humanity by His sacrifice. Christians are justified not by works in accordance with obedience to the Law, but by faith. And, in his Jewish and Judaistic understanding of the Law, the Old Testament is the Letter that kills, whereas true Christians are servants of the new Covenant of the Spirit that gives life. These were Paul's teachings, and the former Pharisee and student of Gamaliel searched urgently through the Old Testament itself for passages that would support his ideas. What for him had been a book of the Law and of the history of Israel was now transformed into a single great promise, the prehistory of Christ, in which nothing had any final meaning, but was, rather, always only a prophecy that had now been fulfilled, and in which everything "is written for us" (1 Corinthians 9:10, cf. Romans 15:4) and precisely the most significant and holy events, sacraments, and laws are only temporary

---

[34] I am grateful to Rudolf Bultmann for pointing this out to me. I do not have any access to specialist literature on this issue at the moment. Cf. Deuteronomy 18:15; John 1:45, 6:14, and 6:26ff.; and Acts 3:22ff.

Figura | 95

foreshadowings and figurations of Christ and the Gospel (1 Corinthians 5:7): *et enim Pascha nostrum immolatus est Christus* [for Christ sacrificed is our Passover lamb].[35] This was how Paul, in whom the practical and political combined in exemplary fashion with a faith endowed with a high level of poetic creativity, managed to transform the Jewish idea of the resurrection of Moses in the Messiah into a system of historically real prophecy, in which Christ resurrected simultaneously fulfills and annuls the work of his predecessor. Whatever the Old Testament had to sacrifice in legal authority and in historical-national autonomy, it gained in new and dramatically concrete contemporary relevance. Paul did not produce a fully consistent interpretation of the entire Old Testament. But those few passages about the exodus from Egypt, about Adam and Christ, and about Hagar and Sarah reveal in adequate measure what he wanted to say. The controversies about the Old Testament over the course of the ensuing years saw to it that his ideas and interpretation did not fade. Of course the influence of the Jewish-Christians who were faithful to the Law soon eroded. But a new and stronger resistance emerged on the part of those who wanted either to eliminate the Old Testament entirely or to interpret it in a strictly abstract and allegorical way. Had they succeeded, Christianity would have lost its connection to providential world history, this-worldly concreteness, and also, in all likelihood, some of its immense and universally persuasive power. It was in this struggle with those who despised the Old Testament and wanted to drain it of its meaning that the method of historically real prophecy again proved itself and successfully secured its own validity precisely in terms of the way Christianity understood the promise of Christ.

At the same time, there is yet another factor that we consider significant for the massive expansion of Christianity that subsequently took place, especially in the western and northern parts of the Mediterranean countries. As we have said, the Old Testament was transformed as a result of figural interpretation from a book of laws and a national history of Israel into a series of figures of Christ and of Redemption, not unlike those with which we are familiar from the processions of prophets in medieval theater or in the cyclical representations of medieval sculpture in Western and Northern Europe. In this form and in this context, in which the national history and the national character of the Jews was eclipsed, the Celtic and Germanic nations, for instance, were able to accept the Old Testament. On the one hand, it was a part of the universal religion of redemption; on the other, it was a necessary component of a vision of world history that was similarly grand and unified and that was communicated to them along with this religion. In its original form, as a book of laws and as the history of such a foreign and distant nation, the Old Testament would have remained inaccessible to them. This was of course

---

[35] Sedulius, *Eleg.* 1.87: *Pellitur umbra die, Christo veniente figura* [the shadow is dispelled by the day, the figure by the coming of Christ].

an understanding to which they came after the fact; it lay completely outside of the frame of reference and thinking of the first apostles to the Gentiles and the Church Fathers. They would also not have encountered the problem so quickly, because the early pagan converts lived among the Jews of the Diaspora and, exposed to their influence and as part of a Hellenistic population that was extremely well disposed to accept religious experiences of any sort, they had already long since acquainted themselves with Jewish history and the Jewish religion. But this perspective is no less important for being possible only in retrospect. It was not until quite late, in all likelihood after the Reformation, that the Old Testament came alive to European Christianity as Jewish history and Jewish Law. At first it appeared to be a *figura rerum*, or a historically real prophecy, the prehistory of Christ for the newly converted peoples, and as such it gave them a sense of the basic concept of world history. Because of its very specific connection with faith, this concept became extraordinarily powerful, and it remained the sole legitimate view of history for nearly a millennium. This meant, however, that the way of understanding on which figural interpretation was based necessarily became one of the most important constitutive elements of the Christian understanding of history and reality and of its concept of concrete reality in general. This thought leads us to the second of the tasks mentioned at the beginning of the chapter, namely to the need for a more precise definition of figural interpretation, and thus to the job of distinguishing it from other related forms of interpretation.

Figural interpretation creates a connection between two events or persons in which one signifies not only itself but also the other—and that one is also encompassed or fulfilled by the other. The two poles of the figure are separate in time, but they both also lie within time as real events or figures. As I have repeatedly emphasized, both figures are part of the ongoing flow of historical life. Only the act of understanding, the *intellectus spiritualis*, is spiritual. But this spiritual act must deal with each of the two poles in their given or desired concrete reality as past, present, or future events, respectively—and not as abstractions or concepts. These are completely secondary, since both promise and fulfillment are real and concrete historical events that either occurred in the Incarnation of the Word or will occur in the Second Coming. Of course purely spiritual elements are also involved in this kind of ultimate fulfillment, since "My kingdom is not of this world." But the coming world will likewise be a real kingdom, not an abstract and immaterial entity. This world will fade away only as *figura*; its *natura* will remain (cf. above, p. 85) and the body will be resurrected. Insofar as figural interpretation takes one thing for another and insofar as one thing represents and signifies the other, it belongs, broadly speaking, to the allegorical forms of representation. But it is also clearly different from most other forms of allegory that we know because of the concrete historicity of both the sign and the signified. The majority of the allegories that we find in either literature or the fine arts represent

Figura | 97

either a virtue (for example, wisdom) or a passion (jealousy) or an institution (the law), or at most a very general kind of synthesis of a historical phenomenon (peace, the fatherland). Never, however, do they capture the full concrete historicity of a particular event. The allegories of the late antique and medieval traditions—from Prudentius's *Psychomachia*[36] to Alain de Lille and the *Roman de la Rose*—are of this type.

Similarly, or, if one prefers, conversely, allegorical interpretations of historical events in the world[37] are usually read as obscure representations of philosophical doctrines. In biblical exegesis, this kind of allegorical method remained in constant competition with figural interpretation. Such was Philo's method, for example, which was also practiced by those catechetical schools in Alexandria that were influenced by him.[38] This method rested on a venerable and widespread tradition. Various philosophical schools had already taken over the Greek myths (especially those of Homer and Hesiod) and, in enlightened fashion, interpreted them as veiled depictions of their respective physical and cosmological systems. Quite a number of other influences followed that were no longer purely rational, but were rather ethical, mystical, and metaphysical. All of the numerous late antique sects and occult doctrines cultivated the allegorical interpretation of myths, signs, and texts. As a result, physics and cosmology gradually yielded to ethics and mysticism. Philo himself, who, following the Jewish tradition, constructed his philosophy as a kind of commentary on Scripture, interpreted the individual events of Scripture as various phases in the constitution of the soul and its relation to the intelligible world. He saw in the fate of Israel in general, as well as in the lives of the individual actors in Jewish history, an allegory of the movement of the sinful soul in need of salvation from its fall through hope to its final redemption. This approach was clearly based on a purely spiritual and extra-historical interpretation that was very influential in the late antique world because it was itself probably merely the most respectable version of a powerful spiritualist movement that was centered in Alexandria. At the time, however, it was not only texts and events that were stripped of their sensuous reality and then interpreted allegorically, occasionally even in a somewhat figural fashion. The natural world in its direct manifestations, such as the stars, animals, and stones, was also read this way. The catechetical schools in Alexandria adopted the method in all of its spiritualist, ethical, and allegorical detail. Origen was a particularly important representative of this

[36] There are other examples of figural interpretation in Prudentius that he nevertheless does not seem to acknowledge and explain, namely, his *Dittochaeon* (*PL* 60:90ff).

[37] We must understand here both actual events in history as well as legendary and mythical ones. Whether that which is to be interpreted actually occurred or is merely taken to have occurred is a matter of indifference for my project.

[38] On this subject, see most recently Émile Bréhier in his *Les Idées philosophiques et religieuses de Philon d'Alexandrie*, 2nd ed. (Paris: J. Vrin, 1925) 35ff.

school, which, like the figural approach, as we know, had a robust afterlife in the Middle Ages. Yet, regardless of the fact that some hybrid forms occurred, the two are decidedly different. The spiritualist approach also transforms the Old Testament, causing the Law and history of Israel to lose their national and popular character. These are replaced with a mystical and ethical doctrinal system. As a result, the text loses its concrete quality to a far greater extent than when it is read with the figural approach, and it is deprived of its historicity as well. This kind of exegesis dominated for a long time and determined one of the levels of the fourfold meaning of Scripture, the moral level, entirely—and often a second one, the analogical level, too. Nevertheless, I believe, without of course being able to prove it conclusively, that alone, without the support of the figural approach, it would hardly have had any impact on the newly converted peoples at all. Its effect was always somewhat scholarly and indirect, even abstruse, except when the rare, great mystic occasionally breathed life into it. But as a result of its origin and nature, it was restricted to a relatively small circle of intellectuals and initiates; they were the only ones who could take pleasure in and be sustained by its teachings. By contrast, figural historically real prophecy had a task in history. It had by necessity become genuinely relevant, owing to the specific historical situation out of which it had emerged—namely, the separation of Christianity from Judaism and the particular circumstances of the mission to the Gentiles. It captured the imagination and the innermost feelings of those nations with the force that comes with a unified and teleological interpretation of world history and a providential plan for the world. Its success simultaneously opened the way for less concrete forms of allegory, such as the Alexandrian form. But although this and other spiritualistic forms of interpretation may be older than the figural approaches of the Apostles and the Church Fathers, they are unmistakably late forms. Figural interpretation, on the other hand, while certainly not primitive or archaic in any way, represented, in its dynamic concrete historicity, a new beginning and a rebirth of creativity.

In addition to the allegorical forms I have just discussed, there are other ways of representing things that could be compared to figural prophecy. These are the so-called symbolic and mythical forms of representation that are often considered characteristic of primitive cultures and that are in any case often found in those cultures. A great deal of material about them has come to light recently. But because so little thorough analysis of it has been completed, we must be careful about what we say. What is characteristic of these forms—and Vico was the first to recognize and describe this—is that the object of the representation must always be something enormously important, even sacred, that determines the lives and thought of those who believe in it. However, this force is not only expressed or, as it were, imitated by the sign or symbol. It is actually present in and contained by the symbol in such a way that the symbol itself can act and be acted upon in

Figura | 99

its place. Whatever influences the symbol is considered to sustain are also sustained by that which is symbolized; under these conditions, the symbol acquires magical powers. The kinds of symbolic or mythical forms existed in the Mediterranean cultures of late antiquity. But having for the most part lost their magical power, they had been reduced to allegories. The process is similar today; traces of it survive in our legal symbols, in heraldry, and in national emblems. Of course, both in late antiquity and still today, new and universally valid ideas over and over again create symbols that have what we might call real magical power. Such symbolic or mythical forms intersect with figural interpretation in several ways. Both lay claim to being able to interpret life in general and to endow it with order; both are only conceivable in religious or related spheres. Yet differences are also immediately apparent. Symbols by necessity possess magical powers; *figura* does not. *Figura* must always be historical; the symbol is not. There is of course also no dearth of magical symbols in Christianity, but *figura* as such is not one of them.[39] The two forms are, moreover, completely different from one another in that historically real prophecy refers to the interpretation of history and is thus a moment of textual interpretation from the start. By contrast, symbols pertain directly to the interpretation of life, and originally, no doubt, mostly to nature. In this juxtaposition, figural interpretation is a product of late cultures and is much more indirect, complicated and freighted with history than the symbol or myth. Viewed in this light, *figura* has a rather ancient feel to it, since an advanced civilization must first reach its very highest point, indeed, it must already show signs of old age, before exegesis (which is itself the product of a tradition) can become something like figural interpretation.

As the result of both of these distinctions, the one concerning allegory, the other concerning symbolic and mythic forms, figural prophecy can be seen in a double light. On the one hand, it is youthful, newborn, and sure of its purpose as a concrete interpretation of world history capable of giving that history form. On the other hand, it is ancient, the late interpretation of a venerable text that is freighted with history and that has matured over hundreds of years. Its youthful dynamism invested figural prophecy with an unparalleled power of persuasion. With this, it won over not only the late cultures of the Mediterranean, but also the relatively young peoples of the West and the North. Moreover, its antiquity endowed these peoples and their understanding of history with something that was oddly enigmatic, and it this enigma that I will now undertake to explain more precisely.

[39] There are many intermediate forms that are both figures and symbols. The Eucharist, which is the real presence of Christ, is the most prominent of them; the cross as the tree of life, *arbor vitae crucifixae*, is another one whose meaning is well known. We see examples from the fourth-century poem *De Cruce* [On the Cross] in Labriolle (n. 23 above) 424, through the Franciscan spiritualist Ubertino da Casale and Dante and beyond.

Figural prophecy consists in an interpretation of one inner-worldly event by another. The first event points to the second, the second fulfills the first. To be sure, both remain concrete events that have taken place within history. Yet, when seen from this perspective, both also have something provisional and incomplete about them. They point to one another and both point to something in the future that still is to come. This will be the actual, complete, real, and final event. This is the case not only for Old Testament prefiguration, which points to the Incarnation and the proclamation of the Gospel. It is also the case for the Incarnation and the Gospel themselves. For these too are not yet the final fulfillment, but rather also a promise of the Last Days and the true Kingdom of God to come. In this way, whatever happens, happens. But it also remains, in spite of its powerful facticity, no more than an allegory, veiled and in need of interpretation, even if the general sense and direction of this interpretation are given by faith. In this way, no specific event in the world ever achieves the kind of closure that is found in both the naïve and the modern-scientific notions of an accomplished fact. Rather, whatever happens remains open and uncertain, pointing to something that is still obscure. The relation of the living individual towards events of this kind is that of someone who is being tested and who lives in a state of hope, belief, and expectancy. The provisional nature of events in figural understanding is also fundamentally different from the modern idea of historical progress; here, the provisional nature of history is steadily and consistently interpreted as part of a never-ending horizontal sequence of future events. In figural understanding, however, meaning must at all times be sought vertically, from above, and events are understood individually, not as part of an unbroken sequence, but as torn apart from one another, and always waiting for a third thing that has been promised but has not yet come to pass. And whereas in the modern notion of linear progression facts are always guaranteed in their autonomy, but their meaning is always fundamentally incomplete, in figural interpretation facts are always subordinated to a meaning that is fixed in advance; they orient themselves according to a model of events that lies in the future and that thus far has only been promised. The formulation is reminiscent of Platonizing ideas about an original that is located in the future (recall the phrase *imitatio veritatis* [the imitation of the truth] above, p. 89), which brings us to the next point, namely, that this very future original, even if it is incomplete as event, is already perfectly fulfilled in God and has always been so as the result of His eternal Providence. The figures in which He cloaked it and the Incarnation in which He revealed its meaning are thus prophecies of something that exists for all time, but which remains veiled for human beings until the day when they can behold the Savior *revelata facie* (with his face revealed), both with their senses and in their hearts. The figures are thus not only provisional. They are at the same time also the provisional form of something that is eternal and for all times. They signify the future not only as

Figura | 101

a matter of fact, but also as eternity and as that which has been timeless from the very start. They point to something that is to be interpreted, and which will of course be fulfilled in the concrete future, but also to something that is always also already fulfilled in God's Providence, where no temporal difference exists. This eternity is already figured in the figures, so to speak. They are thus simultaneously provisional fragments of reality and part of a veiled reality for all time. This dialectic is especially obvious in the *figura Christi* (figure of Christ) that is the Sacrament of the sacrifice, the Last Supper, referred to in the *Pascha nostrum* (our Passover lamb).[40] This sacrament, which is both a figure and a symbol and has already existed in history for a very long time—in fact, since it was first instituted in the old covenant—shows us in its purest form the simultaneity in figures of what is present to our senses, what is provisional and veiled, and what is—from the very beginning—beyond all time.

IV. On Figural Representation in the Middle Ages

Figural interpretation or, to state it more inclusively, the figural understanding of events, was widespread and had a deep impact into the Middle Ages and beyond. This fact has not escaped the attention of scholars. Not only theological works dealing with the history of hermeneutics, but also studies of art history and the history of literature have discovered ideas of figuration along the way and have engaged with them. This is of course especially true of art historical work in the field of medieval iconography and of the literary history of religious drama from the same period. But the peculiar nature of the problem does not appear to have been recognized. As a result, the figural and typological structure and the issue of historically real prophecy have not been clearly enough distinguished from other allegorical or symbolic forms of representation. In his very learned dissertation on Gonzalo de Berceo's *El Sacrificio de la Misa* (Washington, The Catholic University of

---

[40] The fourth-century text *De sacramentis* gives the following lines in place of the prayer, *Quam oblationem*, in the Roman Mass: *Fac nobis . . . hanc oblationem ascriptam, ratam, rationabilem, acceptabilem, quod figura est corporis et sanguinis Christi. Qui predie . . .* [Make for us this offering consecrated, approved, reasonable, and acceptable, which is a figure of both the body and blood of Christ, who on this day . . .]. Cf. Dom. F. Cabrol in *Liturgia: Encyclopédie populaire des connaissances liturgiques*, Réné Aigrain, ed. (Paris: Bloud et Gay, 1931). Cf. also a much later text, the thirteenth-century *Rhythmus ad Sanctam Eucharistiam*: *Adoro te devote, latens deitas, / Quae sub his figuris vere latitas . . .* and later, *Jesu quem velatum nunc adspicio, / Oro fiat illud quod tam sitio, / Ut te revelata cernens facie / Visu sim beatus tuae gloriae* [Humbly I adore thee, hidden Deity / which beneath these figures art concealed from me . . . Jesus whom thus veiled I must see below, / When shall that be given which I long for so, / That at last beholding thy uncovered face, / Thou shalt satisfy me with [thy] fullest grace?] (*Collected Hymns, Sequences and Carols of John Mason Neale*, J. M. Neale, trans. [London: Hodder and Stroughton, 1914] 63).

America, 1933), T. C. Goode makes a promising start. And, although he does not deal with the fundamental questions, H. Pflaum provides a clear understanding of the issues. He had already encountered the problem of figuration in his study of religious disputation in European medieval poetry (Geneva-Florence, 1935); more recently, in the journal *Romania* (63:519ff.), Pflaum was able—on the basis of his correct understanding of the French *figure*—to provide an accurate interpretation of several old French verses that the editor had misunderstood and thus to restore the text. There may be other examples that I have missed.[41] In any case, I do not believe there has been a thorough-going treatment of the question up to now. But such a study seems indispensable if we are to understand the mixture of spirituality and a sense of reality that characterized the European Middle Ages, a mixture that is very hard for us to comprehend.[42] Figural interpretation continued to play a role for most European peoples up through the eighteenth century. We find traces of it not only in Bossuet, where its presence is only natural, but also decades later in the religious authors cited by Groethuysen in his book on the origins of the bourgeois spirit in France.[43] A clear understanding of its nature—such that we could distinguish between it and other related, but dif-

[41] There are many allusions to it in Étienne Gilson's *Les idées et les lettres* (Paris: J. Vrin, 1932), especially 68ff. and 155ff. He also refers to the role of the figurative in the medieval philosophy of history in his essay, "Le Moyen Âge et l'Histoire," in his book, *L'Esprit de la philosophie médiévale* (Paris: J. Vrin, 1932). He does so there, however, not with any great emphasis, since his main interest is in working out the medieval roots of modern ideas. Cf. also, for German religious drama, T. Weber's 1909 Marburg dissertation, *Die Praefigurationen im geistlichen Drama Deutschlands* and Ludwig Wolff's essay, "Die Verschmelzung des Dargestellten mit der Gegenwartswirklichkeit im deutschen geistlichen Drama des Mittelalters (*Deutsche Vierteljahrsschrift für Literaturwissenschaft und Geistesgeschichte* 7 [1929] 267ff). On figural elements in the character of Charlemagne in the *Song of Roland*, cf. Albert Pauphilet's well-known essay ["Sur la Chanson de Roland"] in the journal *Romania* 59 [1933] esp. 183ff.

[42] There are of course countless analyses of the fourfold meaning of Scripture. Yet none of them emphasizes what seems to me to be the essential point. It is logical that medieval theology differentiates among the various forms of allegory in clear ways (for example, Petrus Comestor in the prologue to the *Historia scolastica*). But it attributes only a more or less technical and not a fundamental meaning to these distinctions. Even a major modern theologian like the Dominican, Father Mandonnet, who gives an outline of the history of symbolism in his book, *Dante le Théologien* (Paris: Desclée, de Brouwer & cie., 1935, 163ff.), considers the knowledge of these distinctions necessary only as technical preliminaries to textual understanding and does not attend to the various different structures of the idea of reality contained in the text.

[43] The foundations of figural interpretation were already in ruins by that time; even religious personnel for the most part no longer understood them. As [Émile] Mâle tells us in his *L'Art religieux du XIIe siècle en France* (3rd ed. [Paris: Colin, 1928] 391), Montfaucon interpreted the figures of the Old Covenant lined up on the sides of several church porches as Merovingian kings. In a 1696 letter from Leibniz to Burnett (in Gerhardt's edition, 3:306), we find the following passage: *M. Mercurius van Helmont croyait que l'âme de Jésus Christ était celle d'Adam, et que l'Adam nouveau réparant ce que le premier avait gasté c'était le même personnage qui satisfaisait à son ancienne dette. Je crois qu'on fait bien de s'épargner la peine de réfuter de telles pensées* [Monsieur Mercurius van Helmonst believed that the soul of Christ was Adam's soul and that the new Adam, repairing what

Figura | 103

ferently structured forms—would allow us to be more precise and incisive in our overall understanding of the documents of late antiquity and the Middle Ages and could—in individual cases—even solve some real mysteries. Might the themes that appear so frequently on early Christian sarcophagi and in the catacombs not be figures of the Resurrection? Or, to cite one of Mâle's examples in his massive and important work, might not the legend of Maria Aegyptica, whose representations in the museum at Toulouse he describes (op. cit. 240ff.), be a figure of the people of Israel as they went out of Egypt and as a result be open to an interpretation like the one that was generally given in the Middle Ages to the psalm *In exitu Israel de Aegypto*?

But individual interpretations do not exhaust the significance of the figural approach. The extent to which it lies at the very foundation of the interpretation of history in the Middle Ages and even often plays a role in the way that everyday realities of the period are understood, will not have escaped the attention of anyone who has studied the medieval period. The entire system of analogical thinking that extends into every sphere of medieval spirituality is closely bound up with the structure of figuration. As the image of God, man himself takes on the character of a *figura trinitatis* [a figure of the Trinity] in interpretations of the Trinity beginning with Augustine's *De Trinitate* and extending approximately up through Thomas Aquinas (*Summa* 1.45.7). It is not entirely clear to me to what extent aesthetic ideas were determined by figural thinking, just how far, that is, the work of art was understood as the *figura* of a fulfillment in reality that had yet to be attained. The question of artistic imitation did not arouse much theoretical interest in the Middle Ages. But the notion that the artist, as a figure of God the Creator, as it were, was able to realize in the world something whose original was alive in his own mind became all the more important.[44] Such thoughts are, as one can see, indebted to Neoplatonic ideas. I have not been able to find any final, decisive answer to the following question in the texts to which I have access here (the most important specialized works are lacking): To what extent were this original and the work of art based on it considered to be figures for a reality and a truth whose fulfillment lay in God? I would nevertheless like to cite several passages that I happen to have ready to hand and that suggest something in the direction of which I am thinking. In an essay about the representation of musical tones in the capitals of the Abbey of Cluny (see *Deutsche Vierteljahrsschrift für Literaturwissenschaft und Geistesgeschichte* 7 [1929] 264), L. Schrade quotes the explanation given by Remigius of Auxerre of the word *imitari*: *scilicet persequi, quia veram musicam non potest humana*

---

the first Adam had spoiled, was the same person paying off his original debt. I believe that one would do well to spare oneself the work of refuting such thoughts].

[44] Thomas Aquinas writes of the architect: *quasi idea* (*Quodlibetales* 4.1.1). Cf. on this topic, Panofsky (n. 15 above) 20ff. and the note on 85. Also, cf. the quotation from Seneca in note 15 above.

musica imitari [to follow this up of course: because human music is not able to imitate true music]. The idea behind this is in all likelihood that in the creation of art, the artist produces an imitation or a shadowy figuration of a true reality that is also a sensuous reality (in this case, of the music of the heavenly choir). In *Purgatory*, Dante praises the works of art there that were created by God Himself—which represent examples of the virtues and the vices—for their perfectly fulfilled sensuous truth, next to which human art and even nature pale (*Purgatory* 10 and 12). His appeal to Apollo includes the verses:

> O divina virtù, se mi ti presti
> Tanto che l'ombra del beato regno
> Segnata nel mio capo io manifesti!

> [O godly force, if you so lend yourself
> To me, that I might show the shadow of
> The blessed realm inscribed within my mind.]

—*Paradise* 1.22–24 (Trans. Mandelbaum 379)

Here, his own poetry is described as a true *umbra* [shadow] of the truth, chiseled into his mind. Dante's theory of inspiration occasionally contains statements that can be explained in the same way. But these are all only suggestions, and a study seeking to clarify the relationship between Neoplatonic and figurative motifs in medieval aesthetics would have to be based on a far broader collection of material. But my statements so far allow us to conclude this much: We must, in fundamental ways, distinguish the structure of figuration from other forms of imagery. Roughly speaking, we can say that in Europe, the figurative method goes back to Christian influences, the allegorical to ancient pagan ones, and that the first is applied for the most part to Christian materials, the second, rather, to ancient ones. We would not even be mistaken if we were to designate the figural approach as primarily Christian and medieval, while the allegorical method, which relied for its models on late antique pagan authors or authors who were not yet thoroughly Christianized, tended to appear when classical, pagan, or even strongly secular influences were on the rise. Yet, such claims are still too general and imprecise to capture the plethora of phenomena in which cultures interpenetrated over the course of a millennium, an abundance that does not permit simplistic categories of this sort. Both profane and pagan material was also interpreted figuratively already very early on. Gregory of Tours, for example, used the legend of the Seven Sleepers as a figure of the Resurrection; the waking of Lazarus or the rescuing of Jonah from the whale was also read in this way. In the high Middle Ages, the Sybils, Vergil, and the figures in his *Aeneid*, indeed, even the characters from the cycles of mythic sagas from Brittany (Galahad in the *Queste del Saint Graal*, for example) were absorbed into figurative

Figura | 105

readings. Some extremely diverse amalgamations of figural, allegorical, and symbolic forms were the result. All of these forms, applied to both classical and Christian material, can also be found in the text in which all medieval culture is contained and which is the culmination of this culture, namely, the *Divine Comedy*. As I will now attempt to show, figural forms are in principle the ascendant ones in the poem; they are decisive for its entire structure.

At the foot of the mountain of Purgatory, Dante and Vergil meet an old man of venerable appearance. His face is illuminated—as if by the sun—by four stars that signify the four cardinal virtues. He inquires sternly as to their right to make this journey, and it becomes clear from Vergil's respectful answer—he has already bidden Dante to kneel before the man—that this is Cato of Utica. For after explaining his divine mission, Vergil continues as follows:

> Or ti piaccia gradir la sua venuta;
> Libertà va cercando ch'è sì cara,
> Come sa che per lei vita rifuta.
> Tu 'l sai chè non ti fu per lei amara
> In Utica la morte, ove lasciasti
> La veste ch'al gran dì sarà sì chiara.

> [Now may it please you to approve his coming;
> He goes in search of liberty—so precious,
> As he who gives his life for it must know.
> You know it—who, in Utica, found death
> For freedom was not bitter, when you left the garb that will be bright on
> the great day.]

—*Purgatory* 1.70–75 (Trans. Mandelbaum 219)

Then Vergil implores Cato to favor him by invoking the memory of his former wife, Marcia. The latter rejects the request with no less severity; the wish of the *donna del ciel* [woman in Heaven], Beatrice, is enough. He then orders that, before his ascent, Dante's face be wiped clean of the smoky marks of Hell and that he be girded around the waist with reeds. Cato then appears again at the end of the second canto, where with stern words he reminds the souls, who have just arrived at the foot of the mountain, of their way, for they have forgotten both it and themselves as they listened to Casella's song.

Cato of Utica is the figure that God has placed as the guard at the base of Purgatory: a pagan, an enemy of Caesar, a suicide. This is quite astonishing and the very first commentators, such as Benvenuto of Imola, were already taken aback by it. Dante mentions only a very few pagans, those freed from Hell by Christ, and among them we find here this enemy of Caesar, whose accomplices, those who murdered Caesar, are lodged firmly in Lucifer's jaws, next to Judas. As a suicide, Cato seems no less guilty of having committed the crime of "violence against oneself" than those who suffer horrendous punishments for the same sin in the seventh circle. The puzzle is solved when Vergil says of Dante that he is seeking freedom, which is so dear, as you well know, you who scorned life for its sake. Cato's story is removed from its earthly political context, treated just as the patristic exegetes of the Old Testament treated the individual stories of Isaac and Jacob, among others, and is made into a *figura futurorum* [figure of what is to come]. Cato is a *figura*. Or better, the earthly Cato, who in Utica gave up his life for freedom, was a *figura*, and the Cato who appears here in *Purgatory* is that figure revealed, or fulfilled, the truth of that figural event. For the political and earthly freedom for which he died was only a *figura futurorum*, a prefiguration of that Christian freedom that he has been placed here at the foot of Purgatory to defend and for the sake of which, here too, he resists all earthly temptations. This is the Christian freedom from all evil impulses, the freedom that leads to true control over oneself, the freedom for the sake of which Dante has girded himself with the reeds of humility until he in fact secures it at the very top of the mountain where Vergil crowns him master over himself. Cato's freely chosen death in the face of political servitude is introduced here as a *figura* of the freeing of the soul from the servitude of sin, and thus of the eternal freedom of those of God's children who despise all earthly things. How Dante came to choose Cato for this role can be explained by the position above all party loyalties that he held among the Roman writers who took him to be the ideal image of virtue, justice, piety, and love of freedom. Dante found him praised this way equally by Cicero, Vergil, Lucan, Seneca, and Valerius Maximus. It must have been Vergil's sentence in *Aeneid*, Book 8 (l. 670): *secretosque pios, his dantem iura Catonem* [distant far th' assemblies of the righteous, in whose midst was Cato, giving judgment and decree], the praise, that is, that was expressed for Cato in the work of a poet who wrote on behalf of the Empire, that made such a great impression on Dante. How great his admiration of Cato was is clear in several passages of the *Convivio*; that his suicide must be judged in a special way was something he found addressed already by Cicero in a passage he cites in his *De monarchia* (2.5),[45] where he speaks of it in the, for Dante, so important context of examples of Roman political virtue. There, he wants to demonstrate that Roman rule was legitimate because it was virtuous and served the interests of justice and freedom for all humanity. It is in this chapter that he writes the sentence: *Romanum imperium de fonte nascitur pietatis.* [The Roman empire is born of the fountainhead of piety (Prue Shaw translation, 40).][46]

---

[45] Here see Nicola Zingarelli, *La vita, i tempi e le opere di Dante,* 3rd ed. (Milan: F. Villardi, 1931) 1029ff., and the literature cited in the notes.

[46] Cf. J. Balogh in the *Deutsches Dante-Jahrbuch* 10 (1918) 202.

Figura | 107

Dante believed in a preordained accord between Christian salvation history and Roman secular monarchy. It is thus not surprising that he of all people applies figural interpretation to a pagan from Rome; elsewhere he takes his symbols, allegories, and figures from both of these worlds without distinction. There is no doubt that Cato is a *figura*—not in the way that the characters in the *Roman de la Rose* are allegories, however, but a figure of the kind I have described above, a fulfilled figure that has already become true. The *Divine Comedy* is a vision that regards figural truth as already fulfilled and proclaims as much. This is precisely what is so special about it. That is, following the logic of figural interpretation, it joins the truth that it has witnessed in its vision with earthly and historical events in a precise and concrete way. The character of Cato as a stern, just, and pious man who, at a crucial moment of both his own fate and the providential history of the world, valued freedom above life, is preserved in all its full historical and individual force. This is not just an allegory of freedom, however. No, he remains Cato of Utica, just as Dante saw him, as a unique individual. Yet he is, at the same time, also removed from the earthly and provisional realm in which he considered *political* freedom to be the highest good—in the same way as the Jews saw the strict observance of the Law as the highest good—and is set into a state of final fulfillment. Here it is no longer earthly deeds of civic virtue or of the law that are at stake, but rather the *ben dell'intelletto* [spiritual good], the highest good, the freedom of the immortal soul in the eyes of God.

Let me try to illustrate the same thing in a rather more difficult case. Vergil has been taken by nearly all early commentators to be an allegory of Reason, of natural, human Reason, which leads to a just earthly order—in Dante's mind, to secular monarchy. The early commentators did not object to a purely allegorical interpretation, for they did not feel that allegory and real poetry contradicted one another (as we believe today). Modern interpreters have often resisted this claim, valuing instead the poetic nature, humanity, and individuality of the figure of Vergil without of course being able to deny that Dante's Vergil "means something" or to bring that "something" into seamless alignment with his humanity. Recently—and not only for the figure of Vergil—several scholars (L. Valli, on the one hand, and Mandonnet, on the other) have wanted to return to a greater emphasis on the purely allegorical or symbolic dimension of the poem, thereby eliminating its historical meaning as "positivistic" or "Romantic." But there is no either/or here, no choice to be made between a historical and a hidden meaning in the poem. It is both at once. The figural structure preserves the historical event even as it reveals its meaning. And it can only reveal this meaning when the historical event is preserved.

The historical Vergil is both a poet and a guide in Dante's eyes. Indeed, he is a guide *because* he is a poet, because in his poem, the *Aeneid*, and in Aeneas's descent into Hell the political order that Dante considered to be exemplary, namely, the *terrena Jerusalem* [earthly Jerusalem],[47] the universal peace that came to pass during the Roman Empire, is prophesied and glorified, and also because the founding of Rome as the predestined seat of worldly and spiritual power is honored there in song in light of its future mission. But he is also a guide *as poet*—above all because his work triggered and inspired the work of all the great poets who came after him. Dante emphasizes this not only for himself. He also introduces a second poet, namely Statius, to show the same thing in the most pointed of ways. The same theme is addressed in the encounter with Sordello, and perhaps also in the much debated line about Guido Cavalcanti (*Inferno* 10.63). Moreover, the poet Vergil is also a guide because, in addition to temporal prophecies, he proclaimed in the Fourth Eclogue the coming of the eternal, timeless order, the Coming of Christ, which was to coincide with the rebirth of the temporal world. This he of course did without sensing the significance of his own words, but still in such a way that those who came later could be inspired and their understanding of the truth illuminated by his text. Moreover, Vergil led the way as a poet because of his description of the realm of the dead; he was thus a guide through the afterlife because he knew the way. But it was not only as a poet that he was destined to lead. He was also so destined because he was a Roman and a human being. He was endowed not just with eloquent speech and lofty wisdom, but also with precisely those qualities that enable one to lead—the same qualities embodied in his hero, Aeneas, and in Rome overall, namely, *iustitia* [justice] and *pietas* [piety]. Finally, for Dante, the historical Vergil already embodied the fullness of earthly perfection that destined him to be a leader and made him capable of guiding Dante up to the very threshold of insight into divine and eternal perfection. The historical Vergil is for Dante a *figura* of the figure of Vergil as the poet-prophet as leader-guide, now fulfilled in the world beyond. The historical Vergil is "fulfilled" by the Vergil who dwells in Limbo, the companion of the great poets of antiquity who, at Beatrice's request, takes up the position of Dante's guide. Just as he once, as a Roman and a poet, had followed the advice and decision of the gods and allowed Aeneas to descend into the underworld to learn the fate of the Roman world, just as his poetic work became a guide for those who came after him, so too is he called here to serve as guide for a no less significant undertaking. For there can be no doubt that Dante sees his mission as equal to that of Aeneas. He has been summoned to reveal to a world out of joint the just order that was revealed to him on his journey. And Vergil has been summoned to show and interpret for Dante the true order on earth whose laws extend to and are fulfilled in the world beyond, an order whose goal, which is the heavenly community of the blessed, he had anticipated in his

---

[47] In *Purgatory* 32.102, Dante construes *quella Roma onde Cristo è Romano* [the Rome in which Christ is Roman; Mandelbaum translation, 369] as the fulfilled Kingdom of God.

Figura | 109

poem, but whose innermost divine kingdom he was not allowed to enter—
for the meaning of his anticipation had not been revealed to him during his
time on earth. He died a nonbeliever without revelation, and God would not
have anyone led by him enter His kingdom. He may lead Dante only up to
the threshold of this kingdom, but only to that border of which his just and
noble poetry had allowed him to catch a glimpse. "You were the first," Statius
says to Vergil, "to send me to drink within Parnassus' caves and you, the first
who, after God, enlightened me. You did as he who goes by night and carries
the lamp behind him—he is of no help to his own self but teaches those who
follow. . . . Through you I am a poet and, through you, a Christian" [*Purgatory* 22.64–69 and 73–743; Mandelbaum, 319].[48] Just as, in his earthly form
and influence, Vergil led Statius to salvation, so too does he here, as a fulfilled
figure, lead Dante to salvation. For Dante too has taken from him the lofty
poetic style and been saved from eternal damnation by him and set upon
the road to salvation. Just as he once inspired Statius, without himself seeing
the light that he carried and proclaimed, so too does Vergil now lead Dante
to the very threshold of the light of which he may know, but which he is not
himself permitted to see.

Vergil is thus not an allegory of an attribute or of a virtue, of an ability
or a power, or of a historical institution. He is neither Reason nor Poetry
nor the Empire. He is Vergil. But he is of course not Vergil in the way that
later poets tried to depict a human figure caught up in his concrete life in
the world—as Shakespeare did for Caesar or Schiller for Wallenstein. These
poets show their earthly characters in the midst of their lives on earth, calling
an important epoch of earthly existence up before our eyes and interpreting
its meaning in terms of those lives. For Dante the meaning of any life is to
be interpreted according to its place in the providential world history that he
has captured in the vision of the *Divine Comedy*, once the general outlines
of that vision have been preserved in the revelation that is given to every
Christian. In the *Divine Comedy*, Vergil is the historical Vergil himself, to be
sure. But he is also no longer just this. The historical Vergil is only a *figura* of
the fulfilled truth that the poem reveals, and this fulfillment is more, more
real and more significant, than the *figura*. In an entirely different way than
in modern poetry, a character becomes more real in Dante's poem in direct
relation to how completely it is interpreted, how accurately it takes up a place
in the eternal plan of redemption. And for him, unlike the ancient poets of

---

[48]Numerous scholars since Comparetti have dealt in detail with the claim that Vergil was often
considered one of the prophets of Christ. There is some new material about this issue in the *Festschrift*-volume *Virgilio nel medio evo* in the series *Studi Medievali* (N.S. 5 [1932]). I would like to
mention especially Karl Strecker, "*Jam nova progenies caelo dimittitur alto*" (ibid. 167), where a
bibliography and some material about the general structure of figuration may be found. See also
Émile Mâle, "*Virgile dans l'art du moyen âge*" (ibid. 325), and especially plate I. Also Luigi Suttina,
"*L'effigie di Virgilio nella Cattedrale di Zamorra*" (ibid., 342).

the underworld for whom earthly life was real and the life below only a play of shadows, it is the Beyond that is the true reality. The world below is only an *umbra futurorum* [a shadow of things to come]. Of course this *umbra* [shadow] is also a prefiguration of the reality beyond and must be found again fully in it.

What I have said here about Cato and Vergil holds true for the *Divine Comedy* in general. It is based entirely on the idea of figuration. In my book, *Dante: Poet of the Secular World* (1929), I attempted to show that it was Dante's project in the *Divine Comedy* to "represent the entire earthly, historical world . . . as already subjected to God's final judgment, so that each soul occupies the place assigned to it by the divine order. However, the individual figures, arrived at their ultimate, eschatological destination, are not divested of their earthly character. Their earthly historical character is not even attenuated, but rather held fast in all its intensity and so identified with their ultimate fate"(86). When I wrote this, I lacked the details of the historical foundation of my claim, which is a claim that can already be found in Hegel and on which I based my interpretation of the *Divine Comedy*. It is more hinted at than directly recognized in the introductory chapters of that book. I now believe that I have found this foundation. It is precisely the figural interpretation of reality that dominated the worldview of the European Middle Ages, even as it also was engaged in an ongoing battle with purely spiritualistic and Neoplatonic tendencies. The idea was that earthly life was thoroughly real, with a reality of the kind that the Word entered into as flesh. But even in all of its reality, this life is only an *umbra* and *figura* of the actual, future, final, and authentic truth that, both unveiling and preserving the figure, contains true reality. In this way, every earthly event is to be considered as neither a final reality and an end unto itself, nor as one event in a series, whereby new events always emerge as the result of earlier events or of a combination of events. Rather, the earthly event is to be viewed, first, as standing in an immediate vertical relation to the divine order in which it is contained and which will itself, at some future point, be a reality that occurs. The earthly event is thus a historically real prophecy, or *figura*, of a part of a divine reality that will occur in the future and that will at that point be perfected in all its immediacy. Yet this reality is not only in the future. Rather, it is always present in the sight of God and in the Beyond. The revealed and true reality is always and eternally present there, beyond time. In his work, Dante attempts to capture all of earthly reality in this light, both poetically and philosophically. The grace of the divine powers had come to his aid—this is the vision of the poem—precisely when he was threatened by the ruin of his confusion in the world. He had partaken of this special grace already in his youth because he was destined for a special task. Very early he had been permitted to see in Beatrice, a living being, the Revelation incarnate (here, the structures of

Figura | 111

figuration and Neoplatonism become entangled, as is so often the case). As a living being, albeit in veiled fashion, she designates him as chosen, greeting him with her eyes and her mouth; in death she did the same, but in an unspoken and mysterious way.[49] Departed and now blessed, Beatrice finds for the confused Dante—for whom she is Revelation incarnate—the only salvation still available for him. She is indirectly his guide—and in Paradise, directly—as she shows him the divine order revealed. This order is the truth of earthly figures. Everything he sees and learns in the three realms is true and concrete reality, the reality in which the earthly *figura* is contained and interpreted. When he sees the fulfilled truth while he is still alive, he is both himself saved and at the same time able to announce to the world what has happened and to indicate to that world the correct path to follow.

Of course this insight into the figural character of the *Divine Comedy* does not offer a universally valid method for interpreting every individual disputed passage. Yet we can deduce several basic principles of interpretation from it. We can be sure that every historical or mythical character that appears in the poem can only mean something that was intimately connected with what Dante knew about that individual's historical or mythical existence, connected, that is, in the way that figure and fulfillment are connected. We must take care not to give these characters only a conceptual or allegorical meaning and to deny them their earthly and historical existence. This is particularly the case for Beatrice. In the nineteenth century, Romantic realism overemphasized her humanness and tended to make the *Vita Nova* into something like a sentimental novel. Now a reaction has set in and scholars are making every effort to find ever more specific theological concepts into which she may be completely absorbed. But this is also not an either/or situation. For Dante, the literal meaning and historical reality of a character do not contradict that figure's deeper meaning. Rather, they figure it. Historical reality is not annulled by this deeper meaning. Rather, it is confirmed and fulfilled in it. The Beatrice of the *Vita Nova* is an earthly figure. She really appeared to Dante, she really greeted him and, later, really denied him this greeting. She mocked him, mourned a dead friend and her father, and then really died. Naturally this kind of reality can only be the kind of reality that Dante experienced—for a poet forms and transforms in his consciousness those events that have happened to him. We can only work with what was alive in this consciousness and not assume any external reality. Moreover, we must keep in mind that, for Dante, even the earthly Beatrice was from the very first day she appeared to him a miracle sent from Heaven, an incarna-

---

[49] The words *converrebbe essere me laudatore di me medesimo* [this would entail praising myself] in the *Vita Nova* (28) allude to 2 Corinthians 12:1. Cf. [Charles Hall] Grandgent in the journal *Romania* 31 [1902] 14, and Michelle Scherillo's commentary [*La Vita Nuova e il Canzoniere*, 2nd ed. (Milan: Hoepli, 1921) 233].

tion of divine truth. The reality of her earthly person is thus not, as is the case with Vergil or Cato, derived from specific facts that belonged to a historical tradition, but rather from his own experience, and this experience had shown him that the earthly Beatrice was a miracle.[50] Yet, an incarnation and a miracle are also things that really occur. Miracles occur on earth and the Incarnation is a thing of the flesh. The alien nature of the medieval idea of reality has led modern scholars to the point where they do not distinguish between figuration and allegory, and mostly understand only the latter.[51] Even as astute a theological scholar as Mandonnet (op. cit. 218–19) accepts only two possibilities: Beatrice is either no more than an allegory (this is his position) or she is *la petite Bice Portinari* [little Bice Portinari], a claim at which he jeers. Quite apart from the misconstrual of the essence of poetic reality that is obvious in this kind of judgment, it is above all astounding that he sees such a deep split between reality and meaning. Is the *terrena Jerusalem* [earthly Jerusalem] not historical reality merely because it is a *figura aeternae Jerusalem* [figure of eternal Jerusalem]?

In the *Vita Nova*, Beatrice is thus a living human being viewed from the reality of Dante's lived experience—just as she is not an *intellectus separatus* [separate intellect] or an angel in the *Divine Comedy*, but, rather, a blessed human being whose body will be restored to her at the Last Judgment. There is no theological concept associated with the Schools that would grasp her in her entirety. Many of the events of the *Vita Nova* do not fit into any allegory. And there is the additional problem in the *Divine Comedy* of having to distinguish her in some precise way from several of the other characters in *Paradise*, the "Testing Apostles," for example, or St. Bernard. In any case what is special about her relationship to Dante cannot be grasped in this way to anyone's satisfaction. Most older commentators saw Beatrice as Theology. In recent years, scholars have attempted to identify in her a more specific aspect of the theological. But this too has led to exaggeration and mistakes. Even Mandonnet, who used for Beatrice the very broadly understood term, *ordre surnaturel*, which he develops in opposition to Vergil, becomes overly subtle

---

[50] The title of the book indicates as much as does his first designation of her as *la gloriosa donna de la mia mente* [the glorious lady of my mind], the name mysticism, the significance of the number nine with its reference to the Trinity, with the effects that derive from it, and much more. Occasionally she even appears as a *figura Christi*; here we need only think of the significance of her appearance behind Monna Vanna (24) and the events that occur in connection with the vision of her death (23): eclipse, earthquake, and the hosannas of the angels, as well as the welcome given to her when she appears at *Purgatory* 30. Cf. Galaad in the *Queste del Sainte Graal*, in Gilson (n. 41 above) 71.

[51] To avoid misunderstandings, I want to mention here that Dante and his contemporaries called this figurative meaning "allegory" as opposed to designating what is termed allegory here as the moral or tropological meaning. Readers will certainly understand why in this historical study I have stayed with the terminology as it was developed by the Church Fathers and which they preferred.

Figura | 113

in the subcategories he invents, makes mistakes,[52] and forces his concepts. The role that Dante assigns to her is completely clear from her actions and from how her person is described. She is a figure or incarnation of Revelation (*Inferno* 2.76: *sola per cui l'umana specie eccede ogni contento da quell ciel che ha minor li cerchi sui* [the sole reason why/the human race surpasses all that lies/beneath the Heaven with the smallest spheres; trans. Mandelbaum, 65], *Purgatory* 6.45: *che lume fia tra il vero e l'intelletto* [the light between your mind and truth; Mandelbaum, 240]), that God in His Grace and out of His love sends to man to redeem him and that becomes his guide to the *visio Dei* [the vision of God]. Mandonnet forgets, however, to mention that she is an incarnation of divine Revelation, not Revelation itself—this in spite of the fact that he cites the relevant passages from the *Vita Nova* and from Thomas Aquinas, among them the salutation: *O Donna di virtù, sola per cui,* etc., mentioned above. One cannot address the "supernatural order" as such in this way, only its embodied revelation, only that part of the divine plan for salvation which is precisely the miracle through which human beings are exalted above all other living creatures. Beatrice is an incarnation, she is the *figura* or *idola Christi* [image *or* form of Christ], her eyes reflect His doubled essence (*Purgatory* 31.126), and she is thus also a human being. Her humanity is of course by no means exhausted by such explanations. Her relationship to Dante can likewise not be fully expressed by considering it from any dogmatic point of view. My comments are merely intended to show that as helpful and indispensable as theological interpretation is, it by no means obliges us to sacrifice Beatrice's historical reality. Precisely the opposite.

With this I bring my study of *figura* to a provisional end. My aim was to show how a word branches out from its semantic meaning and into a world-historical situation and how the structures that emerge out of this situation can remain effective for many centuries. The world-historical situation that led Paul to undertake his mission among the Gentiles did much to shape figural interpretation and paved the way for the broad impact that it went on to have in late antiquity and the Middle Ages.

---

[52] He denies, for example, that there is a smile on her face in spite of *Purgatory* 31.133ff. and 32. Mandonnet's explications of Beatrice may be found op. cit. 212ff.

8

Typological Symbolism in Medieval Literature

In Dante's third heaven, the heaven of Venus, the soul on whom Dante apparently wishes to focus our attention, is introduced to him by one of her companions in this manner: "Now, I will satisfy the ultimate desire which this star has suggested to you; you wish to know who is hidden in this light which shines about me like a sunbeam in pure water: this soul is Rahab, and her splendor gives to our ranks the seal of supreme beatitude; she was the first to be received into this heaven when Christ liberated the souls from Hell; it was most fitting that she should be in one of the heavens as a trophy of the victory that was won with both hands; and this because she contributed to the first conquest made by Joshua in the Holy Land, a remembrance which means little to the Pope" (*Paradise* 9.109–26). And then, the speaker continues with a violent attack against the avarice of the clergy.

This passage is full of problems. Rahab, in the second and sixth chapters of the book of Joshua, is the harlot who hides in her house the two spies sent by Joshua into the town of Jericho—who saves them by deluding their pursuers, declares to them her faith in the God of Israel, helps them to escape by means of a red cord through the window of her house, which is on the townwall, and makes them swear that the Jews would spare her and her parents and all her family in the house. The men asked her to bind to the window, as a sign, the scarlet rope by which she had let them down; and thus only Rahab the harlot and her house were spared when all of Jericho, men and women, were put to death by the victorious Jews entering the town.

Now, why does the splendor of this harlot confer on the third heaven the highest degree of beatitude? Why is the explanation of her position able to fulfill the ultimate desire which the star of Venus has suggested to Dante? Why was Rahab the first to be received in this star when Christ liberated the souls of the old Covenant? What is meant by the victory won with both

Reprinted from Auerbach's English original (1952) as reprinted in his 1967 Gesammelte Aufsätze *(see Appendix: Original Publication History of the Essays in This Collection) with minor editorial changes in punctuation and orthography. The reader should note that by "figuralism," "figuralistic," and "figurative," Auerbach intends their more common equivalents "figural" and "figural interpretation."—Ed.*

hands? And what has the avarice of the Pope to do with his forgetting the glory of Joshua in the Holy Land?

All these problems are easily resolved if you consider the figurative or typological interpretation of the book of Joshua which, in a constant tradition, fully developed already in the writings of Tertullian, is explained or alluded to in an infinite number of commentaries, sermons, hymns, and also in Christian art. The book of Joshua, especially its first chapters, has always been one of the most popular objects of figurative interpretation; Joshua was regarded as a figure of Christ (the identity of the names Jesus and Joshua is emphasized as early as Tertullian), and when he leads his people over the Jordan (just like Moses leading his people out of Egypt) he figures Christ leading mankind out of the slavery of sin and perdition into the true Holy Land, the eternal Kingdom of God. Concerning Rahab, all ancient commentators consider her as a type of the Church; her house alone, with all its inhabitants, escapes perdition, just as the Church of the faithful will alone be saved when Christ appears for the Last Judgment; she found freedom from the fornication of the world by way of the window of confession, to which she bound the scarlet rope, the sign of Christ's blood, *sanguinis Christi signum.* Thus she is *figura Ecclesiae,* and the scarlet rope, like the posts struck with the blood of the Lamb in Exodus, becomes the figure of Christ's redeeming sacrifice. The conception of Jericho as eternal perdition was supported by the parable from Luke 10:30 (a certain man went down from Jerusalem to Jericho, and fell among thieves) generally interpreted as a figure of the Fall of Man. In the same manner, the victory gained with one and the other hand alludes to Joshua's victory won with the help of Moses' outstretched hands, the figure of the victory of Christ on the cross with his hands outstretched on the *arbor vitae crucifixae.* Thus, Rahab, or the Church, stands, in our passage of the *Paradise,* as a trophy of both victories, that of Joshua and that of Christ; of the victory of Joshua inasmuch as Joshua prefigures Christ, and of that of Christ inasmuch as Christ is the fulfillment of Joshua (*implere*); both entities in the figurative or typological relationship are equally real and equally concrete; the figurative sense does not destroy the literal, nor does the literal deprive the figured fact of its status as a real historical event. Obviously, the last sentence of our passage, namely that the Pope has forgotten Joshua's glory in the Holy Land, is also to be understood in a two-fold and typological manner. It is not only the Holy Land in its concrete and geographical sense which the Pope neglects by fighting against Christians instead of liberating it; he has also, for the sake of the *maledetto fiore,* the golden florin of Florence, lost all memory of the city to come, *eterna Jerusalem.* And now, the meaning of the passage has become completely clear: the first elect soul in the heaven of Venus is Rahab, a figure of the Church—that is, of the bride in the Song of Songs—in love of her bridegroom who is Christ—a symbol of the highest form of love—and this view, as Folchetto says, will satisfy the ultimate desire the star of Venus has prompted in Dante's mind.

The method used here for the interpretation of the first chapters of the book of Joshua does, of course, not apply only to this text, but is part of an entire system which embraces the whole of the Old Testament. When Saint Paul came to the conviction that a man is justified by faith alone, not by action according to the Jewish law, and that God is not the God of the Jews alone, the character of the Old Testament was changed completely—this was no longer the law and the particular history of the Jews, because "all these things happened to them in *figura* only": thus the Old Testament became a series of prefigurations of Christ, of his Incarnation and Passion, and of the foundation of the Christian Church. Saint Paul himself gave a few figurative interpretations (the conception of figurism as such was not unknown to the Jewish tradition), and the whole system developed so rapidly that we find it completely worked out, with an incredible abundance of details, in the earliest patristic literature. You will realize that this method of interpretation involves an approach to human and historical phenomena entirely different from ours. We are apt to consider the events of history and the happenings of everyday life as a continuous development in chronological succession; the typological[1] interpretation combines two events, causally and chronologically remote from each other, by attributing to them a meaning common to both. Instead of a continuous development, the direction and ultimate result of which is unknown to us, the typological[2] interpreter purports to know the significance and ultimate result of human history, because this has been revealed to mankind; in this theory, the meaning of history is the fall and redemption of Man, the Last Judgment, and the eternal Kingdom of God. We, on the other hand, are able to explain to a certain extent every single historical fact by its immediate causes and to foresee to a certain extent its immediate consequences, moving so to speak on an horizontal plane; with the typological[3] approach, on the contrary, in order to explain the significance of a single historical event, the interpreter had to take recourse to a vertical projection of this event on the plane of providential design by which the event is revealed as a prefiguration or a fulfillment or perhaps as an imitation of other events. In view of the fact[4] that education and culture were almost entirely ecclesiastical up to the fourteenth century, that the conception of human history, as taught by the Church, was dominated by the interpretation of the Scriptures, and that this interpretation was entirely figurative and based on the trilogy: Fall of Man, Incarnation of Christ, Last Judgment—in view of all these facts it is evident that the figurative conception of history had to exert a deep and lasting influence on medieval spiritual life, even on laymen. Sermons, religious poetry (lyrical and dramatical), Church sculpture—that

---

[1] Changed in the 1967 rpt. from "figurative" in the original version.—Ed.
[2] See previous note. —Ed.
[3] See n. 1 above.— Ed.
[4] Changed to "facts" in the 1967 rpt. —Ed.

is to say, the three most important means of popularizing knowledge in the Middle Ages—were entirely impregnated with typology.[5]

May I draw the attention of my readers to the important difference which obtains between typology[6] and other similar forms of thinking, such as allegorism or symbolism. In these patterns, at least one of the two elements combined is a pure sign, but in a figural relation both the signifying and the signified facts are real and concrete historical events. In an allegory of love or in a religious symbol at least one of the terms does not belong to human history; it is an abstraction or a sign. But in the sacrifice of Isaac considered as a figure of the sacrifice of Christ, it is essential, and has been stressed with great vigor, at least in the occidental tradition, that neither the prefiguring nor the prefigured event lose their literal and historical reality by their figurative meaning and interrelation. This is a very important point.

Dante's mind was deeply rooted in this tradition, and I believe that not only many particular passages in the *Commedia* can be explained in this manner, but that the whole conception of the great poem has to be considered from this angle. It is not difficult to prove that the community of the blessed in the *Empireo*, in which Dante's *Paradise* culminates, is arranged according to a figurative pattern. Not only the world of the Christian religion, but also the ancient world is included in Dante's figural system; the Roman empire of Augustus is for Dante a figure of God's eternal empire, and the prominent part Vergil plays in Dante's work is based on this assumption. Dante is not the first to subject all the material of human history to the figural conception; biblical history, Jewish and Christian, came to be seen as universal human history, and all pagan historical material had to be inserted and adapted to this framework. Especially Roman history was interpreted by Saint Augustine and other patristic authors as a path of Christian universal history and of the plan of Providence. Medieval authors followed this tradition, and very often used it for political purposes, in the long struggle between *imperium* and *sacerdotium*. So did Dante, and most of his figures taken from Roman history are connected with his political ideas, as the following example shows.

At the foot of the mountain of the *Purgatory*, Dante and Vergil meet a venerable old man, who, with severe authority teaches them how to prepare for the ascent, as the guardian who controls access to purification. It is Cato of Utica. The choice of this particular character for such a function is very astonishing. For Cato was a pagan; he was an enemy of Caesar and the monarchy; his allies, Caesar's murderers Brutus and Cassius, are put by Dante in the deepest Hell, in Lucifer's mouth by the side of Judas; moreover, Cato committed suicide, a crime for which horrible punishment is meted out in another circle of the Inferno. And yet Cato has been appointed as guard-

---

[5] Changed in the 1967 rpt. from "figural interpretation" in the original version. —Ed.
[6] See previous n. —Ed.

ian of the *Purgatory*! The problem becomes clear to us by the words with which Vergil addresses him: "I pray you, allow my companion to enter; he is in search of liberty, that precious good you know so well—you who have despised life for it; you know it well, because death was not bitter to you in Utica, where you abandoned your body that will be so radiant on the last day." From these words, it becomes obvious, that Cato is a *figura*, or better still, that the historical Cato is a *figura* of the Cato in Dante's *Purgatory*. The political and earthly freedom for which he died was only a shadow, a prefiguration of Christian freedom from evil which leads from the bondage of corruption to true sovereignty over oneself, the *libertas gloriae filiorum Dei*—a freedom which Dante finally attains at the top of the *Purgatory*, when Vergil crowns him as master over himself. Cato's choice of voluntary death in order to avoid slavery is obviously considered by Dante not as a crime, but as a *figura* of this liberation. Of course Dante was inspired in the choice of Cato for this part by Vergil's sixth book, where Cato is represented as a judge of the righteous in the netherworld (*secretosque pios, his dantem jura Catonem*) and he was encouraged to treat Cato in a special manner by the universal admiration expressed for him even by authors who were his political opponents. Cato was one of the classical examples of Roman virtue on which Dante based his political ideology of universal Roman monarchy. But the manner in which he introduced Cato and justified his part is independent of Vergil and is clearly figurative. Both forms of Cato are real and concrete, the historical and the eternal form; his function in the Beyond presupposes the reality of his historical role. Cato is not an allegory or a symbol of liberty, but an individual personality: he is raised from his preliminary status, where he considered political freedom as the highest good, to the final perfection of his form, in which civil virtue or law have lost their value, and in which the only thing of importance is the *ben dell'intelletto*, the true highest good, the liberty of the immortal soul in the sight of God.

In striking contrast to earlier poets who dealt with the other world, the inhabitants of Dante's three realms have not lost the individual shape and strength of their earthly character; on the contrary, their individual character presents itself with an intensity and concreteness superior to what it was during the various stages of their earthly careers; and this realism in the Beyond is allowed to survive in spite of the fact that they have left history for an eternal, and eternally unchanging, situation. This powerful realism is based on Dante's conception that God's judgment develops and fixes the complete and ultimate form of the individual—a conception which is in concordance with Thomistic anthropology—and which at the same time is figuralistic, in that God's judgment endows an earthly figure with its own final and absolute perfection.

Earlier poets never used figurism in such a universal and audacious manner; they confine figuralistic treatment in most cases to the poetical illustration of sacred history; figurative interpretation of other events or of life in general was mostly unconscious.

From the very beginning of Christian art and poetry, the *figurae* have a tendency to appear in series. These series of figures can be found already on the early Christian sarcophagi; we find for example the liberation of Joseph from the pit, the liberation of Jonah from the belly of the whale (after three days), and the resuscitation of Lazarus (also after three days) represented side by side as figures of Christ's Resurrection. But the full development of figurative series in Christian poetry is rather a medieval phenomenon than one of late antiquity. So far as I can see, the Latin hymnologists of the Carolingian period—especially the inventor of the sequences, Notker Balbulus—were the first to use this form consciously; and the great master of what I may call figurative eulogies is Adam of St. Victor; the twelfth century is the apogee of figurism and especially of figurative series. The praise of the Virgin, for instance, in many of the sequences of Adam and his imitators, consists of just such series; she is represented successively as Sarah laughing at Isaac's birth, Jacob's ladder the top of which reaches to heaven, Moses' burning bush which is not consumed by the flames, Aaron's rod that budded, Gideon's fleece soaked with dew, the Ark of the Covenant that contains the celestial manna, the throne or the bed of the true Solomon who is Christ, Isaiah's rod coming out of the stem of Jesse, Ezekiel's gate looking towards the East which shall be shut because the Lord has entered by it; she is the garden enclosed, the fountain sealed, the fountain of gardens, the well of living waters from the Song of Songs, and so forth.

A student of medieval French literature may remember here the figurative series in the mystery plays, especially the most famous of them, the *Jeu d'Adam* with its procession of prophets. These prophets are not prophets in the restricted sense in which we normally use this word, but Old Testamentary personalities in general: besides Isaiah, Daniel, and Jeremiah, there appear Abraham and Moses, David and Solomon, Balaam and Nebuchadnezar, and others. Each of them begins with one Latin sentence isolated from the text of the Bible, and then goes on to explain the sentence in French as an announcement of Christ. Isaiah for example will not present the whole of his prophecy concerning the future of Jerusalem and the king of Babylon, but is introduced exclusively for the sake of one sentence: *egredietur virga de radice Jesse*, etc., which was considered as a prediction of the Virgin and Christ, just as Abraham is introduced for the sake of the promise God made to him, and Aaron for his budding rod. This is pure figurism; as I have mentioned before, the Old Testament becomes a succession of isolated prefigurations, or, if you prefer, figural prophecies of Christ. In this system even Adam may become not only a *figura* but a figural prophet of Christ. His sleep during which Eve, the mother of mankind in the flesh, was created out of one of his ribs, prefigures Christ's death or sleep before his Resurrection, when one of the soldiers with a spear pierced his side, and forthwith came there out blood and water, symbols of the sacraments of the Church, the mother of mankind in the spirit. Adam's sleep is the mystical sleep of contemplation or ecstasy; when he awakens he starts prophesying: "Therefore shall a man leave his father and his mother and shall cleave unto his wife, and they shall be one flesh"; this passage has been constantly interpreted as a figure of the union of Christ and the Church. This is one of the most ancient and venerable figures, one of the few introduced by Saint Paul himself (Ephesians 5:29–32): *sacramentum hoc magnum est, ego autem dico in Christo et in ecclesia.* [This is a great sacrament, but I speak in Christ and in the Church.]

This interpretation of Adam as a figurative prophet predicting Christ and the Church has become an unbroken tradition. I became aware of it for the first time when reading a sermon of Saint Bernard, the second in Septuagesima. The *Jeu d'Adam*, it is true, does not present Adam in the procession of the prophets, but in another passage of the play he outspokenly predicts Christ. After his Fall, when he gives himself up to despair and long-winded self-accusations, he sees one ray of hope: "There will be no salvation for me except by the son who will be born of the virgin"—*Deus . . . ne me ferat ja nul aïe, fors le fils qu'istra de Marie.* In his deepest despair, he becomes conscious of the future redemption; he has knowledge of the future. This blithe anticipation of the future may appear to us as medieval naïveté, as a lack of historical perspective—the same historical naïveté with which Adam and Eve or, in other plays, other biblical personalities are realistically depicted as Frenchmen of the twelfth and the thirteenth centuries. And, of course, there is indeed implied, in such phenomena, a naïveté and lack of historical perspective; but such an evaluation would not be exhaustive. The figurative interpretation, in spite of its stress on historical completeness, derives its inspiration from the eternal wisdom of God, in whose mind there does not exist a difference of time. In His sight, what happens here and now has happened from the very beginning and may recur at any moment in the flow of time. At any time, at any place, Adam falls, Christ sacrifices himself, and humanity, the bride of the Song of Songs, faithful, hopeful, and loving, searches for Him. A personality who is a *figura Christi,* as Adam is, has knowledge of the providential future—Christ knew that Judas would betray him, just as another figure of Christ, Charlemagne, *Charles li reis, nostre emperere maignes* [Charles the king, our great emperor], in the *Chanson de Roland*, knows from the very beginning that Ganelon is a traitor. The eternal coexistence in God's mind of all historical events is a conception best expressed by Saint Augustine's doctrine that God keeps present in his mind all things past and future in their true reality—that therefore it is not correct to speak of God's foreknowledge, but simply of his knowledge—*scientia Dei . . . non . . . praescientia sed tantum scientia . . . dici potest* [the knowledge of God cannot be called foreknowledge but only knowledge; Augustine, *De diversis quaestionibus ad Simplicianum* 2.2.2]. Figurism gives the basis for the medieval fusion of realistic naïveté and other-worldly wisdom.

9

On the Anniversary Celebration of Dante

Dante's poetic fate is so astonishing that one would have to despair of the laws governing intellectual history to imagine that this fate had already run its course. In every age the poetic sources of a cultural sphere penetrate the deepest layers of popular consciousness. Homer and the Greek tragedians, the heroic lay and Shakespeare, have all been absorbed in their entirety. In Dante we have a poet who must surely be deemed the *fons et origo* of modern poetry. His name and image live on. Yet in his native country, his work has only partly been internalized and absorbed. In the rest of Europe, it has no resonance at all.

This fate began to take shape immediately after his death. Dante's impact was massive: he singlehandedly established the expressive possibilities and the landscape of all poetry to come, and he did so virtually out of thin air, without any tradition behind him and with no fellow travelers at his side. But this impact, though immense, was not direct. Dante was transmitted to the Romance countries and to England through Petrarch, and it was only in Shakespeare's less intense and much refracted form that he reaches us today.

I believe that Dante is far from having achieved his maximum impact even now. No nation has had the strength needed to absorb him. Boarding a vessel that was far too small for the task, everyone followed him into open waters, and then lost sight of him altogether. No later generation proved a match for the powerful force of his character, which erupts into view fully formed and self-fashioned. As a consequence, his truest impact remained limited to a very few. The poetry of subsequent eras oscillated between the two poles of aimless elemental power and rational connection. No poet who could give adequate form to Dante's incandescent fullness ever appeared again.

In Dante the individual was born anew. The individual life of the person had been buried since the fall of antiquity. With Dante, this powerful stream of life was liberated and came to light in the most compelling form the world has ever seen. Then there was his fate, which cut the poet off from his customary and beloved surroundings and denied him the slightest of earthly satisfactions. Dante was as unhappy as anyone endowed with so elemental an intensity can only ever be. He was permitted to enjoy little of what a more fortunate lot grants to other mortals. His earthly love was tragic. His beautiful city, to which he was attached like a young lamb to its flock (*Paradise* 25), banished him. His political aspirations came to naught, and he remained lonely and poor, obliged to "climb another's stairs" (ibid., 17.58–59). In a later era such a man would have been torn apart from within. He would have become accusatory or indignant. And just as he would have protested his earthly surroundings, so too would he have rebelled against his lot. Yet Dante's faith was as unshakeable as his misfortune was unforgiving. No failure could perturb him. So free of doubt and so unconditionally certain was his proud passion that he felt he was one with God. His world and God's world were one and the same. At the end of time stood the Last Judgment, and Dante knew what God's verdict would be. And so, full of impatience and eager to hear this final judgment, he projected his earthly surroundings into the realm of eternity and created the Dantean world *sub specie aeternitatis*. And he did so with the sure knowledge that this was merely his charge, that he was but a herald of things to come, and that he was only God's vessel.

But what shape did this world of Dante's assume? It is the earthly world, in all its sensuous vigor. Even the landscape remains earthly, only it is enhanced to the point of being fantastically prodigious. This is especially true of the people who inhabit it. They have forfeited none of their earthly sense of self. On the contrary, everything particular about them is heightened to a supernatural degree; and it is from these particulars that they reap either damnation, expiation, or salvation. "I am in death as I was in life," Capaneo says (*Inferno* 14), and the same holds for all of Dante's characters. Even in *Paradise* individual passions and affections are expressed in the liveliest of bodily acts and gestures. It never crossed Dante's mind to suggest, the way the German mystics did, that in order to be acceptable to God one must sacrifice one's particularity. Particularity is all-decisive. Character and fate are one, and the destiny of the autonomous self lies in its freedom of choice. The self was created by God in all of its particularity; but the freedom to decide is left entirely up to the self.

This is the secret of Dante's inner commitment, namely his conception of human particularity as something that is intimately bound up with fate. Most reprehensible of all to Dante are people with no personal character, people who pass through their lives without putting themselves on the line and risking humiliation: they do not warrant so much as a thought. A distinctive and particular humanity is the *sine qua non* of any human life. Without it not even evil can come about. But tempting though it may be, we need to beware of detecting in Dante a form of individualism in the modern philosophical sense. Only submission to the divine will leads to salvation, and the proudly indignant characters of the *Inferno* stand on no other footing than that of unfounded defiance. Fate is the only arbiter. Fate is God. And in and of itself the person has no value.

I am keenly aware that an analysis like this only begins to hint at the sensory fullness of Dante. But this much should be clear: that this poet who has kept scholars occupied for centuries, when he is viewed from a loftier perspective, is completely *unproblematic*: the world is closed for him; the order of things is complete; the way is steep, but the direction is preordained.

Now we can see clearly the distance that separates Dante from later centuries. The division of body from soul is not to blame, for at least Michelangelo and Shakespeare still managed to produce a sensuous image of the soul's inner workings. Rather, the separation of fate and character in human consciousness is at fault. As long as we seek out the justification of our existence and our actions anywhere else than in our fate, or at least in our metaphysical aspirations, and as long as we apply our own standards—be these earthly and rational, like virtue and justice, or otherworldly and mystical, like self-renunciation and the repudiation of life—we will never find anything else in the *Divine Comedy* beyond a measure of poetic beauty and prolific matter for scholarly footnotes. Only once the cultural community in which we live takes on a closed form again, one from which it can draw sufficient strength and courage to acknowledge that its destiny is its final arbiter, only then will a commemoration of Dante be more than a celebration by scholars and enthusiasts.

10

Dante and Vergil

... perhaps your Guido disdained him

—*Inferno* 10.63

It is unlikely that any of us would today still want to claim that the traditions of classical antiquity perished with the mass migration of peoples, the so-called "barbarian invasions," and were resurrected only later by the Humanists. We no longer equate the classical Latinity of the end of the Republican and Augustan eras with all of antiquity, and we are doing our best to discover traces of its survival other than Ciceronian Latin and philosophical eclecticism. For us, the history and intellectual activity of the early Middle Ages seem to testify best—albeit in an often indistinct way—to what was ultimately the most successful afterlife of the thought and institutions of late antiquity, which are visible in frequently incongruous, but for that very reason deeply historical forms that are organically linked to the past. Just as we have increasingly come to understand that the real history of Latin lies in the history of the Romance languages, and that classical Latin is, by contrast, an artificial construct (the imitation of which is a historicist endeavor and an aestheticizing one at that), so too does the art of the Middle Ages appear to us today as a clear extension, development, and continual reshaping of ancient Mediterranean traditions. Across the disciplines, scholarship on the early Middle Ages today tends to read artifacts as signs of the persistence of the traditions of the ancient world. Though often present only at a subterranean level and frequently in unrecognizably disfigured forms, they are ultimately triumphant and eminently visible as a kind of "vulgar"—or popular—antiquity, if we may be permitted the term. Here, as in the case of the hotly contested term "vulgar Latin," the word "vulgar" is not meant in any pejorative sociological sense, as if vulgar antiquity or vulgar Latin were proper only to the lower classes, or to the *Volk*. Rather, the word suggests only that the process occurred at the level of the unconscious, the historical, and the organic rather than as a result of conscious, historicist, and learned activity.

It goes without saying that in "vulgar," or late antiquity, individual classical authors and their texts played a less significant role. This is so because antiquity lived on not as the product of a culture of reading or study, but, rather, by way of institutions, habits, and oral transmission. Whereas the historicist goddess of memory, Mnemosyne, insists on fidelity to the original text, here the crucial feature was the ongoing reformulation of traditional materials—and amnesia concerning their origins. Culture and erudition in fact came to an abrupt halt, and the ideas that were held of the authors of antiquity became confused and increasingly dim—if they ever existed at all. Vergil was the sole exception. To be sure, knowledge of his life and his *oeuvre* was likewise muddled and imprecise, having undergone the same strange and unexpected metamorphoses as the ancient tradition writ large. But some essential elements of his identity did live on and their impact continued to be felt as the figure of Vergil evolved into a popular legend in ways that, despite their distance from the original, never really became entirely uncoupled from it. This is the version of Vergil that we ultimately see recaptured in Dante's rendering of him, for Dante found his way back to Vergil in more intensely true and unadulterated ways than scholars and positivists could ever have achieved. Modern scholarship found this Vergil, whose extraordinary fate was unlike that of any other ancient writer, worthy of note from the very start. A great number of studies of this phenomenon began to be published as early as the 1830s, at a time when no scholar would ever have thought of engaging in research into the medieval afterlives of the ancient world. Domenico Comparetti has given us a full account of this work in his well-respected and still oft-cited book, *Vergil in the Middle Ages* (1872). Comparetti's erudition and deep familiarity with the material are compromised, however, by political chauvinism and even more so by his failure to parse the vast era of the "Middle Ages" according to either immanent or external categories.

It is almost paradoxical that Vergil became the poet of the *Volk* and ultimately a legendary figure, for his education, learnedness, and high cultural and social standing make him anything but a "popular" poet in the conventional sense of the term. This paradox was first and foremost the result of external factors. Vergil was *the* poet of the Roman Empire. It was he who replaced the ancient Roman national sense of identity (which in the confines of its original urban boundaries and its indigenous, agrarian virtues had in any case long since lost its currency) with the new ideology of Rome's global mission. He did so by linking the political situation of his own time to the legendary prehistory of the ancient world, thereby creating the myth of the world's divinely ordained progress toward the ultimate goal of the *Pax Romana*, the condition of universal peace under Caesar's rule. This reading of his work guaranteed that Vergil would become a permanent feature of the primary school curriculum, where he naturally maintained pride of place for as long as the Western Roman Empire reigned supreme. During these years, his popularity was more or less assured, since grammatical instruction was frequently based on examples from his texts as well as on commentaries on his works. Pedagogy at the primary school level thus kept Vergil alive during those admittedly brief periods when the actual substance of his poetry had no meaning. And these periods were brief. Indeed, in many parts of Italy and especially in Naples, we can say that his influence never disappeared altogether. The dream of the Roman Empire had been seized upon very quickly by the barbarian nations. Recently a number of scholars have shown its links with both political aspirations and apocalyptic visions throughout the entire Middle Ages. Such connections had their basis in the peculiar doubling of the significance of Rome as the traditional seat of worldly empire, on the one hand, and as the seat of the Papacy, on the other. Here again, it was precisely Vergil's work that seemed to legitimate the idea of the *sacrum imperium* and to prove that world history was unfolding in an uninterrupted and deliberate fashion. The allegorical approach, methodologically so significant for the spiritualist movements of late antiquity and the entire medieval period, had been applied to his work. As early as the fourth century, a proclamation of the dawning of a new blessed age and the prophecy of the imminent coming of Christ were found in the verses of *Eclogue* 4. Sibyl-like, Vergil thus gradually became a kind of pagan prophet and crypto-Christian, or at least an inspired, if unwitting seer of God's truth. His reputation, still well deserved today, as a poet entrusted with the most deep-seated of wisdom's secrets both paved the way for and reinforced this pious, if erroneous claim. The descent into Hades in the sixth book of the *Aeneid*, together with the eschatological myths that permeate all of his texts, imbued Vergil's person with the aura of a magician, in whose service both the powers on high and the powers below stood. Local Neapolitan tradition (which became very influential beyond Naples in later years) had it that he was a kind of patron saint or *genius loci* of the city, an actual conjurer whose great and beneficent magic could be deployed to purely practical ends. He was widely viewed as both a sage and a prophet of Christ. Such theories explain the impact he had on speculative thought about the history of the world in late medieval times. For, as both the poet of the Roman Empire and the herald of Christ's Incarnation, he seemed to bear witness to the meaning of the phrase: the fullness of time. Our Savior had appeared in the fullness of time, when the world was at peace under Caesar's rule. This was the natural condition of the secular world, it was thought, which would be restored and thus made ripe for Christ's return as soon as that world, unified and in peace, was resurrected under imperial rule. This was more or less the most common version of these doctrines and one that was passionately defended at precisely the same time as the medieval empire was headed toward its final decline. Of the many polemical treatises that espoused this claim, Dante's *On Monarchy* was the most important and best known. Indeed, one of the many ways to understand the *Divine Comedy* is as a brief on behalf of an empire of this Vergilian kind.

Meanwhile, however, Vergil had also taken on another and this time, authentically artistic meaning that was more directly accessible and could be more easily understood. It is significant—and instructive—to note that German medieval courtly-love lyric, *Minnesang*, had no direct affinity with any of the ancient poets whose texts were known at the time; not even Ovid provided this tradition with any material. But its very first encounter with Vergil produced the *Divine Comedy*, the event of the greatest consequence for the history of literature after antiquity, bar none. "It was from you, and you alone," Dante tells Vergil, "that I learned the noble style for which I have been honored." Here, Vergil's fate comes full circle. He was a farmer's son from a provincial town near Mantua, and his early poetry took rural matters as its subject. The unsullied and elegant simplicity of the Italian countryside and the moderation of his life stayed with him even as he ascended to the highest echelons of society, and their spirit lives on in the learned and mythical depths of his work. Artistically elaborate and saturated with the enigmatic lore of the Mediterranean peoples, his poetry accorded so closely with a sensibility shared by so many that for centuries it was used to teach children the standard form of their own mother tongue. What is more, it continued to kindle men's imaginations for more than a thousand years after his death, for, even after the modern nations had produced their own vernacular literatures, it was the power of Vergil's forms that succeeded in uniting these new efforts both amongst themselves and with the European tradition. In order to prove this claim, we must now clarify exactly what it was that Dante learned from Vergil specifically about poetry.

Originally Dante belonged to an Italian literary movement that he called the *dolce stil nuovo*. It was a movement that, with a swiftness of growth unparalleled in literary history, conjured perfection out of a void. The flowering of medieval verse during the first quarter of the second millennium in France, Germany, and Spain had passed Italy by. Apart from several belated and insignificant imitative texts, there was neither an Italian national epic nor a courtly novel nor a love-poem tradition. It was not until the thirteenth century that the unique form of vernacular religious poetry known as *laudes* emerged in central Italy in connection with the Franciscans. The aristocratic love poetry of the *stil nuovo* emerged only in the second half of the thirteenth century as well. As a young man, Dante composed verse that belonged to this school, and it was also in this context that he undertook the *Divine Comedy*. The *stil nuovo*, which is a version of *Minnesang*, had its origins in Provençal lyric and especially in the work of its late practitioners. Unlike their predecessors, whose verse was relatively naïve and characterized by a refreshing modesty, these Italian poets preferred the complexity of conflicting emotions and a language heavy with images both esoteric and obscure. The poetry of the Italian *stil nuovo* is also obscure, but less capricious; its systematic tendencies place it in closer proximity to the contemporary philosophy of Scholasticism. Nevertheless, most of its poems, and especially those that seem the most beautiful, are so difficult to understand that some scholars have resorted to the idea that they must represent some kind of secret code that, while ultimately decipherable, made it possible to keep dangerous ideas hidden from the ecclesiastical and political authorities.

Dante's early poetry is equally difficult to understand. Even the handful of the most famous poems that almost everyone knows and that can be understood purely intuitively are less easy to interpret when compared with others that appear to express something quite similar, but in a highly idiosyncratic fashion. From the very beginning, Dante nevertheless differentiated himself fairly strongly from his companions. Like them, he may well have intended for his poems to have an allegorical meaning, or even several kinds of allegorical meaning in addition to their literal one. But in his case, the literal meaning or idea is not neglected in as absurd a way as it is by his peers. Rather, in almost every case the literal meaning yields a poetic idea; whatever lies concealed in the literal is less hidden there on some rational basis than it is entirely immanent in it. As a result, once we have understood the literal sense, we have understood its meaning too. Indeed, as soon as one reads, one understands, before—and even in the absence of—any detailed interpretation.

Herein lies the poetic power of Dante's genius. For I do not want to be misunderstood as suggesting that we have Vergil's influence rather than Dante's inborn gift to thank for it. His astonishing natural talent, far superior to anything possessed by any of his contemporaries, is visible in Dante's ability to absorb all the intellectual goods from the past that are at his disposal and to deploy them where he needs them. Antiquity meant nothing either to the other poets of the "sweet style" or to the scholars of the period, for whom the ancients were little more than bookish resources to which clear access was in any case blocked by faulty textual transmission. This was initially also the case for Dante; he was determined to become a scholar and pursued this goal with much more distinction and more systematically than his contemporaries. His erudition in fact displays all the distinguishing marks of the educational system of his time: the reception of tradition in whatever obscure and haphazard forms it was available and with no attempt to verify its authenticity or merit; an inability to understand either the beliefs of the ancients or their historical context; and the medieval allegorical method, applied to each and every text. Yet, the ancients—and especially Vergil—were also something else, something more, for Dante, something that resembled a theory of art. Of all his contemporaries, he alone regarded the ancients in this way. His relentless reading and rereading of Vergil led to a true reawakening of the Roman poet's voice in Dante's soul—a soul unique in its sensitivity to language and to verse—for the first time in ages, to the point that it became impossible for Dante to write poetry without hearing this voice.

Vergil's voice gave Dante something that the *dolce stil nuovo* lacked but that he greatly needed: simplicity. Already in Provence, the courtly love lyric had long since lost its original naïve purity of expression and had become learned, weighed down by its own tradition; it used highly ingenious, yet in the end completely conventional terms to capture extraordinarily subtle feelings and events. The Italian *dolce stil nuovo* intensified this penchant for the artificial and the obscure. Its practitioners all came from the leading social circles of their native cities. Their aristocratic sensibility, derived partly from this social position and partly from their unusual intellectualism (accessible to only a few), is witnessed by their exaggerated antithetical formulations, their propensity for obscure images, and their efforts to define the main duties of courtly love in nearly Scholastic terms. From Vergil Dante learned, rather, the art of expressing one's thoughts in poetry. These thoughts—together with the lessons that poetry itself could teach—no longer appeared as some kind of strange, disruptive, and potentially crippling intrusion into the text, but were absorbed into its mytho-poetics and thus became part of the very substance of the poem itself.

The widely endorsed modern stance (which is perhaps already no longer quite so modern) holds that the didactic elements of the *Divine Comedy* are unpoetic and should be distinguished from its actual poetry, indeed discarded, and that we ought to take pleasure only in the poetic parts as such. On the contrary, it cannot be emphasized too strongly that there are no poetic parts of the *Comedy* that are free-standing in this way, since for Dante, poetic beauty is identical with the vision of divine truth. This is why genuine knowledge is as beautiful as real beauty is true. Every line of his great poem is undergirded by this aesthetic, which grew out of a unique version of high Scholasticism that was Dante's own. But for the ability to execute it, to saturate poetic form with truth, he is indebted to Vergil, who was for him as much a philosopher as a poet. Here, it is irrelevant just how wrong Dante might have been when he thought this way; he often erred in the details. But he was not as mistaken in his overall understanding as we have come to believe. The message of Vergil's work—which consisted in a belief in the coherence of a providentially shaped world history in both its origins and its ends, the doctrine of Rome's mission on earth, and the prophecy of the coming of Christ—is conveyed in Dante's poetry in ways that are neither dogmatic nor allegorical. Rather, this message is visible in the very fabric of his narration of events. Images derived from real life are steeped in divine wisdom; there is no need for dogmatic gymnastics to make their truths clear. In its obedience to set rules derived from tradition, Dante's language is marked by supreme artifice. But it is uncomplicated in its effect. He does not deal in riddles. The profound wisdom of his words can thus be understood as fully (if in different ways) by the simple and childlike mind as by the reader who contemplates them in pursuit of their deeper meanings. What Dante took as a model of the high style he pursued with a sublime simplicity, the absence of everything that smacked of a merely playful profundity, and the complete absorption of doctrine into meaningful events. But it was under Vergil's tutelage that he freed the poetics of the *dolce stil nuovo* from its pedantic, even snobbish esotericism. We must be grateful first and foremost to Dante's own eye and skill for the fact that, in spite of the real difficulty of interpreting its meaning and substance, the *Divine Comedy* is very seldom obscure at the level of form. Its sentences and syntactic flow are decisive and clear, its metaphors vivid and concrete. But that his natural talent found expression and avoided the traps of capricious abstraction and fragmentation in which his brilliant friend Guido Cavalcanti had been caught is all to be attributed to the impact of Vergil's voice. Both Dante's temperament and his subject prevented him from attaining the pure and airy transparency of his master, it is true. But he far surpassed him in the sublimity of his passion. They nevertheless shared a true devotion to the real, to a kind of natural harmony that impressed upon their sentences the common mark of necessity, permanence, and everlasting stability.

There was another dimension of Vergil's work that served as the basis of a natural relation to the *Minnesang* tradition and to its subsequent, more intensely self-reflective forms. This was the story of Dido. Among the ancients, the concept of love did not include the sentimental and almost supra-sensory dimension created by the courtly-love tradition. In spite of being the most powerful of the physical instincts, there is nothing in the ancient representation of love that suggests that love is anything more than an instinct; it is simply more natural, but also more impersonal and cooler. This lack of feeling is the case even in ancient depictions of erotic frenzy. The story of Dido in the *Aeneid* is an exception or, perhaps better, it was this story that paved the way for the changes that were to come. Her tragedy was individualized, sentimental, even novelistic, and thus much closer to the lofty ideals of courtly love than, say, Ovidian love poetry. At the same time, the impact of Dido's love story on *Minnesang* is visible in that genre's return to the concrete and the individual. In the lyric of the *dolce stil nuovo*, there is practically nothing left of its actual subject, love. Completely buried in abstractions, the real substance of love is so profoundly suppressed as to have vanished altogether. Only a poet familiar with the art of the fourth book of the *Aeneid* could have used its secrets to create the encounter with Francesca da Rimini in *Inferno* 5.

But Vergil was Dante's teacher and master not only in the art of poetry. He was also his guide through the Underworld and up the mountain of Purgatory, and thus one of the three main figures in this magnificent poem. It is he who appears to Dante when he is confused and in distress to lead him through the Underworld up to the light. It is Vergil whom Beatrice plucks out of Limbo, the abode of the pagan heroes and sages, calling him to the task of saving Dante. What an odd concept for our sensibility! A Christian has lost his way; the heavenly dispensers of grace choose a pagan poet to lead him back to the right path and to ensure him eternal salvation by preparing him to behold God. Vergil's entirely exceptional position during the Middle Ages, which I noted above, becomes visible in this mission. The role that Dante assigns him in the *Divine Comedy* in fact allows a kind of synthesis to occur, a blending of all of the traditions and legends that had enveloped and obscured Vergil's person over the course of thirteen centuries. Here, precisely that person becomes a palpable unity once again, unquestionably quite different from the historical original, to be sure, but nevertheless organically related, despite the historical transformations, and in whom the original is visibly maintained.

In the *Divine Comedy*, Vergil is initially a sage. The aura of the clever magician with which he had been endowed in the popular mind remains; he knows the route into the Underworld, recognizes the ghostly figures there, and has power over them. But now it is the Christian God who has entrusted him with this power so that he might undertake the task of preparing a soul for redemption. In the sixth book of his *Aeneid*, upon which Dante relied for many of his mythical themes, the Sibyl bequeaths her enigmatic wisdom to Vergil's hero, Aeneas. The gift lives on in the *Divine Comedy* in the disposition of the divine order. Vergil will not be saved, for he did not believe in Christ while alive on earth. But he is found worthy of being selected for the task; he is in fact the sole pagan predestined for it because he was the only one who, having understood the truth of the secular world, linked it to the anticipation of redemption in the advent of Christ. Himself unmindful of the truth, Vergil lit the way for those who were to come. For this reason he embodies God's eternal wisdom, as it is witnessed in the course of secular history, more completely and perfectly than anyone else. From the very beginning, as noted above, Dante's doctrine defined Rome as the chosen leader of the world, with the emperor as its master. The coming of Christ occurred at the moment when Rome's imperial dominance of the world was firmly established. Its political form, universal Roman monarchy, embodied secular justice and peace on earth—this was both a requirement for and the precondition of God's kingdom. Whatever wisdom and justice could achieve in this world had become real in Rome; when joined by a belief in the Savior and in mercy and by the longing for eternal salvation as both are offered in the revelation and Incarnation of Christ, the ideal form of earthly existence was attained. Living in this world, man lived in the true order ordained by God, the order that prepares his eternal salvation. Falling away from the integrity of a Roman imperial peace meant that man would be left to live an unlawful and unjust life that would disrupt all levels of society and communities of men and thereby endanger the spiritual well-being of every individual. This stance is clearly rooted in the political situation of Dante's time; his targets were the Pope and his desire for secular power, on the one hand, and the divisive particularism of the princes and the urban states, on the other. As both the poet of empire and the imperial Roman mission and the prophet of Christ's redemption of the world, Vergil thus occupied an important position in Dante's system; he was the symbol of a wisdom that both understood the true worldly order and anticipated the other-worldly order as well. This is why Vergil is named as Dante's guide along the path to the world beyond, the preparatory path that leads to the very threshold of the heavenly kingdom—which only those who believe can enter and this only by means of revelation.

These are the essential outlines of Vergil's role in the *Divine Comedy*. I have scarcely touched on the rich and intricately interwoven system of meanings associated with it. To explain these would require extensive interpretation, and we would soon lose our way in the jungle of scholarly polemic. But Vergil is not only a vehicle for a message or a symbol of a sublime and far-reaching idea. Even though he is technically but the shadow of one who has passed away, he is also a living human being in the *Divine Comedy*. In the poem, his personality, the image of his very being as it appeared to Dante, emerges with enormous clarity.

Dante always felt a great sense of gratitude—indeed, a *need* to be grateful—especially towards those to whom he owed intellectual debts. We might see this as a form of respect for tradition, a kind of Vergilian *pietas* that is characteristic of Romance peoples. It is visible in the scenes in the *Divine Comedy* with Brunetto Latini and in the encounter with the poets, Guido Guinizelli and Arnaut Daniel, and in many other passages as well, not least in the words with which Dante greets Vergil as his savior at the beginning of the poem. But the most touching and beautiful of all these testaments to beholdenness is the way in which he tries to create a Vergil who is the object of his appreciation by stripping him of what had obscured him over time. Beatrice addresses the Roman poet: "*O anima cortese mantovano.*" In the person of Dante's Vergil, this *cortesia*, the greatest virtue of those who had endorsed the *dolce stil nuovo*, far exceeds what the term was understood to mean by the poets of that school, and comes to signify the inner virtue of one who is always prepared to do what is right—even if he will not reap the rewards of his deeds. And Vergil will not reap these rewards, for he is banned from God's kingdom. Thus, whatever he does for Dante—and for that kingdom—is done by virtue of a kind of *cortesia* sustained by understanding and modesty and a selfless and sovereign greatness of soul that seeks no reward other than his own awareness of it and his countenancing of the good. For, more than any other character in the *Divine Comedy*, Vergil has himself to thank for his insight and his integrity. His courage and gentle heart, his self-restraint and firmness of judgment, his majestic, yet unassuming wisdom, all create in him the fatherly humaneness that reveals itself over and over again in ever new ways and in every gesture and word. Dante endowed his Vergil with all the candor of a man who has attained the highest form of human education, the same candor that enchants us in Vergil's work itself. It is for this reason that his Vergil is, in spite of all the bizarre traits that the Middle Ages mistakenly bestowed upon him, a fundamentally true Vergil. But it was not enough for Dante to express the mutual love that he and his master had for one another directly, as he does on many occasions. He also created another figure in his poem who has a relationship to Vergil that is similar to his own so that he could show in that figure's interaction with Vergil, as in a bright mirror, the characters and their relationship. This character is Statius, the author of the *Thebaid*, from the second half of the first Christian century. Statius encounters our two pilgrims of the underworld in the fifth circle of Purgatory. He does not recognize them and thus does not know that it is Vergil's soul that stands before him. When asked about his own fate, Statius answers by praising Vergil, to whom he is indebted for his fame as a poet and for his secret conversion to Christianity (this is Dante's invention). Vergil indicates to Dante that he should remain silent, but a spontaneous movement on Dante's part reveals the truth and Statius kneels down in front of Vergil. "Brother," Vergil says, "do not do that. You are a shade, a shade is what you see." And Statius answers as he stands up: "Now you can understand how much love burns in me for you, when I forget our insubstantiality, treating the shades as one treats solid things."[1]

---

[1] *Purgatory* 21.132–36 in the *Divine Comedy*, A. Mandelbaum, trans. (New York: Knopf, 1995) 316. —Trans.

11

The Discovery of Dante by Romanticism

Speaking about a poet and not allowing the poet himself to speak, indeed, not even speaking about him, but rather *triton ti apo tou poiētou*, speaking only of those who have spoken about him, must certainly seem a rather stilted, roundabout, and uninspiring affair. Yet the history of Dante reception and the vicissitudes of a reputation that is, after all, now some six hundred years old, have an integrity, a life and shape of their own, entirely apart from the *oeuvre* that serves as its occasion. In fact this history reflects the vicissitudes of Dante's spirit back to us in ways that his poetry hardly can, for even the most beautiful and finest poetry is never as perfectly and exclusively a mirror of the times as the history of readings of that poetry is. Moreover, we become skeptical about our own readings in a productive way when, considering a poem through this kind of lens, we are provoked to reflect on our own prejudices and our own all too ephemeral judgments.

From this six-hundred-year-long history of Dante readings, I have singled out for consideration a relatively limited period, namely that of Romanticism and its precursors. This is, of course, the most important period of all, as it was the time when Dante was discovered anew—and refashioned into the form in which he essentially still exists for us today. Prior to this moment, it had been a long while since anyone had concerned himself with Dante, not since Michelangelo in fact, who was often inspired by and even sustained by the *Divine Comedy*. After him, Dante gradually vanished from sight, his magnificence too sublime to be sensed by periods such as the late Baroque and the Enlightenment, with their cold rationality and academic aloofness. Of course, it was not that he was actually forgotten. He was simply neglected and held in low regard. Increasingly, his work came to be seen as an absurd kind of hodgepodge, tasteless, anarchic, and esoteric—in short, unpalatable for learned society—even as it was at the very same time acknowledged that he had in fact achieved something significant, given what were held to be the quite limited (and low) cultural horizons of his time. The most caustic version of this oft expressed judgment was articulated (as one might have anticipated) by a Frenchman, namely Voltaire, who openly mocks the un-

intelligible and uncivilized ingenuities of the *Divine Comedy* and characterizes its author as coarse and bizarre. Yet, even as Voltaire wrote these words,
Dante's rebirth was not far off. It was a rebirth that would deploy as accolades
many of the very same terms the Enlightenment had used to condemn him.
Formerly, to be called a vulgar barbarian poet, the poet of a still primitive
people, had been an indictment; now, the same claim became a matter of
praise. Formerly, the opinion prevailed that garish atmospherics and an extravagance of expression were in poor taste and bizarre; now, good taste was
scorned and the bizarre was extolled. It was not as if this new inclination, the
novel attitude of the pre-Romantics, grew out of some newly discovered dimensions of Dante that then led to a reversal of judgments about him and his
work. Rather, arguments heretofore used to disdain him were now invoked,
in substantially identical form, to justify enthusiastic esteem. For this reason,
both approaches seldom referred to the *Divine Comedy* as a whole and to the
poem's actual purpose. Instead, they addressed only individual passages and
their value as poetry, whereby this value began to be regarded as autonomous
and independent of theological, moral, and philosophical value.

Giambattista Vico was the very earliest and thus a still entirely solitary
spokesman for the Romantic view. He was a Neapolitan. Several decades
Voltaire's senior, he died an old man in 1744. Vico was the real founder of
modern aesthetics and thus a precursor of Romanticism. He was the first
to articulate the movement's ideas, considerably before Herder, with whose
profundity and judgment he nevertheless compares favorably, despite his of
course very different intellectual background and ultimately also despite his
very different intentions. In the course of working on his project to create a
philosophy of history—and, as he explained, a timeless and perfect history
within which all the histories of all the individual nations of peoples in their
origins, evolution, flourishing, decline, and end occurred—he had discovered that the very first men, pre-historic men, so to speak, had not lived in a
blissfully rational and primitive Paradise, as the Enlightenment utopianists
had presumed. Rather, they must have been wild beasts, he claimed, devoid
of any reason. Nevertheless, as a result they were all the richer in a kind of
supremely potent sensuality that endowed them with the capacity to express
everything in a powerfully material and visible language. This language was
full of immensely gripping immediacy and figurative vigor, and was thus the
very image of their vital and animated natures. Its words appeared to be not
so much conventional signs of that for which they stood, but rather the very
things themselves. At the same time, these primitive men's elemental, sensuous powers were domesticated, tamed by their mystery cults and ritual
worship, such that their very first genuine language was not prose at all, but
was rather akin to rhythmic hymns. Their entire lives—their religion, laws,
customs, and deeds—thus played themselves out as a series of fantastically
sensuous formulaic performances. For Vico, these primitive times were the

true era of poetry, the poetic age, when men were "natural poets." The best one could say about later generations of poets was that the more proximate they were to this poetic age, the greater poets they were.

This was how Vico rediscovered Homer (much earlier than F. A. Wolf) as the poet of the heroic—and thus poetic—age of ancient Greece; he then placed Dante side by side with him as the "Tuscan Homer," who thus came to embody the spirit of the era of barbarism revived (such was his label for the Middle Ages). Homer was naïve (in the Schillerian sense), heroic and sublime, free of both Enlightenment calm and the over-subtle ratiocinations of human understanding. So too was Dante. Homer reveled in inhumanly cruel melées and battles. Dante followed him in devising horrible and terrifying infernal punishments. Of course it did not entirely escape Vico's attention that Dante was by far the more thoughtful, doctrinally correct, and academically rigorous of the two, in both design and execution. But, in his utter ignorance of matters concerning the medieval literature of other countries and the civilization of the *trecento*, Vico believed—as some still do today, but without his excuse—that these elements did not constitute Dante's true essence and were thus not worthy of attention. Dante would have been an even greater poet, according to Vico, had he known nothing of Scholasticism or Latin.

Vico's conception of Dante thus already contained the entirety of what the Sturm und Drang generation thought about him and what for the Romantics were widely held truths. But Vico remained a mystery and unknown to these, his descendants. It was thus not he, but rather Herder who inaugurated the new way of thinking. The intimate affiliation of thought with Herder has been pointed out frequently in recent times. Herder too resisted the methodological straitjacket of conceiving of and depicting poetry as the product of reason, declaring it to be, rather, the original expression of the soul of a nation captured in fantastically sensuous forms. But here we of course immediately also see the fundamental difference between Vico and his German heirs. Vico is ever focused on the very most general, not the particular, and only happens upon the one or the other historical artifact as an exemplification, as it were, on his way to developing a metaphysics of world history. Already for Herder, and subsequently even more for the German Romantics, the goal was ultimately to grasp what was particular about the national soul as that soul manifested itself in individual phenomena and to understand it in this way.

Nevertheless, it was in fact Herder who did not know Dante's work in any detail; his expressions of praise are, accordingly, unfounded. One of the earliest of these is interesting. Johann Jakob Dusch mentions Dante several times in his *Letters to a Young Man of Rank Concerning the Fashioning of Good Taste* (1756), claiming, for example, in a statement that was quite characteristic of this transitional moment, that "even the very worst plan, or sketch, defies all criticism when it draws on the ambiance offered by a Shakespeare or a Dante and thereby bullies its way more or less violently into the holy precinct of good taste." It had been Herder's displeasure that provoked Dusch's attempt to legitimate the form of the didactic epic. Resistance came from the new way of thinking that saw in folk epic not didactic rationalism, but rather something that existed as pure poetry on an entirely higher plane. Herder wrote in his review: "How can the author mistake passages of doctrine, slotted into an epic, for a form, for *the* epic form of didactic poetry? There are no such passages in Homer . . . and in Milton, Dante, and Ariosto we must ignore them." Gerstenberg's tragedy, *Ugolino*, appeared just ten years later, and took as its subject a tale from one of the last cantos of the *Inferno*, where Ugolino and his sons, incarcerated in a tower, are left to starve to death. The origins of the popular "German Dante" lie here in this play, and are thus entirely rooted in some of the most horrific passages of the poem. It was on such foundations that subsequent interpretations of Dante by the Romantics were based. Dante is thus not received—in either a practical or a theoretical sense—in the same way that Shakespeare is. Few know his work. By and large their verdict—differentiating itself from Voltaire's only by inverting the evaluative signs—runs as follows: the design of the *Divine Comedy* is unfortunate, or at least no longer appropriate to the times; the structure and doctrines it contains are aberrations that can be explained only by the historical context in which the poet lived. These faults must nevertheless be excused given the heightened poetic power of individual passages, which were of course held to be located primarily in the *Inferno*.

These were also the general parameters of Goethe's reading. He, too, never became truly intimate with Dante; his admiration for the *Divine Comedy* (or at least for some very few passages in the poem) was diluted by his instinctive antipathy for a personality like the Tuscan's that was so fundamentally different from his own. Monotonous, ambiguous, and obscure, filled with repulsive and often detestable coarseness[1]—these were surely the real feelings Goethe experienced in the presence of Dante's verse. When, late in life, he found himself the recipient of numerous translations and scholarly essays on all manner of subjects related to Dante—which required a response—Goethe was unable to muster anything more than a cool reticence by way of acknowledgment. Even his remark to his companion, Eckermann, in 1828—"Dante seems great to us, but he had—by way of preparation—centuries of civilization on his side"—was no longer puzzling by that time, even though it does seem to indicate that he was not entirely ignorant of Dante's actual place in history. Indeed, he looked upon Dante as a product of older cultures rather than merely a primitive poet from some prehistoric era. Still, Goethe had absolutely no connection to or rapport with either the intellectual or the material world of the *Trecento*. His entire

---

[1] Auerbach is quoting here from Goethe's "Tag-und Jahresehefte" (1821). —Trans.

attitude toward Italy (expressed elsewhere in his *oeuvre*) makes this clear. His observations about Dante thus merely reflect his familiarity with one or the other of the works by Abeken, Schlosser, or Rosenkranz, who evaluated medieval Italian poetry by juxtaposing it to medieval German poetry, comparing *Titurel* with the *Divine Comedy*, and the like. There is no indication that he understood in any clear way the conventions of the wider European or Mediterranean cultures contained in Dante's poem. In response, finally, to the penchant that some seem to have had for comparing and finding correspondences between the *Divine Comedy* and Goethe's *Faust*, we cannot say explicitly enough that they are actually worlds apart and fundamentally incomparable. Faust attempts to find himself in countless ways; Dante is led to his God by his guides and along a single, narrow path, any deviation from which would mean the loss of his immortal soul. Faust experiences in himself and in his own worldly endeavors the ever-changing abundance of God's being; Dante observes instead the palpable and eternally fixed architecture of God's plan in a world beyond the here-and-now of any real deeds. The characters and scenes in *Faust* are, finally, the stuff of an individual's soul and its history, unintelligible if they do not refer to the one who experiences them. In the *Divine Comedy*, they belong to an objective order outside the self.

It is between Goethe's early and late remarks concerning Dante that we find the true discovery or, better, the rediscovery of Dante by some of the greatest of the German Romantics. But this rediscovery bore fruit with only a very few of the most prominent figures in Germany and later in Italy. A wider reception was hindered by the speculative and overly generalized nature of the texts written by the great Romantics; uninformed by any thorough study or knowledge of the poem, they were ill prepared to prove their vastly generalizing claims on the strength of close readings. But their reverence for Dante as well as their excellent, if selective and fragmentary translations did inspire an interest in individual passages and revived and popularized a kind of Dante appreciation—which was of course also a beginning of sorts. Thus, the Romantics gave birth to what must really be called a Dante cult. His name began to appear next to Shakespeare's and Goethe's, sometimes even bundled together with Shakespeare and Cervantes to become a triumvirate of modern European poetry. Now, and for the first time since the twilight of the hegemony of the Catholic Church and its philosophy, the integrity of the magnificent poem became visible. The Schlegel brothers, Friedrich and Wilhelm, Schelling, and Hegel stopped seeing the *Divine Comedy* as little more than an anthology of beautiful passages and began to experience it instead as the most powerful and unified poetic edifice of our age. Overly inclined to speculative constructs and failing to attend faithfully to their object (the text), however, their aphoristic criticism was often off the mark and their important conceptual frameworks devolved into overly subtle interpretive caprice. Friedrich Schlegel, for example, at first saw Dante as a Gothic primitive in his *Essay on Ancient Greek Poetry*, with the peculiar structure of the massive poem indebted to "barbarian" Gothic concepts. Still, he formulated these claims, common enough in the early Romantic period, from the new and ingenious, if somewhat odd, perspective that is already audible in his choice of the term "concept." Thinking of Scholasticism and of early medieval allegorical systems, he believed, that is, that unlike the art of the ancients, which emerged directly out of nature, medieval art originated in "concepts." Such a notion may seem somewhat strange and exaggerated. But in fact, apart from the interesting resonances it has with Schiller's treatise on naïve and sentimental poetry, there was in Friedrich Schlegel's commentary on Dante a discovery, or perhaps better, the kernel of a new kind of historical insight. That is, he no longer saw the Middle Ages in the same light as the entire eighteenth century had done, from Voltaire through Vico and Herder, namely, as an age of primitive barbarism. Rather, he sensed that it could be understood more as the effective blending of the unmediated vital forces of childlike races, on the one hand, with, on the other, the legacies of late antiquity and with ideas and fantasies inherited from time immemorial but now practically frozen into ghostly versions of themselves. Indeed, elsewhere Friedrich Schlegel anoints Dante as the founding father of the old style of modern art on the basis of having united religion and poetry, just as the ancients had done. He thus set the tone for the discussion that both his brother, August Wilhelm Schlegel and, most importantly, Schelling took up, arousing their appreciation for the connection of religion and poetry, and enabling them, under its aegis, to now see the entire *Divine Comedy* as an undivided whole. Friedrich was not destined, however, to pursue this idea. Indeed, his early admiration for Dante seems to have given way to a certain aversion to him in later years.

August Wilhelm Schlegel had a far more intimate and also a more professional relationship to the *Divine Comedy*. In 1818 Friedrich called his brother the doyen of Dante scholarship. August Wilhelm not only wrote about Dante. He also—and more importantly—translated him. His translations were the finest before Stefan George's, even though he—understandably, but with unfortunate consequences—tended to render the rhyme of only the first and last lines of the *terza rima*, leaving out the middle line, which announces the rhyme for the next stanza. His translations were published as fragments, never as a whole, and in a number of different venues; they did not appear together until the collected works edited by Böcking, where they may be found in the third volume. The elder Schlegel was nevertheless terribly preoccupied by them and returned to and revised them time and again. His work clearly influenced any number of other translations that date from the beginning of the century. His intention had been to translate the *Divine Comedy* in its entirety. The only significant portion of this plan ultimately realized is from the *Inferno*. Mere fragments of the *Purgatory* and next to nothing from the

Paradise survive. This is a curious state of affairs, for he wrote to Schiller in 1795 that he found "the final stanzas of the *Purgatory* to be the most beautiful and most charming sections of the entire poem," and he praises the *Paradise* as "the most difficult, profound, sublime, and splendid part" of the *Divine Comedy*. Such claims, made at a time when it was, again, primarily the *Inferno* that was most commonly taken to be what was meant when one referred to the *Divine Comedy*, bear witness to Schlegel's real familiarity with the magnificence of the poem as a whole. Indeed, he describes it as his task in this project "to penetrate into the very mainspring of this foreign thing, to discover what it really is, and to eavesdrop on how it came to be." And yet, August Wilhelm never completed the great Dante book that had been the subject of so much planning and that his brother had expected him to write. His scattered translations and readings amount to little more than the effusions of an amorphous enthusiasm, at the center of which Dante stands as the great prophet of the Catholic Church and is praised (as Waiblinger so mockingly wrote) as the axis upon which the whole world of Romanticism turned. As a result, in about the year 1800 an entirely imponderable, indeed hapless craze for Dante took hold in circles around the Schlegel brothers. Even Caroline, August Wilhelm's wife, had the indecency to praise him to the detriment of his master, Vergil.

The most significant words written about Dante at this time came from Friedrich Wilhelm Joseph Schelling, and they may be found in his essay "Dante's Relationship to Philosophy," which had a significant impact upon the Schlegel brothers and others, above all, Hegel. (Karl Vossler has recently reminded us of this piece in his contribution to the *Festschrift* for Leo S. Olschki.) It would in the end undoubtedly have been more appropriate for Schelling than for August Wilhelm Schlegel to give us the great book on Dante that Romanticism still owes us. Indeed, the former begins where Friedrich Schlegel had left off, describing the *Divine Comedy* at the very opening of his essay as the sacred place where poetry and religion commingle. He then goes even further, suggesting, in response to the question of the *Commedia*'s genre, that the poem belongs to no genre: it is comparable to nothing but itself; the very identity of Dante's age in its entirety is its theme, he claims. Schelling was the first to understand the core issue of the poem when he explained that the modern world, whose poetry the *Divine Comedy* exemplifies in prophetic fashion, is a world of individuals in which everything begins with the particular. This world demands that individuals become universal by virtue of their extraordinary particularity; when contingency reaches its perfection, it becomes universal, absolute once again. A relation thus emerges in Dante between the allegorical and the historical "as a result of individuals having become timeless because of the positions in which the poet has placed them, positions that are themselves timeless." Moreover, Schelling explains, the knowledge that Dante collects in his poem provides an image of the universe that, in the utter harmony of all things, produces the most authentic and beautiful of visions, or, as the Romantics called them, "fantasies." Following directly upon such precise claims, he offers a number of intensely speculative, even mystical observations. In the pervasiveness of Trinitarian logic in the *Divine Comedy*, for example, he sees the symbolic expression of the inner forms of a typology of all science and poetry; Hell is the realm of Nature, Purgatory represents History, and Paradise is Art. And, in spite of the fact that he reiterates that the poem, rather than being the individual product of a specific period, embodies the exemplary in its absolute universality, theology represented as an architectonically planned system rendered *in concreto*, he goes on to attempt a description of the generic norms of its individual parts, calling Hell "sculptural," Purgatory "painterly," and Paradise "musical." We can sense what he means, but the labels are less than compelling and ultimately remain unenlightening.

Be that as it may, Schelling's essay undoubtedly contains the most significant set of observations about Dante and his poem produced by Romanticism narrowly defined. It is not just that he understood the importance of seeing the *Divine Comedy* as an integrated system and in its entirety. The Schlegel brothers had already done this. Rather, it is the fact that he was the first to suggest that its characters enter into and manifest a kind of eternity as a result of the specific space that they are made to occupy in the poem. Here he grasps the very essence of the *Divine Comedy* and thus connects with its true meaning. For the poem has one core meaning, which is of course not a veiled political or heretical or any other kind of particular meaning. (If finding this kind of meaning is one's goal, then one will always find an endless supply of meanings.) Rather, the all-encompassing crux of the poem's significance is this: our earthly and historical world in its true and eternal form is a manifestation of God's judgment. Schelling was the first critic to grasp this truth since the collapse of the Catholic ideological world order with its ecumenical reach, since the Middle Ages, that is, when of course this truth was self-understood. His insights nevertheless remained without echo. To be sure, August Wilhelm Schlegel took over from him the Trinitarian approach and the notion of allegory, but he overlooked Schelling's essential point, which remained without resonance for the rest of the century—but for a single and admittedly powerful exception, namely Hegel. Hegel wrote only a single page about Dante in his *Lectures on Aesthetics*. But this page, free of Schelling's speculative detours and capturing Hegel's ideas in a very few, select words, provides what I believe to be the most crucial point that can be made by way of synthesis about the *Divine Comedy*:

> Instead of a particular event, the *Divine Comedy* has for its subject matter the eternal action, the absolute end and aim, the love of God in its imperishable activity and unalterable sphere, and for its locality Hell, Purgatory,

and Paradise; into this changeless existent it plunges the living world of human action and suffering and, more particularly, the deeds and fates of individuals. Here, in the face of the absolute grandeur of the ultimate aim and end of all things, everything individual and particular in human interests and aims vanishes, and yet there stands there, completely epically, everything otherwise most fleeting and transient in the living world, fathomed objectively in its inmost being, judged in its worth or worthlessness by the supreme Concept, i.e., by God. For as individuals *were* in their passions and sufferings, in their intentions and their accomplishments, so now here they are presented for ever, solidified into images of bronze. In this way the poem comprises the entirety of objective life: the eternal condition of Hell, Purgatory, and Paradise; and on this indestructible foundation the figures of the real world move in their particular character, or rather they *have* moved and now in their being and action are frozen, are eternal themselves in the arms of eternal justice. While the Homeric heroes have been made permanent in *our* memories by the muse, these characters have produced their situation for *themselves*, as individuals, and are eternal in themselves, not in our ideas. The immortality created by the poet's muse counts here objectively as the very judgment of God in whose name the boldest spirit of his time has pronounced damnation or salvation for the entire present and the past. This character of the subject-matter, already independently finished, must be followed by the manner of its portrayal. This can only be a journey through realms fixed once and for all, and although they are invented, equipped, and peopled by the same freedom of imagination with which Homer and Hesiod formed their gods, still they are meant to prove a picture and a report of what has really happened.

—G.W.F. Hegel, *Aesthetics: Lectures on Fine Art*, T. M. Knox, trans. (Oxford: Oxford University Press, 1975) 2:1104.

With this single page Hegel brings the story of the rediscovery of Dante by Romanticism to its close. What followed was an era of conscientious and well meaning activity with regard to the details, interpretations, and translations of the poem, as well as assiduous research into its author's fate, all of which adhered far more closely to the *communis opinio* of the Romantics than it did to Schelling's or Hegel's ideas, especially in terms of its general orientation and impact. Things were much the same in France, where Dante was celebrated only as the Romantic poet *par excellence*, as the poet of the sublime, the grotesque, and the gruesome, by the leading minds from Chateaubriand to Sainte-Beuve—this in spite of the efforts of a select few true scholars, such as Villemain and Fauriel, who resisted such prejudices, all of which were of course based on the *Inferno*. In England there arose, as a result of the influence of the Italian émigré exiles—above all, Ugo Foscolo, but then also Mazzini—a considerable interest in Dante that is still alive today, and important research has been done there. Yet, even in the exquisite and passionate tendencies of a Shelley we can observe the popularized prejudices of Romanticism. During the post-Romantic and Pre-Raphaelite period in England there then emerged the ghastly misreadings of the entirety of the *Divine Comedy* as some kind of clandestine treatise and politically subversive tract.

In Italy itself, a new surge of enthusiasm for the native son had welled up beginning at the end of the eighteenth century, driven in crucial ways not only by the forces at work in the rest of Europe, but also by political tendencies that were specifically nationalistic in origin. For Dante was the first poet to reawaken the Italo-Roman sense of the world and transform that sense into a specifically Italian national ideal. It was also in Italy that Hegel's ideas took root and flourished later on. They were especially significant for the most important of the later Italian critics of the nineteenth century, namely Francesco de Sanctis's, whose interpretation of the *Divine Comedy* far surpasses those of all the German Romantics in its philology and its understanding of the details. Yet, Hegel's comprehensive conception seems to have eluded de Sanctis's reach. To the best of my knowledge, Schelling's and Hegel's great insight into the *Divine Comedy*, namely that its charge was to probe deeply and dispassionately into the essence of the secular world, was soon forgotten. It has only recently been recalled. Elsewhere I have tried to show how significant their thesis is for a reading of the poem. Should this perspective succeed in emerging as the dominant way that Dante and his *oeuvre* are understood today, there will be a veritable Dante renaissance, a renewal of the poet and his work that will finally achieve and maintain what he so longed for on his own behalf: *vita tra coloro che questo tempo chiameranno antico* [(a) life among those who will call this present, ancient times (*Paradise* 17.119–20)].

12

Romanticism and Realism

la seconda bellezza che tu cele
[the second beauty that you still conceal]

—Dante, *Purgatory* 31.138

It is certainly widely recognized that the most characteristic literary achievement of the nineteenth century was that it was the first age to attempt to represent human beings in the full range of their everyday reality. It was due solely to this endeavor, which we call Realism, that it became possible for literature to maintain a vital connection to the other ways in which contemporary society expressed itself—to its science, its economics, and its thoughts and desires (most of which it fulfilled). By contrast, the poetic works more narrowly defined that originated in that century (and especially in its second half) were often tragically irrelevant to the inner and outer lives of the people of the time. At first, these works continued to produce occasional poetic images by way of embellishment, and perhaps also a vague sense of a world that transcended the everyday. But this higher world was in no substantial way linked to the everyday, and thus remained a matter of indifference for it. Later, even this influence on the general run of things waned and, in the second half of the century, precisely the works of free, creative imagination and lyrical genius considered to be the most important lost both their readership and any connection to the wider national audience. The small circle of their admirers that survived retained only a dubious authority.

By contrast, the works of the Realist tradition, despite at first encountering occasional resistance, generated a completely different kind of enthusiasm and broad-based engagement. One might initially be tempted to associate the turn to Realism with the spirit of the empirical sciences and with positivism in general, as well as with materialism, capitalism, socialism, industrialization, and the new global market. This view is certainly legitimate. But it is insufficient and even misguided as soon as one assumes on this basis—as might seem obvious and correspond to one's initial impressions—an opposition between Realism and Romanticism. Such initial impressions do not withstand further investigation, for there are in fact close and immediate connections between the first works of Realism and the intellectual foundations of Romanticism. Even looking at the matter from a strictly chronological perspective raises doubts about whether positivist trends could have been the source of these writers' interest in empirical evidence and the material world in general: after all, the first great works of modern Realism, namely the novels of Stendhal and Balzac, began appearing before 1830, at the height of French Romanticism and well before Comte, Renan, and Taine.

The reader will grant, I hope, the designation of the Frenchmen Stendhal and Balzac as the first Realists. Germany at this time had not yet reached a stage of development where reality could become a focal point, and in England both a historical sensibility and the satirical-moralistic tradition still held too strong a grip. In contrast, Stendhal and Balzac (the latter more directly and to the exclusion of all else) were concerned with depicting the reality of their earthly worlds exactly, by capturing not just the spirit of the age, but also (as it were) its very embodiment. They observed the layeredness of the social world in detail and sought to lay hold of the real existential conditions of each and every individual living human being without excluding anything in principle, and also without subjecting their material to any kind of analysis that could prevent their readers from recognizing their own, their actual, reality as in a mirror.

But did such an endeavor really have no precedent in earlier times? Had there not been—to stay with the French tradition—a realistic tradition in comedy ever since Molière and a representation of reality in all of its breadth in the novel since Sorel, Scarron, Furetière, and Lesage? At first glance, it is clear that these precursors are more limited in the areas of reality to which they provide access and that they shape the everyday experiences they depict more strictly according to certain norms from either the rationalist or the romance tradition. Insofar as they were realists, then, they did not in the least attain the kind of significance in the literature of their day as the Realists of the nineteenth century did in theirs. But perhaps these differences can be understood as differences more of degree than in principle. One might argue that the expansion of the kinds of material that occupied Realism and the sudden dynamism that it brought to the representation of what had up to that point been a relatively rigid everydayness were motivated quite naturally by the impact of the French Revolution and its aftermath, which caused disturbances in the social order and, by introducing violent disruptions and rearrangements of the social classes, generated a rich field of dramatic problems and events, and that these representations were more interesting as a result. This might seem adequate as a way of interpreting the great works of nineteenth-century Realism, for it places them in the context of the expectations of the times out of which they emerged, and explains how, through the particular conditions of their age, they arrived at new subject matter and the possibility of new expressive forms. The works thus acquire greater significance and can be viewed not so much as something entirely new but as the final fruits of a preexisting artistic genre made possible by a different set of external conditions.

Looking at the issue only in this way nevertheless misses the essential point. It is not just the extent of the everyday that is decisive in the realism of Stendhal and Balzac and in their European and American successors. Rather, what is decisive is that they undertook the depiction of human beings *both* as they lived in the midst of their material everydayness *and* in the richness and depth of their inner humanity, with the intention of moving the reader to participate emotionally as fully as possible in the fate of these individuals by means of tragic pity. The conditions of everyday life and the very most unique personality traits of individuals were not dealt with in isolation, apart from their inner tragic existence. They were not depicted in order to have a humorous or moralistic-didactic effect, or to delight the upper classes with colorful and quasi-ethnographic images of the lower rungs of social life. Instead, precisely as the result of a broadly conceived presentation of the everyday, human passions appear with the full force of their travails, and the individual human being appears with his own great and tragic dignity. The maltreated and humiliated seminarian Julien Sorel, for example, who experiences all kinds of comic mishaps, is a tragic hero; poor Goriot in the squalid everydayness of the Pension Vauquer is one as well; and the aged Grandet is not comical in the same way as Molière's miser. Such representations had never existed before—or at least not for a long time. One might conceivably believe (although it is doubtful) that Molière had sought to transcend the limits of the merely comical; or grant that the genre of the *comédie larmoyante*, particularly Diderot's significant new developments, was pathbreaking to a certain degree; or see in works like *Manon Lescaut* some first steps in the direction of what we are exploring here. But in terms of the extent of the everydayness and the depth of human tragedy, and, above all, in the interweaving of the two, no earlier work realizes any of these in a way that compares with the Realism of the nineteenth century. Its entirely new and unique contribution consists in the way it embeds the tragic within the everyday.

For centuries tragedy had been restricted to that particular faculty of the human soul that appeared to belong, sociologically, only to the highest class of kings and heroes, which, in terms of poetics, could only be represented in the high style. Everydayness was so completely banished from the ambit of this class that the tragic hero could never mention a handkerchief or even ask the time of day. It was Realism that discovered the sphere of the tragic within a realm that had until then been home only to the base and the comic. It thus more thoroughly and radically shattered the barriers that separated the styles than all contemporary poetic prefaces, dramas, and historical novels taken together had been able to do. Perhaps what I claimed earlier to be the connection between the first works of modern Realism and the intellectual foundations of Romanticism is clearer now. The modern Realist novel destroyed ancient, classicistic aesthetics and its concept of human dignity with a radicalism that one finds in no other genre. In comparison, the identification of the sublime and grotesque à la Victor Hugo and his friends looks like mere decoration; indeed, Hugo's Romantic historical sensibility seems almost ludicrous. In turn, the concrete manifestations of Romantic irony as they came to the fore in Germany now appear in a new light, at first as a detour, but then, once they have been given their due, as capable of illuminating authentic reality. Compared to the powerful shadows of Shakespeare and Cervantes (which certainly appear no less powerful as a result of the comparison), what we see emerging in nineteenth-century Realism is something entirely new. Here, everydayness does not merely interrupt tragedy. Rather, it is the very home of the tragic itself.

Leaving aside the question of whether Stendhal and Balzac were conscious of its significance, I believe that we must evaluate these two writers in terms of the criteria provided by the traditional theory of style and its problematics. In my estimation, these criteria explain and justify an interest in specific formal features of their art, for otherwise the preoccupation with these authors as individuals in the most extreme detail—as is typical of Stendhal criticism (indeed, he invites such an approach)—could easily become frivolous and snobbish and have no point. After all, how else could we legitimate our special interest in, say, a particular individual as opposed to all others if not by claiming to see revealed in that person with unique clarity a particular moment of intellectual history, or, say, a manifestation of God's hand in history? We must in fact assume that it is just such a feeling that helps to account for our being seduced into an intense preoccupation with any particular work or individual from the past. But we cannot be content with just this feeling; we must supplement it with an effort to understand its origins as well as to locate the object of our fascination more precisely in its own history. This is the true task of the historical disciplines, a task that transcends itself in the course of being accomplished.

Independent of the question, then, whether Stendhal and Balzac were aware of the fact—a question to which I shall return—I perceive their historical significance to lie in their radical rupture with the separation of styles, and thus in one of the basic tenets of Romanticism. Of course, their genre of choice—and the very form of the novel (*Roman*) itself—always possessed the potential for being Romantic. Even without the tragic realism of content that Stendhal and Balzac depicted, the novel was not a classical form of art. It lacked the strict unity of action and the quasi-sculptural highlighting of each individual sentence and word; in short, it lacked what we would designate as the properly classical features of pathos and formal rigor. And while the genre of the novel existed prior to Romanticism and its precursors, it was only the historical sensibility of Romanticism and, to an even greater extent, tragic Realism that brought out its latent romantic nature by revealing its ability to put the principle of the mixing of styles into action in a radical but effortless way. Beyond this one basic tenet of Romanticism, however, the realistic novel is also intimately connected to all other Romantic tenets insofar as they are themselves, like it, organically interconnected and grow out of a common source, namely, a feeling for life.

For do we not see, beginning with Herder and Rousseau, the attempt to regain the authentic reality of the individual subject and the world—be it in resisting rationalism and rule-based aesthetics, civilization and social castes, or in outrage against the empty and excessively submissive world of tradition, or in the return to nature, mankind, and feeling? Does not reality seem to have been overly structured in the classicizing, rationalist era to the point of forfeiting its authenticity? This desire to regain a sense of self and world is apparent in the entire range of creative works produced by the new spirit that came to be called "Romantic." The Romantic historians, for example, no longer differentiated between being fixated on facts and collecting and studying sources, as the Maurist Benedictines had done, and a purely rational, systematic presentation like Voltaire's. Rather, they united the two. For them, any given document opened a window not just onto the fact to which it testifies but, in the particulars of its form, onto the embodied spirit of a past epoch as well. Each document thus inspires the unmediated presentation of an epoch, which the historian then aims to make real and concrete. In turn, the Romantic philologists no longer inquired into normative use and grammatical rules, but into the very origin and inner intention of languages and literatures themselves; they too wanted to surrender themselves to the truth of reality. The earlier formulas that had guided philology, "It is thus" and "So it should be," gave way to the new formulas: "Thus it was," and "That is how it came to be," or "This is how it developed." Political theorists and economists likewise no longer sought to find the best forms of the state in their own rational constructs, but instead strove to understand existing states and economies according to their national, geological, historical, and social roots and the possibilities that arose organically from these foundations. Reality was their starting point and their goal. Poets, finally, did their best to free themselves from all formal conventions, all traditional embellishments, and everything that smacked of reasonableness, utility, didacticism, pleasure, and amusement. They gave themselves over instead to the very most immediate experiences of feeling, nature, and introspection. And even if, especially in Germany, this endeavor focused more on interiority and ideality than on what I referred to earlier as the "embodied" spirit of the age, here, too, the point of departure was a desire for the genuine reality of a pulsating life force—Schiller's *Luise Millerin* is, after all, a German work of 1783.

This list of pre-Romantic and Romantic motifs could be extended and explored in even greater detail. Seen in this context, the rebellion against the traditional separation of styles is not arbitrary, isolated, or idiosyncratic, but rather one of the basic features of the time and one that sheds interpretive light on all the others and is in turn illuminated by them. The separation of styles was thought to distort and degrade both ways of looking at human beings—the high and the low, the tragic and the comic—in equal measure; it seemed to tear the very nature of humanity asunder in arbitrary ways. Only by dismantling the distinctions this separation imposed was it possible to regain what was most lacking in the traditions of rationalism and classicism, namely a true inner life. Classical aesthetics had drawn selectively from reality, choosing only what seemed useful for the purposes of instruction or pleasure; such bits of reality, cobbled together out of isolated data into units of instruction and delectation, might have occasionally awakened the memory of real experiences. But they were never able to evoke the totality of life as it raced by. Against this background, the forces of individualism, historicism, and lyricism rose up as with a common will to capture the concreteness of human interiority and the spirit of the world through its living body. It was this common effort that gave birth to the radical mixing of styles and, consequently, to the realistic novel. The mixing of styles obviously attained its richest and purest fulfillment in the representation of contemporary reality. After all, the present offers itself and its reality in a more immediate and comprehensive fashion than any historical subject. Introspection is depicted more genuinely, precisely, and radically when the subject is one's contemporary or even one's own self. In turn, the surrounding world appears more genuine and authentic when it is presented from the perspective of the person who actually experiences it. So it was that Realism was born out of the essence of Romanticism. Later intellectual movements might have transformed it in various ways, enriching its material and refining its methods, often also rendering it crasser and flatter. But they did not create Realism; they found it ready-made.

It is astonishing that Realism has hardly been researched or even considered against the background of its origins as I have discussed them here. In all likelihood, the reason for this lies in the fact that even its creators, Stendhal and Balzac, were themselves unaware of the relationships I have sketched out. Both remained distant to their more (strictly speaking) Romantic contemporaries. Stendhal disdained Chateaubriand's style, and he wanted to write precisely and concretely, in the manner of the *code civil*. His entire demeanor, his simultaneously cool and hedonistically passionate nature, had little in common with the pathos-laden and sentimental generation of a Lamartine or a Hugo. And yet in the 1820s, during the theater wars, Stendhal did write a small pamphlet entitled *Racine and Shakespeare*, in which—in his own unconventional way, to be sure—he defended the Romantics. And Balzac, sixteen years younger than Stendhal, always insisted on his classicistic taste and love of Racine, even if there is no trace of it in his work. In fact, his lack of attention to form, his effusiveness of feeling, and his penchant for melodramatic invention and commentary all make him appear—at least initially— more Romantic than Stendhal. There thus at first seems to be almost nothing in either author that testifies to the motives that were the immediate origins of their work, motives that could be interpreted in support of our thesis. And yet, each in a very different way harbors the spirit of Romanticism.

First Stendhal. Stendhal seems to despise the very everydayness that he depicts. He views characters who are caught in it as either subaltern fools or rogues, or—mostly—both. The actual course of the everyday world, the course of history itself, is for him base and full of chicanery. What stands in opposition to it as the object of his affection and wonder is a unique form of autonomy that is beyond the day-to-day. It is the essence of the "happy few," and it can appear as love or heroism, as a sovereign *esprit* and freedom of soul, or as a *divin imprévu*. But it is a freedom that never really engages seriously with the everyday. Rather, it despises it and strives with all its energy to exercise sovereign control over it, both from the outside and from above. Tragedy as such plays itself out only between and among the "happy few," while base reality occurs—or ought to occur—well beneath them. Its irruption into the upper reaches is never allowed. Rarely in fact do we see the lower realm, the real course of the world, depicted as inorganically as in Stendhal. For him, this is the site of caprice, chance, and competition. Seldom are human actions and thoughts so relentlessly portrayed as a network of abjection, hypocrisy, prejudice, vanity, and routine. Stendhal needs the everyday only as a random foil; its impact is rarely truly tragic. Instead, it is nearly always grotesque, arbitrary, and external. Consider, for example, the consequences that follow from the scene in which Fabrice del Dongo kills the actor Giletti, or the intrigue of the mock birth that deceives Lucien Leuwen and leads to his separation from Madame de Chasteller.

And yet, Stendhal paints these everyday events with a penetrating exactness—and this is striking. Each figure, each situation is constructed with a kind of sociological precision. The freedom of the "happy few" is tied to very specific conditions in the real world, and it is only in relation to those realities that their conflicts are even possible and can be understood. This feature of Stendhal's writing is easy to see when we consider the way the *Princesse de Clèves* or *Manon Lescaut* or even *Adolphe* presents conflicts in a more abstract, moral, and indirect relationship to the specific realities that produced them. How easy it would be to transpose one of those novels into a different milieu without having to change it in any essential way! One could summarize them with abstract formulations like: "the story of a woman who . . . ." or "a novel about a young man who. . . ." This is unthinkable in Stendhal's work. One would have to add specifics of time, place, and social status to the description, but even then one could hardly get a picture of the whole. The most minute of everyday details penetrates stubbornly into the fates of his heroes, as Stendhal uses his often exaggerated psychological and sociological acumen to illuminate them, relentlessly, in all their particularity. Both he and his characters might despise these details, but that does not change a thing. They must do battle with them anyway, even if they rarely emerge victorious—and if they do, it is never for long. The *divin imprévu*, the inner freedom of the "happy few"—these are of little use. They, too, must turn to the petty tactics of hypocrisy and intrigue in their struggles and borrow their weapons from the arsenal of a despicable everydayness. They, too, must run with the wolves. Stendhal's heroes thus exhibit that curious mixture of deep-seated idealism and enthusiasm, on the one hand, and cold, diabolical calculation, on the other. The combination has confused many readers. The extreme indifference of their calculations often feels absurd and stands in stark contrast to the spontaneity of their youth. Yet, being both forceful and forced, such indifference can never succeed, because mere contempt can never engage actively with the reality of life. Whoever merely disdains the world would have to withdraw from it entirely.

This conflict with everydayness brings to mind Rousseau's stance. Both authors are motivated by the same loathing of petty calculations, of social hypocrisy, and of constrictions imposed on nature and the feelings. Even so, Stendhal wants to be active in the world. Indeed, he hopes to attain fortune and success. He thus encases his sensibility in the cold armor of indifference. But this indifference no longer has the carefree spirit of the era before Rousseau. True, there is much in Stendhal that recalls that time, its rationalism and its playful pre-Rousseauian serenity. At least, *he* would want to call all this to mind. His hedonism, his tendency to ideological philosophizing, his treatment of women figures, his wittiness, the careful precision of his style which avoids vagueness and pathos—all these things are, or seem to be, of the eighteenth century; the skeptical old gents, like Mosca, del la Mole, or Leewen, are holdovers from the *ancien régime*, living their lives with wit and an air of superiority. And yet, time and again something does not quite fit. Stendhal's style is not matter-of-fact like the *code civil* and also not witty and light-hearted. Rather, his coolness constantly comes off as deceptive, his sentences are fractured, erratic, and nihilistic. The aphoristic formulations of the seventeenth and eighteenth centuries degenerate into paradoxes in Stendhal. Finally, his relationship to the supposedly cold, calculated, and despicable realm of everydayness is certainly not the same. The age before Rousseau never loathed or despised the world of the everyday; it was simply beneath its dignity. Isolated bits could be selected out for instruction or pleasure and the rest simply ignored. But it is an odd kind of disdain that can rise to a passionate engagement with its object and then strive to uncover and depict its concrete details. Indeed, such a stance begins to be tragic. And so it is for Stendhal's heroes: disdain for the world becomes deadly serious. The events that knock them to the ground are not simple intrigues to be countered with calculation and ingenuity; rather, given their quantity, consistency, and ubiquity, they approach the power of tragic fate. Moreover, the heroes of the novels—René, Obermann, Adolphe—are all self-portraits of the author, hidden confessions and wishful projections at one and the same time. They are handsome and elegant figures following a noble destiny and close to attaining fortune and success. By contrast, Stendhal was an unattractive and awkward fellow whose phlegmatic constitution often paralyzed him physically and spiritually when he most needed strength, and whose life was not without its misfortunes. It is well known how deep the wounds were that his phlegma inflicted on his ambition and pride. He was in the end a Romantic who dared to engage with the real world. And he experienced concretely, time and again—for he was both brave and stubborn—the truly Romantic tragedy that comes with living in that world: he was more capable than his most capable contemporaries, and yet less capable than the most random *dummkopf*. No wonder, then, that it was precisely Stendhal who discovered Realism, no wonder that his form of tragedy should have emerged out of disdain for the everyday rather than out of the immediacy of the everyday itself. This tragedy of an ultimately empty autonomy vis-à-vis the everyday remained his Romantic legacy, living on through Madame Bovary, Frédéric Moreau, and perhaps even beyond.

In the case of Balzac, things are apparently more straightforward. Here there is no doubt that we confront the fullness of the most authentic of realities, which he then takes completely seriously. The tragedy of his characters grows out of this context. His most perfect creations are embodiments of the tragic impulses that he sees in the bourgeois reality of his surroundings. And even when his macabre exaggerations go beyond what a normal person could experience in everyday life, at their core they remain yoked to reality. He had no success in representing any actual freedom or true subjectivity. His depictions of purity of heart or integrity of spirit are truly paltry, since they never escape the material realm. He is most at home with figures whose drives and impulses he depicts in the midst of a thoroughly material and down-to-earth world; each is a distinct character that he represents with an at times childlike, but always powerful imagination. This imagination concerns itself, moreover, only with the givens of the empirical realm; it can intensify, combine, and contrast its material data, but it never invents anything beyond what is already there. Balzac's imagination does not even know much about the greater freedoms that can occur on the level of subjective reality. In spite of all this, however, the word "imagination" is unavoidable when describing his work. Undoubtedly Balzac collected a great deal of empirical evidence and often attempts methodical analyses of situations and characters. But he never stops there. The precision with which he presents facts—when, for example, he depicts the worlds of finance or agriculture—is, it turns out, unreliable, because he lacks the necessary forbearance. At any moment, a heated event can break into the analysis and destroy the calm atmosphere of a factual account. What dominates Balzac's work is, in fact, the synthetic imagination about which he himself spoke, although seldom very clearly. This imagination is a striking phenomenon. It is unlike Zeus's daughter, for it does not possess the abilities Goethe praised in his poem "My Goddess" (1883); rather, it is to be associated with those individuals whom Goethe compares with the "other" unimaginative creatures and "poor races":

All die andern
Armen Geschlechter
Der kinderreichen
Lebendigen Erde
Wandeln und weiden
Im dunklen Genuß
Und trüben Schmerzen
Des augenblicklichen
Beschränkten Lebens.
Gebeugt vom Joche
Der Notdurft.

[All the remaining
Races so poor
Of life-teeming earth.
In children so rich.
Wander and feed
In vacant enjoyment,
And 'mid the dark sorrows
Of evanescent
Restricted life,
Bow'd by the heavy
Yoke of Necessity.]

—*The Poems of Goethe*, Edgar Alfred Bowring, trans. (Middlesex: Echo Library, 2006 [1883]) 271.

The imagination that Goethe envisions could only look on such creatures serenely and playfully, as in a midsummer night's dream. But there are no dreams or jokes for Balzac. His imagination takes those who are caught in the everyday completely seriously, even granting them their own imaginative potential as a way of giving their everyday existence a tragic, or at least a melodramatic turn. And yet, without a doubt, it is imagination—and not reason, science, or Christian love—that deals so earnestly with the everyday here. Yet, we must ask: What could have so transformed and enriched the force of imagination that it should now try its hand at giving shape to everyday reality and see in Goethe's "other races so poor" the captivating world of the human? I would reply: The imagination was transformed by the modern European spirit's discovery—in the period whose high point we call Romanticism—that reality itself is in a state of perpetual becoming, and that there is nothing but life all around us. This is a discovery that Goethe helped to bring about. What Balzac presents, then, is not mere reportage or critique, but life. And life demands imagination in order to be depicted in unmediated fashion and in its entirety.

The impulses that led Balzac to turn the powers of his imagination to the reality of his own time were part of his basic character. Reality was spread out before him like a bounteous feast before a glutton, and he consumed it with reckless abandon. He had his start, as we know, in the lower forms of the popular novel, a melodramatic mixture of inauthentic feelings and sham reality. These forms had arisen because the high style of classicistic genres failed to satisfy the public's demand for a literature that involved the emotions directly. And while this tradition left its trace in some of Balzac's masterpieces, he was able to liberate the genre from its more sordid origins and inauthentic subject matter. His somewhat coarse but warm and magnanimous heart, and the directly sensual quality of his writerly talents, introduced him to what were to become the real subjects of the modern epic. They also led him to reject decisively the theatrical mixing of styles fashionable in French Romanticism, against which he often polemicized, as in the Preface to *La Peau de chagrin* [*The Wild Ass's Skin*]. For this reason, he was unaware that his own tragic realism, which was for him a "primal experience," was Romantic in a deeper historical sense. Of course he entitled his masterwork *La Comédie humaine* [*The Human Comedy*]; the reference here back to the greatest medieval monument to the mixing of styles makes it easy for us to interpret his project in terms of Romanticism. But the context that caused Dante to call his work a "comedy," even as he considered it a sacred poem, was certainly not one that was apparent to Balzac.

Tragic realism has developed considerably since the nineteenth century. With the exception of kitsch, in which it had a persistent afterlife, the mixing of styles is no longer an issue for realism, and the opposition between empty ideality and reality, which was a holdover from a mentality that kept stylistic levels separate, has all but disappeared. The task that tragic realism faces now is the task of creating a sense of an ideal order from reality itself, one capable of bringing about tragic catharsis. One might object that contemporary realism is not even aware that this is its mission. But it does incessantly search for true reality, and this search will and must continue. Having passed through the periods of Romanticism and positivism, the realistic novel is even now finding new techniques with which to begin to address the question of actual reality in earnest. In addition to the novel, tragic realism has turned to cinema, now that the stage is too limited a setting. This new medium displays amazing possibilities, each year surpassing all prior expectations; and even if its results are often disappointing, it is clearly full of promise as the century of reading gives way to that of sight and sound. There are two paths forward. In the novel we have a form that allows us to see a recollecting consciousness creating the earthly realm as a projection, as the quivering silhouette of a world that is constantly being destroyed and then created anew. Such a world initially seems chaotic and bizarre, but its thematic allusiveness offers the promise of a vaguely intuited higher order. In cinema there is a new way of constructing external reality, of manipulating and combining multifaceted events and bringing together what is temporally dispersed. Such a collapsing of time and space into one another never existed before. While not undermining all prior aesthetic traditions in their entirety, the cinema does, in my opinion, shake them to their foundations and forces upon them a complete transformation. Common to both these directions is, finally, the tendency to do away with the continuous unfolding of individual events or of a small number of unified actions as was, in the past, common practice in novels and stageplays, carefully culling these out of a wealth of events. Instead, the contemporary novel and cinema present a large number of occurrences, images, or fragments of actions that, rather than following temporally or causally one after the other or leading to the kind of conclusion we might have expected in earlier times, relate to each other only loosely. Everywhere we find complexes of miscellaneous events that, according to earlier conceptions of the unity of action, would have no place there, and which break into the reality that is being represented. Indeed, the very idea of unity of action is disappearing. Earlier methods of separating an episode out from the totality of events in the world in a clean way seems, in the twentieth century, to falsify the authenticity of the real. Furthermore, for our century any apparently objective representation of reality will appear falsely conceived or artificial if it seems to bracket out the experiencing consciousness, or if it seems to intervene in reality in only instrumental ways. Instead, a new existential precision must remain at all times intimately bound up with the experiencing subject itself. This development is clearest in many modern novels as opposed to cinematic drama, which though it does use these new techniques, employs them only as a means to the end of presenting a traditional, even if usually rough and poorly constructed, unified plot—doing so probably out of consideration for an audience that is only gradually learning to understand its own place in this new reality.

These new techniques are appropriate, as I said, for the concrete depiction of true reality. They have far surpassed the positivistic amassing of empirical data and thereby have also destroyed its claims to autonomy. A new desire for totality and unity can thus be felt, even if it cannot yet be proclaimed as law. For many, the world is still too chaotic, and they respond to what they see by calling it the newest phase in the ongoing dismantling of bourgeois culture and by crying out for order. Of course, insofar as it is intelligible, true reality can only be represented as ordered. But order could hardly arise out of a merely programmatic will to orderliness, for any such order would necessarily be too narrow, no matter where the origins of its laws lay. And it would be trying to force reality into a mold, which would be futile. Instead, the ordering of reality must emerge out of reality itself, or at least out of the living human being's engagement with it. Only in that case will it be capacious, firm, and flexible enough to grasp and embrace its object.

There once was a form of tragic realism, long before Romanticism, that was able to grasp our chaotic world as an authentic reality with its own inner order. I am referring to the tragic realism of the Middle Ages and to its source in the story of Christ. This form of realism achieved the most radical destruction of the separation of styles since antiquity, and brought about the most radical instantiation of tragic realism that has ever been seen. It originated in God's sacrifice of Himself to earthly reality. The reality of our world has changed so significantly that any recourse to this earlier notion would be absurd. But how else could an order and truth of reality even be imaginable if not by seeing God in it?

13

Marcel Proust and the Novel of Lost Time

L'univers est vrais pour nous tous et dissemblable pour chacun.
(The universe is true for all of us and different for each one of us.)

—Proust

Marcel Proust was born in 1871 and first came on the scene in the 1890s; when he died in 1922, he was one of the world's greatest literary names. The eruption of his work—distinguished by its huge proportions, its complexity, and a difficulty caused by the unparalleled extravagance of its web of language—into the world was so sudden and so thorough that it is difficult not to see it as the result of some kind of spell that had been cast. For how else might we explain the way that in those restless times, hundreds of thousands, all across Europe, gladly made their way through thirteen densely printed volumes, enjoying page after page devoted to conversations with no identifiable theme, to a few trees, to an act of waking up in the morning, and to the inner development of a jealous feeling, so that they might take pleasure in the variety of an individual's emotions that lay hidden in every sentence? All the more astonishing is the fact that a great number of Proust's admirers are not French. We have to assume that these individuals have a perfect control of the foreign language they are reading, a language that, in this case, has reached the very apex of its tradition and is now using that tradition's devices to experience a second youth and to flourish in subtle ways. For even at its very best, a translation functions, as we know, only as an aid to understanding the text; it can never replace or stand in for the original.[1]

"The text." My choice of words is deliberate, for Proust's novel is a text. It is not only modern. It is also "text-like" (*texthaft*), enduring, and unmistakable, like a famous manuscript. No story of the centuries past seems so overwhelmingly historical, so covered with patina, so finally and irrevocably

---

[1] This essay was written in 1925. Since then, the final, fourteenth volume (*Le temps retrouvé*) has begun to appear in serial form in the current number of the *Nouvelle Revue française*. The first two volumes of the German translation have also appeared with Verlag Die Schmiede in Berlin.

over, so mummified, antique, and eternal as the one he gives to us in his representation of Parisian society around 1900 and of the intelligent and sickly young man who inhabits it. And this is so in spite of the radical novelty (it is without precedent) of the nervous and pedantic lilt of his sentences, with their lurching and penetrating pulse, and of the magnificent internal organization of the book, and also in spite of the fact that the mindset of the book has nothing at all typical or universally valid about it. Rather, the young man whose voice we hear is extraordinarily isolated and monomaniacal and suffers from a plethora of obsessions and tics. And this is not all. In point of fact, everything that this narrative "I" says is the result of a single obsession, a single vision, the empirical existence or facticity of which can be maintained with the same certainty and authority as, for example, the reality of Hell in Dante's poem. Yet, Dante and Vergil walk on two legs in Hell; that is, they know that other worlds exist, including the one from which they have come and still others that they will soon face. Even the souls of the damned know that there is a life other than theirs; almost every word they speak, even as it expresses their torment and despair, has in its awareness and memory of the earthly sphere something salutary and liberating about it, like a breath of fresh air that wafts in through an open window on a cool day. In Proust, there is nothing of this sort. Permanently and hermetically sealed off in a rotten social structure (that is nevertheless the prevailing one) and in the domain of hypersensitive powers of observation that are so logical as to drive one both mad and into atrociously digressive trivialities, the gargantuan novel paces back and forth, as if in a cage, between a very small number of motifs and events, without seeing or hearing the sounds of the world that races by it right next door. It is as if a mentally ill person, held captive in a room that is tastefully and sumptuously appointed, were to give a clever and objective description of this room, including an exact account of both its décor and his activities in it down to the very last detail, holding forth all the while with pedantic solemnity about what he has described as if it were the only thing of any importance in the world.

It is not that Proust did not have eyes to see and ears to hear. Of course he did, and he had them to such a degree that any of us would be proud to possess even the tiniest portion of his vast and unparalleled powers of perception. But whether it is because he knew enough to keep a respectful distance from what did not concern him, or because, whenever he did happen onto something, he instantly imbued it with his concentrated and sharp wit in such a way that, as in the fairy tale, it immediately lost its ordinary taste and the nature normally associated with it, and, like a pig in a sty, became a creature of his own creation. Regardless, the earthly world that he seems in fact to be talking about in his book—a world that we thought we too knew and that, as if in a dream, we believe we have found again and keep on trying to identify—this earthly world is made, in his book, out of some strange, unexplored, and mysteriously concocted substance. There have of course been other, earlier poets who have created a world in something like this way. But Proust's world was always something quite different. For those writers always announced in advance, for example, that they were poets and wanted to make something up, and it was obvious that they quite self-consciously maintained a certain point of view. They altered the normal course of earthly events so radically, even violently and demonstratively, that those events seemed quite crudely and arbitrarily distorted and as a result incomplete, full of gaps, or simply and utterly mad. In these cases, we are always aware that there is another and truer world—the real world—in addition to the one they present to us. In Proust, there is nothing of this sort. He narrates in an entirely simple way, always doing his level best to give us reality in its true, complete, and un-histrionic form. His obsessive focus on just one thing is so intense that it thoroughly recreates the world and does so with no external means—which is to say, he creates the world by eavesdropping on his own feelings and then making these feelings and the internal process that a sense impression initiates in him—and this alone—into the stuff of what he represents. Like no one before him, he renders sensuality with utter and concrete veracity. This is why, in Proust, phenomena like a dress or a meaningless conversation, which we normally observe in an inattentive or summary way and by means of a system of hackneyed analogies, suddenly seem surprisingly profound, transformed and renewed, capable of absorbing the entirety of earthly existence into themselves in spite of—or, perhaps better, because of—their apparent artlessness.

It is strange, but also apparently inextricably linked with this kind of sensuous savoring of things and this complete immersion in the experience of one's own feelings, that Proust's narrator is distinguished by a particular spiritual profile, an intellectualism, and a cryptic and unfathomably eccentric way of thinking. It is not enough that this way of thinking is completely old-fashioned, that it smacks of the prewar period and often borders on the ridiculous. More than that, it is narrow and petty—a fact that one nevertheless acknowledges only against one's will in those very few moments when one succeeds in breaking free of the atmosphere of the book. It is a way of thinking that reflects the final stage of the flowering of traditional bourgeois intellectuality during the last century. Saint-Simon (of whom Proust was very fond) defended this mentality assiduously as—in equal parts and justifiably—enchanting and drenched in the ignoble stench of rotting social forms. And indeed, this rich and hyper-sensitive Parisian—here we are of course always speaking of the "I" of the novel and not of Proust himself—adopts a frame of mind that, unfazed by the turbulence of the world, is not in principle any different than that of a Joris-Karl Huysmans or an Oscar Wilde. It is a frame of mind that belongs to the *fin de siècle* (there is no adequate German expression here) and that is impressionistic, decadent, egotistical, dandy-like—one could think of any number of abominable words with which to characterize the period, were one so inclined. His social station naturally corresponds to this disposition. By birth a bourgeois, he belongs to a family well known for its service to the state as well as for its wealth and property, which goes back many generations. His personal charm assures that all doors are open to him and allows him entry even into the exclusive circles of the great families of the historic nobility. Everyone considers him unusual, a person of privilege. But his health is poor, and he suffers from constrictive feelings of *angst* and all manner of nervous disorders. He is incapable of making decisions, indeed, of doing anything at all. His sensitivity is so extreme that, for no reason that can be determined, he sometimes cannot leave the house for weeks— even though time and again he makes plans to do so. His moral compass is equally unbalanced. His consummate intellectualism, his profoundly elegant sensibility and ability to empathize fully with those around him, and his tact and respect in domestic affairs stand in disturbing contrast to his equally consummate and inconsiderate egocentrism, his reserve in the most intimate matters of the heart, his inability to confide in or trust anyone, and his observational powers, always overly keen, aloof, and capable of dragging the worst out into the daylight in often petty ways. He can only love what he either does not possess or is afraid to lose. As soon as he is sure that he has a secure hold on someone, he loses all interest; he or she becomes a matter of indifference to him. Mind you, he is seldom not jealous; even the most unlikely occasion immediately triggers suspicion. Above all, he suspects homosexual lapses on the part of all of the men and women with whom he deals. He is in fact preoccupied with homosexuality in general in the very keenest of ways, as if with a graven image or idol around which his thoughts constantly dance. This narrating "I" is thus neither pleasant nor even interesting for a time period that is still too close to his own.

But this is only the case as long as one forces oneself (and force is necessary; nothing else works) to look at him only as the object of narration. When, at the same time, he is also seen (as he must be seen) as the one who is himself doing the narrating, everything changes. His powers of perception and veracity are so great that he becomes far more than, indeed, far superior to the character whose actions he represents. He even himself claims at one point that there are many people inside him, all rolled into one. This is one of those odd moments in the text where the superiority of the narrator over the figure who is being narrated becomes especially clear, when the entirely mysterious pathos that emerges from its sources in earthly life rises—both pithily and luminously clearly—to the surface. Proust writes: "I remained closeted with the little person inside me, the melodious psalmist of the rising sun, of whom I have already spoken. Of the different persons who compose our personality, it is not the most obvious that are most essential. In myself, when ill health has succeeded in uprooting them one after another, there will still remain two or three, endowed with a hardier constitution than the rest, notably a certain philosopher who is happy only when he has discovered between two works of art, between two sensations, a common element. But I have sometimes wondered whether the last of all might not be this little manikin, very similar to another whom the optician at Combray used to set up in his shop window to forecast the weather, and who, doffing his hood when the sun shone, would put it on again if it was going to rain. I know how selfish this little manikin is; I may be suffering from an attack of breathlessness which only the coming of rain would assuage, but he pays no heed, and, at the first drops so impatiently awaited, all his gaiety forgotten, he sullenly pulls down his hood. Conversely, I dare say that in my last agony, when all my other 'selves' are dead, if a ray of sunshine steals into the room while I am drawing my last breath, the little barometric manikin will feel a great relief, and will throw back his hood to sing: 'Ah! Fine weather at last!'"[2]

This little inner "manikin"-weatherman is infinitely more tenacious and made of better stuff than the one who keeps to his bed, his body tormented by *angst*, the one whose body the weatherman inhabits. Likewise, the narrator is, as object, infinitely superior to his "I." The "I" is fearful; he suffers. The narrator is free to roam the world, uncoupled from the pitching deck of time as it unspools, and deeply immersed in the internal course of his emotions and in the melody of their expression. Untouched and untouchable, the narrator takes the regal path. We, of course, have no idea where this path will ultimately lead, but we do know that its innumerable twists and turns and scenic views are themselves destinations, for they represent the steps of purification and liberation that are required by any historical event and that are available to whoever truly understands it. It is for this reason that Proust's narrator can achieve what the entire generation of his author could not: he is able to find humor in the truth of things without forcing it out of them by means of violent sarcasm or caricature. Laments and sounds of joy, tears and laughter, well up in delightful and truly graceful ways out of those moments of people's lives in the society in which they are embedded, moments that seem incidental—the way they talk, their gestures and movements—but which are in fact who and what they properly are.

I could fill pages with quotes in support of this point. But one would actually have to know the countess of Guermantes, Aunty Léonie, Françoise, Charles, Bloch, Morel, Aimé, and all the others very well before one could fully appreciate even one sentence about them. It is impossible to describe them in any other way than the way Proust himself did. One cannot introduce them to a reader with a few descriptive phrases, for to do so would

[2] [Translation is from *The Captive* (*La Prisonnière*), C. K. Scott Moncrieff, trans., vol. 5 of *In Search of Lost Time* (*À la Recherche du temps perdu*). (London: Chatto and Windus, 1992) 4–5. —Trans.]

destroy what makes them so rich—and thus destroy them entirely. Next to Proust's characters, the figures that populate the stage of the great realistic novels of the nineteenth century are mere extras, whose essence one catches only a glimpse of at the very last minute and then finds the appropriate place and role for by stressing this or that detail. The great purposelessness and apparent lack of choreography that characterize Proust's novel, which never demands anything of any of its characters in terms of what would have to happen to allow the plot to develop in one way or another, gives them the freedom to do as they see fit. For Proust, there are none of the limitations that are necessary in Stendhal or Flaubert (not to speak of many others), limitations that are the result of the architecture, of the fixed pragmatic plan of their works. A fantastical object, almost like a vine, it shoots up, entirely on its own; the hand of its author remains nearly imperceptible. If other great poets, disdaining description and analysis, have, with just a few words, made a character captured in his moment of tragedy unforgettable for the ages, this perhaps more sublime approach certainly does not befit Proust's novel. Next to it, almost all the novels that we know seem to be no more than novellas. *Remembrance of Things Past* is a chronicle from memory. In it, the secret and often disregarded links between events take the place of the empirical sequentiality of time. Looking back and also deeply into himself, Proust's biographer of the soul perceives these links to be the real ones. The events that lie in the past no longer have any power over him, and he never acts as if things that happened long ago have yet to happen, or that decisions made long ago still remain to be made. It is for this reason that there is no narrative tension, no *peripeteia*, no raging and looming of events that then find resolution and peace. This chronicle of the inner life flows along with a kind of epic uniformity, for it is only memory and self-examination. The novel is the authentic epic of the soul; truth itself ensnares the reader in a long, sweet dream in which he suffers a great deal, to be sure, but in which he also enjoys a release and a sense of calm. This is the pathos of the earthly course of events, a real, inexhaustible and ever-flowing pathos that at once oppresses and sustains us without end.

PART III

Passionate Subjects, from the Bible to Secular Modernity

14

Passio as Passion

In his lecture on "passion" and "feeling" ("'Passion' und 'Gefühl'"), now published in *Archivum Romanicum* 22 [1938] 320–49, Eugen Lerch has attempted to provide a comprehensive description of the evolution of the meaning of *passio*. It is a word whose development reveals many layers of meaning. He proposes the following scheme:

Whereas our modern understanding of passion (*Leidenschaft*) is essentially active, in antiquity and for a long time thereafter the meaning of *passio* (Greek: *pathos*) was—in accordance with these origins—essentially "passive." This older idea was the result, first, of a linguistic dance of the seven veils, one might say, since both *pathos* and *passio* do in fact mean "suffering." Second, it grew out of Stoic and Christian views; both considered the passions to be maladies of the soul. Finally and most importantly, the early absence of a category of feeling that identified it as a legitimate sphere of a human being's inner life, one commensurate with reasoning and the will, also endowed *pathos* with a passive inflection. As a result, both during antiquity and then on into the eighteenth century, feelings and sensory perceptions (both of which *are* in fact "passive" states of suffering) were folded in with the passions and both of them designated as *pathē, passiones*. It was only when Shaftesbury, Rousseau, Mendelssohn, and others developed an autonomous category of feeling that sentiment, feeling, emotion, and so on, were able to free themselves, as it were, from what is called *passion* in French and *Leidenschaft*, or passion, in German. Only then could these words successfully display an active purpose regardless of their etymological roots.

Auerbach cites numerous texts here from the ancient Greek and Roman traditions, as well as from the medieval and late medieval periods and the sixteenth and seventeenth centuries. When they are available, I cite from previously published translations of these texts and note the source (see Appendix: Sources for Translated Citations). Unless so noted, other translations are my own. I am grateful to C. J. Gordon, Alesya Raskuratova, and Rachel Schaffer for helping me locate the published translations cited here. I would like to thank C. J. Gordan, David Hult, Hermina Joldersma, Julia Lupton, Sally Poor, Ann Marie Rasmussen, Julian Smith-Newman, and John H. Smith for assistance with the remaining translations.—Trans.

Lerch's account is well documented and the substance of his argument clearly laid out. There is much that we can learn from his essay. The psychological meaning that antiquity expressed with the words *pathos* and *passio* is always based on the idea of "suffering" and these words in fact correspond far better to what these days we call "feelings" and "sensation" than to what we understand by the word "passion." For us, the passions are violent, heated affairs. For this reason, they are also always active. And yet, precisely these properties were *not* originally included in the semantic fields of *pathos* and *passio*. Lerch's argument thus fails to answer the question of how ardor and violence and activity, in short, how the features that we moderns associate with passion, came to be part of *passio*'s semantic field. Surely these meanings did not gain prominence merely because what we call "feeling" had been subtracted from them, thereby creating room for new content. Rather, there must be something in the history of the word itself that made *passio* ready to take on this sense. Lerch seems to assume that *pathos-passio* always *also* meant "passion"—in addition to other things. But understanding the term in this way, in the way, that is, that it is commonly used today, is at odds with his own unambiguous and irrefutable claim that it was, rather, passivity—the enduring of suffering—that was characteristic of and distinguished *pathos-passio*. It was only later that *passio* developed, gradually and haltingly, into what we today understand by the word "passion." *Pathos* signifies a state of being "overcome by" and "fraught with," of being "the recipient of" and having to "endure." On this basis, the term was taken to refer to the following spheres, or parts of them: everything characterized by sensation, everything that experiences change, phases of development, and conditions that recur in cyclical fashion. All of these occur in—to use Aristotelian terminology—the realms of animals, plants, heavenly bodies, and so on, and in matter in general. Further, *pathos* is present in and is the result of acts of perception and experience (as both knowledge and event), of sensation and feeling, and, finally, also in what we refer to colloquially as states of illness, suffering, misfortune, and pain.[1] Words that are used to mean the opposite of *pathos* when it is understood in this way include *praxis* (action), *poiēsis* (making), and *ergon* (deed). In this context, however, *pathos* means "passion" only insofar as it can be understood as something that overcomes someone who is subjected to it, as an illness or a feeling might do. There are, moreover, other Greek words, *epithumia* (desire) and *mania* (madness; in Latin: *cupiditas* and *furor*), for example, that are far closer to the kinds of activity and violence to which modern "passion" refers. Yet, these also do not capture its meaning fully, for they lack the possibility of the sublime. Modern "passion" is more

---

[1] Cf. Lidell-Scott-Jones, *A Greek-English Lexicon* (Oxford: Oxford University Press [n.d.]). See also specialist dictionaries, especially Bonitz's index of Aristotle's works: Hermann Bonitz, ed., *Index Aristotelicus* (Berlin: G. Reimer, 1870).

than desire, obsession, or frenzy. At any given time, it may involve the possibility of—or even have as its principal element—a kind of grand creative ardor that spends itself in either struggle or surrender. Next to this kind of "passion," the moderation that we associate with reason often cuts a pathetic figure indeed. As far as I can tell, antiquity did not have a separate word for "passion" when it is understood in this way, in spite of the fact that the substance of its meaning was of course well known at the time, in the mystery cults and in Attic tragedy, and above all in Plato. In the *Phaedrus* (265b), Plato designates the force that overcomes lovers, the *erōtikon pathos*, as one of the four types of divine madness, *theia mania*.[2]

In general we can say that, although antiquity divided up the fields of meaning somewhat differently from modernity, it recognized and developed all the elements of the inner life with the utmost precision. The same can be said for "feeling." In the theoretical debates about the feelings, *pathos* was not the only option; there was also the very ambiguous concept of *thumos* (*kata phrena kai kata thumon* [in mind and heart])—as well as *enthumion* [inner thought], and then *aisthēsis* for "perception," *daimonion* for "inner feeling," and the conceptual pair *hēdonē kai lupē* [pleasure and pain]. I cannot pursue this topic any further here. I only want to stress that it would be rash to draw any conclusions about the development of a concept like feeling based only on the absence of a term that corresponds to it exactly. There is in fact also no Latin word that corresponds to our word "thought." The term *cogitatio*, for example, attested to since Cicero, intersects as little with the semantic field of our word "thought" as the word *sensus* does with our "feeling." In fact, it is in some cases quite possible to use a word derived from the Latin *sentire*, namely, *sententia*, for "thought." The Latin, "quid Plato de pulchro senserit," can be nicely rendered as "Plato's thoughts about the beautiful."

But let me now return to *passio* and try to establish how it was that the modern meaning of "passion" took on the shape it now has within this word. As I have already indicated, in ordinary usage *pathos* originally meant sickness, pain, suffering, and—in terms of the psychological vocabulary coined by Aristotle—everything that can be passively perceived, received, and endured; here, sense impressions and perceptions, sensation and experience, stronger and weaker feelings are included. In addition to passivity, Aristotle attributed ethical neutrality to pathos; in other words, it was not possible to praise or blame people for their *pathē*. The use of the word in this way—to mean suffering in general, but also in the context of experiencing heat and cold, pain and joy, love and hate, and so on—persisted for a very long time,

---

[2] Thucydides refers to *erotikē lupē* [an "affront in love"] at 6.59.1. [Thucydides, *History of the Persian War*, 4 vols., Charles Forster Smith, trans. (Cambridge, MA: Harvard University Press, 1976) here 3:285.] Compare also Bultmann in his *Theologisches Wörterbuch zum Neuen Testament* under *lupē*, where issues analogous to the question of *pathos* are addressed.

in spite of the many and quite different layers of meaning that accrued to the corresponding word *passio* in late Latin. Examples are "illness" up until the Renaissance, the "Passion of Christ" even today, as well as "feeling" or "sensation" in the Aristotelian psychological tradition (whose terminology has proven surprisingly tenacious). We find *passio* as a purely passive and often also ethically neutral feeling not only in Scholasticism, but also very much later, well into the eighteenth century (cf. Lerch's collection of quotes, 332–34). In sum: The characteristic features of this layer of the word's development, the oldest one available to us, are passivity and ethical neutrality, as noted above.

And yet, there was—already in the dialectic of Aristotelianism—the distinct possibility that an active meaning could be mobilized for the concept of *pathos*. Being neither active nor productive of effects, something that "suffers" or allows things to happen to it is in a state of potentiality, of *dunamis* [power]. It is prepared to receive the effect and the impact of whatever is producing the effect that sets it in motion, or changes it. It thus moves, and this movement too is designated as *pathos*. A *pathos* of the soul could quite easily become a *kinēsis tēs psuchēs* [a movement of the soul], in Latin, *motus animi*. During the Middle Ages, these ideas, of which I can give only the simplest account here, were developed further particularly by Thomism.[3] Generally, however, they had little impact on everyday speech. The way the Stoics went on to develop and shape them was all the more momentous as a result. For them, the *passiones* became an agitation, a state of being that was in motion, but in an aimless and undirected way; the passions destroyed the composure of the wise human being. The word *passio* thus acquired a distinctly pejorative meaning. As far as possible, one was to avoid being affected or moved in one's inner being by the hustle and bustle of worldly events. The wise person (the sage) was obliged to avoid confronting the world, at least internally, and

---

[3] A passage from Boethius, *The Consolation of Philosophy* 5.4, is instructive in this context: *Praecedit* (that is, the perceiving activity of the spirit) *tamen excitans / Ac vires animi movens / Vivo in corpore passio*. [And yet in living bodies passion's might / Doth go forth before, whose office it is to incite, / And the first motions in the mind to make] Boethius, *The Consolation of Philosophy*, "I. T.," trans. (1609), rev. by H. F. Stewart (Cambridge, MA: Harvard University Press, 1962) 393. We are not really dealing with psychology here, but, rather, with epistemology; *passio* means "sense perception." But it is *excitans* [inciting] and *movens* [stirring into motion]. The passage contains a polemical defense of the Aristotelian doctrine of the spontaneous cognitive power of the soul against the Stoic claim that the soul only receives impressions (the theory of the *tabula rasa* on which sense impressions deposit their inscriptions like a writing stylus). An example of the further development of the Aristotelian relationship of the agent doing the action to the one who suffers the effect of the action, as I described it above, may be found in Dante's *Convivio* III, 10, at the beginning: "Dov'è da sapere" [Here we must know] [*Le opere di Dante Alighieri: Edizione Nazionale*, Franca Ageno, ed. (Florence: Le Lettere, 1995)]. Cf. on this point the commentary in Busnelli and Vandelli's edition (Florence 1934) 1:376. There may well be Stoic, perhaps even mystical, motifs echoing in Dante's words here.

to eschew disturbances emanating from it. He was to remain *impassibilis*, impassive, at all costs. Here, the original contrast with *actio* recedes into the background and *passio* becomes the opposite of *ratio*; the restive *passiones* are now contrasted with reason's stillness, its calm. For the first time, the German word for passion, *Leidenschaft*, is appropriate, partly because of the association with movement, partly because of the tempestuousness that the Stoics always assumed to be involved in passion. Images of storms and whirlwinds of passions find their origins here, and the obviously deprecatory word *perturbatio* begins to be used. This is the second stage, or layer, of the development of the meaning of *pathos-passio*. It is characterized (again) by tempestuousness and comes close to suggesting activity; it also lends itself to being evaluated in a negative way. This stage has *de facto* been much more influential than the first Aristotelian one, since it lives on even now in the popular conceptions of morality shared by a great many groups. It also appears in almost all subsequent ethical systems in one form or another. We also often discover—especially in late Scholasticism and during the Renaissance—uses of *passio* in which the Aristotelian and the Stoic concepts operate alongside each other, simultaneously and in myriad combinations.

The impact of the Stoic meaning of *passio* was nevertheless that much greater because it influenced the Christian authors of late antiquity from the very start. Ambrose writes, for example (*De Noa et Arca* 15:51; *PL* 14:385): *Caro nostra diversis agitatur et freti modo fluctuat passionibus* [Our flesh is aroused by diverse passions and is ever unquiet like the sea]. Augustine (*De civitate Dei* 8.17) uses a similar image: *passionum turbelis et tempestatibus agitari* [tossed by the whirlwinds and tempests of emotions]. He defines *passio* as a *motus animi contra rationem* [mental agitation that is contrary to reason], and explains that, in Latin—at least in the use of the term by the Church—*passio* is to be understood *non nisi ad vituperationem* [only in a pejorative sense].[4] This is unmistakably Stoic. Christian writers equate the *passiones* with the *concupiscentiae carnis* [bodily desires], often with the sins themselves.[5] Augustine is determined, however, to distance himself from the Stoic doctrine of the passions (*De civitate Dei*, 9.4ff.), claiming that there are also *bonae passiones* [good passions]. Ambrose (*De Noe et Arca*, 24:88, 402)

---

[4] Augustine, *De nuptiis et concupisc.* 2.33. *Nisi* is not securely transmitted, but the meaning requires it. [For the English translation of the citation from the *City of God* above, see Saint Augustine, *City of God Against the Pagans*, 7 vols., David S. Wiesen, trans. (Cambridge, MA: Harvard University Press, 1968) here 3:79. The translation of "Marriage and Desire" follows that text as translated by Roland J. Teske, S.J., *The Works of Saint Augustine*, Boniface Ramsey, series ed. (Hyde Park, NY: New City Press, 1998) 24:7.—Trans.]

[5] This occurs already in the Vulgate. See Romans 1:26, Romans 7:5, Thessalonians 1:4–5. Also see, for example, John Cassian, *De institutis coenobiorum* [Institutes of the Coenobia] V, 2 and *Collationes patrum in scetica eremo* [Conferences] V, 19 and 20. There is a Provençal text that translates the word *peccata* from the *Liber scintillarum* [The Book of Sparks] as *passios*. Cf. Bartsch, *Chrestomathie provençale*, 6th ed., 258, and *PL* 88:600.

does the same (*omnis enim affectus qui est praeter deformis delectationis illecebras passio quidem est, sed bona passio* [To be sure, every emotion which exists, other than the enticements of a degrading pleasure, is indeed a passion, but a good passion])—which sounds, rather, closer to Peripateticism. The two tendencies thus already intersected, even merged with one another at that time, as we see in Augustine. The Stoic moral teachings were in any case quite close to the Christian ones at the time.

And yet, the two systems were also already fundamentally different. The Christian authors contrasted the *passiones* not with the tranquility of the wise person, but, rather, with submitting to injustice. Their goal was not to withdraw from the world as a way of avoiding suffering and passion. Instead, they intended to prevail over the world precisely by suffering. The ways in which the Stoics and the Christians meant to escape the world thus differ profoundly from one another. Rather than a Stoic degree-zero of extraworldly passionlessness, the goal of the Christian flight from the world lay in counter-suffering, a passionate suffering within—and thus in opposition to—the world. Christians fought the flesh, the evil *passiones* of this world, not with Stoic apathy or with "the good feelings" (the *bonae passiones*) as a means of attaining something like an Aristotelian centeredness, or Golden Mean. Instead, they deployed something entirely new, something that was, until that time, completely unheard of, namely, a *gloriosa passio* [a passion full of glory] that consisted in a burning love of the divine.[6] Whoever is *impassibilis* is not perfect, Ambrose (*Commentary on the Gospel of Luke* 10: 177 *PL* 15:1848) says. Rather, that person is *perfectus in omnibus* [perfect in all things] *quem caro iam revocare non posset a gloria passionis* [whom the flesh is not actually able to recall from the glory of suffering]).[7] The Sicilian mar-

---

[6] Leo Spitzer has alerted me to the following passage from Malebranche, *Entretiens sur la métaphysique et sur la religion* 11.14: "Je crois de plus que Dieu a figuré, même par les dispositions du corps, celles de l'âme sainte de Jésus, et principalement l'excès de son amour pour son Eglise; car Saint Paul (Eph. 5:25–33) nous apprend que cette passion violente de l'amour, 'qui fait qu'on quitte avec joie son père et sa mère pour sa femme', est une figure de l'excès de l'amour de Jésus-Christ pour son épouse." [And I believe, moreover . . . that by means of the dispositions of the body God even represented the dispositions of the holy soul of Jesus, and principally the surplus of His love for His church. For St. Paul teaches us that this violent passion of love which causes us to leave our father and mother for our wife, is a representation of the surplus of love of Jesus Christ for His bride [Ephesians 5:31–2].] Nicolas Malebranche, *Dialogues on Metaphysics and on Religion*, Nicholas Jolley, ed., David Scott, trans. (Cambridge: Cambridge University Press, 1997) 214–15.]

[7] Jesus was *impassibilis* before the Incarnation. Bernard de Clairvaux writes on this issue: *Beatus quippe Deus, beatus Dei filius, in ea forma qua non rapinam arbitratus est esse se aequalem Patri, procul dubio impassibilis, priusquam se exinanisset formam servi accipiens* (Phil. 2:6–7), *sicut miseriam vel subjectionem expertus non erat, sic misericordiam et obedientiam non noverat experimento. Sciebat quidem per naturam, non autem sciebat per experimentiam. At ubi minoratus est non solum a se ipso, sed etiam paulo minus ab angelis, qui et ipsi impassibiles sunt per gratiam, non per naturam, usque ad illam formam, in qua pati et subjici posset. . . .* [Blessed is God, blessed the Son of God, in that form in which he does not think it robbery to be equal with the Father (Phil. 2:6). I do not

tyrs cried out as they were being led to their deaths (*Acta Bolland* 8.6 [Jean Bolland, *Acta Sanctorum* 8.6]): *Deo gratias, qui nos pro suo nomine ad gloriosam passionem perducere dignatus est* [Thanks be to God, who thought it fit to lead us to a glorious passion in his name].

Anyone who insists that there is a distinction between the meanings of "suffering" and "passion" (in German, *Leiden* and *Leidenschaft*) has thus failed to understand clearly the dialectic between the two terms as Christianity understood it. It was God's love that moved Him to take human suffering upon Himself. This is a *motus animi*, a movement of the soul, beyond measure and without end.[8] Whereas the Passion of Christ seldom appeared as a theme in the second half of the first millennium, it was a frequent motif after the Christian Renaissance of the twelfth century, when the idea of Christ incarnate once again began to overshadow the notion of Christ the King (*rex gloriae*). In a passage that is often cited by his contemporaries and that used to be well known, Bernard de Clairvaux speaks of the martyr:

> Enimvero non sentiet sua, dum illius (Christi) vulnera intuebitur. Stat martyr tripudians et triumphans, toto licet lacero corpore; et rimante latera ferro, non modo fortiter, sed et alacriter sacrum e carne sua circumspicit ebullire cruorem. Ubi ergo tunc anima martyris? Nempe in tuto, nempe in petra [the reference here is to a commentary on Song of Songs 2:17: 'columba mea in foraminibus petrae'], nempe in visceribus

---

doubt that he was impassible before he emptied himself and took the form of a servant (Phil. 2:7), for just as he had not experienced wretchedness and subjection, so he had not known mercy or obedience by experience. He knew by nature, not by experience. / He became not only lower than himself, but also a little lower than the angels (Heb. 2:9; Ps. 8:6), for they too are impassible, though by grace not by nature. He lowered himself to that form in which he could suffer and be in subjection] (*Tract. de grad. humil.* 3:9; *PL* 182:946) ["On Humility and Pride," in *Bernard of Clairvaux: Selected Works*, trans. and with a foreword by G. R. Evans (New York: Paulist Press, 1987) 99–143; here 108–109]. After the Resurrection, Christ is again *impassibilis*. Cf. Bonaventure, *Breviloquium* 4.10 (*Opera omnia*, A.C. Peltier, Aug. Taur., 7.294: *Christi corpus . . . primo fuerat passibile et mortale, postea autem impassibile et immortale* [Christ's body . . . [which] had been subject to pain and death had risen impassible and immortal. "The Breviloquium," in *The Works of Bonaventure*, vol. 2, Jose de Vinck, trans. (Paterson, NJ: St. Anthony Guild Press, 1963) 174]. On God's *impassibilitas*, cf. Isidore 7.1.24 which Spitzer discusses in his rich note in *Romania* 56, 123ff. In this sense, *passibilis* is sometimes rendered with the word *sensibilis*; the two terms appear to be nearly synonymous in the *Stimulus Amoris* (cf. the edition of Bonaventure cited above, 12: 636–37.) See also the *Roman d'Eneas* 2883: *Sire . . . ge voil saveir, se ce puet estre . . . veir que cil . . . aient forme corporel, passible seient et mortel* [Lord, . . . I want to know if it can be . . . true that these men . . . have corporeal form, [if they] are mortal and subject to passion]. By contrast, see Dante, *Inferno* 2.15: *sensibilmente*.

[8]Of course this is not a divine *passio*, for God is *impassibilis*. A Renaissance love dialogue explains: *. . . quello affetto suo voluntario non è suggetto a passione, come il nostro, non essendo in lui difetto d'alcuna cosa.* [That affect [e.g., love] which is willed by [God] himself, is not subjected to passion, as our human affect is, since there is no defect of any kind in him; *Trattati d'amore del Cinquecento* [Treatises on Love from the Fifteenth Century], Giuseppe Zonta, ed. (Bari: G. Laterza, 1912) 39.]

Jesu, vulneribus nimirum patentibus ad introeundum . . . Non hoc facit stupor, sed amor.

[While gazing on the Lord's wounds he will indeed not feel his own. The martyr remains jubilant and triumphant though his whole body is mangled; even while the steel is gashing his sides he looks around with courage and elation at the holy blood pouring from his flesh. Where then is the soul of the martyr? In a safe place, of course; in the rock, of course; in the heart of Jesus, of course, in wounds open for it to enter . . . Insensibility does not bring this about, love does.] *Serm. in Cant.* 61 [Walsh and Edmonds, trans., 3:147], *PL* 183:10.[9]

The martyr takes shelter in Christ's open wounds. These wounds light the fire of love in him and allow him to triumph, ecstatically, over the torments inflicted on him. His own agonies are witnesses to Christ's love. Bernard writes (*Epist.* 107.8; *PL* 182:246): *Amavit, inquam, amavit: habes enim dilectionis pignus Spiritum, habes et testem fidelem Jesum, et hunc crucifixum* [I say he loved us. As a pledge of his love you have the Spirit, and you have a faithful witness to it in Jesus, Jesus crucified]. Cistercian mysticism—which had the greatest influence on similar movements in later centuries—developed within the framework of commentaries on the *Song of Songs*. For us a deeply arcane interpretative form, it is primarily allegorical, but also partially typological and figural. It nevertheless yields a powerful and rich love, abundant and sweet, of a kind that we can hardly understand anymore. Bernard writes in *De diligendo Deo* [On Loving God] 3.7 (*PL* 182:978):

Facile proinde plus diligunt, qui se amplius dilectos intelligunt: cui autem minus donatum est, minus diligit. Judaeus sane, sive paganus, nequaquam talibus aculeis incitatur [amoris], qualis Ecclesia experitur, quae ait, 'Vulnerata caritate ego sum: et rursum, Fulcite me floribus, stipate me malis, quia amore langueo' (Cantic. 2, 5) . . . Cernit Unicum Patris, crucem sibi bajulantem; cernit caesum et consputum Dominum majestatis; cernit auctorem vitae et gloriae confixum clavis, percussum lancea, opprobriis saturatum, tandem illam dilectam animam suam ponere pro amicis [suis]. Cernit haec, et suam magis ipsius animam gladius amoris transverberat, et dicit: 'Fulcite me floribus, statipe me malis, quia

[9]Cf. here Meister Eckhart, Sermon 107, Pfeifer, ed., 3rd ed. (Göttingen 1914) 353: *Ez wundert vil menschen, wie die lieben heiligen in sô grôzer süezikeit sô grôz liden getragen haben. Wer des wunders wil ledic weden, der erfülle daz die heiligen mit grôzem flîze erfüllet hânt unde hânt Jêsû Kristô mit inhitziger minne nâch gevolget* [Many wonder how the beloved saints were able to bear such great trials with such great sweetness. Whoever wants to become free of [this] wondering, he should bring to fruition that which the saints have brought to fruition with great eagerness and imitate Christ with soul-warming love.]

amore langueo.' Haec sunt quippe mala punica, quae in hortum introducta dilecti sponsa carpit ex ligno vitae, a coelesti pane proprium mutuata saporem, colorem a sanguine Christi. Videt deinde mortem mortuam . . . Advertit terram, quae spinas et tribulos sub antiquo maledicto produxerat, ad novae benedictionis gratiam innovatam refloruisse. Et in his omnibus, illius recordata versiculi, "Et refloruit caro mea, et ex voluntate mea confitebor ei" [Ps. 27:7][;] passionis malis, quae de arbore tulerat crucis, cupit vigere et de floribus resurrectionis, quorum praesertim fragrantia sponsum ad se crebrius revisendam invitet.

[The more surely you know yourself loved, the easier you will find it to love in return. Those to whom less has been given love less [Lk. 7:47]. The Jew and the pagan are not moved by such wounds as the Church experiences. She says, "I am wounded by love" [Sg. 2:5], and again, "Surround me with flowers, pile up apples around me, for I am sick with love" [Sg. 3:11]). . . . She sees the Lord of majesty [1 Cor. 2:8] struck and spat upon. She sees the Author of life and glory [Acts 3:15] transfixed by nails, wounded by a lance [Jn. 19:34], smeared with abuse [Lam. 3:30], and finally laying down his precious life for his friends [Jer. 12:7; Jn. 15:13]. She sees these things, and the sword of love pierces her soul more deeply [cf. Lk. 2:35], and she says, "Surround me with flowers, pile up apples around me, for I am sick with love [Sg. 2:5]. . . . These are beyond a doubt the pomegranate fruits which the Bride brought into her Beloved's garden [Sg. 6:10]. They were picked from the Tree of Life [Gn. 2:22], and their taste had been transmuted to that of heavenly bread, and their color to that of Christ's blood. At last she sees the death of death. . . . Under the ancient curse [Heb. 6:8] the earth had produced thorns and thistles; now she sees it burst forth into bloom again under the renewed grace of a new blessing. And as she beholds all this, she remembers the verse: "My flesh has bloomed again, and willingly shall I praise him" (Ps 27:7). She desires to add to the pomegranate fruits which she gathered from the tree of the Cross some of the flowers of the resurrection whose fragrance more than anything else invites the Bridegroom to visit her more often.] [Evans, trans., 179–80]

Just as Christ was drunk with the wine of charity (*ebrius vino charitatis*), when he sacrificed himself (*Sermo de diversis* 29, *PL* 183:620), so too does the soul become drunk when it immerses itself in its *passio* and *resurrectio*. *Suavissimum mihi cervical*, writes one of Bernard's successors, *bone Jesu, spinea illa capitis tui corona; dulcis lectulus illud crucis tuae lignum. In hoc nascor et nutrior, creor et recreor, et super passionis tuae altaria memoriae mihi nidum libentur recolloco.* [Good Jesus, the crown of thorns on your head is to me the sweetest pillow, the wood of your cross a sweet bed. In this, I am born and suckled, created and recreated, and I gladly return to that place to take refuge on the altar of memory of your passion.][10]

The main starting point for Cistercian Passion mysticism is nevertheless the following verse from the Song of Songs (1:12): *Fasciculus myrrhae dilectus meus mihi, inter ubera mea commorabitur.* [My beloved is a bundle of myrrh to me and he will linger between my breasts.] Referring, on the one hand, to the cup of myrrh before the Crucifixion (Mark 12:23) and, on the other, to the story of Joseph of Arimathia and Nicodemus, who took Christ down from the cross and wrapped Him in a linen cloth with myrrh and aloe, the *fasciculus myrrhae* [bundle of myrrh] is read as a figure of Christ's crucified body and thus of the Passion, which—like myrrh—is both bitter and healing. It ought thus always to be held between the beloved's breasts and against her heart, which is to say that the Church and the soul should never cease meditating upon the Passion.[11] The grape clusters of Cyprian wine in the next verse (*botrus Cypri dilectus meus mihi.* . . .) [my beloved is a cluster of Cyprian grapes to me] are then interpreted as signifying the Resurrection because of their sweetness, which gives joy to the heart. Bernard's commentary on these verses (which contains a variant of this tradition that renders only the drink as the Passion and the anointing of Christ's body already as a figure of the indestructibility of the body) must have been hugely influential at the time. Both Bonaventure and Suso cite its main passage:

> Et ego, fratres, ab ineunte mea conversione, pro acervo meritorum, quae mihi deesse sciebam, hunc mihi fasciculum colligare et inter ubera mea collocare curavi, collectum ex omnibus anxietatibus et amaritudinibus Domini mei. . . . Ubi sane inter tot odoriferae myrrhae huius ramusculos minime praetermittendam putavi etiam illam myrrham qua in cruce potatus est; sed neque illam qua unctus est in sepultura. Quarum in prima applicuit sibi meorum amaritudinem peccatorum; in secunda futuram incorruptionem mei corporis dedicavit. Memoriam abundantiae suavitatis horum eructabo, quoad vixero; in aeternum non obliviscar miserationes istas, quia in ipsis vivificatus sum. (*In Cant.* 43; *PL* 183:994)

> [As for me, dear brothers, from the early days of my conversion, conscious of my grave lack of merits, I made sure to gather for myself this little bunch of myrrh and place it between my breasts. It was culled from all the anxious hours and bitter experiences of my Lord. . . . Among the teeming little branches of this perfumed myrrh I feel we must not forget the myrrh which he drank upon the cross and used for his anointing at

[10] Gilbert of Hoyland, *PL* 184:21, on Song of Songs 3:1. [The translation here is based on Martin Elsky's translation of the "Passio" essay in *Criticism* (Summer 2001), with some alterations. —Trans.]

[11] On this tradition, see Bede, for example, in his *Cant. Cant. alleg. expos.* [Commentary on the Song of Songs], 2.4, *PL* 91:1097.

this burial. In the first of these he took upon himself the bitterness of my sins, in the second he affirmed the future incorruption of my body. As long as I live I shall proclaim the memory of the abounding goodness contained in these events; throughout eternity I shall not forget these mercies, for in them I have found life.][Walsh and Edmonds, trans., 221–22]

On the basis of these citations, which are only examples, we may conclude that the meanings of "suffering" and "actively creative and ecstatic love-passion" were closely aligned with each other. It would take a separate essay to discuss individually the motifs that occur again and again: *ebrietas spiritus* [drunkenness of the spirit], *suave vulnus charitatis* [the sweet wound of love as charity], *gladius amoris* [the sword of love], *pax in Christi sanguine* [peace in the blood of Christ], *surgere ad passionem* [rising up to passion], *calix quem bibisti amabilis* [the cup, worthy of love, from which you drink], and so on. The penchant for Passion mysticism becomes even more intense over the next centuries. In what we might call the "classical" mysticism of Bernard, the Passion nearly always appears in connection with other love motifs, depending on the occasion and the context, whether it be in association with the early life of Christ, or with the Resurrection, or—as in connection with witnessing God's love—as a matter of the efficacy of the Holy Spirit. Both the depiction and the bodily enactment of the Stations of the Cross and the ecstasy that they produce in those who meditate on them are always tempered by a certain moderation.[12] In the age that followed, a far more powerful and concrete emphasis on the Passion and on Passion mysticism gained acceptance; not least, in all likelihood, because of the miracle of the stigmata of St. Francis of Assisi. The Franciscans and the mendicant orders in general appear to have been mainly responsible for this trend. I have very few texts at my disposal here, almost nothing beyond the edition of the works of Bonaventure to which I referred above. And I have no access to the texts of the Franciscan spiritualists at all. But this development is clear even in a figure as moderate as Bonaventure. The passages that prove it are so frequent and extensive that I cannot quote all of them here.

Rather, let me simply indicate the most important ones: in the *Breviloquium*, Part IV, Chapter IX, in the *Diaeta salutis*, Tit. VII, Chapter VII, in

---

[12] Lerch cites as particularly convincing examples of the transformation of the significance of *passio* into an active mode several texts from the eighteenth century (Bonnet, Wieland, Choderlos de Laclos) that mention *passions actives*, "active passions." In *Dangerous Liaisons*, Valmont recommends the "active passions" as the sole way to achieve happiness. Bernard de Clairvaux says of Jesus already in his sermon on the Passion (in *Feria quarta Hebdomadae Sancta* [The Four Holy Days of the Week] 11, *PL* 183:268: *Et in vita passivam habuit actionem, et in morte passionem activam sustinuit, dum salutem operaretur in medio terrae.* [In life, he performed passive action, in death, he endured active passion that he might achieve salvation on earth.] [The translation here is based on Elsky (n. 10 above), with some alterations. —Trans.])

the seventh chapter of the *Itinerarium* (*De excessu mentali et mystico*) [The Journey of the Mind to God (On Mental and Mystical Ravishment in which Repose is Given to the Soul that Rises Toward God in Ecstatical Love)], the foreword of the *Lignum vitae* [The Tree of Life], the sixth chapter of *De perfectione vitae* [On the Perfection of Life, Addressed to Sisters], the chapter entitled *De specialibus orationibus* [On Special Prayers] (2.23) in the probably apocryphal *De profectu religiosorum* [On the Progress of the Devout], the foreword and the sixth *Feria* [feast day] of the *Meditationes Vitae Christi* [Meditations on the Life of Christ] and the first several pages of the *Stimulus Amoris* [The Spur of Love] by his student, Jacob of Milan [Giacomo Capelli]. There is doubtless much that I have overlooked,[13] for everywhere one turns, one is confronted with an extensive elaboration of the Passion and with the extreme intimacy of what "suffering" and "passion," *passio* and *fervor*, are taken to mean. *Christus homo hunc (ignem charitatis) accendit in fervore suae ardentissimae passionis—devotionis fervor per frequentem passionis Christi memoriam nutritur—transfige, dulcisssime Domine Jesu, medullas animae meae suavissimo ac saluberrimo vulnere amoris tui animam (Mariae) passionis gladius pertransivit—in passione et cruce Domini gloriari desidero—curre, curre, Domine Jesu, curre et me vulnera.* [Christ as man lights this [the fire of charity] with the heat of his most burning suffering—the heat of devotion is fed by the frequent recollection of the suffering of Christ—pierce, most sweet Lord Jesus, the marrow of my soul with the most sweet and most healing wound of your love just as the sword of the Passion penetrated the soul [of Mary]—I long to be glorified in the Passion and on the cross of the Lord— hurry, hurry, Lord Jesus, hurry and wound me.] I have selected just a few sentences here, and there is much more that is relevant that cannot be cited in such brief compass, since it only makes sense in context. *Crux* [cross], *vulnera* [wounds], and *gladius* [sword], and so forth, were of course not the only words that stood for *passio*. Often any one of the countless images that medieval theologians derived from their allegorical and figural interpretations of Scripture did so as well. For example, we often read the following for *fervor*: *ardor* [heat], *amor* [love], *ebrietas* [intoxication], *dulcedo* [sweetness], *suavitas* [charm], *excessus* [excess], and so on. I will give just one more example of the kind of metaphorical language that derives from biblical hermeneutics, namely from Chapter Six of the text *De perfectione vitae ad sorores* [Holiness of Life], in which Bonaventure, addressing a nun, paraphrases Isaiah 13:3:

---

[13] In the *Ottimo Commento* on *Paradiso* 11.118, in the context of a description of the life of Saint Francis, I find the following: *Da quella ora* [that is, since the time when Christ appeared to him in San Damiano] *innanzi l'anima sua fu tutta liquefatta, e la passione del Crucifisso nel suo cuore fu mirabilmente fitta.* [From that moment, his entire soul softened and the Passion of the Crucifixion miraculously became set in his heart.]

(Haurietis aquas in gaudio de fontibus salvatoris): Quicumque desiderat aquas gratiarum, aquas lacrymarum, iste hauriat de fontibus Salvatoris, id est de vulneribus Jesu Christi. Accede ergo tu, o famula, pedibus af- fectionum tuarum ad Jesum vulneratum, ad Jesum spinis coronatum, ad Jesum patibulo crucis affixum, et cum beato Thoma apostolo non solum intuere in manibus eius figuras clarovum, non solum mitte manum tuam in latus eius, sed totaliter per ostium lateris eius ingredere usque ad cor ip- sius Jesu; ubique ardentissimo amore crucifixi in Christum transformata, clavis divini timoris affixa, lancea praecordialis dilectionis transfixa, gladio intimae compassionis transverberata, nihil aliud quaeras, nihil aliud desideres, et nullo alio velis consolari, quam ut cum Christo tu pos- sis mori in cruce; et tunc cum apostolo Paulo (Gal. 2:19–20) exclames, dicens: "Christo confixus sum cruci; vivo iam non ego, vivit vero in me Christus."

["You shall draw waters with joy out of the Saviour's fountains." In other words, if the grace of tears, the tears of thanksgiving, the tears of fervent piety are sought, such tears must be drawn from the Saviour's fountains, i.e., from the . . . wounds of Jesus Christ. Draw near, O handmaid, with loving steps to Jesus wounded for you, to Jesus crowned with thorns, to Jesus nailed to the gibbet of the Cross. Gaze with the Blessed Apostle St. Thomas, not merely on the print of the nails in Christ's hands [. . .] neither let it be sufficient to put your hand into the wound in His side; but enter bodily by the door in His side and go straight up to the very Heart of Jesus. There, burning with love for Christ Crucified, be trans- formed into Christ. Fastened to the Cross by the nails of the fear of God, transfixed by the lance of the love of your inmost heart, pierced through and through by the sword of the tenderest compassion, seek for nothing else, wish for nothing else, look for consolation in nothing else except in dying with Christ on the Cross. Then, at last, will you cry out with Paul the Apostle: With Christ I am nailed to the Cross. I live, now not I; but Christ liveth in me.][14]

[14] [The translation cited here is: *Holiness of Life, Being St. Bonaventure's Treatise* De Perfectione Vita ad Sorores *Englished by the late Laurence Costello O.F.M. and Edited by Fr. Wilfrid, O.F.M.*, 2nd ed. (London: B. Herber Book Co., 1928) 62–64.] For anyone familiar with the propensity for anti- thetical paradoxes in European love poetry beginning with the Provençal poets and extending up through Petrarch (for example: *Pace non trovo, e non ho da far guerra* [I find no peace and I am not one to make war]), it is difficult to avoid the impression, when reading medieval texts, that it was the great paradoxes of the Passion that created the fertile soil out of which those forms were able to grow. The following text may be relatively late (it is from the *Stimulus Amoris* from the second half of the thirteenth century and thus approximately contemporary with the rise of the *dolce stil nuovo*), but it makes clear that similar motifs were being used already since the beginning of the twelfth century: *Si ergo, anima, carnem diligis, nullam carnem nisi carnem Christi ames. Haec enim pro tua et totius humani generis salute est super aram crucis oblata, cuius passionem in corde rumines*

It is not only the way that "suffering" and "passion," *passio* and *fervor*, begin to converge that appears significant to us in these mystical texts, but rather and above all, the fact that both states are so sought after: *desiderium et gloria passionis* [the desire for and glory of suffering].[15] In stark contrast to all of the ideas of the ancients, and especially those of the Stoics, *passio* is celebrated and longed for here. St. Francis of Assisi's life and his receiving of the stigmata unite passion and suffering, the mystical leap of the one to the other, in the most concrete of ways. The passion of love leads, through suffering, to an *excessus mentis* [departure from reason] and thus to a union with Christ. The person who is without *passio* is also without Grace. Whoever does not sacrifice himself, in empathic suffering, to the *passio* of the Savior lives in a hardening of the heart, an *obduratio cordis*. (We often find instructions in the mystical treatises on how to overcome this condition.) And yet, as important and influential as Lerch's main criterion is, namely, the active quality of *passio*, we must be careful not to exaggerate it. The stance of the soul is dynamic and potential rather than truly productive; it is more receptive and full of longing than really active; it is decidedly bride-like. No matter what kind of tempestuous and enrapturing love or passionate submission the soul may achieve on its own, victory ultimately always belongs to the power of Christ, or Grace. This is where activity begins. The wounds of love, the *fervor spiritus* [ardor of the soul] and the *unio passionalis* [passionate union], are gifts bestowed by Grace. One can perhaps prepare oneself to receive Grace, one

---

quotidie. Huius enim passionis Christi meditatio continua mentem elevabit . . . O passio desiderabilis! O mors admirabilis! Quid mirabilius quam quod mors vivificet, vulnera sanent, sanguis album faciat, et mundet intima, nimius dolor nimium dulcorem inducat, apertio lateris cor cordi coniungat? Sed adhuc mirari non cesses, quia sol obscuratus plus solito illuminat, ignis extinctus magis inflammat, passio ignominiosa glorificat. Sed vere mirabile est, quod Christus in cruce sitiens inebriat, nudus existens virtutem vestimentis ornat, sed et eius manus ligno conclavatae nos solvunt, pedes confossi nos currere faciunt . . . [If therefore, my soul, you love the flesh, love no flesh but the flesh of Christ. For lifted up on the altar of the cross, this flesh, whose suffering you should contemplate daily in your heart, is for you and the salvation of the entire human race. For uninterrupted meditation on Christ's suffering will elevate the mind. . . . O suffering to be wished for! O marvelous death! What can be more wondrous than that death may restore life, that wounds may heal, that blood may make you fair, and cleanse your inner being, that great pain brings great sweetness, that an opened side may join heart to heart? But may you not cease to look with wonder because a darkened sun shines more than usual, that an extinguished fire burns more brightly, that shameful suffering glorifies. But it is truly marvelous that Christ thirsting on the cross intoxicates; that nakedness adorns virtue with its garments, not to mention that his hands nailed to the cross unbind us and his pierced feet allow us to run. (The translation here is based on Elsky's translation (n. 10 above), with some alterations. —Trans.)] The passage is already almost too ornate.

[15] Here, also see [Heinrich] Suso, *Horologium Sapientiae* [Clock of Wisdom], ch. 14. (I consulted the edition prepared by J. Strange, ed. nova [Cologne 1861]). To understand this passage, one must note that the rose is a symbol of divine joy. Cf. M. Gorce, O.P., *Le Roman de la Rose* (Paris 1933) 29–36. Passion mysticism is also very developed among the German women mystics, including Mechtild von Magdeburg and Margaretha Ebner.

can wish that it would come, and even pray that it does. Indeed, the desire for Grace can be so intense that it can force its own fulfillment—just as Jacob prevailed over the angel. But in this case, Grace must have already been present in the one who prayed for it:

> *Regnum coelorum* vïolenza pate
> Da caldo amore e da viva speranza
> Che vinca la divina volontate;
> Non a guisa che l'omo a l'om sobranza,
> Ma vince lei perché vuol esser vinta,
> E vinta vince con sua beninanza.

> [*Regnum celorum* (the Kingdom of Heaven) suffers violence,
> From ardent love and living hope, for these
> Can be the conquerors of Heaven's Will;
> Yet not as man defeats another man:
> The Will of God is won because It would
> Be won and, won, wins through benevolence.]

—*Paradise* 20.94–99 (Trans. Mandelbaum 417)

Here the *passiones* are and remain something that the soul endures and by which it is overcome. Both the original meanings and the Aristotelian tradition are to this extent preserved. What is new and to a certain degree active in the Christian concept is the idea that spontaneity and the productive force of love can be aroused by *passio*. (This is also fundamentally Aristotelian.) And yet, love always originates in some more-than-human force, be it lofty and celestial, or low and creaturely, and is thus always received or endured as an either magnificent or terrifying gift.

The claim that *passio* has a "positive value" in the tradition of mystical love ecstasy also requires caution and qualification. All Christian thought and especially all mystical ideas move between two poles that stand in opposition to one another. The love of God is a love that torments, even when He responds to it, for God overpowers the soul. Were He to take the soul into His heart, "[it]would perish from His more powerful being" and suffer a *Liebestod* full of real torment, but also of real rapture at one and the same time. By way of explanation, I want to cite some lines from Jacopone da Todi's *Cantico dell'amor superardente* [How the Soul Complains to God of the Over-Ardent Love Infused in Her]:

> Amor di caritate, / Perchè m'hai si ferito? / Lo cor tutto partito, / Et che arde per amore? // Arde et incende, e nullo trova loco; / Non può fugir però ched è ligato; / Sì si consuma come cera a foco; / Vivendo mor, languisce stemperato: / Dimanda di poter fugir un poco, / et in fornace

trovasi locato. / Oimè do' son menato / A sì forte languire? / Vivendo si
è morire, / Tanto monta l'ardore.//Nante che io il provassi dimandava /
Amar Jesu, credendo ciò dolzura. / E'n pace di dolcezza star pensava, /
Fuor d'ogni pena possedendo altura: / Provo tormento qual io non sti-
mava, / Chel cor si mi fendesse per calura. / Non posso dar figura, / Di
che veggio sembianza; / Che moio in delettanza, / e vivo senza core.

[Love, that art Charity, / Why hast Thou hurt me so? / My heart is smote
in two, / And burns with ardent love.//Glowing and flaming, refuge finding none, / My heart is fettered fast, it cannot flee; / It is consumed like
wax placed in the sun; / Living, yet dying, swooning passionately, / It
prays for strength a little way to run, / Yet in this furnace must it bide and
be: / Where am I led, ah me! / To depths so high? / Living I die, / So fierce
the fire of love.] [Beck, trans., 363]

All of these motifs also occur in profane love poetry, as we know—often
so powerfully that we can legitimately doubt whether we are dealing with
secular literature here at all. To be without love is to be unworthy of a noble
heart. Love is the path to all virtue and knowledge. Yet, it is as much rapture
as torment. Suffering and passion are one; lovers suffer not only when they
long for the beloved, but also when the beloved is nearby. When the beloved
greets the lover, her words cause him such distress that he thinks he might
die. These are all well known subjects in love poetry. Even if they gradually
become secularized and superficial in numerous ways, they are documented
from the time of the Provençal poets up through Dante and Petrarch and well
into recent times. They are, moreover, vigorously resurrected in their original
form wherever a powerful mystical movement arises. In spite of the fact that
they are often of earlier origin, the metaphorical language of mysticism—the
images of fiery consumption, of being wounded and pierced, of drunken-
ness, imprisonment, martyrdom, and so on—are also universally present in
this specifically mystical variation. Brother Francisco Tressati da Lugnano,
who provided me with the early seventeenth century edition of Jacopone that
I am using, can cite passages from later secular poets (Petrarch, Bembo, etc.)
whose verses run parallel to those by Jacopone.

I believe—and the reader will already have understood my thinking in
the course of what I have elucidated so far—that Passion mysticism, in its
close association of *passio* and ecstasy, also influenced the development of
passio-passion. It was this form of mysticism that prepared *passio* to accom-
modate the modern sense of "passion," giving it (e.g., *passio*) an advantage
over the competing expression, *affectus*, in this respect. What *passio*-passion
adopted from Passion mysticism was, in my estimation, an intensification of
what "suffering" meant in a doubled, dialectical sense, insofar as it can mean
rapture and transport at one and the same time. This is what Meister Eckhart (see note 9 above) calls *inhitzige minne* [ardent love]. The influence is

incontestable in terms of content, for the binary dialectical form of "passion" also developed in secular love poetry in close association with mysticism, in which love experiences are described as *martiri* [martyrdoms], *tormenti* [torments], *dolce furori* [sweet furies], and the like. Nevertheless, the impact on the profane usage of the word *passio* is attenuated at first. Dante of course describes what he experiences on the day that his lady appears in the world in his *Rime* LXVII: *E' m'incresce di me sì duramente* [I pity myself so intensely]—an experience that he relates unmistakably to the rapture of Paul at Acts 9—as a *passion nova* [new passion] that leads to a mystical *Liebestod*.[16] And at the beginning of the *Convivio*, he refers to the mystical work of his youth, the *Vita Nova*, with a combination of terms familiar from mystical texts: *fervida e passionate* [fervent and empassioned]. We can likewise conclude from one of his Latin letters (*Exulti Pistoriensi*, Critical Edition, 417) that *passio* was commonly used to mean "erotic passion" (*Liebesleidenschaft*)—at least in the colloquial usage of certain circles. Boccaccio, finally, uses the words *passione* and *passionato* for erotic suffering and passion, occasionally speaking of the *piacevolissima passione d'amore (suavissima passio amoris)* [the very most pleasing suffering of love (the sweet suffering of love)]. But these are the only examples from the Italian thirteenth and fourteenth centuries to which I can refer.[17] In the overwhelming majority of cases, Dante himself uses the term *passio* in the Aristotelian sense when he contrasts it with *actio*, and occasionally with a Stoic connotation when he opposes it to *ratio*. The same is true of the rest of the theoretical writers of the late Middle Ages. In their work, *passio* means suffering (without the secondary dialectical meaning), feeling, experience, and sometimes passion in a purely pejorative sense (as the Stoics understood it). Here, the Aristotelian meaning is by far the dominant one, with the Stoic sense only weakly present, and the mystical one entirely absent. At the time, *passio* was a technical term that smacked of the Schools, and for this reason, love poetry never used it at all. Even Jacopone always speaks of *croce* [the cross] and not *passione* [passion]. Dante, whose understanding of the high style incorporated the philosophy of the Schools, did not have any lasting influence, since it was directly after his time that an early Humanist and anti-Scholastic tendency began to prevail. Petrarch, who uses a great number of images derived from mysticism in the *Canzoniere*, never uses *passio*. In the high style, the word could be accepted to mean "passion" only after the influence of the Aristotelian Scholastic tradition had abated. *Passionatus* was less closely affiliated with this tradition, yet at the time it too meant "passionate" only in a strictly pejorative, Stoic sense—albeit with a new slant that suggested "biased" or "prejudiced." Dante already uses it this

[16] One must take care here—as always with Dante—with the meaning of *novo*, which depends on passages from Ezekiel and Paul. E. Eberwein drew my attention to this fact.

[17] I do not have access to the Catalan examples which Spitzer cites (cf. *Romania* 65, 124).

way, employing the verb *passionare* (*De monarchia* 1:11): *bene repellentur, qui iudicem passionare conantur* [those who try to stir up a judge's emotions are rightly rebuffed]. Other passages may be found in a report about the College of Cardinals at Pisa (1409), cited by Du Cange (*concilium . . . fuit ex personis . . . passionatis contra iustitiam Suae Sanctitatis* [the council . . . was made up out of those . . . biased against the justice of His Holiness]), as well as in the *Imitation of Christ* and in several Italian texts that are cited in the Tommaseo-Bellini dictionary.[18]

In the sixteenth century, when the power of the Thomist-Aristotelian Schools declined and both the Stoic and the mystical movements began to become important for literature, the modern meaning of *passio* as passion began to establish itself, doing so by relying on amorous suffering and erotic passion, as I have already indicated above. But it was still to take a long time for this meaning to become established as the only authoritative one. For *passio*-passion, nourished by mystical and Stoic sources, had to wage a battle on two fronts—not only against its own Aristotelian meaning (as experience, feeling, or a suffering entirely free of passion), but also against the competition provided by *affectus, affectio*. One still finds various shades of Aristotelianism in Montaigne,[19] Th. de Bèze,[20] Garnier,[21] and Lecoq,[22] for example. These are still present later in the Scholastic psychological systems of the seventeenth and eighteenth centuries. In turn, both the Italian and the French equivalents of *affectus* compete with *passio*-passion in the love treatises of the Italians. Finally, even in two such different writers as Alexandre Hardy and Honoré d'Urfé, I have never come upon *passion* (although I have found the words *feux* [fire], *flammes* [flames], *blessures* [wounds], and, above all, *affections* [affections]) in my examination of their works). Yet, *passio* as "passion" and specifically as erotic passion *has* been used in Italy since Boiardo[23] and Lorenzo de' Medici[24] (I do not recall any such usage in Ariosto and Tasso)

[18] Later, the meaning of "biased preference" becomes an epistolary flourish. Guez de Balzac and Descartes write at the end of their letters: *que je suis passionnément* [I remain yours, passionately] or *avec une très ardente passion, votre très humble* [with a burning passion, your most humble . . .]. This corresponds to our German *vorzügliche Hochachtung* [with the utmost respect] or to the term *Vorliebe* [preference] that a businessman uses to maintain that he remains at our disposal. In 1724, Prince Eugene closes a letter to Vico with the words: *E sono con parzialità* [And I am with partiality yours], etc. See Vico, *L'Autobiografia* [2nd ed., Benedetto Croce and Nicolini Fausto, eds. (Bari: G. Laterza, 1929)] 180.

[19] See the *Lexique de la language des Essais*, in volume five of the edition published by the city of Bordeaux (Bordeaux 1933).

[20] Cf. Darmesteter-Hatzfeld [eds.], *Morceaux choisis . . . du XVIe siècle* [Paris: C. Delagrave, 1929] 315.

[21] Ibid. 342 and 349.

[22] Ibid. 327.

[23] For example, in his *Orlando in Love* 1.2.19, and 1.13.49.

[24] For example, in his description of the origin of Italian love poetry, which can be found in d'Acona's and Bacci's *Manuale della letteratura italiana* 2.85ff.

and in France most prominently in Marguerite de Navarre,[25] who in addition to *passion* uses *affection, feux,* and *flammes*; nearly everywhere the word occurs, there is also the suggestion of the idea of suffering. While occasionally one notices a somewhat reproachful overtone, there is no doubt that the word consistently means "erotic passion" and the suggestion of reproach is usually forgotten, with sympathy and admiration for the grand events of the heart taking its place. Since then, *passion* has never stopped playing this role[26] and the older meanings have gradually become a thing of the past.

In the French seventeenth century, the word migrates out of the learned sphere into the realm of literature and culture. Here, its meaning is unambiguously and exclusively "passion" in the modern sense of the word, primarily erotic passion, but also the kind of zealous and domineering egoism—self-love—and self-profiling that came to be called *ambition* and later more typically *gloire*. Cartesian psychology, which depended, at least for its vocabulary, on Aristotelian Scholasticism, of course calls all emotions, including the feelings and sensations, *passions*. But despite Descartes' significant impact on educated society, such terms were perceived as part of a technical language and had little impact on everyday speech. No one spontaneously identified either self-satisfaction, cowardice, or the spirit of mockery, on the one hand, or illness, hunger, or cold, on the other, as *passion. Passion* and *souffrance, passion* and *sentiment,* thus go their separate ways. Although Théodore de Bèze could still say, "*Retirez vous, humaines passions*" [Be off, human passions] (see note 20), in Racine (*Iphigénie,* 4.6.1327), we can read: *étouffant tout sentiment humain* [stifling all human emotion]. *Passion* and *sentiment* are in essence already being distinguished here just as they would be in the eighteenth and nineteenth centuries.[27] The difference between them can never be established once and for all, however, since some feelings become desires—and thus passions—as soon as they become extremely intense. And yet, even in the line from Corneille (*Nicomède* 3.4.1310–11)—*J'ai tendresse pour toi, j'ai passion pour elle* [I / am fond of you and deeply in love with her]—which still sounds a bit strange to our ears, there is a clear intensification. Here, *passion* is meant to express a violent, passionate feeling of love as opposed to a

---

[25] See her *Heptameron, passim.*

[26] Cf., for example, Montchrestien in Darmesteter-Hatzfeld, 359, and Régner, ibid. 291. Also see Spitzer [n. 17 above], and Mairet in his *Sophonisbe* play. We find the following sentence in Grimmelshausen's *Simplicissimus* III:19: . . . *wann der Herr nicht selbsten wüßte wie einem Bühler ums Herz ist, so hatte er dieses Weibes Passiones nicht so wohl ausführen oder vor Augen stellen können.* [. . . If you did not know from experience how a lover feels, you could not have told so much about this woman's passion; H.J.C. von Grimmelshausen, *The Adventures of Simplicius Simplicissimus,* 2nd ed., George Schulz-Behrend, trans. (Rochester, NY: Camden House, 1993) 148.]

[27] And yet, as soon as it became an act of conscious theorizing, it was easy for the earlier technical, Aristotelian term *passion* to reappear and be applied to all the emotions. This is the case not only for the eighteenth century (cf. Lerch, 334, and the passages he gives from the *Encyclopédie* and from Rousseau), but occasionally for the nineteenth century as well.

natural, paternal feeling of tenderness, which is unrelated to desire. Later, we often find a deliberate distinction made between *passion* and *sentiment*, as in Saint-Évremond's well-known critique of Racine's *Andromaque*.[28] Finally, as far as Lerch's criterion, namely, activity, is concerned, we find it in Pascal's version of the relation of passion to action, which is expressed in a way that is entirely traditional but that also corresponds to what we call "feeling" today:

> L'homme est né pour penser; aussi n'est-il pas un moment sans le faire; mais les pensées pures, qui le rendraient heureux s'il pouvait toujours les soutenir, le fatiguent et l'abattent. C'est une vie unie à laquelle il ne peut s'accommoder; il lui faut de remuement et de l'action, c'est-à-dire qu'il est nécessaire qu'il soit quelquefois agité des passions, dont il sent dans son coeur des sources si vives et si profondes.

> [Man is born for thought; therefore he is not a moment without it; but the pure thoughts that would render him happy, if he could always maintain them, weary and oppress him. They make a uniform life to which he cannot adapt himself: he must have excitement and action, that is, it is necessary that he should sometimes be agitated by those passions[,] the deep and vivid sources of which he feels within his heart.][29]

In the French seventeenth century, the *passions* are human desires of the grand sort. What is special about this context is that there is a clear tendency to consider these desires tragic, heroic, sublime, and worthy of admiration. At the beginning of the century, there are very often still echoes of the Stoic-pejorative judgment. Soon, however, this judgment's polar opposite emerges, and the terrible and the noble unite to become sublime. We can sense this already in Corneille and Pascal, perhaps also already in Descartes. It culminates in the tragedies of Racine, whose goal it is to excite the passions and to celebrate them as well. It is now possible to have *les belles passions* [beautiful passions] and *les passions généreuses* [generous passions] and critics judge a tragedy in terms of the authenticity, the depth, and the beauty of the passions displayed. The torment and rapture of passion become the ultimate form of life for the spectator as a man of feeling. "Ce n'est point une nécessité qu'il y ait du sang et des morts dans une tragédie: il suffit que l'action en soit grande, que les acteurs en soient héroïques, que les passions y soient excitées, et que tout s'y ressente de cette tristesse majestueuse qui fait tout le plaisir de la tragédie," writes Racine in the preface to his play *Bérénice* (23–24.19–24).

---

[28] *Oeuvres mêlées* II, 320 (Amsterdam 1706). See also I, 65 and *passim*.

[29] *Pensées et opuscules,* ed. Brunschvicg 123 (*Discours sur les passions de l'amour* [Discourse on the Passion of Love, in Blaise Pascal, *Thoughts*, W. F. Trotter, trans.; *Letters*, M. L. Booth, trans.; *Minor Works*, O.W. Wight, trans. (New York: P. F. Collier and Son, 1910) 417].) We should note that here, all inner processes, including the *sentiments*, other than the passions, belong to the category of *pensées*. Cf. Brunschvicg's note.

[Tragedy does not necessarily demand bloodshed and death; it needs no more than an action endowed with grandeur, characters of exalted status, the arousal of the passions and, throughout, that stately sadness which is the source of all one's pleasure in tragedy (Knight, trans., xxiii–xiv).] Later, timidity and hypocrisy combined with incipient sympathy and inchoate remorse caused him to express himself quite differently in the preface to *Phèdre*: *Les passions n'y sont présentées que pour montrer tout le désordre dont elles sont cause* [Passions are portrayed only to show all the turmoil they cause (Racine, *Three Plays*, Chilcott, trans., 143)] for the audience admired, even envied the title character in spite of the horror evoked by her fate.

The glorification of the passions ceased being the target of a Stoic polemic and became instead an ecclesiastical one (Nicole, Bossuet), whose proponents recognized the situation with far greater clarity than the majority of Racine's other critics. They also realized that the most authentic, the most sublime, and thus, from their point of view, the most dangerous passions were *amour* and *ambition*. Pascal uses the word *ambition*, but later writers use the term that is the most characteristic one for the time, namely *gloire*. Bossuet writes, "Dites moi que veut un Corneille dans son Cid, sinon qu'on aime Chimène, qu'on l'adore avec Rodrigue, qu'on tremble avec lui lorsqu'il est dans la crainte de la perdre, et qu'avec lui on s'estime heureux lorsqu'il espère de la posséder? Le premier principe sur lequel agissent les poètes tragiques et comiques, c'est qu'il faut intéresser le spectateur; et si l'auteur ou l'acteur d'une tragédie ne le sait pas émouvoir et le transporter de la passion qu'il veut exprimer, où tombe-t-il, si ce n'est dans le froid, dans l'ennuyeux, dans le ridicule . . . ? Ainsi, tout le dessin d'un poète, toute la fin de son travail, c'est qu'on soit, comme ses héros, épris des belles personnes, qu'on les serve comme les divinités; en un mot, qu'on leur sacrifie tout, si ce n'est peut-être la gloire, dont l'amour est plus dangereux que celui de la beauté même . . . On se voit soi-même dans ceux qui nous paraissent comme transportés par de semblables objets: on devient bientôt un acteur secret dans la tragédie; on y joue sa proper passion; et la fiction au dehors est froide et sans agrément si elle ne trouve au dedans une vérité qui lui réponde." [What, I beseech you, was the Intention of [a] Corneille in his Cid but to make the whole House in love with his Chimène, that every man there should join with Roderique in the Adoration he pays her, that they should tremble, and Sympathise with him when in fear of losing her; and look upon themselves as happy as he did, when in hopes of enjoying his Mistriss? The very First and fundamentall Principle of the Drama, whether for Tragedy or Comedy, is to infuse in the Audience the present Disposition of the Stage; to make each Spectator a party in what is doing. And if either the Poet or the Player have not the skill to move and transport us with the Passion he is labouring to express pray what becomes of him? Does he not presently grow flat and cold upon your hands, tedious and ridiculous? . . . That all his Contrivance tends this way, and the very form and

Design of his great Pains is, that we should be fashioned upon the modell he Sets us in his Hero; that, like Him, We should be Smitten and charmed with Beautifull Faces, and adore them as if they were Divinities upon Earth; In a word, that we should even be proud to sacrifice every thing to their Pleasure and service (Every thing except Glory and Fame, which hath Sometimes the Privilege of being reserved. But) even this Honour, as they have managed the matter, is at least as dangerous an Object of our Love, as even Beauty itself . . . The Actor[s] (who appear to us transported upon such Occasion) are a Glass in which we see our own faces; each Spectator presently turns an Actor in the Tragedy, and plays over his own Passions, though insensible, and unseen: ('Tis manifest he does, from hence; because) all the Fiction and Personating upon the Stage is of itself cold and insipid, and never entertains us delight-fully, till it have found within our selves some Reality.][30] For those associated with the Church, the concept of the passions in seventeenth-century tragedy was thus a dangerous adversary. Passion was not just the ordinary "disarray" that earthly life inevitably entails, but was, rather, itself a kind of religion, a presumed heightening of human existence worth pursuing. Going in search of it demonstrated a greatness and nobility of heart. I have written about this topic before.[31] I am therefore by no means saying much that is very new when I maintain that the sublime understanding of the passions in their binary dialectic represents a secularized and anti-Christian transformation of Passion mysticism. This thought is often articulated in modern literary criticism of Racine, even if any explicitly historical grounding is lacking. It could very well provide the key for comparing Racine with his ancient models.

In any case, the modern meaning of "passion" is entirely current already in the French seventeenth century, and not just in periphrastic metaphors such as *feu* [fire] and *flamme* [flame], but also in the very word *passion* itself. I even doubt whether the emphasis that Lerch places on the development of the meaning of "feeling" in the eighteenth century contributed a great deal to a clearer distinction between feeling and passion (such a distinction is in any case generally valid only for scientific psychology). There were also move-ments, ranging from Pietism to Romanticism, that allowed the feelings to include so much that they again approached being understood as passions, in the end distinguishing themselves from the latter only by virtue of the im-precision and elusiveness of the object of their desires. At one point, Étienne Pivert de Senancour refers to what he calls a *passion universelle*. In the fourth

[30] *Maximes et réflexions sur la comédie* IV. [*Maxims and Reflections on Plays. Written in French by the Bp. Of Meaux and now made English. The Preface by another Hand* (London 1699) 9–13. The passages in the English translation in parentheses here are not cited by Auerbach, but are included to fill out the context. —Trans.]

[31] "Racine und die Leidenschaften" [Racine and the Passions, here Chapter 18]; *Das französische Publikum des 17. Jahrhunderts* [The French Audience of the Seventeenth Century] (Munich, 1933) 47 ff.

letter of his novel, *Obermann* [1804], after a night of melancholy meditation at the lake at Neuchâtel, he writes:

> Indicible sensibilité, charme et tourment de nos vaines années; vaste conscience d'une nature partout accablante et partout impénétrable, passion universelle, sagesse avancée, voluptueux abandon; tout ce qu'un coeur mortel peut contenir de besoins et d'ennuis profonds, j'ai tout senti, tout éprouvé dans cette nuit mémorable. J'ai fait un pas sinistre vers l'âge d'affaiblissement; j'ai dévoré dix années de ma vie. Heureux l'homme simple dont le coeur est toujours jeune.

> [Indescribable tenderness, charm and torture of our empty days; vast consciousness of a Nature which is everywhere overwhelming and everywhere inscrutable; universal passion, advanced wisdom, voluptuous abandonment: all that a mortal heart can hold of deep needs and deep weariness, all these did I feel, all pass through on the ineffaceable night. I took an ominous stride towards the age of decadence; I consumed ten years of my life. Happy is the simple man whose heart is forever young!] [Waite, trans., 20]

Postscript: In response to the objections that Lerch raises on pp. 326ff. of his essay to certain of the details of my note, "Remarques sur le mot passion" [Remarks on the Word "Passion"], which appeared in *Neuphilologische Mitteilungen* 38 (1937) 218, I would like to observe the following: (1) I agree with his thoughts about the survival of the word *passio* in vulgar Latin, namely, that it continued to exist as a scholarly and ecclesiastical word and meant "illness," or the Passion of Christ. I said as much and attribute far more importance to the ecclesiastical usage. Godefroy also cites popular forms of the term. (2) I stand by my explanation of the disappearance in the seventeenth century of *passion* as illness in terms of its status as a lower form of a word that had by then migrated into the high language of the educated classes. Lerch obviously misunderstood me. I did not claim that "suffering" had to disappear to make way for "passion"; rather, the notion of an inferior, physical illness had to make way for a sublime movement of the soul. Lerch's own explanation that *passio* as illness had to give way as a *terminus technicus* does not contradict my argument, but rather supplements it. (3) Lerch is nevertheless correct when he sees—*contra* both Furetière and myself—an echo of Christ's Passion in the turn of phrase *souffrir mort et passion* [to suffer death and passion]. The expression appears already in Crusade songs, as, for example, in the song, "*Chevalier mult estes guariz*" (in Bédier-Aubry, *Les Chansons de croisade* [Paris 1909]) and in Provençal in the work of Raimbaut de Vaqueiras (Marburg 1904) 139:10.

15

The Three Traits of Dante's Poetry

Ladies and Gentlemen:

In spite of his fame, Dante's poetry is not very well known outside of Italy. He is one of the great authors who survive rather by the radiation of their personality and the evocative power of their name than by the reader's knowledge of their work, for the access to this work is very difficult. Many parts of his *Commedia*, commonly called [the] *Divine Comedy*, cannot be understood by the modern reader without a commentary explaining the theological, philosophical-historical, and scientific background of early fourteenth-century Italy and Europe—the background of Dante's time, the later Middle Ages. Of these, the *Commedia* is a poetical encyclopedia, the richest and most complete picture of an entire civilization ever achieved by a single man we know or contained in a single work we possess.

Of course, there are in this great work many passages of such emotional and poetical power that they enter the soul of the reader immediately and spontaneously. But obviously all of this power can act only in the original Italian text, not in a translation. To translate poetry is something very problematical, and very few translations succeed in preserving something of the original beauty. With Dante, the task is particularly difficult. The Italian language, with its abundance of two-syllable or feminine endings, favors complicated and rather entangled patterns of rhymes. It is almost impossible to imitate such patterns in German, French, or English. Add to this the problem of rendering exactly—within the limits of such a verse scheme—all

Transcript of an oral lecture delivered in English in 1948 (see Appendix: Bibliography to the Essays in This Collection). Auerbach's original text is lost. The present version is based on the transcript first made and published by Martin Vialon in 2007, with further minor emendations added, whether in punctuation (these have been silently added) or replacing a missing phrase (these are marked by brackets). More drastic changes—corrections of non-idiomatic expressions for the sake of intelligibility—are signaled in the notes, but these are rare. Translations of Dante's verses have been supplied in brackets. Auerbach evidently expected his audience to follow the Italian originals.—Ed.

the shades of Dante's thoughts and feelings. It is understandable that even the best translations—and there are admirable ones—have not succeeded in winning a large public of non-Italian readers. Thus, as I have said, Dante survives outside of Italy rather as a legend or as a myth. In this image, three traits prevail: first, that of a poet of love, of a highly exalted form of love, the poet of Beatrice; then, as a poet who saw and described the terrible torments and fantastic landscapes of Hell; and third, as an exile expelled from his native city, Florence, a poor political refugee in the towns and principalities of Italy, ever nostalgic, ever unbending in his hatred of the new rulers of his home city. All three aspects are true, but they are incomplete.

As for the first, the exaltation of love and deification of the beloved lady: the earliest symptoms of it had appeared almost two centuries before Dante with the first European lyric poets of the Middle Ages, the Provençal troubadours in southern France. They first created the concept of the inaccessible lady worshipped by a lover unconditionally devoted to her, and also the concept of idealistic love as the highest object of poetry. There is still much discussion and controversy about the origin of this idea of love, unknown to earlier times. Christian mysticism, the cult of the Virgin, Neoplatonic trends, even certain social aspects of feudalism or Arabic influences have been presumed to be its sources. The Provençal poetry of love spread rapidly over southern, western, and central Europe. One generation before Dante, a group of Italian poets, the poets of the so-called "sweet new style" (*dolce stil nuovo*) started developing this Provençal idea of love in an even more philosophical and esoteric way. They wrote beautiful verses of a highly refined style, and it is not easy to decide if *amore* (love), which they consider as a unique source of inspiration and as a unique initiation to a higher and purer life, has anything to do with an earthly object, or if it is a pure Platonic concept of divine beauty and divine wisdom. Many of their highest creations are as difficult to understand as the modern poetry of Valéry or Rilke or T. S. Eliot.

Dante, in his beginnings at the end of thirteenth century, was one of the youngest members of this group. He surpassed all of them by sheer poetical power. He alone succeeded in conferring on the somewhat theoretical and pale motifs of the *dolce stil nuovo* the life and force of personal experience. Even in his first verses, whatever he experiences, whatever happens to him, is a real event causing real emotions. Most of his earlier poetry he inserted in a kind of novella, the *Vita Nuova*, telling the story of his love for Beatrice, whom he first saw when she was nine and who died young. Here we are in the midst of visions and of symbolic meaning. Beatrice appears from the very first as an incarnation of divine beauty or wisdom, *not* as a mere allegory, but as an incarnation. Still, she is a human being. However exalted her personality may be, many of the events seem to happen before our eyes. Let me give you one famous example:

Tanto gentile e tanto onesta pare
la donna mia quand'ella altrui saluta,
ch'ogne lingua deven tremando muta,
e li occhi no l'ardiscon di guardare.
Ella si va, sentendosi laudare,
benignamente d'umiltà vestuta;
e par che sia una cosa venuta
da cielo in terra a miracol mostrare.
Mostrasi sì piacente a chi la mira,
che dà per li occhi una dolcezza al core,
che 'ntenderno la può chi non la prova:
e par che de la sua labbia si mova
un spirito soave pien d'amore,
che va dicendo a l'anima: "Sospira."[1]

[Such sweet decorum and such gentle grace
attend my lady's greeting as she moves
that lips can only tremble into silence,
and eyes dare not attempt to gaze at her.
Moving, benignly clothed in humility,
untouched by all the praise along her way,
she seems to be a creature come from Heaven
to earth, to manifest a miracle.
Miraculously gracious to behold,
her sweetness reaches, through the eyes, the heart
(who has not felt this cannot understand),
and from her lips it seems there moves a gracious
spirit, so deeply loving that it glides
into the souls of men, whispering: "Sigh!"]

—Mark Musa, trans., *Dante's Vita Nuova*, new ed. (Bloomington:
Indiana University Press, 1973) 57

Beatrice, after her death, becomes a protective genius of Dante. In his great poem, the *Commedia*, she, as a representation of divine wisdom, sends Vergil to save Dante's soul, to lead him through the realms of the condemned and the penitent, and is herself his guide in Heaven. And here we have come to the second of the three traits I mentioned: Dante as a poet of Hell. Some legends in the Middle Ages inspired by the haughty somberness of his bearing, and much later some Romantic poets impressed by the power of his infernal landscapes, stressed[2] this aspect. But the *Divine Comedy* is a wander-

---

[1] *Vita Nuova*: Testo critico della Società Dantesca Italiana, Michele Barbi, ed. (Florence: Società Dantesca Italiana, 1960) 26.5–7. —Trans.

[2] "Stressed" for Auerbach's "have stressed." —Ed.

ing through all the three realms of the other world: Inferno, Purgatory, and Paradise. It is also, as we shall see later, a poem of human life on earth.

Its basic scheme is the following: Dante, lost in the forest of sin and of mental anarchy prevailing in this world, but protected by divine powers and destined for a high mission, meets Vergil. Vergil, the Latin poet, has been sent out by Beatrice to Dante's rescue, and as there is no other way both to save him and to show him his future task, Vergil leads him through Hell, then up to the mountain of Purgatory. At the top of this mountain he has to leave him, for Vergil is a pagan and, although a man of supreme wisdom and virtue, [he] is not allowed to enter Heaven. It is Beatrice who, from now on, assumes the leadership through the different grades of beatitude up to the immediate sight of God.

The three parts of the poem comprehend thirty-three cantos each. Together with the introduction, this makes [one] hundred cantos, [totaling] more than 14,000 lines. The stanza, called *terza rima*, consists of three lines, the first and the third having the same rhyme and the rhyme of the second announcing the rhyme of line[s] one and three of the following stanza: aba, bcb, cbc.

While he is wandering through these three realms, the divine order of the universe becomes manifest and visible to Dante. He experiences it as a concrete phenomenon. Of course, it is a vision, not a scientific experience in the modern sense of the term. But it contains all [the] scientific and philosophical knowledge of the Middle Ages in a powerful synthesis. Many critics and aestheticians of the last century have condemned the didactic[3] poetry, poetry that teaches and instructs, and have identified it with dry pedantry. They have tried to solve the problem of Dante by choosing single passages of his work which they admire and by rejecting the rest, arguing that Dante's genius had created these beautiful passages in spite of [his][4] false and absurd general concept of poetry. But in few[5] other works of world literature is the unity of the whole so stringent and so essential for the comprehension of its parts. In no other work is it so suggestive, so powerfully evident in every passage, every *terza rima* being a symbol of the whole structure and reflecting it. Didactic contents are *not* incompatible with poetry. They can assume poetic form and dignity. Otherwise, works such as Lucretius's [*De rerum natura*] could not be regarded as poetry.

The order of the universe as Dante, inspired by Thomistic philosophy, Neoplatonism, and personal experience, conceived it, can be seen as consisting of three parts, distinct but corresponding with each other: the physical, the moral, and the historical or political order. The earth, according to the

---

[3] "Didactic" for Auerbach's "didactical." —Ed.
[4] "His" for Auerbach's "a." —Ed.
[5] "Few" for Auerbach's "the few" —Ed. and trans.

Ptolemaic system accepted in the Middle Ages, is the center of the universe. Immediately after the Creation, one of the highest angels, Lucifer, rebelled against God and was thrown from Heaven down to earth. There, the violence of his fall made him enter deep into its interior, causing a vast hole down to the center of the globe. This hole is Hell, where the condemned in descending graves suffer different kinds of eternal punishment, eternally banished from the sight of God. One hemisphere only is inhabited by men. The other is entirely covered by the sea, but in its center a high mountain emerges whose peak reaches Heaven. It is Purgatory, the mountain of penitence, where the souls destined for eternal beatitude are purified step by step and prepared to enter Heaven. The earth is surrounded by nine concentric heavens symbolizing ascending forms of beatitude, but each of them symbolizing and possessing its own complete form of beatitude, that is to say, its own vision of the highest good of God. Here the two hosts, the angels and the beatified, have their eternal abode.

You may already have realized that the moral order is contained in the physical. In Hell, the condemned are grouped according to the gravity of their unrepented sins; in Purgatory, according to their bad tendencies and dispositions; and in Heaven, according to the profundity of their vision of God, which again depends on their natural dispositions. To elaborate his moral hierarchy, Dante used several philosophical sources, Aristotelian as well as Neoplatonic. For him, the whole Creation is an emanation of God's essence. The innumerable aspects of the Creation and the overabundance of its forms are considered [to be][6] the irradiation and the realization of divine love. The world is created by the force of divine love.

All aspects and theories of the philosophy and science of the Middle Ages are contained in these two orders, the physical and the moral. They are actually present and at the same time are explained during the various stages of Dante's wandering. The third order, the political or historical, is not easy for modern readers to understand. Dante's political ideal is the universal monarchy. He considers the Roman Empire of Augustus as its model—even as a providential form of world government. For Christ appeared on earth under Augustus, when the world was in perfect peace, and to Dante's mind this fact is closely linked with the history of Christian salvation, because Providence, establishing the Roman Empire as the highest political and juridical power, conferred upon it the task of the trial of Christ. This trial, although [a] supreme injustice because of Christ's innocence, is, at the same time, supreme justice as expiation of Adam's sin, as the expiation of the Fall of Man. The Roman Empire therefore has an essential part in the providential drama of Man. Providence has ordained Roman world domination in order to establish perfect justice on earth.

[6]"To be" for Auerbach's "as."—Ed.

The stages of the great drama of humanity are the Fall of Man, the redemption through Christ, and the eventual return of Christ for the Last Judgment. This return will take place when once more complete peace and justice will be achieved on earth under the rule of a Roman emperor. Dante considers the Roman emperors of the German nation of his time as the legitimate successors of the ancient Roman emperors. When he wrote the *Commedia* in the last fifteen years of his life, he was a passionate partisan of universal monarchy under the German emperor. The emperors who in the preceding centuries had followed this policy of universal unity were the Hohenstaufen, or Ghibellines. From their name the imperial party of these times had taken the name "Ghibellines." Being a Ghibelline, or a partisan of world monarchy under the rule of the emperor, Dante not only condemned all particularism, such as the anti-imperial policy of the French kings or the trends towards independence of the Italian towns, but even more strongly he condemned the other great international power of his time, the Pope.

According to the poet, the two great international powers—the Pope and the emperor—had entirely different tasks. The power of St. Peter's successors had to be entirely spiritual, and all earthly or political power belonged rightly to the emperor. This is for him the will of Providence. Last—although not [an] orthodox Catholic, he opposed and condemned strongly the political ambitions of the popes of his time, which had to lead and have led to [the] utter corruption of the clergy, and he places several popes of recent times in the deepest circles of Hell. This political attitude explains also the leading part Vergil plays in the *Commedia*, for Vergil is the great poet of the Roman Empire who had glorified Rome as predestined for world rule. And Vergil was at the same time a prophet of Christ, for one of his most beautiful poems praising the birth of a miraculous child was considered [to be][7] an unconscious prophecy of the birth of the Lord. For Dante, Vergil combined both elements of his concept of history, the Christian and the Roman. Vergil had died unbaptized without knowing of Christ; he could not be admitted among the blessed in Heaven. In spite of that, he is a symbol of supreme human virtue and wisdom as well as a great model of poetry.

These considerations lead us to the third of the above-mentioned aspects of Dante, to Dante as a political refugee. He was born in 1265, a few years after the collapse of the Hohenstaufen dynasty. During his youth, the Guelphs, in power [in][8] his native city of Florence, which was to become [a] center of industrial banking capitalism as well as of literary and artistic life, [had] strongly developed. In his thirties, that is to say about the year 1300, Dante was a famous poet of lyrical songs and a leading personality in Florentine politics. In 1301, he was a member of the government. At that time he was

---

[7] "To be" for Auerbach's "as."—Ed.
[8] "In" for Auerbach's "of." —Ed. and trans.

not yet a Ghibelline. He belonged to a group fighting for municipal independence against the attempts of the Pope and a French prince to dominate the rich city. In November, 1301, the French party succeeded in getting control of Florence. The leaders of the defeated party—among them, Dante—were exiled. Subsequent attempts to regain power were unsuccessful. A few years later Dante broke away from his former political friends. The rest of his life he spent in complete political isolation. It was at this time that he became a radical and uncompromising partisan of imperial monarchy, a perfectly hopeless position. The new German emperors—the first Habsburgs—had no time for Italy and for supernational and ideological tendencies. However, there was one more revival of hope when, in 1308, a new German emperor—Henry VII—came to Italy with an army in order to regain control and to reestablish the imperial idea. But the emperor died during his campaign and his attempt—the last of its kind—failed completely. Nevertheless, Dante remained faithful to his creed.

The *Commedia* is the strongest and the most passionate expression of the medieval idea of a European Christian unity, which had already become obsolete when the *Commedia* was written. When [the] opportunity to return to Florence was offered to him, he declined because he considered the conditions humiliating. Henceforth, he lived in different towns in Italy as a guest of the ruling princes, writing and serving his protectors as a diplomat. He died in 1321 at the age of 56[9] in the town of Ravenna a few days after returning from a mission to Venice. All these nearly twenty years, he never ceased to feel the bitterness of exile, his nostalgia for Florence, and his hatred for her new rulers. Thus, when in Heaven, he meets one of his ancestors who prophesies his future's exile, the verses of the prediction read as follows:

> Tu lascerai ogne cosa diletta
> più caramente; e questo è quello strale
> che l'arco de lo essilio pria saetta.
> Tu proverai sì come sa di sale
> lo pane altrui, e come è duro calle
> lo scendere e 'l salir per l'altrui scale.[10]

> [You shall leave everything you love most dearly:
> this is the arrow that the bow of exile
> shoots first. You are to know the bitter taste

---

[9] Auerbach says "at the age of high 56," most likely meaning "well into his 56th year." (Dante was born around May of 1265 and died on September 14, 1321.) —Ed.

[10] *Paradiso* 17.55–60, in *La divina commedia*, Giorgio Petrocchi, ed. (Florence: Le Lettere, 1994). There are minor differences between the Petrocchi edition and the edition cited but not identified by Auerbach in his lecture. —Trans.

of others' bread, how salt it is, and know
how hard a path it is for one who goes
descending and ascending others' stairs.]

—*Paradise* 17.55–60 (Trans. Mandelbaum 159)

In another passage of the *Commedia*, there is a most poignant expression in his nostalgia:

Se mai continga che 'l poema sacro
al quale ha posto mano e cielo e terra,
sì che m'ha fatto per molti anni macro,
vinca la crudeltà che fuor mi serra
del bello ovile ov'io dormi' agnello
nimico ai lupi che li danno guerra;
con altra voce omai, con altro vello
ritornerò poeta, e in sul fonte
del mio battesmo prenderò 'l cappello.[11]

[If it should happen . . . If this sacred poem—
this work so shared by heaven and by earth
that it has made me lean through these long years—
can ever overcome that cruelty
that bars me from the fair fold where I slept,
a lamb opposed to wolves that war on it,
by then the other voice, with other fleece,
I shall return as poet and put on,
At my baptismal font, the laurel crown.]

—*Paradise* 25.1–9 (Trans. Mandelbaum 497)

His hatred of Florence is expressed in many lines of the great poem, most strongly perhaps in the famous formula concluding the oldest manuscripts: "Here ends the *Commedia* of Dante Alighieri, a Florentine by birth but not by character (*Explicit Comedia Dantis Alagherii, florentini natione, non moribus*).[12]

In addition to these three aspects of Dante, I should like to stress two other points most important for understanding his part in the history of European poetry and civilization. Dante was the first to use his mother tongue or, as people said in his time, the vulgar language, Italian—for the purpose of high,

---

[11] Line 3 in Auerbach's lecture gives the variant reading *più* for *molti*. —Trans.

[12] Auerbach has misremembered the Latin original, which is the title that *introduces* the first posthumous editions of the *Divine Comedy*, and which derives from the (possibly pseudo-Dantean) *Epistle to Cangrande* (10): *Incipit Comedia Dantis Alagherii, florentini natione, non moribus.* —Ed.

or sublime, or philosophical poetry. For many centuries, the literary language of Europe had been Latin. The new, so-called vulgar idioms (French, Italian, Spanish), which in fact still were dialects with no fixed grammar and spelling, were used only colloquially. Two centuries before Dante, a literature in [the] vulgar language had begun to develop in France, also in Spain and in Italy. As yet it was confined to popular poetry and to didactic or religious popularization. And all this was still a dialect, and [it] did not go so far as to create a literary style. Again, it was the Provençal poets who were the first to attain the literary language independent of the variety of the dialects. But their works as well as those of their Italian disciples, the poets of the Italian *dolce stil nuovo*, were restricted to very few topics and to a few traditional forms of short lyrical poetry. Their first attempts to create something like a sublime style are stilted and theoretical.

It seems that, since his early youth, Dante had been concerned with the problem of a high literary Italian style. He wrote a Latin treatise on poetry in vulgar language, *De vulgari eloquentia*. Here he sets up a program which was to serve as a model for many later attempts at creating a national literary language, not only in the Italian peninsula, but also in many other countries. The basic principle from which Dante and his followers in the Renaissance started was imitation—imitation of the classical languages, Greek and Latin. It tended towards an ideal, nowadays to a great extent forgotten, the ideal of a pure literary style, distinctly different from and even opposed to the daily usage. Imitation of Greek and Latin literature is an important aspect of Humanism. Insofar as this concept was applied to the development of the vulgar idioms, it was called "Humanism in vulgar language." Thus Dante, by his treatise *De vulgari eloquentia*, is a founder of the theory of Humanism in vulgar language. And he also is the initiator of its application, for the *Divine Comedy* is the first great work dealing with the most serious and sublime subject written in a high, consciously literary style written in one of the vulgar languages of Europe. Now, Dante was not quite sure whether his poem really deserved to be ranked among the works of highest literary style. He called it *Commedia* (comedy), whereas in marked contrast he designates the *Aeneid* of his master, Vergil, *l'alta tua tragedia*, "your sublime tragedy."

In the Middle Ages, these words—tragedy and comedy—did not mean dramatic works. Tragedy meant a poem of high style with [a] tragic end, no matter if dramatic or epic, and comedy meant low style and [a] happy end. Indeed, Dante's *Commedia* has a happy end. But did Dante really believe that this great work dealing with the other world, the highest matters of faith, and the most tragic conflicts of human life was written in [a] low style? He was doubtful, because his work did not completely realize [the] antique ideal of sublimity. According to classical tradition, everyday realism, [in its subject] matter [and in its] language,[13] was not admitted into the sublime style.

---

[13] Auerbach's lecture here runs, "as well as for matter as for language." —Ed.

People of ordinary condition, such as businessmen or workers or peasant[s], could not be [the] heroes of such works, nor could the problems of their lives be treated seriously. The personalities in poetry of [the] high style— whether dramatic or epic—were kings or mythical heroes. The language was high flown, free from everyday realism, and the events described, heroic or sublime, mostly situated in a remote past. One had to avoid all low realism. Dante was deeply influenced by the classical tradition. He was one of the first men in Europe to understand its aesthetic standards. But in the *Commedia*, he did not follow the classical model in this respect. Contemporary life with all its implications of realism streams into the poem. All the vigorous words and idioms of everyday language are fused in its style, sometimes even in a crude and violent manner. Nevertheless, the impression of a tragic and sublime style prevails throughout.

In this fusion of styles, where the tragic and the sublime prevail, Dante followed not the classical but another tradition. He followed the tradition of the Gospels, where, in a manner revolutionary even from this aesthetical point of view, everyday persons, everyday life, and the most humble circumstances have become one in a story, which, for [believers],[14] is the most sublime of all tragedies. Therefore, in spite of undergoing the influence of those ancient poets, Dante created a more Christian and a more realistic style of high poetry, into which the whole of life could enter without any restrictions. Realizing that this was not high style in the classical sense, he called his poem *Commedia*, and even in a letter addressed to one of his princely protectors, he called its style "humble." But St. Augustine had given the same designation—*sermo humilis*—to the Bible, in order to define the new Christian way of expression, which makes it possible to remain humble and still to be sublime. In spite of the title *Commedia*, there are many passages indicating that Dante knew perfectly well which kind of style he was using. The most striking of these passages is the one I already quoted, in which he calls his poem neither tragedy nor comedy, neither of [the] high nor of [the] low style, but *il poema sacro*, the sacred poem: *il poema sacro, / al quale ha posto mano e cielo e terra* [the sacred poem to which both Heaven and Earth have set their hand, *Paradise* 25.1-2].

The last point I wish to emphasize is closely connected to this tragic realism. Dante's great poem gives a more complete picture of individual men than had been ever before achieved by any single known writer, poet, or historian. On our way through the three realms, several hundred individuals appear before our eyes, men of all times, past and present, young and old, of all classes and professions, of every imaginable social and moral standing. Some of them are famous in history; others were so in Dante's life, but now are known only to very few. Others had never been famous. All these men and women are so strikingly real, so concrete, there is such a correspondence

---

[14] "Believers" for Auerbach's "the believing." —Ed.

between mind and body and behavior, such an intimate relation between their character and their fate, that the unmistakable peculiarity of each individual emerges with incomparable and often terrifying and poignant vigor. Some are given a whole canto, others only a few lines. But almost all of these individual profiles are unforgettable. They live in our imagination. We do not know and are not able to verify, except in a few cases, if Dante's portraits correspond to reality. But the realism of a poet is not that of a photographer; it is the identity of his own vision with its expression. We here are concerned with the energy of his vision and the power of his voice. No one before him had probed so deeply into the identity of individual character and individual fate.

This is almost paradoxical. For individual character in relation to individual fate develops and manifests itself in history, that is to say, in this earthly life of ours. It is almost impossible to imagine individuality outside of life beyond the changes of history. But in the other world, history has ceased. It does not continue. The souls of the deceased are maintained in an eternally unchanging condition. Their activity, that is to say, life itself, the unfolding of the individual character, has stopped. Therefore, it is not astonishing that earlier poets, such as Homer, Vergil, or some Christian poets of the earlier Middle Ages, have described the existence of the dead as a pale, weak, and destitute form of life. In the poems of antiquity, the deceased are mere shadows of what they had been on earth. In earlier Christian poetry, they appear in groups without any attempt being made to characterize the peculiarity of the individual. Dante did the reverse. As he wanders through the different stages of Hell, Purgatory, and Heaven, at the side of Vergil and later of Beatrice, every soul he sees reveals the full force of its former earthly character. Its characteristic traits still prevail in words and gestures, and the main events as well as the leading motives and passions are still present, undiminished by the change from the temporal to the eternal. They even seem intensified, more concentrated than ever. For these souls the presence of a living man, of Dante, is something that never happened before and will never happen again. Most of them desire to give him a full reckoning of themselves, hoping that he may revive their memory among the living, or in order to inform him of their part and place in the eternal order of divine love. Even some of the inhabitants of Hell who would prefer to hide and to remain unknown—they are few, for in Dante's Hell pride and longing [for][15] glory are stronger than other motives—even those few are compelled to reveal themselves against their will. Thus, the *Commedia* displays an infinite variety of human life in spite of the fact that its scene transcends the normal field of human activities: earthly history.

Is there any explanation for Dante's powerful realism in rendering human individuality? First of all, there was his genius, a fact which allows no further

[15] "For" for Auerbach's "of." —Ed.

explanation. Genius is a combination of faculties appearing in certain men and at certain moments, producing works no other man ever imagined. But, we may explain the idea which enabled Dante to display his realistic genius in a description of the other world. That is to say, we still may explain the paradox of human individuality[16] continuing to be alive in the other world, where life and history have ceased to exist. This outlook of Dante's is fundamental for the explanation of the *Commedia*. It is based on the belief that God's judgment does not destroy, but fully completes human individuality. It brings the human personality to ultimate perfection. In Dante's world, man's personality never attains on earth its plenitude, the full range of its possibilities, be they good or evil. The ultimate perfection of the individual form is achieved and revealed only by the judgment of God. The other world therefore does not only show the divine order and hierarchy of the universe as an all-pervading pattern, but, within all that, the perfection and ultimate realization of each human being. God's judgment: it is in each case identical with the full self-realization of the individual on which judgment is passed. Men in their earthly life are only shadows, or—as the medieval theologians used to say—prefigurations of what they are going to be in the other world. They are divided there into groups according to their sins, dispositions, and merits, but each of them, by his reactions, his words and gestures, his memories and wishes, clearly shows that his earthly character survives and has even reached fulfillment. This concept of Dante's is rooted[17] in the Christian belief in immortality, which originally was very concrete and individualistic insofar as it grants immortality to the individual body. Moreover, this concrete concept of human immortality was supported by a philosophical movement of the thirteenth century, the Aristotelian philosophy of St. Thomas Aquinas.[18]

---

[16]"Human individuality" for Auerbach's "the human individuality." —Ed.

[17]"Rooted" for Auerbach's "enrooted." —Ed. and trans.

[18]There is a silent three-second gap in the tape, followed by: ". . . living history and human individuality into the other world and to present the dead as eternally realizing—fulfilling—their earthly being." Presumably no more than a few words of the concluding sentence have been lost. It will have begun something like this: "With this in mind, Dante sought to transport . . ." —Ed.

16

Montaigne the Writer

Michel de Montaigne was the son of a father from the region of Gascogny and of a mother who was a Spanish Jew. The family was wealthy and well-respected. His grandfather, Eyquem, a fish merchant from Bordeaux, had purchased the noble feudal estate, Montaigne, in the province of Guyenne. His father pursued the life of a noble and of soldiering and eventually became the mayor of Bordeaux. His father's son in all the externals, Michel inherited his wealth, was a soldier, worked in municipal administration, and was well travelled. He was also a family man of the proper sort and, finally, like his father before him, became the mayor of Bordeaux. The two also resembled one another physically, with Michel inheriting his father's robust constitution, optimistic temperament, and, he discovered, his tendency to gallstones. But the times had become more difficult. His father lived in the glorious era of the Italian campaigns, the son through the terrible chaos of the Huguenot crisis and the civil wars, which endangered the continued existence of France as a nation for the last time. This crisis, the French wars of religion, began in the 1550s, when Montaigne had just reached his maturity, and ended around 1600 with the triumph of Henry IV, just a few years after Montaigne's death. Whereas the second half of the sixteenth century was the era of Philip II in Spain and Elizabeth I in England, in France it was a tumultuous time of bloody events, a time of unsettling anarchy in the hearts and minds of the land.

But even on this uneven terrain, Montaigne led a life that was never out of balance. He may have been ambitious and restless in his youth, and may have even known passion. He certainly experienced friendship of the truest sort. But by the time we encounter him, these are all long past. When he turned thirty-eight, he withdrew and became a private citizen. From then on, all his external energies were devoted to protecting what he already had. Neither apprehensive nor inflexible, he was invariably prudent and sometimes even a bit accommodating in his actions, which he undertook with intelligence rather than force. He was nevertheless always tenacious and resolute.

What was it that he had to protect? First of all, his property, his family, and his safety. Yet, these were the very least of his concerns, and he took care of them deftly and in a dispassionate and congenial way. It is amusing to read, for example, how he disarmed bands of robbers merely by confronting them with decency and an air of self-confidence. Should his duties become too troublesome or demand too much from him, he was prepared to relinquish them, for his main concern was to protect his inner core, where he kept his mind and his thoughts concealed. He called this place the *arrière-boutique*, the "room at the back of the shop," and he kept it reserved for himself. "We must do like the beasts and scuff out our tracks at the entrance to our lairs," he wrote.[1] This maxim applied not just to his life in the world; indeed, this world was the world of least importance for him. He was a generous, garrulous, and gregarious man and spared himself no adventure. But he was not inclined to hand himself over to others entirely. He gave himself out only on loan, so to speak, and that he did gladly. Inquisitive and a bit condescending, he often makes himself out to be more of an aristocrat than he is. He knows how to display his elevated social position clearly to us, albeit in the most modest of ways. Even his self-criticism and self irony are filled with an agreeable kind of arrogance. He was very private but by no means a hermit. While he occasionally enjoyed company, the "room at the back of the shop" remained a sanctum for his inner self and was off limits. It was there that he was truly at home, with himself. He devoted his own energies, the best efforts of the cleverest man of his time, to securing this place and equipping it with all possible comforts.

Montaigne possessed a pronounced sense of propriety and loyalty. He had a good and wise father, a pleasant childhood, and an unencumbered youth. A stranger to evil thoughts and base actions, he expected the same from others, that they would behave as he had seen his father behave. Loyalty meant serving the king, being obliging to one's friends, and protecting one's family. Respectable behavior included acting in a humane and unaffected way toward one's subordinates, and being candid and respectful to one's superiors. Loyalty also meant obeying established rules and customs; it would in any case be foolish to think that behaving in any other way would do anything other than precipitate chaos. He did not endorse differentiating oneself from one's social peers in any external way; to neglect one's duties or to take on tasks

---

[1] [The citation here is from Michel de Montaigne, *The Complete Essays*, M. A. Screech, trans. (London: Penguin, 1987) I: 39 (276), cited hereafter as "Montaigne," followed by book, essay, and page number. Auerbach cites Montaigne after *Les Essais de Michel de Montaigne*, ed. F. Strowski, F. Géblin, and P. Villey, 5 vols. (Bordeaux: F. Pech & Cie, 1906–1933), cited hereafter by volume and page (here: 1:322). Montaigne refers to the "room, just for ourselves, at the back of the shop" in I: 39 (270); 1:313.—Trans.]

for which one was not responsible, would be pointless, awkward, and would serve no end. It may also have been quite heartening for him to discover that it was possible to perform an office or manage a task just as well as, or perhaps even better than, anyone else—especially if the work was unavoidable—without having to exert oneself or even devote oneself to it unduly. These were the conditions: "If I am occasionally pressed into taking in hand some business foreign to me, then it is 'in hand' that I promise to take it, not in lung or in liver!"[2] And he also acted this way when, in difficult times, he became (indeed, was half forced to become) mayor of Bordeaux. He was a good father to his family, a loyal Frenchman, and a man who understood the great matters of his time. It was his and only his decision not to become a leading personality at court. He preferred not to. He defended himself against everything that would obligate him to undertake duties beyond those that were absolutely necessary, and this was regardless of whether he was being urged by the king, by his friends, by the citizens of Bordeaux, or even by his family. He defended himself just as resolutely and genially against anything that would constrain his spirit as he did against all external enemies.

Montaigne also defended his inner solitude. But what did he believe he possessed in this solitude? What made him value it so intensely? Solitude, it would seem, was his very life; in seclusion, he could be himself; it was his house, his garden, the place where he kept his most precious goods. It was there that he stored anything of any value from among the things that he had taken possession of as plunder, so to speak, in the course of his various forays into the world. There, he mulled them over, processed them, and imbued them with the tangy essence of his wit. But what exactly was the nature of this solitude and what did he actually do when he betook himself to it? It was neither Christian asceticism nor scholarship nor philosophy. It was in fact something for which we do not yet have a name. He surrendered himself to himself, we might say, releasing his inner energies into a state of free play. He did this not merely with the mind, however. The body also played a role. The body could intervene in his thoughts, for example, even in the very words that he began to write.

Next to Montaigne, the rest of the great intellectual figures of the sixteenth century, the leaders of the Renaissance, of Humanism, of the Reformation, and of the modern sciences, the men who created modern Europe, were all, every last one of them, merely specialists. Theologians or philologists, astronomers or mathematicians, artists or poets, diplomats or soldiers, historians or doctors—broadly speaking, they were all *experts*—most often only in one field, but some had several specializations. Montaigne, however, had none. He was not a poet by any stretch of the imagination. And, although he had studied law, he was an indifferent attorney. While perhaps meaningful

[2] Montaigne III: 10 (1135).

in some other context, his observations about the fundamentals of jurisprudence were of no use as far as the profession was concerned. There was, in other words, no professional connection between his practical endeavors and his intellectual work. While they frequently provided him with the stuff of his ideas, these ideas had nothing to do with the field in the courtroom or on the battlefield or as as far as diplomacy or philology was concerned, this in spite of the fact that they derived their seductive concreteness from these and many other fields. Unsystematic and without method, they were not really even philosophical. Montaigne remained a layman even in disciplines of which he seemed to have good knowledge, in pedagogy, for example. It would be impossible to imagine him actually working seriously in any one of the many professions with which he had a passing acquaintance. In any case, what he achieved was not an achievement in any of these fields. It is, in fact, not easy to describe what his achievement actually was, even today. In his own time, what he did and his impact were nearly incomprehensible. For, as we know, every act needs to be addressed to someone who will find it of value; every effect needs an audience. For Montaigne's *Essays*, this audience was in any case not yet present, and he could not have predicted that it would ever exist. He wrote neither for the court nor for the *Volk*, for neither Catholics nor Protestants, not for Humanists or for any actual community. He wrote, rather, for a community that did not appear to exist: for all living people, for anyone who, as a layperson, possessed some education and was keen to justify his existence as an educated man. He wrote for what later would come to be known as the "educated public." In Montaigne's day, however, when one thought of some sort of all-inclusive community (apart from groupings by profession, class, or nationality), only Christendom came to mind. Montaigne was looking for a new kind of community, and in looking for it, he created it. His book was the first proof that such a community did in fact exist.

Montaigne was not aware of any of this. He claimed that he was writing exclusively for himself, as a means to examine and know himself. He wrote also for his friends, he said, so that they would continue to have a clear image of him after his death. Occasionally he even went further and maintained that the make-up of the entire human race could be found in the make-up of a single man. He himself was, in any case, his sole concern, and his only purpose was to learn how to live and how to die. And the latter was the more important, he claimed, for he who has learned how to die also knows how to live. This all sounds very philosophical and it is, in the end. But it would be misleading to speak of Montaigne's philosophy. He had no system, for he also said, for example, that learning to die is useless, because nature takes care of it on her own. He also had no discernible desire to teach—as did Socrates, for example, whom Montaigne resembled quite closely in many other ways—and thus no discernible desire to be considered, objectively, as a model. What he writes, he writes for himself. It applies only to him. Should others find what he has to say useful or pleasing—so much the better.

The profit and pleasure one takes in reading Montaigne are unique and were unknown prior to the *Essays*. They are not precisely artistic, for what Montaigne writes is not poetry. Their subject is too immediate and matter-of-fact for their impact to be purely aesthetic. But they are also not didactic either, for they are no less interesting if one disagrees with them, or, perhaps better, there is hardly any lesson implied in them with which one might disagree. In their effect, the *Essays* most resemble some of the texts from late antiquity that were historical and moral in character, the writings of Plutarch, for example, whom Montaigne held dear. But Montaigne's writings lack any unified direction in the logic even of an individual paragraph. Instead, there is always only deliberation, the careful examination and consideration of examples. There are very few results or conclusions—and in any case, the few one finds do not obligate the reader in the least. Yet we become entangled in these deliberations. For we see Montaigne explaining that he is alive, but must die, and how he goes about beginning to accept this fact. He also explains what he has heard from others, even observed in them, related to the topic. And we are compelled to listen, for he is a good storyteller. We quickly forget what he has just said, for he is already on to another topic, and no doubt he will soon move on yet again to an entirely new one, drawn to it by some random word. Almost without noticing it, the reader slips into Montaigne's ever changing and always highly nuanced—yet also always serene—way of thinking, into the flow of his ideas. It would do violence to this way of thinking to force it into the clutches of a system, by calling it "skeptical," for example. But it has a strong pull and tows one in and under, as the sea does a swimmer—or as wine does when one drinks. Long before Montaigne's way of thinking takes hold of the reader, it took hold of Montaigne himself and, held him fast, forced him to write. For he in fact did not want to become a writer; he was both too modest and too proud to call something like that his profession. "If I were a scribbler ..." (*Si j'étais faiseur de livres ...*). This is how he begins a sentence that is also remarkable for other reasons,[3] for Montaigne *is* the first "scribbler" in our sense of the word. Neither a poet nor a scholar, he is, rather, an author of books (*Buchverfasser*), a writer (*Schriftsteller*). On a lower level, there were of course already such people; they were writers of popular literature, tellers of tales in the tradition of fairytales, legends, *exempla*, the *fabliaux*; they were only vaguely distinguishable from the poets, on the one hand, and from the didactic moralizers, on the other. But insofar as such writers became neither the one nor the other, but remained caught somewhere between the two, they were accorded no social standing or intel-

---

[3] Montaigne I: 20 (100).

lectual merit. Rabelais was already something of a marginal case—and was thus Montaigne's predecessor.

Independent and lacking a profession, Montaigne thus created a new profession and a new social category as well: the "man of letters" (*homme de lettres*), the layman as "writer" (*écrivain*). We are well aware of the heights to which this profession rose, first in France and then in other civilized nations. These amateurs became the leading intellectuals, spokespersons for the intellectual life. They are so generally acknowledged in our day that Julian Benda has called them the *clercs*, christening them the name of those to whom they were initially opposed, namely, the *clerici*, the clergy. This designation suggests—in fact it confirms—that writers have inherited the mantle and duties of the clergy, which is to say, they have become the supreme intellectual and spiritual leaders of modern Europe. From Montaigne to Voltaire, we may observe their uninterrupted ascendancy. By the nineteenth century, writers had consolidated their position and secured a broader influence by means of journalism. In spite of some signs of decline, which have been apparent already for quite some time, it is very likely that they will be able to defend their claim to be the voice of the world in the twentieth century as well.

What are the distinguishing marks of the writer's nature, a nature whose potential Montaigne was the first to make real?[4] We have already defined two negative ones: the absence of professional specialization and the absence of a scientific method. Both can only be observed, and felt, in texts that speak about objects of knowledge that up to that point one was accustomed to seeing analyzed only by specialists. The de-professionalization of knowledge about the most important of such objects had been prepared for by the Reformation. In this respect, we might say that with the writings of the Reformation as it occurred in France—and especially the vernacular version of Calvin's *Institutes of the Christian Religion* (1536)—we were already well on our way to Montaigne. The Reformers addressed themselves to the laypeople. They had to do so, since these laypeople were expecting from them instruction that they could understand. But the writers of the Reformation were nevertheless still theologians, and thus for the most part professionals, and their readers were not just laymen of any sort, but Christian laymen. It was the layman Montaigne who first wrote about the most important matters in a "lay," or "amateur," manner. Even though he was actually not writing *for*

---

[4]I am of course using the word "writer" here in a narrow sense. Naturally we also call the specialist who writes in his field a specialist writer. The word is also used to refer to poets when they are being discussed in either a limited or official way. This is not what I mean here, although most poets are in fact also writers in this narrower sense. The type has become clear, universally known and difficult to mistake, in spite of the inexactness of the way we speak about such issues and also in spite of the near impossibility of understanding what is meant. This is thanks to the many-sided polemics that has emerged both about and against the writer. In Germany, Karl Kraus can be said to be the father and master of the term and the type.

anyone—initially, he wrote only for himself—it was he who created a community of laypeople and his book became the lay book par excellence. Montaigne thus wrote the first book of lay, or amateur, self-reflection.

But his book only gradually took on this role, for it had originally been, rather, a sort of commentary on his reading. He read a great deal: the ancients, the Italians, and his contemporaries, above all, historians and moralists. His father belonged to a generation that still believed in the Humanist ideals and saw to it that Michel learned Latin before he learned French. Montaigne was thus "educated"; he understood the art of reading and read with such lively empathy and understanding that it occurred to him to note down his own experiences with the subjects about which he was reading and to compare them with what he had just read and also with passages from his earlier reading. The result was a kind of colorful reflection on the issue at hand. And it would have remained no more than that, had not a kind of constant self-provocation always taken Montaigne a step further.

This provocation is both the secret of his great talent, his unique gift, and it was the means by which it was brought to light. His modesty is completely genuine, I believe, when he writes that he only really came to understand this talent when he found himself not only being pleased by what he wrote,[5] but also being recognized in the world for it. This was a process quite different from the quest for stylistic perfection that was the standard by which writing was judged at the time. But it is not only the nonprofessional, lay manner of Montaigne's writing and its disorderliness that are astounding, but above all, the positive aspects of his achievement. He was a contemporary of Tasso (whom he, like others at the time, still considered to be mad) as well as of the Spanish Golden Age and the Pléiade. The dominant trends of the time were Humanism and a kind of manneristic Petrarchism, as well as a distinct predeliction for self-conscious formal artificiality. Montaigne's talent revolved around his power to lay things bare. He speaks about the most concrete of things, albeit in a completely subjective way—but still, *telles quelles*, just as they are. He never paraphrases and is only occasionally metaphorical (since metaphors distract the imagination). He avoids periodic style. In the architecture of his sentences, intonation often replaces conjunctions, which allows the clauses to seem causally, finally, consecutively or concessively linked, according to their meaning. His invocation of Tacitus is thus justified. Meaning creates the connections rather than the other way around. Some of his sentences are long, to be sure, but not intentionally periodic. And his words are plain, bare, and random, or at least not sought out according to any aesthetic criteria. When French is not sufficient, the dialect of Gascony must step up—he says so himself. And yet, the result is not, as in Rabelais, a kind of frenzy of excess, for Montaigne harbored no anti-aesthetic or aesthetically

[5] See Émile Faguet, *Seizième Siècle: Études littéraires* (Paris: Lecène, Oudin et Cie, 1894), 369ff.

revolutionary tendencies.[6] He did not flaunt his treasures and sought nothing special in his freedom from linguistic prejudice other than, perhaps at most, the expression that did justice to the topic at hand. The result is the most perfect bareness of the things themselves. And, because he was himself his own object, he also himself appears utterly naked. Had he not continued to respect at least some of the rules of decorum—and he did so against his will, as he admits in the foreword—he would have anticipated much of what some contemporary writers have taught us in our own time. What Montaigne was made of, what he thought and felt, comes across with no pathos, with no discernible artifice, and in a tranquil and comfortable way. It is luminously obvious in his writing. But it became so only gradually. Only after he had recognized his abilities did he disengage himself from the specific text that he had read, become more daring and richer in his expression, and begin to speak at greater length and less circumspectly about himself. He takes pleasure in his own thoughts, which become more diverse and more deliberate even in their complexity. He says whatever occurs to him, trusting implicitly that the integrity of his person is robust enough to maintain the integrity of the whole. He diagrams his inner humanity, to which his external human form of course also belongs, as that exterior is seen from the inside.

What Michel de Montaigne consciously thinks about, then, is the existence of Michel de Montaigne and, with it, the end this existence necessarily anticipates, namely death. Montaigne was a Christian of the Catholic confession; a Catholic priest stood at the foot of his bed when he died. He disliked the Huguenots because he was an enemy of all disturbances of the peace and did not believe that revolutions could bear any fruit. He represents the uncertainty of all knowledge—which is an all too positive and orthodox way of characterizing skepticism—in such a way that revelation and faith are almost always invoked in the end. Yet, we have reason to suspect that he was not a believer. We can *only* suspect this, however, and nothing more, for the final verdict is not ours to make. But we do have his book, as Saint-Beuve so correctly maintained, and we can certainly pass judgment on it. It is not the work of a believer. He assigns faith its place, to be sure, but for the most part, life and death are discussed as if faith did not exist. Montaigne writes profoundly and perceptively about Catholicism, including things that were soon forgotten, or that at least receded into the background, for example, about the relationship between the body and the soul.[7] But there is almost no trace of hope or salvation in the *Essays*. Typically, he wrote about religions as if they were nothing more than customs and traditions; their evolution, their instability, and the

[6]Quite the opposite in fact. He often appears, at least in theory, to anticipate Malherbe. See, for example, *Les Essais* 3:112: "la maniement et employte…." [its being handled and exploited, *Essays* III: 5 (987)].

[7]See *Les Essais* 2:419: "Les Chrestiens ont une particulière instruction" [Christians have their own special teaching, *Essays* II: 17 (727)].

fact that they were the products of men's hand, so to speak, were his empha-ses. At the time, this approach was perceived as a masked attack on Christi-anity, and these famous moments certainly had this effect. But it is not clear that Montaigne himself would have come to such a conclusion. It may be that we unjustly judge the original intention of the author on the basis of the evidence with which we are familiar from subsequent receptions. I consider it eminently likely that Montaigne suppressed the possibility of making the analogy to Christianity—and not simply as a matter of political conservatism or discretion, but, rather, because he never thought of it, for he considered himself a Catholic, respected his faith's forms, and never either tried or was able to deny revelation. He even submitted his book to the Roman Inquisi-tion, which initially—and in spite of some hesitations—judged it quite safe. However this may be, the spirit of the Essays is thoroughly un-Christian, for death is discussed as though there were no life after death and no salvation.[8] The man who wrote this book did not know Christ the Redeemer, and we cannot imagine him kneeling in prayer. What he wrote about religion were the observations of a respectable and diplomatic man, not those of a believer. Montaigne's attitude toward death may be compared to that of Socrates or of the men of late antiquity. From the latter he differs insofar as he makes no grand statements about death, but he is unlike both in his very concrete idea of mortality. Relentlessly fighting off the use of hackneyed phrases that dis-semble, he is the very least cliché-ridden writer one can imagine. Montaigne speaks with a horrifying concreteness about his own death, which he senses lurking within himself and for which he waits.

Montaigne senses his own death within himself. It is the enemy against which there is in the end no defense. Death will drag him out of the canny room in the back of the shop, the *arrière-boutique*, where he keeps himself hidden, and then fling him out into the void, as it has done to many others before him. But at least he will not be intimidated by death—as long as he is not yet confronted directly with it. Montaigne is a brave and intelligent man and knows that merely looking the other way is no good. He thus does ex-actly the opposite. He thinks constantly and in the most concrete way about death and tries to get used to the idea, just as a trainer leads a horse up to the hurdle before which the horse had balked. This is what Montaigne calls "flattering death" (*flatter la mort*). And it works. He becomes so used to death that it becomes part of his life. He gets to know it so well that he no longer fears it. Or perhaps better: He has been so overcome by fear that he no longer feels it. In any case, this is the point at which a series of uncanny ideas occurs

---

[8] *Essays* III: 9 (1099): "I lower my head and plunge, devoid of sensation, into death, neither contemplating it nor exploring it, as if into some voiceless, darkling deep, which swallows me up at one jump and in an instant overwhelms me with a powerful sleep entirely lacking any sensation of suffering." In *Commerce* 18 (1928) 43 ["Montaigne"], André Gide claims that this is the most astounding and commendable sentence in all of the *Essays*.

to him, doubly uncanny in their brilliance and in their icy and brittle lack of romanticism: Life is a journey on horseback; taking leave of one's companions, a kind of annoying and intrusive ceremonial act, and the possibility of death in a rented room surrounded by strangers whom one has paid in cash to take care of one's final affairs, but to whom one is not obligated in any way to be polite, so that the tranquility of dying will not be disturbed—such things fill his mind, and he discusses them in the same uninhibited way as he discusses the impact of his illnesses on his urine. He always sensed that he was on a journey, on the road from one place to another; it was a feeling that, in the end, must have never left him. It is in this sense that we can read words like the following, in which his entire work is contained: "I am not portraying being (*l'estre*) but becoming (*le passage*)."[9]

Montaigne's familiarity with death nevertheless does not vitiate his life. It does not lessen his ability to make himself comfortable, at home, in his *arrière-boutique*. We may compare him with a gourmand or an epicure who knows that he has only a short time left to seek his pleasures. With double the fervor and the kind of methodical deftness that only necessity can bring to a task, he uses the time of his existence to sample it all.

When he enjoys life, it is himself that Montaigne is enjoying. Initially this is so in the most unmediated "animal" sense. That is, he takes pleasure in breathing, eating, drinking, and digesting, in the places he travels to and where he lives, in what he owns and in his social standing. He is delighted at every sign that he is alive; everything that is his must serve the comfort of his interior "home," even his illnesses. He has kidney stones, for example, and the colics they produce are horrendous. Yet he is able to make his peace with them; he calls a truce and flatters them by attending to them in his thoughts and with his words the same way he treats death. In the end, he feels at home in his illnesses too, and they become close friends. They are among his possessions, a part of him, and perhaps not his worst part after all, for they teach him to enjoy his health. What a wonderful feeling it is when he is well, when the fit passes! Now he is free for a time and can eat and drink and move about as he likes. He pays no attention to his doctor's instructions, disdains medicine, and refuses to purchase health at the cost of his pleasures—which are of course the only reason one might want to have one's health to begin with. Others who are his age are not so well off. Perhaps they feel less pain. But for all of that, they are continuously weighed down by their illnesses. Montaigne, however, is healthy as long as he is not overcome by an attack. Before he became ill, he feared illness. He was familiar with the disease he might inherit and was afraid. Now that it is there, he discovers that it is not so dreadful a thing. Perhaps dying is the same.

[9] *Essays* III: 2 (907).

Yet, the pleasure Montaigne takes in his body is only one aspect of pleasure, indeed, an incentive for taking further pleasures in himself. He can feel himself living; as he becomes aware of himself, he becomes intoxicated by his own existence. The constant immediacy of the possibility of his own death gives his life a magnificent coherence, welding all aspects together and making him at home in himself. It prevents him from dissipating his energies and makes real that which is currently most true about him in an ongoing way. Whatever Montaigne is, then, he is thanks to death, and he wants to be in possession of himself at every moment—since any moment could be his last. His courage and the tranquility of his temperament prevent him from becoming desperate about his pleasures. He is always composed and equipped to be, to exist, rather than to do or to achieve. His *Essays* are a symptom of his existence.

Montaigne's existence consists in what he has been given in life. He does not try to change or better his lot, but rather accepts and acquiesces to it as it is. He considers human customs, institutions, and rules all equally idiotic and strange. They are as variable as opinion and thus have no legitimacy and no permanence. With no foundation other than the fact that they obtain at any given time, they are mere habit. Whoever understands this does not elect to rebel any more than the dull-witted and clueless do not choose to accept what happens to them out of sheer stubbornness. Montaigne sometimes seems to want to ally himself with them. The revolutionaries and troublemakers stand in the middle; it is the halfwits who see the injustice and absurdity of present conditions, but they do not understand that every new situation would be equally as unjust and absurd, or that the bedlam caused by change is certain to bring, at least initially, only losses caused by chaos and the melées. As for himself, Montaigne holds his peace and accommodates himself to existing circumstances, both for logical reasons and out of loyalty. He admires Socrates, who submitted to his judges and to the laws of Athens, even though they did him wrong. For Montaigne, things were simpler. His position is agreeable—if one considers the adversity of the times. He does not seek martyrdom. He tries always, by whatever means necessary, to find a way to escape avoidable harms, but there is no reason to doubt that he would also have stayed true to his principles had they turned against him. As it was, his existence seemed quite tolerable. He sat in his tower room in Montaigne, or he traveled around France, Italy, and Germany, always on horseback, without worrying about his health. Great men and kings sought his services; he either turned them down—always politely—or offered his services in a cautious way. He had a respectable wife and a daughter about whom he had few worries, and several pleasant neighbors and friends. People were happy to read whatever it occurred to him to write about, and, once he had decided to let his writing see print, there was a constant demand for further editions. "If I were a scribbler. . . ." In the end, he became involved with a young woman, a companion, Mademoiselle de Gournay, in Paris, who loved and admired him. She became his so-called *fille d'alliance* (adoptive daughter) and was closer to him than anyone since the death of his friend, Étienne de la Boétie. She would be the one to organize the papers and texts that he would leave behind. He was content. Everything should stay as it was as long as possible. Every additional hour was an hour won.

Montaigne did not write very much, about a thousand pages over the course of twenty years. He reread what he had written. Adding some things, removing others, he improved it. Of course he denied that this was what he was doing, but it is clear from the Bordeaux manuscript that has survived—which is actually not a manuscript, but rather a copy of the 1588 edition that he went back over and annotated himself—that he even undertook stylistic revisions. He examines himself, gives full expression to all that he has in terms of intellectual assets, introducing himself, as it were, to a public. He has his own thoughts about just about everything, and while these thoughts are often doubtful and inconclusive, the path that has led him to his doubts and indecisions is one that he has constructed himself, in the process creating a problem or a combination of problems in this way for the very first time. His lack of prejudice and independence of mind are almost frightening, and all the more impressive as he is not really up to much with them. He says what occurs to him and leaves it at that. But this is precisely what provokes the reader, in whom what Montagine has written then readily solidifies into a far coarser, far more systematic and more active way of thinking than the delicate, nearly intangible substance that was Montaigne's. Buried deep in his civil, often even somewhat chatty words there lies a stimulant, some kind of drug, a drink of death or of life, depending on what one decides. It is the poison of freedom, of the abandonment of any fixed position, and of human autonomy. When Montaigne is out in society and among people, he is civil and well mannered. But when he is alone, he is very different. Conventions, customs, laws, and religions vanish. I am alone, I have to die. This world is not my home, I am only passing through, but where I have come from and where I am headed—I do not know. What is the only thing that is mine? My self.

It is here that an extraordinary word begins to take the lead, a word that has led to several interpretations that are both superficial and wide of the mark: *virtus, la vertu,* "manliness" or "virtue." Of course, he gets both the word and the idea from late antiquity, from Plutarch and Seneca. It derives from the Stoic tradition and everything that comes with it, with its admiration of the deaths of Socrates and Cato side by side, the pathos-laden rubbish of exempla in ancient encomia, which he both cites and critiques with an earnestness that is quite naïve. At least Montaigne adopted the humanistic cult of virtue first; several uncritical critics, unable to bring Stoic rigidity together with the nearly indecent and indiscrete directness of his self-portrait in a harmonious way, have proposed that he progressed from Stoicism to skepticism. To some extent this is correct, insofar as he only gradually developed into what he essentially was. But neither word is really appropriate for him; "skeptic" is inadequate and "Stoic" is simply wrong.[10] He was a soldier and capable of performing physical tasks in spite of his illness; when he had to be, he was brave and indifferent to privation. But there is no trace in him of Stoic rigor, of the autonomy of reason, of an identity of reason and nature, or of moral asceticism. He mourned the passing of his youth, longed for it, and refused to recognize the wisdom of age. To be in such a sorry state as to prefer the wretched wisdom and virtue of old age (born of impotence) to the vital energies of youth—well, he hoped to never be so far gone. From a certain perspective, one could perhaps say that he revived the ancient ideal of the wise hermit. But he did so entirely without a program or platform. Quite the contrary: he was sociable, interested in everything, and passionate about traveling. His isolation is only interior, and even then he is not standing on principle. When he is alone, he is in his element, he is content and not actually suffering from any romantic or sentimental wound. He is in fact so content with isolation that it resembles more a state of sin than one of virtue. But neither is truly the case. Being alone is merely his natural element, like water for a fish.

And this is also where we discover Montaigne's famous concept of virtue: "Even in virtue our ultimate aim—no matter what they say—is pleasure. I enjoy bashing people's ears with that word which runs so strongly counter to their minds. When pleasure is taken to mean the most profound delight and an exceeding happiness, then it is a better companion to virtue than anything else; and rightly so. Such pleasure is no less seriously pleasurable for being more lively, taut, robust and virile. We ought to have given virtue the more favourable, noble and natural name of "pleasure," not (as we have done) a name derived from *vis* (vigour). There is that lower voluptuous pleasure which can only be said to have a disputed claim to the name and not a privileged right to it. I find it less pure of lets and hindrances than virtue. Apart from having a savour which is fleeting, fluid and perishable, it has its vigils, fasts and travails, its blood and its sweat . . . and [is] accompanied by a satiety of such weight [that it amounts to repentance]." [11]

Desire as virtue: this is not Stoic. Nor is it Epicurean or skeptical. It is more full of life than those late antique forms of individual ethics, more so than any position founded on reflection alone. It could be that the page on which we

---

[10]See Lanson, *Les Essais de Montaigne* (Paris 1930) 122ff. I only discovered this book many years after completing this essay in 1929.

[11]*Essays* I: 20 (90). Elsewhere (I: 25 [Trans: I: 26 (181)]) he writes: " . . . that the gods place sweat on the paths to the chambers of Venus rather than of Pallas." Of the ancient authors, Lucretius echoes most resonantly here. I nevertheless think that he may have only provided the material for the claim. Montaigne is interested in something else.

find this quote is suspicious. There is much about it that smacks of antiquity. But anyone who knows Montaigne well will have to admit that his point here is not to value virtue over love. Rather, he wants to measure both against pleasure to see how much pleasure each guarantees. In such a comparison, this is a measure that we cannot conceive of without reference to sensuality and life, and this is the case with all of his thought. Life, in its historical and natural facticity, is neither rejected nor disdained. Precisely the opposite. Montaigne, for whom desire is virtue, plunges deeply into living sensuality, for it is only in the living sensuality of the world that he can understand and take pleasure in himself. As strange as it may sound, this is the legacy of Christianity, a transformation of practical Aristotelianism within Christianity, based on the story of Christ, which was itself rooted, in a very un-antique and untheorized way, in the torments of the sensual world. The Renaissance inherited this realism from the "waning of the Middle Ages." It was a realism that consisted in a desire for the next world that was inextricably bound up with the imprisonment of living man in the earthly condition, in other words, the Christian realism of the Middle Ages. And yet, for Montaigne, the prison of this embrace is no longer only involuntary. It is in fact not actually compelled at all. Rather it is an abundance of freedom. For the world into which he was born and which he would leave—not gladly, of course, but without fear—made him the gift of this abundance of freedom when it gave him the gift of the fullness of life. The world gave him countless opportunities to test this freedom, but no law. The virtue which he enjoys is not a law, and it is surely not the "moral law in me." The master of this virtue is neither God nor man. Rather, it is Montaigne himself. It obligates no one to anything. It allows man to be free, but leaves him alone.[12]

This is what the "I" that is the subject of the *Essays* looks like, then. The book succeeded in finding an audience at the end of the sixteenth century—an audience that was of necessity a lay one. It could be that the universal fatigue in the face of the wars of religion played a role here. The *Essays* had a neutral, even sovereign effect. They are not the occasional thoughts of Montaigne on this or that subject, thoughts with which he demands that we agree. Rather, they concern his entire person, which was a person suited to the task of creating an entirely new kind of human being. In the place of the believer or the doubter or the rebellious Christian there emerged the new type of the *honnête homme*, the honest man, capable of fulfilling all formal demands and simply letting things be. But other forces soon pushed the *honnête homme* of the seventeenth and eighteenth centuries in other directions; in the end, this type became more dynamic, more bourgeois, and pettier too.

---

[12] It is easy to see here how Pascal could follow Montaigne and how much more distant Enlightenment thinkers were from him, even though they borrowed a great deal. It is a Christian "human condition" (*condition de l'homme*) that is still everywhere clear in Montaigne.

But Montaigne is everything other than bourgeois and enlightened. At his core is something other than the canny reserve of the *honnête homme* who quickly forgets the nakedness of his existence in the midst of the chatter of the world and the endless drift of its affairs. This man soon invents formulas and words for death that endow death with significance as a social function, thereby allowing him not to look at it directly. But for Montaigne, the layman and the first writer, things were different. He was still enough of a Christian that he was always reminded of the *condition de l'homme*. Full of desire, he immersed himself deeply in the thought of death. While he did not tremble, he also did not hope. He drove his horse to the very edge of the abyss until it no longer balked—and did so not harshly, with spurs and a whip, but gently and consistently by merely applying pressure with his thighs. This was how he flattered freedom, without forgetting that he was its servant. This memory was what allowed him to enjoy the pleasures of this freedom to the fullest. He was unique, with himself, for himself, and in the world—and entirely alone.

17

On Pascal's Political Theory

Il est juste que ce qui est juste soit suivi, il est nécessaire que ce qui est le plus fort soit suivi. La justice sans la force est impuissante; la force sans la justice est tyrannique. La justice sans force est contredite, parce qu'il y a toujours des méchants; la force sans la justice est accusée. Il faut donc mettre ensemble la justice et la force; et pour cela faire que ce qui est juste soit fort, ou que ce qui est fort soit juste.

La justice est sujette à dispute, la force est très reconnaissable et sans dispute. Ainsi on n'a pu donner la force à la justice, parce que la force a contredit la justice et a dit que c'était elle qui était juste. Et ainsi ne pouvant faire que ce qui est juste fût fort, on a fait que ce qui est fort fût juste.

—Pascal, *Pensées* 298, ed. Brunschvicg.

[It is right that what is just should be obeyed; it is necessary that what is strongest should be obeyed. Justice without power is helpless; power without justice is tyrannical. Justice without power is gainsaid, because there are always offenders; power without justice is condemned. We must then combine justice and power, and for this end make what is just strong, or what is strong just.

Justice is subject to dispute; power is easily recognized and is not disputed. So we cannot give power to justice, because power has gainsaid justice, and has declared that it is she herself who is just. And thus being unable to make what is just strong, we have made what is strong just.]

—Pascal, *Pensées,* W. F. Trotter, trans. (New York: Dutton, 1954) 85.
Translation adapted.

I would like to thank Sam Arkin for assistance with securing materials for this translation.—Trans.

These sentences comprise fragment 298 in Brunschvicg's edition of Pascal's *Pensées*.[1] They capture the frailty of positive law very clearly. To analyze them in terms of style poses no difficulty, and their structure becomes immediately obvious when we arrange the text in the following way:

It is right that what is just should be obeyed:
It is necessary that what is strongest should be obeyed.

Justice without power is helpless:
Power without justice is tyrannical.

Justice without power is gainsaid, because there are always offenders;
Power without justice is condemned.

We must then combine justice and power, and for this end make
what is just strong,
or what is strong just.

Justice is subject to dispute,
Power is easily recognizable and is not disputed.

So

we cannot give power to justice, because power has gainsaid justice and
has declared that it is
she herself (*elle*) who is just.

And thus,

being unable to make what is just strong,
we have made what is strong just.

Reading the text this way allows us to understand immediately how Pascal develops his idea by placing symmetrically arranged pairs of antithetical propositions (*isocola*) in playful dialogue with one another. There are six such pairs. The first three describe the problem. Out of this problem there emerges a challenge that can be met in different ways. The fourth pair describes these different ways, and the following syllogism is the result: Either A or B had to be done. A was impossible; thus B was done. The second statement (e.g., that A was impossible) is emphatically underscored; the reason for this impossibility is given in the fifth pair of *isocola*, which is not entirely symmetrical, since its second part is longer and more direct, and the second statement itself appears twice in the lines that complete the syllogism—and the entire fragment. The conclusion is divided into two steps: *ainsi* (thus) and

---

[1] On this same topic, see Jacques Maritain, "The Political Ideas of Pascal," in *Ransoming the Time* (New York: Scribner's, 1941) 33ff., and Romano Guardini, *Christliches Bewußtsein* (Leipzig: Verlag Jakob Hegner, 1935) 139ff.

et ainsi (and thus), with the first (*ainsi*) containing a dramatic elaboration of the second (note the emphasis on *elle*), while the second (*et ainsi*) repeats once again that A was impossible, endowing the conclusion contained in the final pair of antithetical *isocola* with a tone of bitter satisfaction

This brief analysis betrays something about Pascal's style, namely, its unique fusion of logic, rhetoric, and passion. The development of his thoughts appears simply to follow a logical method, nothing more. But the rhetorical play with the two concepts in symmetrically constructed antithetical propositions injects a kind of dramatic tension into the business—such that when, at the end, power emerges from the battle of the concepts with its head held high and its voice clearly heard (*et a dit que c'était elle. . . .*), its triumph becomes *the* major event.

A modern critical reader not very familiar with Pascal could become suspicious of the argument's antithetical form, regardless of how effective it is. He might remark that the argument seems not entirely free of sophistry and ask whether Pascal is not treating two entirely different meanings of the word *juste* (just) as if they were the same. At the beginning, *juste* surely means "true, natural, and absolute law." Later, however, when it falls into the hands of power, it signifies, rather, "established positive law." What is contingent on power is thus of course not really law; at best, it only passes for it. As obvious as this reasoning might seem to the modern reader, however, it is not the way Pascal understood it. He actually believed, as we shall soon see, that on this earth, power is not only real and positive law, but justifiably legal as well. In order to understand Pascal's thought as he intended it, we must inquire how it came to take on the form that it did. For, as unified and simple as his thought appears to be (in spite of its highly rhetorical nature), in fact it is made up of a variety of influences and experiences.

One such influence was Montaigne. From him Pascal borrowed—occasionally word for word—the idea that the dominant factor in law is neither reason nor even natural agreement among all men but, rather, merely custom. According to Montaigne, however, custom is contingent on time and place; it is thus always changing. What is permitted, even praised, in one country or age counts as a crime in another; indeed, even absurd, arbitrary, and apparently unjust ways of living may be sanctioned by custom. We must nevertheless obey custom and the law based on it, Montaigne says, not because it is just, but, first, because this law is the one that is in force and, second, because one cannot hope for anything better. The disorder that accompanies any change is inevitably evil, and it is not worth foisting this evil either on oneself or on others, since the new custom will be neither better nor make any greater sense than the former one. This was the logic that Pascal adopted from Montaigne. But even as he did so, he changed the emphasis a little, placed the accent differently. An entirely new argument was the result. For Montaigne, the variability of custom was neither frightening nor even a reason for despair. His free, venial, and accommodating manner allowed him to move about courageously, even comfortably, in a world full of uncertainties. He had no need of stability or absolutes. I even doubt that he would have felt comfortable with anything of the sort. But Pascal did have such needs and pursued them with an often violent passion. He demanded security in the here-and-now, a durable orderly world of absolutes, and could not tolerate fluctuations or variability of any sort. These he dismissed without hesitation as evil, indeed, as the embodiment of Evil itself.

In addition to their differences in temperament, it may well have been the differences of the times and conditions in which Montaigne and Pascal lived that were responsible for the different ways in which they considered such issues. Montaigne's was an age of political and religious struggles. He observed how untrammeled historical forces actually evolved over the course of their conflicts with one another and how customs changed. But he was still able to hope that some kind of permanent compromise might result from these struggles and changes (even if he did not approve of them) and that this compromise, if not necessarily good, might at least be moderate and could be tolerated. Pascal, however, lived at a time when absolutism was nearing its zenith, that is, under a system in which a single source of power was beginning to rule in unimpeded and apparently entirely arbitrary ways, as if it were the established law. Still, it seems to me that it was the peculiarities of Pascal's temperament, rather than his times and his situation, that produced his much harsher judgment of custom and that led to his tendency simply to dismiss custom as evil and to replace it, almost imperceptibly, with an entirely different concept, namely, power.

Of course, we can also derive this idea from Montaigne, if we are so disposed. He does claim that we must obey the law not because it is just, but because it is what is enforced, which is to say: because it has power. But for Montaigne, the law has power and is valid only because it is based on custom. Pascal is inclined to strip custom of its autonomy because he considers it to be a mere function of power, established only by force. Here, we see Pascal addressing a problem that Montaigne never considered, namely, the relationship of custom to power. He calls custom without power a grimace, and takes a certain satisfaction in collecting examples in which this grimace must yield to power; indeed, he is happy to reduce custom in general to mere *imagination* or *opinion.* Pascal is thus not at all sensitive to the historical development of customs, for which Montaigne had offered a very beautiful image: *elles groissent et s'anoblissent en roulant, comme nos fleuves* [they grow and become more noble as they flow, like our rivers]. For Pascal, customs originate in the arbitrariness of power and in "the caprice of legislators." By repeating this kind of arbitrary act at any given moment, power could oust the prevailing custom. Montaigne never speaks categorically about power, but it is clear from the general direction of his ideas that he would have defined power only as the executor of custom. For Montaigne, two differing customs, both of them supported by power, could easily come into conflict and destroy each other. But there is no place in his *Essays* for naked power that is not endorsed by custom or that rests solely on the whim of those in charge. Pascal, on the other hand, bestows on pure power, which custom arbitrarily creates for itself, the ability to create its own law. He even claims with a kind of bitter triumph, as we shall see, that it is right that this should be the case, because there is no law other than the one which power has in its hands. What would happen, he asks, if we were to try to settle differences according to merit or law? Our differences would be insolvable. Who goes first, you or I? You have four footmen, I have one. One has only to count; the situation is clear.

This is where the second set of ideas that was significant for Pascal as he developed his understanding of law begins to be important, namely the ideas about the fundamental corruption of human nature as these were espoused by Port-Royal. Montaigne of course also occasionally asserts that we have lost our original innocence, or nature, and that all we have left are artifice and custom. But he nevertheless ultimately does rely on this nature, or perhaps better, on this nature as history has transformed it into custom. In fact, he trusts custom as much as he trusts nature itself, and allows the flow of historical life to engulf him—and is willing to be engulfed by it, just as a swimmer is caught up in water or someone who drinks gives himself over happily to the wine. Pascal, on the other hand, allied himself with the radical form of Augustinianism endorsed by the gentlemen of Port-Royal, according to which the world is fundamentally and necessarily evil and stands in the sharpest possible contrast to the Kingdom of God. In this situation, one must decide whether to follow the one or the other.

I do not wish to discuss the ideas of Port-Royal from either a historical or a philosophical perspective here. There is a rich secondary literature on the topic from the last century, running from Sainte-Beuve to Laporte, which is quite adequate for that purpose. Suffice it to say that before Pascal these ideas did not include a political theory.[2] At most, they contained instructions about what stance a Christian should take toward the world. On the one hand, he was to detach himself from it; on the other, he was to submit to it—with detachment understood as a spiritual, internal affair and submission as a matter of outward deportment. Anyone who could also remove himself from the outside world by entering a monastery was encouraged to do so. Here, as in everything, a Christian ought to follow God's will rather than his own, for God's will is more likely to be identified with certainty in the external circumstances of one's life than in the movements of one's inner life, which fluctuate by definition. Thus, when an important social position

---

[2] The fact that Port-Royale was involved with political movements and problems at the time in a variety of ways in no way contradicts this claim.

with many responsibilities or familial circumstances forbids one from retiring from the world, the believer should remain at the post to which God's will has assigned him. But even within the world, one can detach oneself by turning one's heart away, refusing to participate in the world's pleasures and appetites, participating instead in its sorrows and suffering its woes—since suffering is the most secure bond we have with Christ. External submission, however, consists in acknowledging the political and social institutions of this world, obeying the secular powers, and serving them in accordance with one's situation in life. For even though the world has yielded to concupiscence and is thus evil, a Christian has no right to condemn it or even to resist it by any worldly means, since he is himself in the same state of sinfulness, and the evil of this world is the just punishment and penance that God imposes on fallen man. The injustice of this world is God's true justice, and we must bear it happily. Indeed, when God permits true right to prevail, He does so not out of justice (*iustitia*), but as an act of mercy (*misericordia*). Such sentiments, which reject the possibility of criticizing worldly institutions, appear to preclude the development of a political theory. For, as evil as it may be, the world was established by God; it is the duty of the Christian to submit to it. Port-Royal did not concern itself with political theory, and Pascal would hardly himself have come to anything resembling such a theory had external circumstances not imposed the problem of politics upon him with such urgency that it was impossible to avoid.

The circumstances are well known: They concerned the sequence of events that we know today as the struggle between Port-Royal and the Jesuits. If a Christian is obliged to submit to the world, then his obligations are all the greater in terms of the obedience he owes to the Church. The Church is the community of believers established by God; it has authority over the teaching of doctrine and the administration of those sacraments that are indispensable to anyone seeking salvation. To stand outside the Church or to break away from it entirely of one's own free will, as the Protestants did, was a thoroughly horrifying thought for Port-Royal. But if corruption gains power within the Church, indeed, if evil powers succeed in beguiling and enthralling the heads of the Church (the bishops and the Pope) such that they become these powers' willing instruments and, on the basis of their authority and the duty to obey, force the few true believers (whom God has judged worthy of true knowledge) to publicly and solemnly condemn what appears to them to be, and what they are absolutely sure is, the essence of belief, indeed, if the Church, supported by secular power and itself acting as a secular power, desires to destroy what is right by force, then a situation emerges in which there is no way out. There is a crisis with—quite literally—no possibility of redemption. This was the situation in which Port-Royal found itself during the years when Pascal was most closely associated with it. He thus experienced the majority of the crises that must have seemed to him to be the very triumph of evil in the Church. It was during these years that the problem of the relation between justice and power became of particular relevance to him and it was then, too, that he wrote the fragments of the *Pensées*, as well as the other shorter texts in which his political theory can be found. Montaigne's theory of the prevailing law as merely a matter of custom now joined with the radically Augustinian view of the world as a realm of evil to produce the system in which, as we saw above, custom is understood as the pus that has leached out of power, as it were, the pure caprice of Evil.

Pascal was of course always one to carry things to extremes. In his final years, during the crisis at Port-Royal, he gave in to this tendency entirely and was utterly convinced—and was supported in this conviction by ecstatic visions and a miracle—that he was doing God's work. Among the extreme ideas that arose in his mind, three are closely related to one another, and these constitute what I call his political theory: his hatred of human nature (and thus of his own nature); his unmasking of existing law as purely arbitrary and evil; and his acceptance that this evil law was the only one with any legitimacy.

Pascal's hatred of human nature arose from radical Augustinianism. In his famous distinction between use (*uti*) and enjoyment (*frui*), the saint taught that we ought not to love creatures for their own sake, but, rather, for the sake of their Creator. We owe them transient love (*amor transitorius*) and not enduring love (*amor mansorius*). Above all, we must not love ourselves for our own sake, as this would be to set ourselves above God, which, he writes, had been Adam's sin. That God is the only lasting object of our love, that all things worthy of being loved are united in Him, and that all created things are worthy of love only insofar as they are a reflection of His being, is universal Christian doctrine, and was even a widely held doctrine in pre-Christian times. But these teachings underwent a shift of emphasis for Port-Royal and especially for Pascal in his last years, a shift that invested them with a strange radicalism and peculiar severity. We read that toward the end of his life, Pascal behaved with a certain coldness to those closest to him. He was not able even to tolerate their affection for him because it represented a theft of their affections from God. He quite often made a point of saying this openly and, when he did, emphasized that loving God's creatures instead of God necessarily leads to disappointment, even despair. For, he wrote, the object of such love is transitory, both in itself and in terms of the individual qualities that are the reason we loved the object to begin with. The thought of the transitoriness of the things we love was intolerable for Pascal; the idea that the treasures to which our heart clings are dwindling by the minute and are in constant danger of being torn away from us in their entirety filled him with horror. Whatever is transitory and thus necessarily returns to a state of nothingness counts, for Pascal, as nothing. This includes heaven and earth, relatives and friends, even one's own body and mind. God alone endures and is unchanging, immutable. Only He is worthy of being loved. Human frailty and mutability are the consequence of Original Sin and of Adam's inordinate self-love, the wicked and grotesque error that he bequeathed to his descendents and which represents what is most despicable in us. In spite of his obvious imperfection and mortality, every individual necessarily considers himself the center of the universe. Loving nothing so much as himself, he judges everything from his own point of view. This is clearly a horrible mistake that deserves our scorn. Indeed, it is at this point that the word "hatred" begins to resonate through Pascal's writings in a way peculiar only to him.

Other Christian writers of course also use the word in this way. It occurs already in the Gospels in certain exceptional passages in St. Luke and St. John. But I can scarcely believe that hate ever dominated the entire context of the thought of man's love for God to the extent that it does in Pascal. His famous remark about the hateful self is by no means his most drastic statement of this kind. He maintained that one ought to love only God and hate only oneself, and that Christianity teaches self-hatred, which is the only true virtue. Somewhat more temperate formulations can be found scattered about in his writing, but it is these more direct utterances that determine the tone of the *Pensées*. Obviously Pascal's self-hatred refers not merely to the self that happens to be Pascal, but to the self of every individual human being, because everyone participates in this same transitoriness and in this same horrific self-love. Hatred of the self and of all human beings by no means came naturally to Pascal. He was capable of passionate, even jealous attachments, and it was a struggle for him to resist his own high regard for—his pride in—himself (a pride to which he, from an earthly point of view, was more entitled than most others). His religious radicalism triumphed over his natural predisposition only by force—a predisposition itself marked more by an inclination to violence than by anything else. Even in the radical form that it takes in Pascal, the motif of self-hatred and the hatred of all human beings can undoubtedly be justified as dogma within the Christian tradition. Nevertheless, when this motif, justifiable in and of itself, is isolated from other Christian ideas and is overemphasized, as in the case of Pascal, it runs the risk of standing in direct contradiction to Christian ethics. The commandment that one ought to love one's neighbor as oneself assumes that one loves oneself; if this were not the case, then one would "hate one's neighbor as one hates oneself." Moreover, a certain coolness toward Creation in general is latent in such ideas, especially when they are formulated in such an extreme fashion. Mutability makes not only the human race, but all of created nature unworthy of our love. In Pascal, the great physicist, nature was able to call up curiosity, admiration, and fear—but not love. There are few men of religion, few mystics, and few idealistic writers who distance themselves as radically as he does from the thought that the things of this world are reflections of divine wisdom and beauty. This is surely the reason why Pascal so vigorously rejected all attempts to prove the existence of God on the basis of natural phenomena.

The second idea to be considered here—namely, the unmasking of earthly law as merely arbitrary and evil—is closely connected to the first. For this follows from the corruption of human nature, independently of any experience and purely on the basis of logic. Corruption is only capable of breeding further corruption. Our law and our politics—with politics understood in the broadest possible sense to include all worldly activity—can only be evil. And they *are* evil, as we know from experience. Thus neither reason nor justice can prevail, only violence and chance. Pascal was a member of the bourgeois citizen class of *la robe*, or officialdom; he was a man of great intelligence and discriminating judgment. Although many honorable positions were open to him and his social peers, the way to any kind of political freedom or political responsibilities was barred. During the era when absolutism had reached its perfection, the entire population, all classes included, was merely the object of politics, not its subject or agent. Indeed, it was at precisely this moment that Pascal's class had even the last remnants of its political autonomy destroyed in the unrest of the Fronde. But it would be difficult to prove—and is in any case unlikely—that any sense of dissatisfaction resulting from these circumstances contributed to his political views. Even though the tradition of his family would have certainly justified it, he distanced himself completely from any participation in the Fronde. Yet, at any other time it would be impossible to imagine that a man of his social standing and intellectual stature would have both thought and acted politically as he did. He was convinced that all political institutions were based on delusion, chance, and violence, and he stated as much in the cutting and paradoxical way peculiar to him, which, it seems to me, occasionally allowed themes other than Christian ones to become audible. Pascal's was a critical attitude that may indeed have been intended to legitimate radical Christian conclusions. But it was also capable of having an effect that far exceeded such goals. In his *Trois Discours sur la condition des Grands* [Three Discourses on the Situation of Great and Powerful Men], he proves to a great lord that his prestige and power are based not on any natural or authentic right, but merely on the will of the legislators. If these legislators were to think about it again or in a different way, Pascal argues, the lord would end up impotent and poor. The lord's position is thus legitimate—as is any institution that is recognized by positive law, once it exists. Yet for the same reason, only outward deference and obedience are due to the lord (for it is foolish and ignoble to deny these to laws and institutions), but not respect from within. For, even though a prince may use his power in an honest and benevolent way according to how such things are understood in this world—which he is duty-bound to do—his rule is always opposed to God's kingdom. The goods of love lie in God's hands. He is the king of charity. The man who administers and distributes the goods of this world is the king of *concupiscentia* [desire for worldly things], and even if he rules his kingdom in a decent fashion and strives to do no more than this, he will be eternally damned—although he will of course be damned as a decent man. *Si vous en demeurez là, vous ne laisserez pas de vous perdre, mais au moins vous perdrez en honnête homme* [If you remain there, you will not be able to avoid loosing your soul, but at least you will loose it as an honest man.] The borders of the Kingdom of Grace and salvation lie far beyond those of any merely earthly decency.

Pascal returns to these ideas in the *Pensées*. There, he describes the absurd contingency of all human institutions in a way that would immediately seem exceedingly revolutionary if we failed to view them within the Augustinian framework. To give an example: According to both human and divine law, murder is the worst crime of all. But if my neighbor, whom I ought to love, lives on the other side of the river where another prince rules, and if this prince happens to be involved in a conflict with my prince, then I may kill him and, in fact, I am obligated to do so. He lives on the other side of the river! This is the basis—the only basis—of my right to kill him. The entire age of absolutism, the age of cabinet wars in which the people had no role other than to endure them, is captured in these words. It is remarkable to observe just how widespread such thoughts were at the time (even if others did not formulate them quite so directly) and how perfectly compatible they were with a total and hyperbolically expressed loyalty to the king. There has never been a more nominalist era than this one. At the same time, this is of course all based on Pascal's extremely pointed version of the idea of the world's corruption. Original Sin and Christ's sacrifice made the world into the perpetual murderer of Christ, the human race lost its original nature, and any random *opinion* or *imagination* at all can become its second nature. Yet what actually becomes second nature at any given time is decided by the right of whoever is stronger, whoever is in charge. Real power is the sole earthly phenomenon for which Pascal shows a certain kind of respect, even approval—even if this respect is of course so bitter and insidious as to sound cynical at times. He respects the law of the wicked because of its lack of distortion, its sheer clarity, and on occasion he elaborates on this respect in considerable detail. It is not so very vain to dress in an elegant manner, he says at one point, for it shows that you have many people at your beck and call: the tailor, the embroiderer, the barber, the valet. This is not a matter of deceptive externals, but of real power. To dress well is to display it. The common folk are thus thinking clearly when they show respect for power and its external signs— even though their motives are wrong. They believe they must respect power because it is just, but this is a fallacy. Power is to be respected not because it is just, but for its own sake, simply because it exists. It is nevertheless dangerous, Pascal claims, to enlighten the people about their mistake.

Here we are quite close to Pascal's third idea, the idea that provides the foundations of his argument about the legitimacy of right based on power. But before going into this idea, I must introduce something of a digression. I do so because I need to qualify my claim that Pascal recognizes nothing on earth besides power. For there is actually one other realm that earns his respect, a realm situated between the earthly order of power and the Kingdom of divine charity. This is the realm of human thought, the earthly intellect, which he occasionally juxtaposes with the realm of power, as he does in the *Discours sur la condition des Grands* and in fragments 332 and 793 of the Brunschvicg edition of the *Pensées*. Here, Pascal carefully distinguishes these three realms from one another. The material realm is infinitely distant from the realm of thought. This "infinite" distance symbolizes the infinitely more infinite distance that separates the realm of thought from the transcendent realm of divine love. The greatness proper to each of these realms individually has no validity or influence in the others; earthly potentates, geniuses, and saints each have their own domain, and each remains outside the practical jurisdiction of the others. Pascal's acknowledgement of the human intellect, which seems to have something of a Cartesian hue, corresponds to his understanding of the human being as a thinking reed (*roseau pensant*). In the antithesis between human grandeur and misery, thinking is where man can be great. And thus it is that Pascal can also occasionally call "intellectual greatness" "natural greatness" (*grandeur naturelle*) when he opposes it to material power—even though he really recognizes only a nature that is fallen. The point is not terribly easy to understand. Indeed, the realm of human thought represents a total quandary for Pascal's political theory since, in the end, it is not possible in practice to distinguish clearly between it and power in such a way that the one has no influence on the other. Either there is something in the world—namely, human thought—that can successfully oppose power, or else power can quash it. Here, Pascal is of course thinking primarily about forms of thought, such as mathematics and physics, which are more or less unpolitical. But even here, as we know from ample experience, thinking and power can come into conflict. Pascal himself discussed one such example, the case of Galileo, in his eighteenth *Provincial Letter*. It is thus not sufficient to distinguish in theory between these two realms and to declare that the potential practical infringement of power on the realm of thought is an act of tyranny, an act that in the long run will neither be able to repress the truth nor be justified in trying to do so. Such a claim would justify the revolution of the intellectuals—and this is exactly the opposite of Pascal's intention. Logically, he would have to reduce science and the intellect to the same low level as all other human things, and to categorize their activities and achievements as mere *opinions* and *imaginations*—just as he had done to everything else on the earth that depends—justifiably—on power. But this was something that this great mathematician and physicist, who was actively involved with the work of Descartes, Roberval, and Fermat, could not bring himself to do. It was much easier for Montaigne.[3]

Nevertheless, when Pascal discusses politics, he does not mention the human mind. The inconsistency thus does not emerge. I can conclude my digression here. In the earthly political realm as Pascal describes it, power alone—which is to say, evil—rules, and does so justly. He goes much further in elaborating this paradox—which is the third of the ideas that I listed above—than either Augustine or his friends at Port-Royal, and he also became much more deeply involved than the latter in the practical affairs of the earthly world.

The moral code of the decent man (*honnête homme*) dictated submission to the prevailing political and social powers. One had to acknowledge one's proper place in the existing order. Adopting an attitude that coincided perfectly with one's position in this order was an ethical and aesthetic ideal that was just emerging at the time. Pascal's friend Méré played a significant role here. It was an old set of Christian ideas that was gaining renewed significance at the time and that gave the moral code I have been discussing its theological foundation and thus its greater depth. The argument runs as follows: It is a Christian's duty to endure this world and especially its injustices, since it was precisely Christ's sacrifice to have endured injustice of His own free will. It is the mission of the Christian to imitate Him in this respect. This is especially the case when it comes to political authority, for Christ submitted both in principle and in the Passion to the power of the state. Thus, even though it was committing an injustice of the very highest sort, the state authority that carried out the Passion acted legitimately insofar as its job, in accordance with the divine order of salvation, was to carry out the Passion in a manner that was legal, that followed the laws of the state. Christ's sacrifice was also just in God's eyes as the expiation of Adam's sin. Every Christian must reenact Christ's sacrifice; whoever is deemed worthy of enduring injustice, especially at the hands of the state, is also worthy of participating in Christ's sacrifice and should rejoice in this fact. The joy one takes in suffering injustice may be limited only by love of one's neighbor. This is to say: We cannot wholeheartedly wish that someone will commit an injustice against us, since such a wish would also imply that we desire that he commit an injustice— and it is a great sin to wish that one's neighbor do anything of this sort.

While this doctrine, which Port-Royal supported in theory and still more in practice, concerns the kinds of injustice that occur in the world, it avoids any political critique. It teaches that we must endure the events of the world

[3] Similarly, we can find such demands for freedom of thought in the theoretical writings on the absolutist state by other thinkers who were more or less contemporaries of Pascal. The historical context of such ideas is most likely linked in many cases to the enforcement of the power of the centralized state over movements of religious fanaticism that were more particularistically oriented. In such contexts, the centralized state endorsed its idea of religious tolerance.

regardless of whether they are just or not. It does not concern itself theoretically with the question whether injustice does or does not occur sometimes or always or even in a particular case. To be sure, Port-Royal adhered in Augustinian fashion to the idea that the world is evil in its entirety. But it did not explore the possibility that the individual legislator or particular government might be swayed by God's Grace and mercy such that either often or even occasionally there might be some justice in the world, or whether this was never the case. And it certainly did not pursue such questions by means of or according to the standards of human reason.

But Pascal did undertake such an inquiry, and he did so on the basis of Montaigne's, Méré's, and his own experiences. He combined the negative outcomes of these experiences with an extreme Augustinianism, and thus developed, as it was his nature to do, the Christian idea described above into a tragic paradox of a most imposing and dangerous kind. On the basis of both rational analysis and his own experience, Pascal determines that the institutions, and indeed the entire progress of this world, are based on chance and caprice, and that our whole earthly order is nothing but madness (*folie*). He claims that he is serving faith when he proves that misery and injustice, arbitrariness and folly, are the very foundation of our life, and then goes on to argue that a Christian must obey these follies in the full and detailed awareness that they are follies, and that he must do so not because he respects them, but because he respects God's will. God's will subjected the human race to these follies in order both to punish mankind and to open up the road to salvation—even as He also makes that road more arduous. The foolish laws are thus the just laws—and the only ones we deserve. As far as I know, none of this can be contested dogmatically. Yet, there is an inappropriately heavy emphasis on certain points, and a presumptuous—or so it would seem to a Christian—introduction of insights based on reason that takes the logic to a point where faith, ruthlessly driven into the arms of paradox, almost necessarily transforms into its opposite. In French *folie* means both "folly" and "madness." I thus do no great violence to Pascal—and exaggerate only slightly—when I summarize his thoughts on this matter in the following way: The order of the world is one of madness and violence. A Christian must obey this madness and may not lift a finger to correct it, owing to the fact that madness and violence rule the world by God's will. This is the true justice that we deserve. The triumph of madness and violence, the triumph of evil on earth, is God's will. It is of course difficult to find many people who will live with this paradox and desire to remain Christian. But Pascal also says—in what is once again an overstatement that is nevertheless dogmatically speaking unimpeachable—that the Christian religion is the only religion that is contrary to nature and contrary to common sense (*la seule religion contre la nature, contre le sens commun*). In the eighteenth century Voltaire and others took these thoughts of Pascal's as their starting point for an enlightened polemic against Christianity. It is obvious how close this kind of reasoning is to Pascal's.[4]

At this point one might be inclined to conclude from all of this that the Christian who adheres to these views—to Pascal's ideas as well as to the more moderate stance of Port-Royal—would not be able to fight for justice and truth. This is not the case. Pascal himself did. He was the author of the *Provincial Letters*, one of the most important polemics in Christian literature, and for that matter in all of literature. The Christian may fight, indeed he must fight, as soon as he is convinced that it is not for his own cause that he fights, but rather for God's. The Church itself fought in its early years, and even the Church triumphant fought for the sake of truth against its enemies, both from without and within. But when can a Christian be sure that it is really the truth for which he is fighting? When, that is, can he be certain in the midst of this earthly darkness and confusion that God's Grace is with him and that God has chosen him as the instrument of His cause? In Pascal's favorite Psalm, the 118th, it is written: I am a sojourner on the earth: hide not thy commandments from me (*Incola sum in terra non abscondas a me mandata tua*). Pascal in fact gave us a document that addresses both the signs by which a Christian can be sure that he is fighting for God's cause and the conviction which he must have when he does so. This text deserves to be included, in my estimation, among the greatest of the great texts of Christian ethics. It consists in a fragment of a letter, first published by Faugère. The date and addressee are unknown, but it appears to have been written in 1661 and to have been directed to one of Pascal's fellows at Port-Royal during the controversy over the signing of the Formulary one year before Pascal's death.[5]

This letter begins with a criticism of the behavior of some of his comrades in arms. They are acting, he says (more or less), as if they were fighting on their own behalf and not in God's name. They seem to have forgotten that it is the same Providence that reveals truth to some and withholds it from others; they seem to believe that they serve some God other than the God who permits obstacles to be placed in truth's way. It is for this reason that they are dissatisfied and grumble about both the adversities that they confront and the victories of their enemies. This kind of behavior is the result of willfulness and conceit, Pascal explains. For when our self-centeredness leads us to desire something fervently, we are angered by anything that hinders us, because it represents something foreign, something that does not originate within and is not caused by us and that opposes our ends. But if it is really God who is acting through us, we will never experience any feelings of this

---

[4]See, for example, Voltaire's protest against Pascal's claim that we should love only God and not His creatures in letter 25 of the *Lettres Philosophiques*, or Chateaubriand in his commentary on Pascal, and Rousseau in his *Génie du Christianisme* (Part Three, Book 2, Chapter 6).

[5]Cf. Pascal, *Pensées et Opuscules*, 244–47.

sort, nothing that does not derive from the same principle as the one that determines our actions. There is then no such thing as foreign opposition to us, for the very same God who inspires us permits others to oppose us. It is thus not our spirit or intellect that fights against the intellect that stands outside and opposed to us. Rather, it is one and the same spirit, for it is God who both produces good and permits evil. Being aware of this fact bestows peace upon our soul, and this kind of inner peace is the surest sign that it is really God who is acting through us. That is, it is far more certain that God permits evil (as bad as that evil may be) than that He has chosen to do good through us—regardless of how important believing this is the case might seem to us. We must always fear that it is not God, but our own secret egotism that is directing what we do. Self-examination never produces clear results; in fact, it often deludes us. And so it is far safer to examine our outward conduct than our inner motivations. When we endure external obstacles with patience, this indicates that there is an identity in our souls between the one who is the source of our will to fight and the one who permits opposition to our struggle. And because there can be no doubt that it is God who permits this opposition, we may most humbly hope that it is also He who induces us to fight. Some individuals nevertheless act as if they were charged with assuring that truth will triumph rather than with understanding that our only mission is to fight for it. The desire for victory is all too natural and human. But when this natural desire conceals itself beneath the desire to secure truth's victory, it is easy to mistake the one for the other and to believe that we are fighting for the glory of God when in fact we are striving only for our own glory. Here again our behavior in the face of external obstacles and the successes of our opponents is the surest test. For, if we desire nothing other than to follow the will of God, we must be just as content when truth is defeated and remains hidden as when it triumphs and is revealed. In the latter case it is God's mercy that triumphs, in the former, His justice. Pascal concludes the entire reflection with a reference to St. Augustine, whose commentary on John 17:25 (O righteous Father, the world hath not known thee [*Pater juste, mundus te non cognovit*]) says that God's concealment is a product of His justice.

There are four main points that this text gives me a special opportunity to emphasize. First of all, it is very characteristic of Pascal—and this distinguishes him from most other mystically inclined thinkers and movements—to distrust his own inner feelings. He is so convinced that self-examination is unreliable and risks being falsified by self-love that he urgently warns the pious believer not to rely upon it exclusively. As I mentioned above, according to Pascal, when someone is deciding whether or not to enter a monastery, he ought not to heed his inner voice alone if important external circumstances speak against it. So here too, in the case of a far more significant and universal problem, one's own acute feeling about what it is right and good to do should not be considered the sole valid criterion. Only perfect peace of mind, based on Christian patience and humility, can prove that the good on whose behalf we think we are fighting really derives from God.

But what are patience and humility based on in this kind of situation? They are based on understanding that only God and nothing else, nothing foreign, permits obstacles to be placed in the path of the good. Nothing external that is capable of rattling us stands in our way. God's will alone determines the course of our struggle. And since our will must coincide with God's will, if we in fact champion what is good, our souls must be governed by the same peace of mind, patience, and harmony that derive from our knowledge that it is one and the same God who is the source of all good and who permits evil.

Here I must warn the reader of a possible misunderstanding: There is nothing relativist about Pascal's position, nothing that suggests that the Christian understands his adversary's point of view. It is not, Pascal argues, as if our opponent "is correct from his own point of view," or even that we must try and understand him. Christian understanding has nothing to do with one's opponent or his concerns at all. It concerns, rather, God alone. His plan for salvation permits there to be a constant series of obstacles placed in its way (e.g., the way of His plan), obstacles that are the result of Original Sin and its ruin of the world. As a result, God's cause on earth appears perpetually endangered and in a desperate situation. Those few who champion His cause are by their very nature just as corrupt as their opponents. It is only by the Grace of God that they are raised above this corruption. But even the possession of Grace is perpetually threatened and never secure.

A third important point is captured in Pascal's proposition that our charge is to fight, not to win. This proposition involves the obligation to fight regardless of the circumstances and with no concern as to whether the prospects for the outcome of the battle are good or not. Such an obligation makes terrible demands on those who fight, demands whose fulfillment goes far beyond what is normally expected of human nature. But anyone who succeeds in adopting this attitude is at least inwardly invincible, and, in the long run, it will also be only with great difficulty that he will be defeated in the real world. Experience teaches us that ordinary human courage fails at precisely that moment when the struggle seems hopeless, at least according to human judgment. But the person who knows for sure that he must fight regardless of the prospects for success is immune to despair and even more so to any kind of panic. And experience teaches us that many important victories have been wrested from a desperate situation—and that these victories have been achieved by people who refused to allow themselves to be defeated from within before they were overwhelmed from without.

Finally, a fourth point: Even if—indeed, especially when—truth is defeated and remains hidden, justice is preserved. For God's justice consists precisely in the fact that He hides the truth. When He lets it be known, He does so out of mercy, Grace, and love. This is a variation of the thought that

I already took the opportunity to develop above, namely, that to suffer injustice is the only justice that is fitting for the human race. From this it follows that in God's eyes there is no one on earth who suffers injustice, or (to put it more precisely) human beings can commit injustice, but can never suffer it. For even if the man who inflicts injustice on his neighbor is really committing an injustice, the neighbor who suffers that injustice is corrupt by virtue of Original Sin and thus deserves to suffer. This idea is absolutely Christian in its essence and its origin. Yet the paradox that one can commit an injustice but can never suffer injustice also has its place in a way of thinking that is not Christian in the strict sense—if, that is, we allow the phrase "original sin" to function as an index of the ways in which we are inextricably bound up in a web of what we have inherited, our historical situation, individual temperament, and the consequences of our individual actions, for it is in such a web that we find ourselves perpetually caught. Here it will be immediately objected that daily experience gives innumerable examples of people who do in fact suffer injustice. It is of course impossible to prove the opposite. We can only reply that, strictly speaking, an individual can examine only his own conscience and decide only for himself whether the injustice done to him was really done unjustly. If he can deny this question, this does not pardon or even justify the one who did him wrong, for the latter is not permitted to inflict anything on anyone, since he is not competent to judge that act's legitimacy and since the power to execute justice is in fact held by him only by proxy. Nor may the defensive position of the victim of injustice be weakened by recognizing the legitimacy of what he has suffered, for insofar as he has had justice done to him, it was tendered at a different level of authority than the one at which he received the injury.

The proposition that, in the sense that has just been described, a person can commit an injustice but cannot suffer one, seems to me to be valuable as a working hypothesis in the field of ethics. At least initially, ethics can only be a matter for the individual, which is to say a matter between me and my conscience. Anyone who succeeds in recognizing that everything that happens to him is just, regardless of the extent to which others were wrong to have inflected a wrong upon him, has not only established a foundation, it seems to me, for ethics in general and for his own individual ethical position, but has also discovered a new and enlightening way of understanding everything that happens in the world. But it is no easy matter to achieve and then maintain this theoretical insight as the basis for one's practical behavior.

Let us return to the fragment that appeared at the outset of this essay. The examination undertaken so far of the influences and many layers of experience that formed the context out of which Pascal's thought emerged was necessary so that we might appreciate the almost classical clarity with which he expressed it. His claim rests on an antithetically expressed juxtaposition of two concepts, whose meaning is taken to be universally understood and established. Yet the antithesis itself reveals that these terms are problematic. On the one hand, power and justice are juxtaposed. On the other, there is—at first—a refusal to define or delimit either term. But in the contest between the two, their true meaning eventually becomes clear, and we ultimately see that they are not opposites at all, but rather that the one is merely a function of the other. When we hear the following sequence: that it is just to obey what is right, that justice without power is without force, that power without justice gives grounds for complaint, and that there are always criminals who fight against what is just, we must assume that Pascal recognizes the existence of some kind of positive law that is different from power and that is—at least in theory—also independent of it. But when he goes on to state that justice is always a matter of debate, but that power is never disputed and is always immediately recognizable even in the absence of an adjudicating body—and this in the absence of any authority either competent or empowered to (even theoretically) decide objectively what true justice might actually be—and when he claims, moreover, that we are always at the mercy of the system of justice that currently prevails and that lies in the hands of those in power and that this system knows no bounds, then, at this very moment, we understand that Pascal was not thinking in the first proposition about any kind of objective or really-existing justice, but about a mere word, an *imagination*. "It is right that what is just should be obeyed." Of course. But is there any justice that exists independently of power? Can we recognize it? No, we certainly cannot. Are those who complain that they are oppressed by power without justice justified in their complaints? Certainly not, for how do we know that their complaints are just? Are those criminals who challenge a law that has no force objectively evil? Who can decide? "Justice is subject to dispute" (*La justice est sujette à dispute*). And what about the power that challenges justice and claims it is power itself that is just? Is the claim unjust? Certainly not. For by what mark can we identify beyond the shadow of a doubt what justice *is* other than that it is what currently rules? There is no justice other than the justice that lies in the hands of the powerful. Is power for this reason "justice"? Is power good? Yes, power is justice, but it is not good. It is evil. Our world is evil, but it is just that this is so. This final thought is of course no longer in the fragment we are considering here. But it can be supplied from other of Pascal's statements, since it provides the key to the whole. The fragment consists in the gradual revelation and clarification of the concepts of justice and power.[6] At first they seem to be in conflict. But one of the two contestants—power—needs only to show itself, needs only to appear in all of its recognizability and indisputability, and justice will stand down, yield its

---

[6] Alexander Rüstow has alerted me to the fact that the formulation "to create harmony between justice and might" is used by Solon in fragment 24.15–17. Plutarch cites this verse in his *Life of Solon*, and Jacques Amyot translated Plutarch. It is thus likely that Pascal was familiar with it.

autonomy without a fight, and submit to power and become its vassal. This is its proper place, at the side of power, and not opposed to it.

The present study of the influences and layers of experience that produced Pascal's thought allows us to understand it in depth and also grants us perfect insight into his masterful way of expressing it. When an idea is taken over, ready-made, merely because it is the coin of the realm and is present in the very air that we breathe—as was recently the case with a great number of ideas in the late nineteenth and early twentieth centuries—its expression usually becomes weak and inexact, since the effort demanded to achieve precision of expression is not considered necessary. A mere allusion, a slogan, a common phrase or two that indicate a certain way of thinking appear to suffice to allow matters to be understood. In such cases, when only one of the ideas in the air needs even to be mentioned to suggest what is meant, things are generally understood quite quickly—or at least there is a general sense of what is at stake. But when an idea is seized upon in the course of the struggles that constitute one's experience and this happens spontaneously and internally, it can become a complete and all-embracing expression that captures the insight perfectly. This expression in turn bars any confusion, any even partial deviation from an exact understanding, while at the same time also permitting many additional layers of deeper understanding. Sentences come into being that are at once so profound and so clear that any reader who aspires to express himself in equally as perfect a way will feel—in addition to admiration—something like envy.

Pascal's political ideas, described as we have described them here, are related to the ideas of other contemporary theorists in a number of respects. Out of the collapse of the medieval Christian foundations of political theory there had emerged two traditions of thought that appear in a variety of combinations and mixtures in those writers. Pascal has nothing in common with one of these traditions, namely the theory of natural law. Nor of course is his thinking in any way related to the older Catholic version of natural law developed by Thomism, for he did not accept the idea of a justice innate in all human beings—except perhaps in the Hobbesian version of natural law as the right of the stronger. But he is very close to the other tradition, the more empirical statecraft, or *raison d'état,* of absolutism, whose founder is taken to have been Machiavelli. Naturally this tradition had lost some of its novelty and wit since Machiavelli's time. His unencumbered elegance, in which Tuscan ingenuity played as much of a role as Humanistic boldness, had yielded in the course of time to juridical and pragmatic-political treatises, a primarily methodical but also often somewhat fantastic system of political rules based on ideas that one either accepted or rejected, but could scarcely love or despise. Pascal's thoughts are quite close to those of the theorists of *raison d'état,* and especially to those of his contemporary Thomas Hobbes. Hobbes too regards human nature as evil. To curb this nature, he likewise demands a strong state based on power, a state not bound by moral laws in the fulfillment of its duties, a state to which everyone owes absolute obedience since only this state can prevent revolution and guarantee peace. For Hobbes, as for Pascal, the laws of the state have no juridical basis other than the state's power. While we may owe them unconditional obedience, we are not obliged to believe in them internally. We owe the state certain sacrifices, but no inner devotion. Hobbes's construct is a security state, pure and simple. What this state must guarantee, in spite of all its apparatus of power, is, as has often been noted, the freedom or, better yet, the inviolability of the individual. Pascal comes very close to all of this. But because he is less concerned with the purely negative idea of the inviolability of the individual and more interested in the positive idea of the immortality of the soul, similar ideas take on an entirely different slant. He may emphasize, as Hobbes does, the necessity and legitimacy of a state based on power, but his theory provides a more profound insight into the nature of this presumptive legitimacy as evil. In Pascal, we nevertheless have not so much a mutual agreement between the state and the individual, which would entail that the individual owes the state obedience and a material sacrifice and that the state owes the individual peace and security, as the submission of the Christian to the evil of this world independent of whether that evil provides him with any compensatory benefit or not. For Pascal, the additional charge or, perhaps better, the natural function of power is to create and preserve peace; he cites Luke 11:21 by way of support. But even if the individual gains nothing in the process and suffers a relentless oppression that knows no peace, he must still show obedience. This goes far, far beyond Hobbes. Here Pascal reaches back well beyond the theoreticians of the Renaissance and Middle Ages to the thought of St. Augustine, while outbidding even him. Augustine taught that all government on earth, all power of one man over another, followed from Original Sin. Without the injustice of Original Sin, which destroyed the natural peace and equality of all men, we would not need the severe counter-injustice of power on earth. A Christian must obey this power, which is imposed upon him as penance, with patience and hope for future deliverance: *donec transeat iniquitas, et evacuetur omnis principatus et potestas humana, et sit Deus omnia in omnibus* [until all wickedness pass away and all lordship and human authority be done away with and God be all in all. Augustine, *The City of God*, William Chase Greene, trans. (Cambridge, MA: Harvard University Press, 1969), 190.] (Cf. *De civitate Dei* 19.15, with reference to Psalms 56:2 and 1 Corinthians 15:24). From this we may conclude that a Christian must also obey power when that power is evil. Augustine did not deal with this borderline case—and it was a borderline case for him—in any depth. When he condemns the power of the state as evil—and it is always the power of the Roman state—he does so because this state was or is pagan and therefore serves false gods. We can conclude from Augustine's chapter on the *pater familias* that in his mind a Christian state was perfectly capable of using its power to good ends, even though the power of one man over another was in and of itself, as an institution, an evil made necessary by Original Sin. But Pascal, who lived in the midst of a Christian system of states, lumped the two orders of evil together. For him, not only is power evil as an institution because of Original Sin, but it follows from this that anytime it is exercised, power will be nothing but foolish and unjust.

In order to arrive at this kind of exceptionally extreme conclusion, Pascal needed the pessimistic and nominalist ideas of the theorists of *raison d'état*. He combined them with Augustinianism[7] and created a system that, despite appearing to be a form of Christianity that has been driven to an extreme, nevertheless contains many secular elements—and even the germs of a revolutionary social criticism. The *raison d'état* theorists had almost all taught in more or less radical fashion—some with approval, others half in disgust—that the state could not adhere to moral laws if it really desired to fulfill its duties. Fraud and cunning, treason and violence were permitted this kind of state, they claimed. Its laws reached as far as its power and were based on it. Pascal adopted the same position. But these theorists were interested in the state for its own sake and valued it as such. Like Machiavelli, they took delight in the state's dynamism and vitality, or at least, like Hobbes, took a keen interest in the benefit that the state, if it were properly constructed, could bring to individuals living in the here-and-now. Pascal was completely indifferent to all of this. The internally dynamic life of the state did not exist for him. If it had existed, he would have considered it evil incarnate. He was not interested in the best form of the state, since he considered all of its forms equally bad. He combined the doctrine of *raison d'état* with Augustinianism and thereby arrived at the paradox of a pure and evil power that one must obey without demur, regardless of any possible benefit that such power might bring, but also without any devotion, or better yet, out of a devotion to God —in the way I have described here.

---

[7] In contrast to Pascal's having combined ideas derived from Montaigne and from Port-Royal, as mentioned above, his combination of *raison d'état* with Augustinianism was in all likelihood an unconscious one, since Pascal was barely familiar with the political theorists of his time, and in any case did not study them in any depth.

18

Racine and the Passions

For the first time since August Wilhelm Schlegel wrote his critique of *Phèdre*,[1] a German of considerable stature has stepped forward and dared to take on Racine.[2] Free of the German prejudice against French Classicism (almost a birthright, it seems), Karl Vossler both loves Racine more and understands him better than his predecessor. A sensibility for the human profundity of Classicism's very formal demeanor is for him completely intuitive. In Germany (and sometimes even in France), this demeanor often had the reputation of being insipid, only "gallant," and in any case unnatural and unpoetic. It is for this reason that Vossler's book represents an excellent, indeed, a unique introduction for anyone who is serious about understanding things French. Schlegel's book is by contrast no longer of any value in the world of Racine criticism, its biased polemic useful only insofar as it documents the fundamentally tense relationship that exists between how the two nations thought (and perhaps still think) about poetry.

For Vossler, there is no such tension. Following the best traditions of French criticism—and even surpassing them insofar as he omits anything that is at all problematic in terms of the work and life of this remarkable, but opaque man—Vossler instead sees a quiet modesty and deep wisdom in Racine and sums up the playwright's essential characteristics in the claim that Racine renounced all earthly concerns in favor of the world Beyond. He links Racine's partiality to the Jansenist teaching of election through Grace to the doctrine of Fate espoused by the ancient Greeks, seeing in this combination the revival of that great tradition of tragedy that the Middle Ages, with its adherence to the inflexible architecture of Catholic dogma, had marginalized because of its unambiguous and unproblematic positioning of man vis-à-vis the powers above. In short, Vossler sees Jansenism as a kind of Protestant attempt to free man from his conscience and to promote him to the posi-

---

[1] *Comparison des deux Phèdres* in *Oeuvres écrites en français* 2 (Leipzig 1846) 333ff.
[2] Karl Vossler, *Jean Racine* (Munich 1926) (= *Epochen der französischen Literatur* 3.2).

tion of being his own judge and thus considers Racine to be *the* great poet of this kind of humane Protestant stance. There would be no sense in arguing that Vossler overlooks what speaks against such a reading; he simply considers such objections beside the point. *Andromaque* is a "sacred hymn," he maintains, *Bérénice* the expression of a "Protestant" interiority reminiscent of Iphigenia, *Phèdre* a drama about penance, with its title character driven by her desire for a pure heart (even the death of Ériphile in *Iphigénie* seems to Vossler to be about penance), and *Athalie* a powerfully humane tragedy of fate.

Vossler explains the lack of sympathy for Racine among the Germans as a matter of the playwright's language and form and points to the indisputable illiteracy of contemporary taste in Germany in this respect. As an antidote, he recommends a way of accustoming one's ear to the perfection of Racine's language that is based on sense perception. One ought to allow the verses to wash over oneself again and again, he writes, and learn them by heart "until they become intuitive to us, whispering to us in our very hearts, allowing us to give ourselves up to them freely and easily."[3] This is an excellent suggestion, and the method will prove its merit—as will that section of Vossler's book that deals with the aesthetic and poetic magnificence of Racine's *oeuvre*—for anyone who might be inclined for any reason whatsoever to turn to Racine. It is, moreover, an approach that will be of value for anyone who finds that his own inability to understand this great poet signals an embarrassing lack of education, one that he would like to amend. Yet, we might in general be permitted to observe—only, of course, to the ever smaller community of people for whom the legacy of the great European literary tradition is still alive— that the senses spring into action on their own, so to speak, whenever the mind discovers something dynamic upon which it can feast. And if Vossler sets Racine alongside Dante, Milton, and Goethe, it is nearly impossible to understand why, even in the best of times in Germany, the French playwright met only with indifference, indeed with rejection, on the part of those who were among the most important adjudicators of such things. For it was not only the Storm and Stress movement or only Romanticism that objected to Racine. No. Even Schiller, shortly before his death, expressed his aversion to Racine in a letter to Goethe. Goethe's silence, his failure to respond when he was already well along in his 50s, was deafening; he offered no objection to Schiller's judgment, not even any sort of moderating reply.[4]

Another book about Racine, this one by a French scholar, appeared at nearly the same time as Vossler's. Its author is Gonzague Truc, a well-respected critic with a well-deserved reputation, who is known for his predis-

---

[3] Ibid. 60.
[4] Schiller to Goethe, January 17, 1804 (cf. also the letter of May 31, 1799).

position to react in a classicizing way (naturally in the French sense of the term).[5] Already several years ago, Truc published a series of essays that dealt with Racine from a biographical and psychological point of view.[6] His work represents a more measured approach when compared with that of Masson-Forestier, whose ill-considered and somewhat tempestuous book celebrated Racine as a "beautiful monster."[7] In Truc's book, we get a comprehensive picture: the *oeuvre*, the poet, the man, and his times. It is interesting that he finds more reason than Vossler to defend Racine against contemporary taste, and, in so doing, provides an excellent juxtaposition of classicizing French versus modern methods of psychological representation in literature.[8] The latter consists, he writes, in descriptive analysis, the former, in a concentrated extract of life. He even goes so far as to make the claim (with which I think I agree) that when one compares Hermione, Doña Sol (*Hernani*), Mme. Bovary, and any heroine in the works of Paul Bourget, only Hermione can be said to be truly alive. "The others, when they are either saying their lines or describing or analyzing themselves, remain merely literary, which is to say 'scientific,' if you will."[9]

From where I stand, it is difficult to judge whether these kinds of polemics are really still necessary in a nation whose most important figures speak of Racine with love and admiration,[10] and whose entire structural formality and ways of expressing themselves in the way they live appear—to the foreigner at least—still strongly shaped by an essentially Racinian sensibility. One might be better off challenging some of the critical trends characteristic of the nineteenth (rather than the twentieth) century. In any case, the tribute that Truc pays to Racine is understandably dedicated to praising him as the poet of the passions. He considers Racine the classical master in this domain, equaled by none of his successors; even among the giants of Classicism, he is the one who depicts the passions at their most horrifying and destructive. "Bossuet exposed the full depth and the nuances of the problem of fate, and considered it resolved. No one went as far as Molière in giving us a portrait of manners, and La Fontaine lay hold of nature in all her simplicity. Corneille extolled the lofty virtues. But Racine clung to that part of life that, trembling and uncertain, casts its shadow on life and, under the pretext of providing reassurance, jeopardized it, perhaps forever. He erected a complete and moving image of love

---

[5] G. Truc, *Jean Racine* (Paris: Librarie Garnier Frères, 1926).

[6] "Le cas Racine" [The Case of Racine] in *Revue d'histoire littéraire de la France* (1910, 1911, 1912); these essays have also appeared in book form.

[7] F. Masson-Forestier, *Autour d'un Racine inconnu* [Concerning the Unknown Racine] (Paris 1911).

[8] Truc (n. 5) 287.

[9] Ibid. 273.

[10] One thinks of Gide or Proust, for example.

in such a way that it only took juxtaposing it to the reality of some kind of intimate experience to apprehend its horrific truth."[11]

I quote this passage word for word here because it seems to me to capture a universal assessment of Racine, one that has persisted for generations among the French. It is an assessment that, *contra* Vossler, I would like to endorse. Like Vossler, Gonzague Truc praises Racine's humanity. But the humanity of which Truc is thinking is one saturated—both by nature and through experience—with the human passions. It is in no way to be mistaken either for asceticism or for a humane greatness of soul beyond all passion. Such thoughts did not even occur to Truc when he was forced to become involved in a polemic against Masson-Forestier's exaggerated claims that Racine was a kind of stunning but villainous beast. The extraordinarily passionate nature of Racine's tragedies was, for Truc, so indisputable that he considered the alleged innocence of the playwright's youth and the pious dignity of his old age to be nothing but an enigma for which there was no explanation. How could such a man have produced such plays? Since then, however, this conundrum has become less baffling for Truc; one can understand the character of the man Racine and his work together, without falling into Masson-Forestier's fairly rudimentary categories.

Gonzague Truc considers Racine so radical and so modern in his devotion to the passions that he takes this devotion to be the explanation for the superficiality of the critique aimed at him by both his contemporaries and by the eighteenth century. Indeed, we have only been able to understand Racine, Truc maintains, since Rousseau opened our eyes to the depths of the human mind and soul in a more general way. This is entirely correct—with the slight modification that each and every audience—and Racine was already working for an audience—has its own way of considering art as autonomous, designed to serve as entertainment. Its charge is, accordingly, to push aside in art anything that might be burdensome, and thus (as Rousseau also thought) to transform any intellectual insight that might be gained from art into a new and more complex kind of pleasure. But if anything is clear to me, it is this: Racine's contemporaries did not understand the compass of his work in the least. Only the Jansenists, when they were his adversaries, seem to me to have gauged him correctly. And the fact that this was the case provides me with the opportunity to offer a few observations that suggested themselves to me as I read Racine.

At the beginning of his career, after Racine had abandoned the Jansenists who had brought him up, Pierre de Nicole wrote a pamphlet against a poet by the name of Desmarets de Saint-Sorlin. Racine thought that it was directed partially against him, and in the two letters that he took the occasion

---

[11] Truc (n. 5) 280.

to write,[12] he responded and displayed the elegant and pointed spitefulness of his youth in its full glory. Some memorable phrases were uttered at the time—by the other side, of course—about this public row: "The maker of novels and the poet who struts the boards," Nicole wrote, "uses poison to murder his audience; his brew strikes not the bodies of his supporters, however. Rather, it poisons their souls. He must thus regard himself as guilty of inestimable numbers of spiritual deaths, which he either caused *de facto* or could have caused with his pernicious writings. The more that he has taken care to shroud the criminal passions that he depicts there in a cloak of decency, the more dangerous he makes them, investing them with the power to take simple and innocent souls by surprise and then corrupt them."[13] Goibaud du Bois wrote even more explicitly (and Racine responded to him as well): "Since, in the end, as everyone knows, the spirit of Christianity acts only to extinguish the passions and because the spirit of the theater labors only to inflame them, if it happens that someone remarks in somewhat coarse fashion that these two spirits—Christianity and the theater—are at odds with one another, it is surely better for the playwrights to say nothing at all so as to prevent themselves from entering into the debate. . . ."[14]

Of this situation Gonzague Truc writes: "Racine belonged to a time when one's conduct was based on the belief that one had to devote oneself entirely to the *querelle* between morality and the theater. This is a debate into which we will never be able to be drawn or be exercised by to the same extent."[15] Yes, of course. But this ought not to prevent us from trying. We might yet succeed in grasping the full sense of these words.

In documents such as these we have some of the first evidence of the struggle between Christianity and secular art, a struggle that is still ongoing today. Up until this point the Church had waged war against either heretics or its political foes. Worldliness as such was not the enemy; it kept to itself, and any messy disturbances that the life of the instincts might produce did not threaten the stability of Christianity in any fundamental way. But here things are different. For the ancient Greeks—as for Shakespeare—earthly desire was natural, either an agreeable or a terrible gift from the gods, but always part of man's earthly fate. The Christian Middle Ages had fought against it, considering desire evil and absolutely base. But now desire had acquired the higher status of an independent, fundamental, and autonomous part of the soul and was even considered admirable and sublime. As such, it threatened to displace Christianity and any other form of pious humility and to substitute for them a kind of metaphysics of the passions. We might do well to recall here

---

[12] In the *Lettres à l'auteur des Hérésies Imaginaires* [Letters to the Author of The Imaginary Heresies].

[13] Cited after Menard's edition of Racine (in the *Grands écrivains* series), 4:258.

[14] Ibid. 292.

[15] Truc (n. 5) 47.

that in the case of erotic passion, this ennoblement was originally due to its connection with the cult of Mary and the tradition of divine courtly love favored by the mystics. The cult of femininity in Europe likewise had its roots in the blending of the chivalric character with the idea of redemption. In the French seventeenth century, however, erotic passion and the cult of femininity freed themselves from such tethers and filled people's minds as both matters of fact and as fantasy images. The audience emerged as an entirely new sociological category, consisting of those who had risen out of the ranks of the commoners (the *Volk*) due not to the nobility of their spirit or blood, but, rather, on the material basis that created the same living conditions and habits for all. This audience of readers and theater-goers saw that, in both novels and on stage, a great earthly passion was a reward, a mark of the most noble and sublime humanity. This allowed the upper echelons of the feudal order to distance themselves from the *Volk* in a much more pronounced and final way than they had before. The *Volk* was bound by its workaday labor and problems to the natural sources of life and so considered its own desires to be concrete, something it was due, and, at times, even poetic (as when, for example, the normal course of events was disrupted by tragic circumstances). But the *Volk* never considered desires to be sublime in and of themselves and, as such, an occasion for rigorous self-examination.

I am speaking here not merely about love. Rather, my subject is the worldly desires in general, as well as an entirely new kind of autonomy and hypertrophy, or enlargement, of the human personality. We see already in the plays of Corneille (not to speak of novels in general) that virtue has become entirely too heroic and so full of pathos that it no longer fits neatly into the frame of a Christian state of mind (or, indeed, into any kind of pious thinking). Racine then devotes all of his energies to expanding and developing the worldly personality to its very highest point of efflorescence, even as he at the same time plumbs it in far greater depth and in a much more tangible way than anyone who came before.

Indeed, how else might we characterize the essence and aspirations of Racine's characters than as a kind of cult of the passions, as the development and sublimation of the instincts, or—to use one of Vossler's terms—as a kind of *Machtpolitik* in the struggle between their hearts and minds? Racine went far beyond the line at which passion stops when its business is to provide a pleasant diversion. It has only been his long-standing reputation that, together with the dulling of the senses that is the result of reading his plays in school, has gradually caused his impact to fade. The human beings who are his characters are possessed of enormous vitality, most of them poised on the dangerous precipice between passion and death. Even his women characters disdain the paltry good of mere life when it is a question of their instincts. *Andromaque* is no pious hymn. It is, rather, a ferocious clash of the passions. Its heroine is no noble soul in the mold of Goethe's Iphigenia. No, she is

Priam's daughter and Hector's widow, a prisoner of Pyrrhus, who, together
with his father, is the cause of all her sorrow. She holds fast to her dignity and to
the honor and integrity of her past with all the strength of a mighty spirit and
follows a naturally conservative feminine instinct as regards the drives, even
as new feelings already stir in her heart. (It was only on the advice of friends
that Racine dropped the scene in which she reveals her love over the corpse
of Pyrrhus). That she wants to die and declares as much in gentle words is not
evidence of a "Protestant greatness of heart," but, rather, evidence of her canniness and readiness to adapt after making a rash decision. The very last thing
we hear of her after Pyrrhus's unexpected and violent death at her side reveals
that she has immediately recovered from her own readiness to die and, unbroken and unperturbed, is prepared to take advantage of the more favorable
circumstances that have now presented themselves. In *Bérénice*, the emphasis is not on heroic self-denial on the part of the queen, but, rather, entirely
on the torment of her passion that, in its infinite sophistication and formal
poetic perfection, reveals all the more powerfully its omnipotence and transcendent *dignitas*. Truc is quite correct to say that the play is "Corneilleian
by accident," that Racine would have preferred a tragic resolution (which his
source in Suetonius did not allow), and that death is merely postponed: " . . .
this suffering, of which one catches a glimpse and which is where one enters,
this already imminent death (which is delayed only that it may become more
exquisite), and this regret torn from a supreme joy snatched away at the very
moment when the lips touch, together constitute sufficiently 'tragic impressions' and cast [the spectator] quite deeply into the 'magnificent sadness' that,
according to Louis Racine, 'constitutes tragedy's greatest pleasure.'"[16] How
typical this talk of "magnificent sadness" is! In *Phèdre*, the queen's purity of
heart and the entire architecture of her self-reproach in the end serve only to
highlight the violence of her desires. For what is her misfortune other than
the fact that both Phèdre herself and the audience must take her mad passion
for Hippolyte in a tragically sublime way? "It is all just so much foolishness,"
Vossler writes. "Hippolyte is not her son and Theseus is thought to be dead.
While this all may be in bad taste, it is not incest and, apparently at least, also
not even adultery. Hippolyte nevertheless does not react to her declarations
of love in any way, and so she really ought to have put it out of her mind, all
the more so, since the young man apparently has other interests."[17] This is
Vossler's very polite—and very German—way of expressing the matter, and
with it, he has hit upon its very heart. The entire tragedy of the play depends
on one's belief in the insurmountability, indeed in the finality and virtually
transcendent solemnity of the life of desire. There is no mention of real penance here; even as she dies, Phèdre regrets that she was not able to commit

[16] Truc (n. 5 above) 82.
[17] Vossler (n. 2 above) 121.

the sin (Truc 115ff). Although Racine certainly would have had Jansenist teachings in mind as he wrote this play, he used them only as a kind of foil to heighten the impact of the opposite point of view. I cannot of course prove any of this conclusively. In the end, it is just something which one feels. Yet—and this is to our advantage—this feeling is shared by many, for the oceans of tears that have flowed in French theaters for Racine's heroes were spilled for the sake of passion, not self-denial. Indeed, what would actors from Mont-fleury to Mounet-Sully, from Champmeslé to Rachel and Sarah Bernhardt have said, had it been announced to them that Racine's tragedies, so long the measure of an actor's fame, took the renunciation of the worldly domain for the sake of the Beyond as their theme?

There is not room here to go into the details of the other plays. It would in any case be child's play to do so. Only *Athalie* deserves a few more words. Here, Racine has changed not the core theme itself, but, rather, his way of handling it. *Athalie* is neither a Christian drama nor even a human one. Rather, it is a fierce clash of instinctual forces. Displaying not even a trace of the traditions of a living essence of Christianity, the play is based on a horrific chapter of the Old Testament that has been dragged out of its dark corner into the light, a chapter that becomes no more humane because one of the parties to the struggle is in the right. In *Athalie*, God is Lord not because he is good, but because he is sovereign. There is no redemptive moment. Even in defeat, a vanquished Athalie rebels and asserts herself in the most radical of un-Christian, indeed, simply inhuman ways. It is for this reason that this tragedy does not mean anything to us in terms of the issues in the history of philosophy that we might think most germane to it. For if it did, the hero would have to submit to death, acknowledging either God or Fate as all-powerful. This power is, however, not merely external; it cannot be proven by fire and sword. Rather, it must reign triumphant in his heart. But *Athalie* is a masterpiece all the same, and Racine's masterpiece in particular. The instincts that are alive in it are, in spite of the elegantly simple psychology of the play, far in excess in both kind and degree of anything in which the audience for whom Racine wrote could have been interested. It is thus a unique and nearly incomprehensible testimony to the power of his poetic character that Racine could—so sparely, so sternly, and so independently of any merely external means—create a play that had such an effect. He brought to life—around 1700 and in France—the full horror of a primitive tribal battle. The dreadful, muffled sounds of the all-powerful and blood-thirsty demiurgic character that steers events in any way it sees fit are not muted by the pure and measured propriety of the diction. The play is not Christian, for its theme is not Christian. Nor is it human, for we Europeans, as humans, believe in a deeper, more personal, and more intimate relation to our fate. *Athalie* remains an unusual fruit of an unusual time. Yet it also grew beyond that time into something not only timeless, but quite alien to the very notion of time—precisely because its abundance of timeliness unhinged it from time and caused it to be transformed, paradoxically, into its very opposite, so that now it never finds any echo, any way of getting under our skin.

For Racine, justice—either divine or earthly—was in fact never the issue, even though he may himself have believed it was. He harbored superficial judgments in this respect; reading the preface to *Phèdre* introduces us to them. There, already caught in the toils of a return to the pious life, he speaks of the virtues and the vices and the ways in which he deals with them in his plays. It seems almost to make a mockery of the issue when he claims that, in the plays, virtue can finally be seen correctly; there, he writes, even the most minor of sins receives its just desert. Hippolyte, for example, for all his innocence (he does not even commit sacrilege in the temple of Diana, as is the case in Euripides) is destroyed in a horrendous way and with no reconciliation. Theseus, so horribly blinded, stands unbroken at the end, with enough composure remaining to him that he is able to pronounce the measured words of a king. Vossler notes that Racine uses the word *expier* (to atone) here, and he is correct. But the feelings that Theseus must be having at this moment (at least according to our sensibilities) would demand a formulation other than the one that Racine used, one that he would have been able to muster, had he so desired. But this was not his concern here. Theseus was no longer of any interest to him, he was no longer important. Thus, the king's last words, while respectable, are only just barely so here as their sound fades away.

Racine was interested in entirely different matters, and his poetic impulse derives from an entirely different sphere as well. It consists, it seems to me, in a new and unique feeling for the essence of the human personality. This feeling had been in preparation for a long time, to be sure, but here it achieves its highest expression, in both sensuous and intellectual terms, developing, however, even beyond this into an almost paradoxically, even hopelessly exaggerated form of itself. Before him, Corneille had already produced figures with a very powerful sense of themselves. But he represented the reasons for this self-esteem as primarily ethical and rational in nature. Racine found the source of this kind of individual strength deeply embedded instead in the instincts. His characters have a pronounced and even vaguely covetous sense of their own personal worth and integrity. What this does not amount to, however, is actually a sense of human dignity in general. Nor is it a matter of objective pride based on tradition or actual achievements that have met with success, for the concept of *gloire* is not in play here. It is not enough, that is, to think of the individuality of Racine's figures as associated with any hollow feeling for the abstract position or rank that they might occupy as a king, princess, or hero. Rather, their dignity and sense of self are grounded in their powerful vitality and in the uninterrupted continuity of their instinctual lives. Even the more reserved female characters, such as Bérénice, Monime, Iphigénie, and Esther, draw for their purity, it seems to me, on a very strong sense of confidence in themselves as embodied human beings. Their intelligence and propriety, their modesty and feminine mystery, all make a sensual impact in the most startling way.

The fact that Racine's figures enjoy a sensuous individuality that is so hypertrophic, so greatly developed, is all the more astounding—and difficult to understand—given that they are represented not by means of special characteristics that mark their unique appearance, but, rather, in entirely typical ways. In a sense, they acquire their character only as the result of the dramatic situation in which they find themselves. Moreover, it is not just their earthly character that remains obscure. No, it is their entirely earthly existence. As opposed to the characters of Greek tragedy, such as Oedipus, who is not just a figural allegory of a king, but visibly behaves in a kingly fashion, it is utterly impossible to imagine Racine's figures involved in even the daily activities that would be appropriate to their position. When such things are mentioned, it is only in the most general and abstract way. The stylistic demands of the age were of course largely responsible for this, but the practice is for all that no less characteristic. All of Racine's characters maintain a kind of unearthly and irreal remoteness; they never go about their daily business or undertake quotidian tasks. They are figural, empty vessels for passions and instincts that have become autonomous. Freed from the shackles of the day-to-day world and not bound to any transcendent sphere, they pursue even the life of their desires in a way that is beyond the here-and-now, their acts tempered only through the formal decency of their upbringing.

We cannot permit ourselves to go into any more depth here about the origins of this kind of emotional life or the impact that it had. We can especially not go into the religious trend that, although opposed to it, was closely related in terms of its internal structure. But the following may nevertheless be said: Racine remained without heirs. This was necessarily the case. Even though his idealization of passion as autonomous reappeared in the novel only in an extremely diluted form, his *oeuvre* did have a significant impact on that genre, as Brunetière already knew. But here too other trends also arose that, while reinforcing that impact, also intercepted and reshaped it, gradually erasing the traces it had left behind. Racine has been misunderstood and despised in Germany ever since our national system of education was founded; for better or for worse, he remains alien to us. For we did not experience any Absolutist age, any century of a Louis the Fourteenth, and we did not have, in our society, a class that, having been liberated from daily routines, was free to both depict and enjoy its desires. Indeed, our occasionally petty bourgeois and occasionally holier-than-thou humility resists this kind of formalistic authoritarianism, under whose regime life has no other purpose than the pursuit of the passions.

19

On Rousseau's Place in History

It seems to me that Rousseau's life and work have been sufficiently researched and also that the polemics about how to interpret him are scarcely productive any more. It is true that we are now confronted with a Rousseau who can be understood in various and contradictory ways, and also that there has been a great deal said about him that misses the mark—some of it by biased critics of his own day, some of it by scholars whose analyses go much too far. But the essential details are both well known and well digested. My contribution to the topic will thus consist not in undertaking any new analysis of those aspects that are the obvious ones when we consider the figure of Rousseau *per se*. Indeed, I am not actually offering a new interpretation at all. Rather, what I propose is a particular way of formulating what actually appears to me to be the opinion that is generally held of him. I do so with the intention of inserting Rousseau into the course of European history over the long term. My aim is thus to position him more precisely in his historical location, while at the same time giving him a larger stage. This formulation takes the following form:

Of the men who are well known in European intellectual history, Rousseau is the first who, despite a thoroughly Christian constitution, was no longer able to be a Christian.

This thesis contains three claims: first, that Rousseau was constitutionally Christian, a Christian *in potentia*, one might say; second, that he was unable to realize this potential Christian religiosity in the here-and-now; and third, that he was the first, as far as we know, to have been beset by this fate. The explanation of these three claims that I would like to give will be brief, since I can assume that his life and work are well known; anything that has to do with them will thus be referenced only in passing. My only reason for explicating these claims—and thus my thesis itself—is so that what I have in mind will not be misunderstood. There is in fact no real need for me to prove my thesis if my assumption is correct that I am merely formulating in a specific way a view that is already generally held.

What I mean by constitutional or potential Christian religiosity can probably be best determined by looking to what it is not. In France during the years that Rousseau lived, we find people who were quite obviously non-Christian for the first time. They felt secure in their lives, which they tried to organize comfortably and cozily according to rules based on reason. They did so not only on their own behalf, but also for the sake of others. Theirs was not a matter of work-a-day altruism, however. Rather, they lived this way because it was socially expedient to do so and because they aspired thereby to improve the world and, in the end, to perfect it. No longer considering themselves marked by Original Sin, the people of this era also no longer considered the world intrinsically evil. Their hopes for the future were thus no longer directed at being delivered from sin or at attaining the good in the Beyond, but rather at living a well-ordered life in the here-and-now. Reason would defeat men's prejudices, and the kinds of knowledge acquired through experience and applied in a systematic way would overcome any obstacles placed in their way by nature. The human intellect would one day perfect the earthly world. Thus, while everything was still subject to error, in principle everything could be set right. If there was any pessimism, it had only to do with the fact that this goal seemed both endlessly far off in terms of time and impossible to reach without difficulty. But in principle it could be reached. Of course anyone who thought this way also believed that both he himself and those who shared his convictions were well on the way to attaining this end.

For the Christian, on the other hand, this world was fallen and essentially evil, with no access to the good and no way of achieving the good on its own. Christians thus saw themselves as sinners. Any good works that they did undertake were undertaken not out of their own free will and were in any case ineffectual in the world. Good works, they reasoned, found their origins, rather, in God's Grace, and served only to reveal this Grace and thus to mark those who undertook them as worthy of salvation—to the extent that it is possible to imagine or prove such worthiness on earth. Moreover, Christians lived their lives on earth full of disquietude and uncertainty. One's condition here is temporary, partial, dimly perceived; fulfillment takes place only in the Beyond. And yet, the here-and-now is also the testing ground for eternity, the place where an irrevocable decision about eternity—the dramatic decision about whether one will ultimately be saved or condemned—is made only once. It is for this reason that de-Christianization drains all the drama out of the events of this world, which now become no more than the earthly course of events that unfolds in a less earnest, less anxious, and more natural way—or at least so it seemed at first. It would be a grave mistake to believe that the life of Enlightenment man in this world initially meant nothing more than a greater and more binding attachment to earthly existence. The elimination of the world Beyond meant that its opposite, this world, lost much of its potency as well. The century of the Enlightenment was not just spiritually impoverished, then. It was also poor in inner-worldly sensuousness, hence superficial in the strictest sense of the word.[1]

One can of course detect traces of a Christian way of life even in the some of the most famous figures of the Enlightenment. In the foolishness of his arguments against the fossils he found in the Alps, for example, Voltaire displays a sort of nervous anxiety that the Flood could actually have occurred. His hatred of the Jews, so out of place in the Enlightenment way of thinking, can perhaps be best explained against the background of his fear of the famous argument of Christian apologetics: What he abhorred in the accursed people was that they were living witnesses to Christendom. Such atavisms are astounding in a man like Voltaire. But they are atavisms nevertheless. They had neither any fundamental impact on, nor did they change his character, which as a result remained a character that corresponded in all of its phases and variations to the image of the non-Christian sketched above.

With Rousseau, things are entirely different. Christian religiosity penetrated into the very marrow of his bones. He was insecure in the world, restless and full of fear. His predisposition to self-contempt and self-humiliation is strongly reminiscent of the Christian sinner's remorse. The enlightened, well-ordered, and comfortable world in which the *philosophes* moved struck him as fundamentally evil, as evil as the world itself.

Rousseau's insecurity in the world can be explained well enough by associating it with sociological and psychological causes, thus obviating the need for a religious explanation, or better, allowing us to consider any motives that may have emerged from a Christian sensibility as secondary manifestations with sociological and psychological roots. He was poor and came from a déclassé family; the chaos of his youth, which was at once material and moral, only intensified his situation as a social pariah. He had only irregular schooling; the little that his genius needed to be nurtured he procured on his own in an entirely unmethodical way. His mastery of the outward forms of social life was imperfect. He was possessed by a pathological need to be recognized and suffered from sexual abnormalities. Yet, for all this, his successes as a writer and as a personality allowed him to gain entry into a society that was unsurpassed in world history for its self-confident way of life and the integrated nature of its forms. Even its disorder was formal and orderly. It is no wonder that the situation in which Rousseau found himself in that world was peculiar. He felt uncomfortable, behaved indecisively, and was conspicuous and difficult to tolerate in public. The consequences of his behavior ensnared him ever more deeply in the world until his self-contempt and insecurity turned into peevish hostility to it, accompanied by delusions of grandeur. Little by little he was overcome by mental illness, the symptoms

---

[1]"Inner-worldly" (*innerweltlich*) is a term most famously used by Max Weber to denote the world of facticity, of the here-and-now, in which men live and work. —Trans.

of which had already been apparent early on. But he never surrendered completely to it. Could one not call this a clinical case, as it were, like those so often observed by psychiatrists (whereby we would still also have to inquire after the role of hereditary causes)? Are we really justified in speaking of it as a matter of "potential Christian religiosity" rather than as an inferiority or persecution complex?

We most certainly are justified. Methodological considerations alone justify doing so, for, like all genuine methodology, such considerations go right to the heart of the matter. Rousseau is a permanent figure in the intellectual history of the world and such permanence can never be explained in sociological or psychological terms. Indeed, any attempt to understand him only psychologically would remove him from the context in which he is universally understood and in which he deserves to be understood, namely, that of intellectual history, and would place him in another context, namely, that of a man afflicted by a certain neurological condition. He assuredly belongs in this latter category. But it is one in which only the psychiatrist sees him and in which he loses the interest that, as Jean-Jacques Rousseau, he aroused. Doubtless he did suffer from a psychological condition, and an astonishing number of people have continued to suffer from it—or from something quite similar. But does this mean that he belongs to their ranks in terms of intellectual history? Perhaps. Perhaps the frequency of this neurological condition, this pathological uncertainty about one's life, can be explained, in other words, by the general crisis of Christianity that still persists today. But only insofar as this is the case—and this is an issue I will not explore here—does Rousseau belong to the ranks of those with this illness or pathology, or perhaps better, they to him. If not, then Rousseau's individuality is not adequately addressed merely via psychological or psychiatric categorization—for such categories ultimately work only *ex negativo* and never tell us anything about the particular intellectual form that these preexisting psychological factors took on when they realized themselves historically in him as a particular person and in him alone. Such a categorization also reveals nothing to us about his historical location or about his relation to other historical figures and to history overall. To place him within this historical topology we must illuminate contexts that are purely intellectual, contexts that are in principle independent of the contingent and existential factors that either enabled or hindered a specific intellectual outcome in this or that individual. Such outcomes can be very different in individuals with the same or a similar intellectual profile.

In terms of the historical aggregate that we are considering here, within European intellectual history, that is, uncertainty in the earthly world is a Christian motif. It becomes especially pronounced in the epochs that are crucial for Christianity, namely those during which large groups of people live out their lives in a safely and peacefully un-Christian way. In times like these, uncertainty becomes a matter of excruciating disquiet in those who are disposed to being Christian. They are stunned, incapable of understanding the serenity that those in their immediate environs seem to feel. We have only to recall the example of Pascal. But for Rousseau it was a great deal more difficult, for he had no Jansenist community of companions to stand by him. In the borderlands between religious confessions, between Calvinist Geneva and Madame de Warens (who was a Catholic), his insecurity became amorphous and then spread uncontrollably. The religious confessions as he had been introduced to them no longer compelled belief. Had they done so, he would without a doubt have been able to find his way. But he was never able to come to terms with the prevailing sense of security that his fellow men felt. He remained forever tormented by it and continually sought to be free from the pain it caused him.

He was also never able to resign himself to being who he was. He considered himself a sinner, though not necessarily as an individual who was good or evil, and also not as someone who occasionally engaged in wicked behavior either by mistake or out of reasonable self-interest. No, he was a sinner, a person who, even as he passionately desired to do good, also bore within himself an inexplicably evil part. He always sought to rid himself of this evil—but in vain. The mad aberrations by which he was beset were only outdone by a kind of self-torment previously unknown. Modernity's greatest and most human teacher of men allowed his own children to go to the dogs, for example. The man regarded—not entirely without justification—as the noblest soul of the century took as his partner a woman who was meanspirited and fatuous in a most inferior way, and he believed whatever ridiculous gossip she or anyone else passed on to him. Moreover, he rewarded every act of kindness shown to him with ingratitude and hatred. These and much else are contradictions that in their madness exemplify, as it were, the image of a Christian sinner who falls, then picks himself up, and then falls again. The image he presents of himself borrows its title from the *Confessions* of St. Augustine and takes this cycle as its subject. In doing so, it creates a concept of man that, in the distance between its two extremes, is a familiar one in Christian ethics, but one that was alien to Rousseau's de-Christianized contemporaries: for unknown reasons, often without purpose and in unmotivated ways, one's acts eventuate in either goodness or depravity—the riddle of their origin remains eternally unsolvable and unsolved.

To Rousseau, the world appeared not just occasionally imperfect, then, but fundamentally evil. Here he was completely at odds with the belief in progress that characterized his age. His hatred of civilization was an only partially secularized theory of original sin. The world is corrupt, its original purity spent for all eternity; it has lost something that can never be found again. Rousseau never hoped to regain this purity by adhering to the disciplinary measures for which he called, and he protested fiercely against those critics who accused him of proposing as much, even to the very end of his life.

And yet his detractors were not entirely wrong. Large sections of his writings can be read as Enlightenment texts—at least in the effects they had. They can be made to yield a system of rules to follow in one's earthly life in the hope of reaching perfection in this world. For he failed to find the path that had stood open to men like him for so many centuries. This was Christology, which reflects back to fallen man the image of the fallen men who live in a fallen world and offers the hope of salvation. This did not appeal to Rousseau. Pascal had still been able to commit to this vision, albeit not without paroxysms of anguish. But for Rousseau, Christian faith hardly even presented a dilemma anymore. What had once been living nourishment was now, for him, a dead letter. He saw in Christendom nothing more than dogma, too confining for an anguished soul, not worthy of a noble mind. A century earlier, a man like Rousseau would still have become a great believer, heterodox perhaps, but still a Christian with the full force of an impassioned heart. There is no need to enumerate the outlets he went on to find, for they are well known. All that matters here is to show that, by Rousseau's time, the Christian churches were no longer able to satisfy the desires that Christianity itself had enflamed in Europe, and thus that the legitimate children of faith could no longer find their way back to their mother.

Now it only remains to explain how it was that Rousseau was the first of his kind. Non-Christians had probably always existed in Christian Europe. After approximately 1500 and in most countries, they could even admit their apostasy in public, as long as they did so discreetly and not in so many words. Entire domains of life—among them the most important ones, such as the economy, the natural sciences, philosophy, and politics—gradually emerged and established themselves at a remove from an all-unifying and all-penetrating Christian religiosity. The appearance of massive numbers of non-Christians in the French eighteenth century is not especially significant in and of itself. What they attained was less the thing itself, which was already a *fait accompli*, than its public recognition and a general consciousness that this was the case. It is for this reason that I find Groethuysen's book about the eighteenth-century bourgeoisie and its *Weltanschauung* and view of life more productive and more essential for intellectual history than actual literary history.[2] But a phenomenon like Rousseau—regardless of how intimately he may have been connected with, and how much he was a product of his times—is also something quite a bit more, something new. For, since the beginning of the crisis of Christian religiosity in Europe—and the exact moment of this beginning has been dated in various ways; I am inclined to locate it very early on, given my belief that in historical occurrences culminating moments and the first signs of crisis coincide—Christians capable of

[2] Auerbach is referring in all likelihood here to Bernard Groethuysen, *Origines de l'esprit bourgeois en France* (Paris: Gallimard, 1927). —Trans.

creativity emerged time and again, Christians who found in the very crisis of Christianity the impetus for their own creative growth. They were the ones who finally burst the bonds of the *una sancta* [the one Holy Church]. Calling forth countless schisms, they nevertheless also always provided for the next new wave of Christian religiosity. That a man of their kind, born in Europe, imbued with humility, alienated from the world, and possessed of a desire to do penance and then be saved, could no longer find a place in any Christian church and also failed to found a new one, and wrote not a single word about the sufferings of Christ, the Fall, or the Last Judgment, even in the midst of all of his outbursts of both hope and despair—this seems to me to be decisive for the changes that Europe underwent in the second half of the eighteenth century.

20

The Philology of World Literature

Nonnulla pars inventionis est nosse quid quaeras.
[It is no small part of discovery to know what you are looking for.]

—Augustine, *Quaestiones in Heptateuchum*, Prooemium.

The time has come to ask what meaning the phrase "world literature" can still have if we take it, as Goethe did, to refer both to the present and to what we can expect in the future. Our planet, the Earth—which is the "world" of world literature—is growing smaller and becoming less diverse. But world literature does not refer merely to what we share or what is common to all humanity. Rather, it concerns how what we share and the great diversity of what we do not share can be mutually enriching. The *felix culpa* of the division of the human race into a profusion of cultures is the precondition of world literature. But what is happening now? What ought we to be bracing ourselves for? Today we are witnessing a homogenization of human life the world over. This is occurring for an untold number of reasons, which everyone knows. The eclipsing of local traditions, a process that originated in Europe and which persists today, is leading to their universal erosion. Of course, the calls for national self-determination are also now stronger and louder than ever before. Yet, in each and every case, everyone who defends the national will is in fact focused on reaching exactly the same goal, namely: modern forms of life. It is thus clear that everywhere—as any impartial observer can tell—the underlying spiritual foundations of individual national identity are in the process of fading away. The civilizations of Europe, or the civilizations founded by Europeans, continue to be the most successful in maintaining their independence from one another; first, because they have been accustomed to fruitful interaction for so long, and then because each of them is of course also sustained by a conscious belief in its own modernity and prestige. Even here, however, the leveling process is advancing more rapidly than before. Everywhere else, standardization is spreading, regardless of whether it follows the Euro-American or the Soviet-Bolshevist pattern. Moreover, no matter how different from each other these two patterns may be, the distinctions between them are relatively minor when they are compared, in their current forms, with the patterns that underlie the Muslim, South Asian, or Chinese traditions. Should the human race in the end succeed in surviving the shock of so violent, enormously rapid, and poorly conceived a process of contraction, then we will have to accustom ourselves to the thought that only a single literary culture may survive in this homogenized world. It may even happen that, within a comparatively short period of time, only a limited number of literary languages will continue to exist, soon perhaps only one. If this were to come to pass, the idea of world literature would simultaneously be realized and destroyed.

If I am correct in my assessment that this situation is both inevitable and the result of large-scale movements, it is clearly not what Goethe intended. He was only too happy to avoid these sorts of ideas. And even if his thoughts did occasionally tend a bit in this direction, it was only for a moment, for he could not have anticipated how quickly and radically what was most disagreeable to him would become reality—well beyond everything he had expected. How brief was the age to which he belonged! Those of us who are a bit older can still tell the story of its demise, for we experienced it first hand. It has only been some five hundred years since the European national literatures overtook Latin culture and acquired a sense of themselves, and scarcely two hundred years since the sense of historical perspective awoke which allowed a concept like world literature to take shape. Goethe, who died only 120 years ago, contributed in crucial ways to the formation of this sense of historical perspective and to the philological scholarship that issued from it. And yet, we can already now observe the dawn of a world in which there will no longer be any practical significance in possessing this kind of sensibility.

The period of humanism associated with Goethe was brief, but it had a great impact, setting in motion much that continues to be felt today as it branches out into ever broader and more diverse contexts. The knowledge of the literatures of the world, both past and present, that Goethe had available to him at the end of his life was considerable compared to what was known at the beginning of his life. But even this knowledge was small compared to the knowledge we possess today. We owe our current assets, as it were, to the impetus that the historicist humanism of Goethe's age gave us, which helped us to both locate the material and develop ways of studying it. But quite beyond this, we owe a debt to that age for our ability to penetrate and evaluate this new material in such a way that it can contribute to the history of the intellectual and spiritual development of humanity in general, and thus to the realization of a unified vision of the human race in all its variety. This was the actual purpose of philology, beginning with Vico and Herder, and it was thanks to it that philology became the leading method in the humanities, pulling into its orbit the history of the other arts as well as the history of religion, law, and politics; in the process, it frequently became intertwined with these other fields in the development of shared conceptual systems and goals. There is no need to recall how much was accomplished in terms of both primary research and secondary synthesis as a result of this collaboration.

How reasonable is it to continue to pursue this kind of activity in light of what are now significantly changed circumstances and prospects for the future? The mere fact that philology continues to be practiced and is even expanding into new areas and traditions does not say very much. Something can continue for quite a long time after it has become institutionalized and part of a routine. This is particularly the case even when people have noticed that something has changed profoundly in the general conditions of their lives and also recognize the full implications of these changes, but, for all that, are not yet in any way prepared to—or even capable of—drawing practical conclusions from what they see. Nevertheless, now as before, there is a small number of intensely committed young people, distinguished by their talent and originality, and interested in pursuing philology and intellectual history, who give grounds for hope, the hope, that is, that they are not being betrayed by their instincts, and that there is both a reason and a future for this kind of work.

These days, scientific research into the realities of the world crowds in on and controls our lives. This kind of research is our myth, one might say; we have no other myth that might be so widely accepted. Of all of these realities, history is the one that concerns us most directly, moves us most deeply, and makes us aware of who we are in the most intimate way. For only in history do human beings appear before us in the fullness of their lives. When I refer to the field of history here, I do not mean merely the past, but rather the progress of events in general, including, in any given case, the present-day. The intellectual and spiritual history of the last several millennia is the history of the human race as it has achieved self-expression. It is with this history that philology concerns itself as a historical discipline. Its archive contains the records of the grand and adventurous leap forward that human beings made to becoming aware of their condition as humans and thus to realizing their inner potential. For a long time, humanity had almost no sense of the goal toward which it was being propelled—even in the certainly very fragmented form this goal takes today. And yet, in spite of the intricacy of its twists and turns, this movement nevertheless seems to have proceeded as if according to a plan. The wealth of conflicts that human beings are capable of is part of this journey. Along the way, a kind of drama unfolds whose richness and profundity excite all the faculties of those who look on. At the same time, the spectacle allows its viewers to make peace with their lot by being enriched by what they have seen. The loss of a purchase from which to observe this drama—a drama that must of course be staged and interpreted if it is to become visible—would be a loss beyond repair. Of course, only those who have not yet fully suffered such a loss would be able to experience it as such. This thought ought not to prevent us, however, from doing everything we can to prevent the loss from taking place.

If the thoughts about the future with which I began are at all justified, the task at hand—which is, first, to collect the evidence and then to present it in a unified and effective way—is an urgent one because we are the only ones, at least in principle, still capable of accomplishing it. This is true not simply because we have so much material at our disposal, but also—and above all—because we have inherited the sense of historical perspective that the task requires, and also because we still live in the midst of and continue to experience historical diversity. Without this experience of diversity, I fear our sense of historical perspective might rapidly lose its vitality and concreteness. We appear to be living, then, at a decisive moment in the evolution of hermeneutical history writing. How many more generations will belong to this moment is uncertain. We are already threatened, for example, by the impoverishment of understanding associated with a concept of education that has no sense of the past. It is not just that this impoverishment already exists; it actually threatens to become hegemonic. What we are we have become in the course of our history, and it is only in history that we can remain what we are, and develop. At this—our—moment in time, it is thus the task of the philologists of the world to demonstrate this truth in such a way that it penetrates deeply into people's minds and becomes impossible to forget. Toward the end of the chapter, "Die Annäherung" [Becoming More Intimate], in his novel, *Nachsommer* [Indian Summer], Adalbert Stifter has one of his characters say: "It would fulfill my highest desire if after we leave this mortal sphere our spirit could survey and embrace the entire artistic expression of the human race from its beginnings to its end." [Wendell Frye, trans. (New York: P. Lang, 1985) 255]. Stifter is thinking here only of the fine arts, and I do not believe that we can speak yet of the "end" of the "human race." But we do seem to have reached an end point that is also a turning point, one from which we will nevertheless also be permitted an overview that has never been possible before.

This idea of world literature and of the philology appropriate to it seems less active, less practical, and less political than its precursor. It no longer includes any talk of intellectual exchange or of the refinement of custom or of reconciliation between nations. This is so partly because it has been impossible to achieve these goals and partly because historical events have already rendered them superfluous. It may well be true that certain distinguished individuals and small groups of highly learned people have enjoyed cultural exchanges of this sort. Indeed, they were—and even still are in our own times—sought on a grand scale. But they have little impact on culture or reconciliation among peoples in general. In the face of the storm of competing interests and of the propaganda that is the result, whatever such encounters may have actually accomplished has faded away in an instant. Dialogue is effective when it takes place after political developments have already led to rapprochement; it then hastens the creation of solidarity and understanding within the group in ways that serve a common cause. In general, however, as I stated at the outset, different cultures have begun to resemble one another much more rapidly and completely these days than a humanist of the Goethean persuasion might want to endorse. And there appears to be no reasonable likelihood that any such differences as remain between the cultures will be able to be settled by any means other than force. The idea of world literature that I am proposing here, which conceives of world literature as a diverse backdrop to a common human fate, no longer seeks, then, to achieve what is in any case already underway (even if it is happening entirely differently than one might have hoped). I accept as inevitable that world culture is in the process of becoming standardized. But I do hope that my understanding of world literature will allow those nations that are in the midst of this fateful convergence to focus with greater precision on what is happening to them in these, their last productive moments of variety and difference, so that they can remain mindful of the process and make it part of their own mythologies. If they do so, their awareness of the abundance and depth of intellectual and spiritual developments over the past millennia will not wither and die. It would be fruitless even to speculate about what long-term impact such an effort might have; the task at hand is only to create the possibility that it might have one. This much may in any case be said, that during a transitional age such as ours the impact I am describing can be very significant. It might even help us accept what is happening to us with greater composure, and allow us to not despise our enemies all too blindly, even when it is our mission to fight them. In this sense, my idea of world literature and its corresponding philology is no less human and no less humanistic than its predecessor. The idea of history on which it is based is also not the same as the earlier idea of history—even though it has its roots in it and is inconceivable without it.

I have argued that we are in principle still capable of meeting the challenge that the creation of a philology of world literature presents. This is possible, first, because we have an infinite amount of material at our disposal (this material is in fact always increasing) and, second, because we still possess the sense of historical perspective that was bequeathed to us by the historicism of the age of Goethe. Regardless of how promising such a project might appear overall, the individual, practical challenges that face us in realizing it are considerable. For instance, in order to complete the task of gaining intimate access to and giving shape to world literature, there must be at least a few scholars who command the material in its entirety—or at least large portions of it—as the result of their own experience and research. Yet, it has become virtually impossible to attain this degree of mastery because of the glut of material, methods, and approaches that we face. We possess texts ranging over six millennia, from all parts of the globe, and in some fifty different literary languages. Many of the cultures with which we are now familiar were still undiscovered one hundred years ago; others were known, but only piecemeal when compared with what we have now. Moreover, even for those epochs that we have been studying for hundreds of years, we have now discovered so much that is new that our conception of them is utterly different from what it was before. As a result, we confront entirely new problems. Finally, it has become clear that we cannot study the literature of any particular age of a civilization in isolation. We must also attend to the factors that conditioned that literature as it developed, to the religious, philosophical, political, and economic circumstances of the time, and to its fine arts and of course its music as well. We must, moreover, stay current in the scholarship in all of these individual fields as that scholarship continues to be produced. The sheer quantity of material leads to the need for an ever more specialized focus; special methods emerge, with the result that each sub-discipline—and each of the many ways it can be understood—develops its own secret code. But that is not all. Interloper concepts and methods, with their origins in the non-philological disciplines and trends, begin to invade philology's domain. They come from sociology and psychology as well as from various philosophical tendencies and from the sphere of contemporary literary criticism too. All these must be worked through, if only so that we can in good conscience dismiss one or the other of the methods that has been proposed as useless for our philological ends. Scholarship that does not limit itself, in a disciplined fashion, to a narrow and specialized field and to a conceptual frame shared by a small number of expert colleagues will find itself adrift in a welter of impressions and demands to which it is nearly impossible to do justice. Yet, it is also becoming increasingly frustrating to restrict oneself to work in a single, specialized field. For example, someone who wants these days to become an authority in Provençal poetry, but commands nothing more than the relevant knowledge in linguistics, paleography, and the history of the time, will hardly be considered even an adequate scholar in the field. At the same time, there are other areas of specialization that have developed so many sub-fields that to become expert in them all would take an entire lifetime. Here the study of Dante is an example—even though one can hardly say that Dante is a field of specialization, since studying him takes one in every possible direction. The same is true for courtly romance, with its three areas of concern: courtly love, Celtic lore, and the story of the Grail. How many scholars can there be who have mastered the entire scope of even just this one field in all of its intricacies and research specialties? Under these circumstances, how can we really conceive of a truly synthetic and systematic philology of world literature?

There are still some individuals who have a magisterial overview of the entirety of a tradition, at least in the case of Europe. But as far as I know, they belong to the generation that came of age before the First and the Second World Wars, and they will be difficult to replace. Since then, there has been a nearly universal collapse of late-bourgeois humanist culture, for which learning Greek and Latin and being familiar with Scripture were still the norm in the schools. And, if I may surmise the following on the basis of my experiences in Turkey, similar developments have occurred in other countries with ancient cultural traditions. As a result, what could formerly be assumed at the level of university study (or in "graduate studies" in English-speaking cultures) must now be acquired only at that point, and this is often too late for it to be satisfactorily learned. Moreover, the center of gravity has shifted within the universities and graduate schools. Modern literature and criticism are much more the norm; of the older periods, preference is given to those that have just recently been rediscovered or are familiar to us from modern literary parlance, as in the case of the Baroque. There is no question that we must learn to understand the whole of history from within the mentality and circumstances of our own times if that history is to become relevant for us. But talented students already have a command of the spirit of their own times. In my opinion, they do not need academic instruction to make Rilke, Gide, or Yeats their own. But they do require help if they want to understand the linguistic forms and material circumstances of life in the ancient world, the Middle Ages, or the Renaissance, for example, and to become familiar with the research methods and resources necessary for exploring these fields. While the questions and categories of contemporary literary criticism are always meaningful as an expression of the spirit of one's own time, and are also often ingenious and illuminating in their own right, only a very few of them are ever really useful in any direct way for historical and philological research—not to speak of being substitutes for traditional concepts. They are mostly too abstract and ambiguous, often also result in an all too exaggerated private jargon, and thus intensify the temptation to which many beginners— and often not just beginners—are inclined to fall prey, namely the desire to master a great wealth of material by introducing abstract organizational categories in a hypostasizing way. This can lead only to the effacement of the object of study, to the discussion of issues that are illusory, and ultimately to absolutely nothing at all.

And yet, as irritating as these phenomena may occasionally be, they do not seem to me to be the real threat, at least not for truly talented students who are genuinely devoted to their task. Some have already managed to acquire the skills that are generally indispensable for historical philological work and to find the proper balance between openness to and independence from fashionable trends. In many respects, they also have an advantage over their predecessors from earlier decades. The events of the past forty years have broadened our horizons, revealed world-historical perspectives to us, and revived and enriched our ways of viewing the structures of inter-subjective interactions in concrete ways. We have been and continue to be participants in a practical seminar in world history, which has allowed us to develop greater insight into historical phenomena than we had before, and a greater ability to imagine them. Indeed, even some of the most outstanding products of historical philology from the late-bourgeois era now seem a bit artificial and narrow in terms of the problems they address. In this sense, we do have it easier these days.

Still, how are we to solve the challenge that synthesis involves? A lifetime seems too short to accomplish even the preliminaries. Although extremely useful in other contexts, organized collaboration is not the solution. For, in spite of the fact that the historical synthesis of which I am thinking can be meaningful only when it is based on a scientific encounter with the material, it is, finally, a product of personal intuition. Thus, only the individual can be expected to achieve it. Complete success in such an endeavor would in fact be at once a scholarly achievement and a work of art. Even determining the place from which one should approach the material (*Ansatzpunkt*), about which I will have more to say below, is a matter of intuition. Executing the project in turn entails giving it a form that must be unified and evocative if it is to reach what is being expected of it here. Surely it is intuition's capacity to produce new combinations that we have to thank if anything significant has actually been achieved in this respect. But, in terms of historical synthesis, there is the additional requirement that, if what it produces is to achieve its fullest effect, this product must also appear to the reader to be a work of art. The traditional objection that the literary work of art must be free in order to gain access to its proper matter—and thus cannot be bound by scientific rules—can scarcely still be raised. For the historical objects of today offer the imagination abundant freedom in terms of the kinds of problems it can address and the ways in which these problems can be formulated, combined, and shaped. Indeed we might say that scientific integrity provides a good way of setting limits. That is, since both trivializing reductionism and grotesque distortion often tempt one to deviate from the object or reality at hand, a scientific approach can help preserve and guarantee something that is actually probable in the realm of the real—since the real is the measure of the probable. Moreover, when we demand that an intellectually synthesizing way of history writing resemble a literary genre, we are well within the European tradition. Ancient historiography was a literary genre, and the philosophically and historically oriented criticism established by German Classicism and Romanticism strove to develop its own version of artistic expression as well.

We must thus return to the question of the individual. How can one person alone produce this kind of synthesis? Not in any case by encyclopedic collecting, it seems to me. A broad frame of reference is a prerequisite; of this there can be no doubt. But this frame must be achieved before the fact, as it were, without being limited by any external purpose, and it must be guided by the instinct of personal interest alone. As we have seen in the last several decades, however, it is difficult to perform the work of synthesis simply by striving to collect all of the materials pertinent to even just one field in complete and exhaustive detail—as is usually done in the grand handbooks on a national literature, a period, or a literary genre, for example. The difficulty lies not only in the sheer abundance of material, which no one person can truly master (in such cases, working in groups *is* to be recommended), but, rather, in the very structure of the material itself. The traditional categories, e.g., chronology, geography, and genre, are indispensable for the preparatory steps. But they are not—or are no longer—conducive to a procedure that is dynamic and unifying. Such categories do not cover the areas with which the synthetic approach is concerned. I have even begun to doubt whether monographs on individual important figures, of which we possess many excellent examples, are still suitable as a point of departure (*Ausgangspunkt*) for the kind of synthesis that I am advocating here. To be sure, the figure of the single author provides a concrete and integral life that is fully realized and complete; this object of study is always better as a focal point than anything that has been entirely made up. At the same time, the single author provides this coherence only at the price of being at once too imprecise and too handicapped by the fruitless ahistoricity to which the very fact of the individual as individual ultimately leads.

The most impressive of the recent publications that consider literature from a synthetic point of view is Ernst Robert Curtius's book, *European Literature and the Latin Middle Ages* (1948). In my view, this book owes its success to the fact that, in spite of its title, it does not begin with a comprehensive or generalizing idea. Rather, its point of departure is a single phenomenon that is precisely, and even narrowly, defined—namely, the survival of the tradition of rhetorical education. Regardless of the huge amount of material that it assembles, the best parts of the book are thus not based on amassing details. Rather, they address everything that radiates out from something that is very limited. At the most general level, the book takes as its object of study the survival of antiquity up through the Latin Middle Ages and the impact that these medieval forms of antiquity had on modern European literature. At first sight, there is very little one might be able to do with such a broadly conceived project. Anyone who undertakes it intending to do more than merely describe the subject matter faces an incalculably large mass of disparate materials that would be nearly impossible to organize. Even finding the form that such a project might take by arranging these materials in mechanical fashion according to predictable categories—such as the influence of a single author, or the survival (in sequence) of the entire tradition over the centuries of the Middle Ages—would be stymied by the sheer magnitude of the material on hand. Only by designating as the starting point a phenomenon that is at once firmly circumscribed, comprehensible, and foundational enough—here, the rhetorical tradition and especially the *topoi*, or "commonplaces"—does it become possible to carry out such a plan. To discuss whether the choice of this specific starting point is entirely satisfactory, or even the best one we might imagine for the purpose, is not the issue here. Indeed, anyone who finds Curtius's starting point inadequate when compared with his intention has to admire what he achieved all the more. That he was able to do what he did was thanks to this methodological principle, namely: In order to conduct a large synthetic project, it is necessary to find a starting point, a tangible hook, as it were, that allows one to lay hold of one's object of study. This point must single out a clearly circumscribed and easily surveyed set of phenomena. And the interpretation of these phenomena must possess an illuminating power that is sufficient to organize and interpret a far broader range of phenomena than the point from which it started.

This method has existed for a long time. For example, the study of stylistics has long made use of it to describe the specificity of a given style on the basis of certain fixed characteristics. Yet, it seems to me essential to emphasize the critical importance of this method in general as the only one available at this point in time that allows us to describe important processes of intellectual history against a broader background in a synthetic and evocative way. It also allows younger, even novice, scholars to do this. In fact, as soon as one has intuitively located an auspicious point at which to begin, even a comparatively modest general knowledge—helped along by a bit of advisement—can be enough. As one proceeds to work out the project, one's horizons will expand in a natural and appropriate way, since the selection of relevant materials is already indicated by where one starts. In the end, the elaboration is so concrete, its elements so intimately and necessarily of a piece, that one does not easily forget what one has learned. The achievement is marked, finally, by unity and universality precisely because of its location at the intersection of many layers and paths.

Naturally, it is not always the case in practice that a general project, problem, or interest preexists the concrete approach one will then take. From time to time, it happens that we first find a specific phenomenon from which to proceed (*Ansatzphänomen*) and are then prompted to recognize and formulate the general problem. This can of course only happen when we are open to that problem in advance. It is essential to understand that a general, synthetically framed interest, project, or problem is not enough. It is much more important to locate a partial phenomenon that is as focused and concrete as possible and that can be described with technical philological terms. For it is only out of the phenomenon that further questions will emerge, so to speak, on their own. Only as a result of locating such a phenomenon do the formulation and execution of the project become possible. Occasionally one such initial phenomenon alone will not suffice; several will be required. But once the first one is in place, the rest will come more easily—particularly if they are (as they must be) not only joined together serially, one after another, but all converging on a common goal. This is of course a kind of specialization. But it is not the specialization that relies on inherited ways of classifying one's material. Rather it is always matched to the specific object at hand. As such, it must itself always be invented anew.

The starting points can be very heterogeneous. It would not be feasible to enumerate all of the possibilities here. What distinguishes a good place to start is, on the one hand, its concreteness and inherent richness, and, on the other, its potential power to shed light in a radiating fashion. The meaning of a word, a rhetorical form, a syntactical expression, the interpretation of a sentence, or a series of remarks made at some moment in time and in some particular place—any of these will do. But the possibility of illuminating areas further afield must also exist, such that one could ultimately study the history of the entire world on the basis of wherever it is that one starts. The scholar who wants to work on the position of the writer in the nineteenth century, whether in one specific country or in Europe in general, may well produce a useful reference work by bringing together all there is to know about the topic, and we ought to be grateful for the production of such a helpful book. But the act of synthesis of which I am thinking is more likely to occur if one begins with just a limited number of remarks that very specific writers made about, say, their readers. The same may be said for such topics as the afterlife and fame (*la fortuna*) of poets. The comprehensive studies of Dante reception in individual countries as they currently exist are certainly indispensible. But something much more interesting might emerge—and I am indebted to Erwin Panofsky for the suggestion—if we were to trace how individual passages of the *Divine Comedy* have been interpreted over the years, beginning with the very first commentaries and then proceeding up through the sixteenth century, and then again since the Romantics. This is how to do intellectual history in a precise way.

A good starting point must thus be focused and have an objective quality. Abstract classificatory categories and notions of what is "typical" are not appropriate. "The Baroque" and "the Romantic," "Drama" and "the Idea of Fate," "Intensity," "Myth," the "Period Concept," and "Perspectivism"—all of these terms are dangerous. They can perhaps be used when the context makes it clear what they mean. But they are much too ambiguous to be used as starting points to designate something specific that can be grasped and kept firmly in hand. Also, the starting point should not be some generalization that is then imposed on the object of study from the outside. Rather it should grow out of it organically, like a part of the whole. The things themselves should be allowed to speak. If where one begins is neither concrete nor clearly delineated, this will never happen. And even if one has the very best starting point, it takes a great deal of skill to stay focused on the object. Everywhere, conceptual clichés lie in wait. Although seldom exactly appropriate, their fashionableness and the way they sound can be seductive; in any case, they are ever ready to interject themselves into our writing as soon as we drift away from the energy that the tangible exerts. It is thus that the occasional writer—and many readers—are led to mistake an appealing cliché for the thing itself. Far too many readers are prone to such substitutions. We must do all that we can to prevent them at every turn from straying away from what is actually meant. The phenomena which lend themselves to synthetic philology have an objective existence of their own. This quality must not be lost sight of in the synthesis, however difficult this may be. The point here is not to enjoy individual details in a quietly contemplative manner. Rather, the goal is to be caught up in the dynamic movement of the whole. This movement can be witnessed in pure form, however, only when the individual elements are grasped in all of their substantive reality.

As far as I know, there have been no attempts to engage in a philology of world literature of this synthesizing kind. Only a few initial approaches have been made by those concerned with Western culture. But the more that the globe contracts, the greater the imperative will be to expand our efforts to engage in synthetic and perspectival work. It is an enormous task to make people conscious of themselves within their own history. And yet, it is actually also a limited undertaking—indeed, even a kind of renunciation—if we consider that we live not just on the earth, but in the world, in the universe. We no longer dare to determine the place mankind ought to take in that universe as earlier ages did. All of that seems quite alien to us now.

Yet, our philological home *is* the earth. It can no longer be the nation. The most precious and necessary thing that philologists inherit may be their national language and culture. But it is only in losing—or overcoming—this inheritance that it can have this effect. We must now return—albeit under different conditions—to what the pre-nation-state culture of the Middle Ages already possessed, to the knowledge that the human spirit itself is not national. *Paupertas* [humble circumstances] and *terra aliena* [foreign soil]: These are the words we find in one form or another in the works of Bernard of Chartres, John of Salisbury, Jean de Meun, and many others. *Magnum virtutis principium est*, writes Hugh of Saint Victor in his *Didascalicon* (3.20), *ut discat paulatim exercitatus animus visibilia haec et transitoria primum commutare, ut postmodum possit etiam derelinquere. Delicatus ille est adhuc cui patria dulcis est, fortis autem cui omne solum patria est, perfectus vero cui mundus totus exilium est* [It is, therefore, a great source of virtue for the practiced mind to learn, bit by bit, first to change about invisible and transitory things, so that afterwards it may be able to leave them behind altogether. The man who finds his homeland sweet is still a tender beginner; he to whom every soil is as his native one is already strong; but he is perfect to whom the entire world is as a foreign land] [*The Didascalicon of Hugh of St. Victor: A Medieval Guide to the Arts*, translated by Jeremy Taylor (New York: Columbia University Press, 1961) 101]. Hugh's intended audience consisted of those individuals whose goal it was to free themselves from their love of this world. But it is also a good path to follow for anyone who desires to secure a proper love *for* the world.

APPENDIX

Sources for Translated Citations

Jane O. Newman

Sources to Chapter 7, *"Figura"*

Aristotle. *Nicomachean Ethics*, H. Rackham, trans. (Cambridge, MA: Harvard University Press, 1934).

Augustine. *Answer to Faustus, a Manichean*, Boniface Ramsey, ed.; Roland Teske, trans. and notes (Hyde Park, NY: New City Press, 2007).

———. *The City of God against the Pagans*, vol. 6; William Chase Greene, trans. (Cambridge, MA: Harvard University Press, 1960).

———. *The City of God against the Pagans*, vol. 4; Philip Levine, trans. (Cambridge, MA: Harvard University Press, 1966).

———. *The City of God against the Pagans*, vol. 5; Eva Matthews Sanford and William McAllen Green, trans. (Cambridge, MA: Harvard University Press, 1966).

———. *Expositions of the Psalms, 33–50*, John E. Rotelle, ed.; Maria Boulding, trans. and notes (Hyde Park, NY: New City Press, 2000).

———. *Expositions of the Psalms, 99–120*, John E. Rotelle, ed.; Maria Boulding, trans. and notes (Hyde Park, NY: New City Press, 2003).

———. *On Genesis*, John E. Rotelle, ed.; Edmund Hill, trans. and notes (Hyde Park, NY: New City Press, 2002).

———. *Sermons 1 (1–19) on the Old Testament*, John E. Rotelle, ed.; Edmund Hill, trans. and notes (Brooklyn, NY: New City Press, 1990).

Catullus. *The Poems of Catullus*, in *Catullus, Tibullus, Pervigilium Veneris*, F. W. Cornish, trans. (Cambridge, MA: Harvard University Press, 1966).

Celsus. *De medicina*, W. G. Spencer, trans. (Cambridge, MA: Harvard University Press, 1960).

Cicero. [Cicero] *Ad Herennium*, Harry Caplan, trans. (Cambridge, MA: Harvard University Press, 1968).

———. *De divinatione*, William Armistead Falconer, trans. (Cambridge, MA: Harvard University Press, 1959).

———. *De natura deorum*, H. Rackham, trans. (Cambridge, MA: Harvard University Press, 1956).

———. *De oratore*, 2 vols.; E. W. Sutton and H. Rackham, trans. (Cambridge, MA: Harvard University Press, 1959).

———. *The Verrine Orations*, L.H.G. Greenwood, trans. (Cambridge, MA: Harvard University Press, 1967).

Columella. *On Agriculture and Trees*, vol. 3, E. S. Forster and Edward H. Heffner, trans. (Cambridge MA: Harvard University Press, 1955).

Dante. *The Divine Comedy*, Allen Mandelbaum, trans. (New York: Knopf, 1995).

Gellius, Aulus. *The Attic Nights*, 3 vols.; John C. Rolfe, trans. (Cambridge, MA: Harvard University Press, 1954).

Lucretius. *De rerum natura*, W.H.D. Rouse, trans. (Cambridge, MA: Harvard University Press, 1966).

Ovid. *The Art of Love and Other Poems*, J. H. Mozley, trans. (Cambridge, MA: Harvard University Press, 1969).

———. *Fasti*, James George Frazer, trans. (Cambridge, MA: Harvard University Press, 1968).

———. *Metamorphoses*, 2 vols; Frank Justus Miller, trans. (Cambridge, MA: Harvard University Press, 1971).

Pacuvius. In *Remains of Old Latin*, E. H. Warmington, trans. (Cambridge, MA: Harvard University Press, 1967).

Petronius. *Satyricon*, Michael Heseltine, trans. (Cambridge, MA: Harvard University Press, 1961).

Pliny. *Natural History*, 10 vols.; H. Rackham, trans. (Cambridge, MA: Harvard University Press, 1952).

Propertius. *Elegies*, H. E. Butler, trans. (Cambridge, MA: Harvard University Press, 1968).

Seneca. *Ad Lucilium epistulae morales*, Richard M. Gummere, trans. (Cambridge, MA: Harvard University Press, 1953).

Terence. *The Eunuch*, John Sargeaunt, trans. (Cambridge, MA: Harvard University Press, 1964).

Tertullian. *Adversus Marcionem*, Ernest Evans, trans. (Oxford: Clarendon Press, 1972).

———. *Homily on Baptism*, Ernest Evans, trans. (London: S.P.C.K., 1964).

Varro. *On the Latin Language*, 2 vols.; Roland G. Kent, trans. (Cambridge, MA: Harvard University Press, 1958).

Vergil. *Aeneid*, H. Rushton Fairclough, trans. (Cambridge, MA: Harvard University Press, 1966).

Sources to Chapter 14, *"Passio* as Passion"

Bernard of Clairvaux. *The Letters of St. Bernard of Clairvaux*, Bruno Scott James, trans. (Chicago: Henry Regnery Company, 1953).

———. *Sermons on the Song of Songs*, in *Bernard of Clairvaux on the Song of Songs*, 4 vols.; Kilian Walsh and Irene M. Edmonds, trans. (Kalamazoo, MI: Cistercian Publications, 1979).

———. "On Loving God," in *Bernard of Clairvaux: Selected Works*, translated and with a foreword by G. R. Evans (New York: Paulist Press, 1987).

Corneille, Pierre. *Polyeuctus, The Liar, The Nicomedes*, 4 vols.; John Cairncross, trans. (Middlesex: Penguin Books, 1980).

Dante. *Monarchy*, Prue Shaw, trans. (Cambridge, MA: Harvard University Press, 1996).

Racine, Jean. *Bérénice,* completed and edited by H. T. Barnwell; R. C. Knight, trans. (Edinburgh-Cambridge-Durham: Durham Academic Press, 1999).

———. *Iphigénie*, William L. Craine, trans. (Baton Rouge, LA: 1982).

———. *Three Plays*, Tim Chilcott, trans. (Hertfordshire: Wordsworth Editions, 2000).

Senancour, Étienne Pivert de. *Obermann*, Arthur Edward Waite, trans. (London: William Rider and Son, 1909).

Underhill, Evelyn. *Jacopone da Todi, Poet and Mystic—1228–1306: A Spiritual Biography*. With a Selection from the Spiritual Songs, the Italian text translated by Mrs. Theodore Beck (London and Toronto: J. M. Dent and Sons, 1919).

BIBLIOGRAPHICAL OVERVIEW

James I. Porter

A fairly complete catalogue of Auerbach's published work is available in his *Gesammelte Aufsätze* (1967) 366–369, which includes lists of his essays, translations (of Dante, Vico, and Croce), as well as reviews and review essays. (One of the more significant of these latter is his review of René Wellek's *A History of Modern Criticism*, vols. 1 and 2, in *Romanische Forschungen* 67.3/4 (1956) 387–97; rpt. *Gesammelte Aufsätze*, 354–63). Another catalogue appears in *Literary Language and its Public* (1965) 391–405. Even so, the corpus of Auerbach's writings keeps growing by the year. His archives have yielded a number of unsuspected original essays and lectures, as well as a sizeable correspondence that is not yet translated, in addition to a newly found second introduction by Auerbach to his translation of Vico's *New Science* (the text, dating from 1947, was destined for a reprint that never appeared). A list of Auerbach's main publications follows below, then a brief overview of the contents of the present volume and their original publication details, and finally a note on the state of current primary research in Auerbach studies, with a select bibliography, by way of a quick orientation for anyone interested in pursuing these leads further.

Auerbach's Major Publications

1913. *Die Teilnahme in den Vorarbeiten zu einem neuen Strafgesetzbuch.* Berlin: Frensdorf.

1921. *Zur Technik der Frührenaissancenovelle in Italien und Frankreich.* Heidelberg: C. Winter.

1924. Giambattista Vico, *Die neue Wissenschaft über die gemeinschaftliche Natur der Völker.* Berlin: de Gruyter. Abridged and translated with an introduction by Erich Auerbach.

1929. *Dante als Dichter der irdischen Welt.* Berlin and Leipzig: Walter de Gruyter. (*Dante: Poet of the Secular World.* Translated by Ralph Manheim. Chicago: University of Chicago Press, 1961.)

1933. *Das französische Publikum des 17. Jahrhunderts.* Munich: Max Hueber Verlag.

1946. *Mimesis: Dargestellte Wirklichkeit in der abendländischen Literatur.* Bern: A. Francke. 2nd expanded ed. 1959. 3rd unaltered ed. 1964, etc. (*Mimesis: The Representation of Reality in Western Literature.* Translated by W. R. Trask. Princeton: Princeton University Press, 1953. Rpt. 2003.)

1947. "Philologie als kritische Kunst." Revised introduction to Giambattista Vico, *Die neue Wissenschaft* (1924). See Vialon 2013.

1949. *Introduction aux études de philologie romane.* Frankfurt am Main: V. Klostermann. (*Introduction to Romance Languages and Literature: Latin, French, Spanish, Provençal, Italian.* Translated by Guy Daniels. New York: Capricorn Books, 1961. A Turkish translation was published in 1944 by Suheyla Bayrav based on Auerbach's manuscript.)

1951. *Vier Untersuchungen zur Geschichte der französischen Bildung.* Bern: A. Francke.

1953. "Epilegomena zu *Mimesis*," *Romanische Forschungen* 65.1/2: 1–18. ("Epilegomena to *Mimesis.*" Translated by J. Ziolkowski in *Mimesis* [rpt. ed., 2003] 559–74.)

1958. *Literatursprache und Publikum in der lateinischen Spätantike und im Mittelalter.* Bern: A. Francke. (*Literary Language and Its Public in Late Latin Antiquity and in the Middle Ages.* Translated by Ralph Manheim. New York: Bollingen Foundation. Distributed by Pantheon Books, 1965. Rpt. Princeton, NJ: Princeton University Press, 1993.)

1959. *Scenes from the Drama of European Literature. Six Essays.* New York: Meridian Books, 1959. Rpt. Gloucester, MA: Peter Smith, 1973.

1967. *Gesammelte Aufsätze zur romanischen Philologie.* Bern and Munich: A. Francke.

Original Publication History of the Essays in This Collection

With four exceptions, each marked with a dagger, the essays translated or reprinted here are drawn from Auerbach's collected essays, *Gesammelte Aufsätze zur romanischen Philologie* (1967). Three of the essays originally appeared in English, while one was originally delivered in English ("Three Traits"): only the sound recording survives (see below)—it is hauntingly beautiful, particularly in the quotations from Dante, which Auerbach reads musically in the original. All four of these essays are marked with an asterisk. Of the remainder, four have appeared in previous translations: "*Figura*," "*Passio* as Passion," "On Pascal's Political Theory," and "The Philology of World Literature." These were simply too significant to omit from any major new collection of Auerbach's essays. All were chosen on the grounds of thematic coherence. One essay appears here for the first time anywhere ("The Idea of the National Spirit as the Source of the Modern Humanities"). The German original, a typescript discovered among Auerbach's literary remains by Martin Vialon in the German Literature Archive in Marbach, is forthcoming. We are grateful to Professor Vialon for generously making his transcription of this text available to the English public in advance of his own critical edition.

1. *"Vico's Contribution to Literary Criticism" (1958). First published in English in *Studia philologica et litteraria in honorem L. Spitzer*, Anna G. Hatcher and K. L. Selig, eds. (Bern: Francke Verlag, 1958) 31–37. Reprinted here with minor editorial modifications. (A revised version appeared in Auerbach's Introduction to *Literary Language and Its Public.*).

2. "Vico and Herder" (1931). Lecture held at the German-Italian Research Institute in Cologne, June 1931. First published in *Deutsche Vierteljahrsschrift für Literaturwissenschaft und Geistesgeschichte*, 10.4 (1932) 671–86.

3. "Giambattista Vico and the Idea of Philology" (1936). First published in *Homenatge a Antoni Rubió i Lluch: Miscellània d'estudis literaris, històrics i lingüístics*, 3 vols. (Barcelona: [s. n.], 1936) 1:293–304.

4. *"Vico and Aesthetic Historism" (1949). Originally read at the American Society for Aesthetics, Cambridge, MA, September 1, 1948. First published in English as "Vico and Aesthetic Historism" in *Journal of Aesthetics and Art Criticism* 8.2 (1949) 110–18. Rpt. with minor revisions in Auerbach 1959, 183–98. Reprinted here with minor editorial modifications.

5. "Vico and the National Spirit" (1955). First published in *Wirtschaft und Kultursystem: Alexander Rüstow zum siebzigsten Geburtstag*, Gottfried Eisermann, ed. (Erlenbach and Zürich: E. Rentsch, 1955) 40–60.

6. †"The Idea of the National Spirit as the Source of the Modern Humanities" (ca. 1955). Edited by Martin Vialon from the original German typescript. (The title, added in hand by Auerbach, reads "Der Volksgeistgedanke als Wurzel der modernen Geisteswissenschaften.") Published and translated here for the first time, with the kind permission of Martin Vialon, who is preparing an annotated critical edition of this essay.

7. "*Figura*." (1938). First published in *Archivum Romanicum* 22 (1938) 436–89. Rpt. 1939 (Florence: Leo Olschki). First translated by Ralph Manheim in Auerbach 1959, 11–76.

8. *"Typological Symbolism in Medieval Literature" (1952). First published in English in *Yale French Studies* 9 (1952) 3–10. Reprinted here with minor editorial modifications.

9. †"On the Anniversary Celebration of Dante" (1921). First published in *Die neue Rundschau* 32.2 (1921) 1005–1006, on the six-hundredth anniversary of Dante's death.

10. "Dante and Vergil" (1931). First published in *Das humanistische Gymnasium* 42 (1931) 136–44.

11. "The Discovery of Dante by Romanticism" (1929). Inaugural Lecture, Marburg University. First published in *Deutsche Vierteljahrsschrift für Literaturwissenschaft und Geistesgeschichte* 7.4 (1929) 682–92.

12. †"Romanticism and Realism" (1933) First published in *Neue Jahrbücher für Wissenschaft und Jugendbildung* 9 (1933) 143–53.

13. "Marcel Proust and the Novel of Lost Time" (1927). First published in *Die Neueren Sprachen* 35.1 (1927) 16–22.

14. "*Passio* as Passion" (1941). First published in German in *Proceedings of the Modern Language Association* 56.4 (1941) 1179–96. First translated with an introduction by Martin Elsky in *Criticism* 43.1 (2001) 285–308.

15. †*"The Three Traits of Dante's Poetry" (1948). Second annual Simmons Series Lecture, Pennsylvania State University, delivered in English and recorded on March 22, 1948. First published in Karlheinz Barck and Martin Treml, eds., *Erich Auerbach: Geschichte und Aktualität eines europäischen Philologen* (2007) 414–25. Original transcript by Martin Vialon (who also supplied the title). Further corrections were made by Jane O. Newman and James I. Porter for this volume based on the recording.

16. "Montaigne the Writer" (1932). First published in *Germanisch-Romanische Monatsschrift* 20 (1932) 39–53.

17. "On Pascal's Political Theory" (1941). First published as "Der Triumph des Bösen: Versuch über Pascals polische [sic] Theorie," *Felsefe Arkivi* 1.2–3 (1946) 51–75; rpt.

with minor changes in *Gesammelte Aufsätze*, 204–21. A revised and enlarged version appeared in *Vier Untersuchungen zur Geschichte der französischen Bildung*, 51–74, and was translated as "On the Political Theory of Pascal" by Ralph Manheim in Auerbach 1959, 101–29. The present translation is based on the 1967 version in *Gesammelte Aufsätze*.

18. "Racine and the Passions" (1927). First published in *Germanisch-Romanische Monatsschrift* 14 (1927) 371–80.

19. "On Rousseau's Place in History" (1932). First published in *Die Neueren Sprachen* 40 (1932) 75–80.

20. "The Philology of World Literature" (1952). First published in *Weltliteratur: Festgabe für Fritz Strich zum 70. Geburtstag*, Walter Muschg and Emil Staiger, eds. (Bern: Francke, 1952) 39–50. First translated, with an introduction, as "Philology and *Weltliteratur*," by Maire and Edward Said in *The Centennial Review* 13.1 (1969) 1–17.

Current Research Fronts in Auerbach Studies

The bibliography on Auerbach is enormous and steadily mounting—and too vast to do justice to here. Particularly promising is the recent archival research, which continues to turn up fresh documentary evidence pertaining to Auerbach's life and career, whether in the form of previously unknown essays (such as "The Three Traits of Dante's Poetry" and "The Idea of the National Spirit as the Source of the Modern Humanities," both printed in this volume), lectures by Auerbach originally published in Turkish, or the considerable correspondence that Auerbach maintained with friends and colleagues before and after his exile from Germany. As the integration of all this material into current views of Auerbach proceeds apace, ever so slowly a more nuanced image of Auerbach is emerging, be this in his intimate relationships with his professional colleagues, in his daily life and situation in Istanbul, or in his self-conception as a Jew. Unfortunately, most of the material is not yet available in English, though fragments of it are.

Barck, Karlheinz, ed. 1987 and 1988. "Eine unveröffentlichte Korrespondenz: Erich Auerbach und Werner Krauss," *Beiträge zur Romanischen Philologie* 26.2 (1987) 301–326 and 27.1 (1988) 161–86.

———. 1988. "Fünf Briefe Erich Auerbachs an Walter Benjamin in Paris," *Zeitschrift für Germanistik* 9.6, 688–94. Partially translated by Anthony Reynolds as "Walter Benjamin and Erich Auerbach: Fragments of a Correspondence," *Diacritics* 22.3/4 (1992) 81–83.

Barck, Karlheinz and Martin Treml, eds. 2007. *Erich Auerbach: Geschichte und Aktualität eines europäischen Philologen* (Berlin: Kulturverlag Kadmos) 480–90. The publication is accompanied by a CD with the sound file of Auerbach's lecture and a valuable introduction by M. Vialon, "Die Stimme Dantes und ihre Resonanz: Zu einem bisher unbekannten Vortrag Erich Auerbachs aus dem Jahr 1948," 46–57. Further materials include Auerbach's correspondence with Fritz Saxl, Siegfried Kracauer, and Martin Buber.

Besomi, Ottavio, ed. 1977. *Il carteggio Croce-Auerbach* (Bellinzona: Archivio Storico Ticinese).

Bormuth, Matthias. 2006. *Mimesis und der christliche Gentleman: Erich Auerbach schreibt an Karl Löwith* (Warmbronn: Ulrich Keicher).

Elsky, Martin, Martin Vialon, and Robert Stein, eds. and trans. 2007. "Scholarship in Times of Extremes: Letters of Erich Auerbach (1933–46), on the Fiftieth Anniversary of His Death," *Proceedings of the Modern Language Association* 122.3, 742–62. (Includes correspondence to and from Walter Benjamin, Traugott Fuchs, Martin Hellweg, Erich Rothacker, Fritz Saxl, and Karl Vossler, in translation.)

Vialon, Martin. 2007. "Erich Auerbachs Brief an Victor Klemperer vom 7. Mai 1949," *Süddeutsche Zeitung* 236 (October 13/14) 16.

———. 2008a. "Wie das Brot der Fremde so salzig schmeckt. Hellsichtiges über die Widersprüche der Türkei. Erich Auerbachs Istanbuler Humanismusbrief," *Süddeutsche Zeitung* 239 (October 14) 16. (Letter to Johannes Oeschger from 1938.)

———. 2008b. "Erich Auerbach schreibt 1938 an Johannes Oeschger über Phänomene der Modernisierung in der Türkei," in Matthias Bormuth, et al., eds., *Brotschrift für Ulrich Keicher im fünfundzwanzigsten Jahr seines Verlages damit der rote Faden nie reisse* (Warmbronn: Christian-Wagner-Gesellschaft) 158–67.

———. 2009. "Verdichtete Geschichtserfahrung: Erich Auerbachs Brief vom 3.1.1937 an Walter Benjamin," in Waltraud Meints, et al., eds., *Raum der Freiheit: Reflexionen über Idee und Wirklichkeit. Festschrift für Antonia Grunenberg* (Bielefeld: transcript Verlag) 123–149.

———. 2011. "Helle und Trost für eine 'neue Menschlichkeit': Erich Auerbachs türkisches Exilbriefwerk," *Deutsche Akademie für Sprache und Dichtung: Jahrbuch 2010* (Göttingen: Wallstein Verlag) 18–47.

Vialon, Martin, ed. 1997. *Erich Auerbachs Briefe an Martin Hellweg (1939–1950): Edition und historisch-philologischer Kommentar* (Tübingen and Basel: Francke).

———. 2007. *Und wirst erfahren wie das Brot der Fremde so salzig schmeckt. Erich Auerbachs Briefe an Karl Vossler 1926-1948* (Warmbronn: Ulrich Keicher).

———. 2013. "Erich Auerbach: 'Philologie als kritische Kunst.' Neue Einleitung zur *Scienza Nuova* (1947): Edition, Kommentar und Nachwort," in Peter König, ed., *Vico in Europa zwischen 1800 und 1950* (Heidelberg: Universitätsverlag Winter) 223–319. (Auerbach's never published revised introduction to his translation of Vico.)

Further new materials by and about Auerbach are published in the appendices to Karlheinz Barck and Martin Treml, eds., *Erich Auerbach* (2007), which also contains a wealth of new directions in research by leading scholars in the field.

Of particular interest are Auerbach's responses to his situation in exile in Turkey and the existence of a significant colony of expatriate German-Jews on the Bosporus who found refuge under the auspices of Atatürk's Westernization efforts. On this, see especially Emily Apter, "Global *Translatio*: The 'Invention' of Comparative Literature, Istanbul, 1933," *Critical Inquiry* 29 (Winter 2003) 253–81; Martin Vialon 2008a, 2008b, and 2011; and Kader Konuk, *East West Mimesis: Auerbach in Turkey* (Stanford: Stanford University Press, 2010). (Konuk's appendix also contains two lectures by Auerbach from 1941 to 1942 hitherto available only in Turkish and translated into English by Victoria Holbrook: "Realism in Europe in the Nineteenth Century" and "Literature and War.")

Auerbach's essay "The Philology of World Literature" remains a touchstone in current debates about the practice of comparativism and the meaning of global literature. See Emily Apter "Global *Translatio*"; and Apter's chapter "Auerbach's *Welt*-Theology," in her *Against World Literature: On the Politics of Untranslatability* (London: Verso, 2013) 193–210.

Auerbach's Jewishness is increasingly attracting valuable attention. See Gert Mattenklott, "Erich Auerbach in den deutsch-jüdischen Verhältnissen," in *Wahrnehmen Lesen Deuten: Erich Auerbachs Lektüre der Moderne*, W. Busch, G. Pickerodt, and M. Bauer, eds. (Frankfurt am Main: Klostermann, 1998) 15–30; Martin Treml, "Auerbachs imaginäre jüdische Orte," in Barck and Treml, eds., *Erich Auerbach* (2007) 230–51; Martin Vialon, "Marginalien zu Erich Auerbachs Lebensbild in Briefen," in M. Vialon, ed. 2007, 30–38; Steven G. Nichols, "Erich Auerbach: History, Literature, and Jewish Philosophy," *Romanistisches Jahrbuch* 58.7 (2008) 161–86; James I. Porter, "Erich Auerbach and the Judaizing of Philology," *Critical Inquiry* 35 (Autumn 2008) 115–47 and "Auerbach, Homer, and the Jews" in *Classics and National Culture*, Susan Stephens and Phiroze Vasunia, eds. (Oxford: Oxford University Press, 2010) 235–57; Galili Shahar, "Auerbach's Scars: Judaism and the Question of Literature," *Jewish Quarterly Review* 101.4 (2011) 604–30; Avihu Zakai, *Erich Auerbach and the Crisis of German Philology: An Apology for Western Judaeo-Christian Tradition in an Age of Peril, Tyranny and Barbarism* (in preparation).

The greatest gap in research on Auerbach remains a concerted inquiry into the earliest phases of his career, including his legal studies, his dissertation, and his abridged translation of Vico's *New Science*. Other areas that remain underexplored are his philosophical background (including Nietzsche) and its application to history, literature, and ethics; his critical interventions in the history of Christian theology (see Jane O. Newman, "Force and Justice: Auerbach's Pascal," in *Political Theology and Early Modernity*, Julia Reinhard Lupton and Graham Hammill, eds. [Chicago: University of Chicago Press, 2012] 159–80) and anthropology (including the influence of Ernst Troeltsch on his thought); his background in sociology; his dialogue with contemporary art historical scholarship (like that of Max Dvořák); and the intriguing editorial history of *Mimesis* and other works, wherever records permit an assessment. (Auerbach was personally involved in the translation of *Mimesis* and supervised changes from the German edition, which could be substantive; see Porter, "Erich Auerbach and the Judaizing of Philology" [2008] for some initial discussion.)

INDEX